WOBURN COLLEGIATE INSTITUTE

2222 ELLESMERE RD. ——— SCARBOROUGH, ONT.

Date	Student	HF	Teacher
	Rohan Thirunavukar usu		
99/00	Julian Kuk	OACX	ECKER
00/01	Irene Wong	OACC	BLASKO

LOAN BOOK NUMBER	

98° - 100%

98-100

EXPERIENCE & EXPRESSION:

A Reader for Canadian Writers

Editor: Alden R. Turner

Copp Clark Pitman Ltd.
A Longman Company
Toronto

ISBN 0-7730-4602-X

Editing: Margaret Larock, Pat Trant, Penny McIlraith
Cover photo: Hans Wendler, The Image Bank
Design: Douglas Frank
Typesetting: Compeer Typographic Services Ltd.
Printing and Binding: Webcom Ltd.

Canadian Cataloguing in Publication Data

Main entry under title:
Experience and Expression
ISBN 0-7730-4602-X
1. Canadian prose literature.   2. English prose
literature.   3. College readers.   4. English
language — Rhetoric.   I. Turner, Alden R.
PE1417.E97 1987   C818'.08   C87-093468-6

Copp Clark Pitman Ltd.
495 Wellington Street West
Toronto, Ontario
M5V 1E9

Printed and bound in Canada.

ACKNOWLEDGMENTS

I wish to thank John J. McDermott of Texas A&M University and Donald McQuade of the University of California at Berkeley for their generous advice and encouragement at the initial stage of my work on this book. I appreciate the perceptive comments and helpful suggestions on the manuscript offered by Chris Bullock of the University of Alberta, Karen Ogden of the University of Manitoba, James C. MacDonald of Humber College, Don Jewison and Murray Evans of the University of Winnipeg, and Patrick Burke and Brian Henderson, my editors at Copp Clark Pitman. During the past ten years, the hard work and dedication of my hundreds of composition and rhetoric students at Texas A&M University, the University of Manitoba, and the University of Winnipeg have convinced me of the genuine value of post-secondary writing courses and programs. I would like to express in particular my gratitude for all I learned from the extraordinary people in the Winnipeg Education Centre's inner-city classes. My interests in the Canadian experience traced in this book are owing in large measure to the knowledge and affection of my father, Robert Turner. The book is for Maria and Caitlin, for the way you say things.

PERMISSIONS

Atwood, Margaret. "Survival." *Survival: A Thematic Guide to Canadian Literature*. Toronto: House of Anansi Press, 1972. Pp. 27–42. Reprinted by permission of the publisher.

Bigelow, Wilfred G. "The Invention of the Pacemaker." *Cold Hearts*. Toronto: McClelland and Stewart, 1984. Pp. 88–109. Reprinted with permission.

Bowering, George. "Between the Lines." *Books in Canada*. April 1985. Pp. 4–5. Reprinted by permission of the author.

Callaghan, Morley. "Why Toronto?" *Our Sense of Identity*. Ed. Malcolm Ross. Toronto: Ryerson Press, 1954. Reprinted by permission of the author.

Carr, Emily. "Century Time." *Klee Wyck*. Toronto: Clark, Irwin, and Co., 1941 [1971]. Pp. 94–96. Used by permission of Irwin Publishing Inc.

Cohen, Dian and Kristin Shannon. "The Next Canadian Economy." *The Next Canadian Economy*. Montreal: Eden Press, 1984. Pp. 179–201. Reprinted by permission of the publisher.

Copland, Aaron. "How We Listen." *What to Listen for in Music*. Rev. Ed. New York: McGraw-Hill, 1957. Pp. 18–23. Reprinted by permission of McGraw-Hill Book Company, New York.

Davies, Robertson. ["Reading Plays"], from "Making the Best of Second Best." *A Voice from the Attic*. Toronto: McClelland and Stewart, 1960. Pp. 155–167. Used by permission of The Canadian Publishers, McClelland and Stewart Limited, Toronto.

Dryden, Ken. ["The Goalie"]. *The Game*. Toronto: Macmillan, 1983. Pp. 115–118. Reprinted by permission of Macmillan of Canada, A Division of Canada Publishing Corporation.

Erickson, Arthur. "Ideation as a Source of Creativity." *A Political Art: Essays and Images in Honour of George Woodstock*. Ed. William H. New. Vancouver, B.C.: University of British Columbia Press, 1978. Pp. 26–33. Reprinted with permission.

Ferguson, Max. ["The Birth of Rawhide."] *And Now . . . Here's Max*. Toronto: McGraw-Hill Co. of Canada, 1967. Pp. 44–51. Reprinted by permission of McGraw-Hill Ryerson Limited.

Forster, E.M. "My Wood." *Abinger Harvest*. New York: Harcourt, Brace, Jovanovich, 1936. Reprinted by permission of Edward Arnold (Publishers) Ltd.

Frye, Northrop. "The Vocation of Eloquence." *The Educated Imagination*. Toronto: Canadian Broadcasting Corporation, 1963. Pp. 56–68. Reprinted by permission of CBC Enterprises and Dr. Northrop Frye.

George, Chief Dan. "Lament for Confederation." Unpublished Speech. (Source: Dawe, Alan. *Profile of a Nation*. Toronto: Macmillan, 1969. Pp. 252–253.) Reprinted by permission of the Chief Dan⋅George Foundation.

Grove, Frederick Philip. "A Storm in July." *The Turn of the Year*. Toronto: Macmillan, 1929. Pp. 95–109. Reprinted by permission of A. Leonard Grove.

Harbon, John D. "Modern Icebreakers." *Scientific American*, vol. 249, no. 6 (December, 1983), 49–55. Reprinted by permission of W.H. Freeman & Company for Scientific American, Inc.

Hemingway, Ernest. "When You Camp Out, Do It Right." From the compilation *Dateline: Toronto* (originally appeared in the *Toronto Star*, June 26, 1920). Copyright © Mary Hemingway, John Hemingway, Patrick Hemingway, and Gregory Hemingway. Reprinted with the permission of Charles Scribner's Sons.

Horwood, Harold. "A Wilderness Lake." *Foxes of Beachy Cove*. Toronto: Doubleday, 1967. Pp. 34–41. Reprinted by permission of the author.

Hutchinson, Bruce. "My Country." *The Unknown Country*. Toronto: Longman's, Green and Co., 1943. Pp. 3–5.

Jackson, A.Y. "The Group of Seven." *A Painter's Country: The Autobiography of A.Y. Jackson*. Toronto: Clark, Irwin, and Co., 1958 [1964]. Pp. 60–68. Used by permission of Irwin Publishing Inc.

James, William. "Habit." *Psychology. Briefer Course.* New York: Holt, 1920. Pp. 142–144.

Lower, Arthur R.M. "The Great God Car." *Canadians in the Making: A Social History of Canada.* Toronto: Longman's, Green, and Co., 1958. Pp. 424–426.

MacLennan, Hugh. "But Shaw Was a Playwright." *The Other Side of Hugh MacLennan: Selected Essays Old and New.* Ed. Elspeth Cameron. Toronto: Macmillan, 1978. Pp. 27–32. Reprinted by permission of Macmillan of Canada, A Division of Canada Publishing Corporation.

Marchand, Philip. "Learning to Love the Big City." *Just Looking, Thank You.* Toronto: Macmillan, 1976. Pp. 143–153. Reprinted by permission of the author.

McClung, Nellie L. "Christmas Day." *Clearing in the West: My Own Story.* Toronto: Thomas Allen and Son, 1935. Pp. 166–171. Reprinted by permission of Thomas Allen & Son Limited.

McCourt, Edward. "The Little Things." *The Yukon and the Northwest Territories.* Toronto: Macmillan, 1969. Pp. 24–25. Reprinted by permission of Mrs. Edward A. McCourt.

McLuhan, Marshall. "The Medium is the Message." *Understanding Media: The Extension of Man.* Toronto: McGraw-Hill, 1964. Pp. 7–21. Reprinted by permission of McGraw-Hill Book Company, New York.

Menzies, Heather. "Computers, Chips, and Automation." *Computers on the Job: Surviving Canada's Microcomputer Revolution.* Toronto: James Lorimer, 1982. Pp. 5–15. Reprinted by permission of James Lorimer & Company Ltd., Publishers.

Mowat, Farley. ["People of the Sea."] "Newfoundland: Centennial Country . . ." *Century 1867–1967: The Canadian Saga.* Ed. John D. Harbron. Toronto: Southam, [Feb. 13] 1967. Pp. 10–11. Reprinted by permission of the author.

Ossenberg, Richard J. "Social Class and Bar Behaviour." *Sociology Canada: Readings.* 2nd ed. Ed. Christopher Beattie and Stewart Crysdale. Toronto: Butterworth and Co., 1977. Pp. 370–377. Abridged from *Human Organization*, vol. 28, No. 1 (Spring 1969).

Penfield, Wilder. "Science, the Arts, and the Spirit." *Second Thoughts: Science, The Arts, and The Spirit.* Toronto: McClelland and Stewart, 1970. Pp. 1–13. Reprinted by permission of the estate of Mrs. Helen K. Penfield.

Plato. "The Allegory of the Cave." *The Republic.* Ed. Edith Hamilton and Huntington Cairns. New York: Pantheon, 1963. Pp. 514–521. [Source: Paul Shorey's translation of *The Republic* by Plato, Cambridge: Harvard University Press, publishers and trustees of the Loeb Classical Library, 1930.] Reprinted by permission of the publishers and the Loeb Classical Library.

Rakoff, Vivian. "The Fatal Question." *Saturday Night*, May 1985. Pp. 30–37. Reprinted by permission of the author.

Roberts, Sir Charles G.D. "In the Deep Grass." *The Watchers of the Trails*. Toronto: Copp, Clark, 1904. Pp. 247–253.

Robertson, Heather. ["Sale Night"], from "Winkler". *Grass Roots*. Toronto: James Lorimer & Co., 1973. Pp. 165–168. Reprinted by permission of James Lorimer & Co. Ltd., Publishers.

Salutin, Rick. ["Marginality"]. "Journey to the Periphery." *Marginal Notes: Challenges to the Mainstream*. Toronto: Lester and Orpen Dennys, 1984. Pp. 1–9. Reprinted by permission of Lester & Orpen Dennys Publishers, Ltd., Canada.

Selye, Hans. "The Mastery of Stress." *The Stress of My Life*. Toronto: McClelland and Stewart, 1977. Pp. 102–110. Reprinted by permission of Mrs. Louise Drevet Selye.

Smith, Allan. "Metaphor and Nationality." *Canadian Historical Review*, 51, no. 3 (Sept. 1970). Pp. 247–251. Reprinted by permission of the author and the University of Toronto Press.

Suzuki, David T. "A Planet for the Taking." *Canadian Forum*, February, 1985. Pp. 6–8. Reprinted by permission of the author.

Swift, Jonathan. "A Modest Proposal." *Irish Tracts, 1728–1733*, Ed. Herbert Davis. Oxford: Basil Blackwell, 1971. Pp. 109–118. Reprinted by permission of the publisher.

Thoreau, Henry David. ["Walden Pond"]. *Walden and Other Writings*. Ed. Brooks Atkinson. New York: Random House, 1950. Pp. 159–161.

Traill, Catharine Parr. ["A Sleigh Ride"]. *The Backwoods of Canada*. London: Charles Knight, 1836.

Woolf, Virginia. "The Death of the Moth." *The Death of the Moth and Other Essays*. London: The Hogarth Press, 1942. Pp. 9–11. Reprinted by permission of the author's estate and the Hogarth Press.

An honest attempt has been made to secure permission for all material used, and if there are errors or omissions, these are wholly unintentional and the Publisher will be grateful to learn of them.

Photo Credits

Chapter 1 — Lori Guzda; Chapter 2 — H. Armstrong Roberts (Miller Services); Chapter 3 — Camera Press by Ray Green (Canapress); Chapter 4 — Harold Clark, NFB Phototeque (Miller Services); Chapter 5 — Calgary Herald (Canapress); Chapter 5 — Manitoba Government Travel and Publicity Bureau (Miller Services); Chapter 7 — E. Beldowski (Canapress); Chapter 8 — NASA (Canapress).

CONTENTS

CONTENT GUIDE

THE EXPERIENCE OF PEOPLE

INDIVIDUALS:

SOCIETY:

THE EXPERIENCE OF CULTURE

LANGUAGE AND LITERATURE:

PHILOSOPHY:

THE EXPERIENCE OF SCIENCE

AUTHORS

Margaret Atwood
Pierre Berton
Wilfred G. Bigelow
George Bowering
Morley Callaghan
Emily Carr
Dian Cohen
Aaron Copland
Robertson Davies
Ken Dryden
Arthur Erickson
Max Ferguson
E. M. Forster
Northrop Frye
Dan George
Frederick Philip Grove
John Harbron
Ernest Hemingway
Harold Horwood
Bruce Hutchison
A. Y. Jackson
William James
Arthur R. M. Lower

Hugh MacLennan
Philip Marchand
Nellie McClung
Edward McCourt
Marshall McLuhan
Heather Menzies
Farley Mowat
Richard J. Ossenberg
Wilder Penfield
Plato
Vivian Rakoff
Charles G. D. Roberts
Heather Robertson
Rick Salutin
Hans Selye
Kristin Shannon
Allan Smith
David Suzuki
Jonathan Swift
Henry David Thoreau
Catharine Parr Trail
Virginia Woolf

SUBJECTS

Americans
Architecture
Art
Bars
Camping
Cars
City Life
Computers
Death
Ecology
Economics
Education
Euthanasia
Hockey

Icebreakers
Mass Media
Music
Nationalism
Native Rights
Newfoundland
Overpopulation
Reading
Regionalism
Rural Life
Stress
Technology
Work
Writing

PREFACE

Experience and Expression: A Reader for Canadian Writers presents non-fiction prose selections for students with a variety of educational backgrounds and fields of interest who are taking English composition and rhetoric courses at Canadian universities and colleges. These courses are relatively recent additions to most post-secondary programs in Canada, and their present diversity and ongoing development require that a good reader meet a broad range of students' and instructors' interests and needs.

The selections of effective writing in *Experience and Expression* feature Canadian literary authors writing on a variety of subjects as well as other prominent Canadians writing on their particular (non-literary) areas of specialization and expertise. These selections are supplemented with some classic examples of British and American prose. The content of *Experience and Expression* is interdisciplinary, the selections having been chosen from well-known books, journals, and magazines to offer readings in a number of fields: literature, art, music, history, philosophy, social sciences, economics, sciences, and sports. The selections also reflect writers' differing social, regional, intellectual, and methodological perspectives. I have tried to introduce students to the rich context for their own writing embodied in the tradition of Canadian non-fiction prose whose remarkably long and distinguished history extends from the early settlers' documentary narratives to the literary artfulness of Sir Charles G.D. Roberts and Morley Callaghan to the contemporary journalism of Pierre Berton and Rick Salutin. All of the selections are by men and women whose considerable experience as writers makes their work worthwhile reading for students of writing. More specifically, learning to write effective prose is a developmental process in which reading plays an important role. Reading non-fiction prose is appropriate for students of rhetoric and composition because this is the form of writing they are required to do most in colleges and universities and then in their careers and professions.

Experience and Expression is not only an anthology of interesting non-fiction reading; *Experience and Expression* also incorporates instructional features that make it a reader well-suited for use in conjunction with complementary rhetorics handbooks and workbooks that develop students' basic writing skills. This reader has been designed to allow instructors and students the necessary flexibility to focus on selections and chapters most appropriate to their own approaches and capabilities. The chapters are arranged in a conventional sequence of rhetorical modes (see "Contents") but some may wish either to vary this order somewhat or to use a primarily thematic approach (see "Content Guide"). The selections within each chapter are arranged to facilitate a progression in student proficiency from a basic to an intermediate to an advanced level; accordingly, each chapter contains readings that range from one or two paragraphs to full-length essays. The readings for some courses or classes may be best chosen at only one of these levels. In the general "Introduction," students review basic principles of the writing process, writing patterns, and writing purposes. The subsequent chapter introductions discuss how they can apply these principles to eight fundamental patterns of thought and expression in their own reading and writing. For each reading selection, the introductory commentary, the "Questions on Content," and the "Questions on Structure and Technique" highlight particular features of the relations between the content and the form of an individual author's writing. The questions have been carefully written to guide students through the inductive process of their own explorations and discoveries within these individual texts as well as the chapters and the book as a whole. The "Suggestions for Writing" that accompany each selection afford students practical opportunities to apply and adapt to their own work what they have learned about composition theory and the practice of others.

The goal of *Experience and Expression* is to offer students an educationally effective and intellectually challenging reader that will assist them in becoming better writers.

EDITORIAL NOTE

Most selections are complete essays, articles, or book chapters reprinted in their entirety from the original text. Selections that are not complete for pedagogical purposes are indicated in their introductions. In a few instances ellipses (...) mark a substantive omission in such edited texts but most ellipses simply show where transitional phrases or sentences that maintain the continuity of a book have been eliminated for overall coherence and cohesion in a selected chapter. Sources for selections from authors' books are indicated in the introductions and all sources are documented in "Permissions."

INTRODUCTION

*"In ordinary life, as in literature, the
way you say things can be just as
important as what's said."*

Northrop Frye

Our experience is made up by what we know about our world. We know about places: towns, cities, and nations. We are aware of the passing of time from the past to the present. We know people as individuals and in social groups. However, what we know extends well beyond this personal and familiar realm of experience. We also know something about a variety of cultural endeavours — literature, philosophy, education, fine arts, communications media, sports, and recreation — and about scientific discoveries in nature and technology. Furthermore, what we know is intricately and complexly interrelated with where, when, why, who, and how we know. Henry James wrote: "Experience is never limited, and it is never complete; it is an immense sensibility, a kind of huge spiderweb of the finest silken threads suspended in the chamber of consciousness, and catching every airborne particle in its tissue." Important questions and answers about this profound web of human experience occupy our thoughts and actions today, just as they have for centuries. What has been said by Plato, Aristotle, Augustine, Shakespeare, and Einstein is only part of a continuing discussion involving innumerable participants, including ourselves and the authors of selections you will be reading in this book. Throughout that discussion great thinkers have also been great rhetoricians, people whose knowledge about the public use of words demonstrates that "what's said" about our experience is significantly related to "the way you say things," as one of our authors, Northrop Frye, reminds us.

The expression of what we know about our experience ranges from the verbal expression of our first words to the conversations we have with friends and family to the "body language" we exhibit in social situations. Many of us may also engage in other forms of expression such as music, dance, drawing, painting, drama, and mathematics. However, writing is probably the most common and useful means for us to express our experience of people, places, and events we have found meaningful as well as wider fields of interest, information, issues, and problems we encounter. Understandably, though, the demands and difficulties of written expression increase along with our experience, even when we have been writing for years. By further developing your understanding of the process, patterns, and purposes involved in both "what's said" and "the way you say things" in your writing, this book will help you to bridge this distance between experience and expression.

THE WRITING PROCESS

A writer does not proceed from experience to expression in one giant leap. Writing is a process whereby a writer takes one step at a time, and these steps may be termed: prewriting, writing, and rewriting.

Prewriting

For many of us, the most difficult task involved in writing is getting started. Instead of sitting and staring at a blank piece of paper or computer monitor, or struggling for hours to write a few opening sentences, or otherwise occupying yourself by making coffee, sharpening pencils, and thinking about plans for your weekend, discover what you know by prewriting. When you have a writing assignment or situation, explore it by using one or more of the following prewriting techniques.

Freewriting is thinking and, at the same time, writing down whatever comes to mind, continuously moving your pencil or pen along the lines on your paper or your fingers on the keyboard for ten or fifteen minutes without worrying at all about your spelling and word choice and sentence structure. Then, read what you have written. Underline any relevant or important words, phrases, and passages with which you may want to work further. You can then use that material as the basis for either a gradual building process through subsequent freewriting sessions or work with another prewriting technique.

Making lists of words and phrases that refer to your experiences and thoughts is another good way for you to discover what you know. Many of your words will suggest other related or associated words that you can then add to your lists. As you are adding words and perhaps deleting other ones, you should examine the relations you see among them. By indicating these relations through groupings and arrangements of your words and phrases, you can make a very useful sketch of a subject.

Journal writing is a classic method of prewriting. Devote a brief period every day to writing a page or two about one particular idea or experience that is important to you. When you are faced with a formal writing assignment, you may choose to write about that subject or some aspect of it. If you cannot think of anything to write in your journal, try freewriting or making lists. Use your journal to discover subjects, to work out your ideas and, generally, to increase your experience with writing itself.

These three prewriting techniques are common methods you can use to explore what you know — your *subject* — but also to learn more about yourself. Therefore, as you are working at the prewriting stage, first consider what you know about a general subject and then try to establish your "real" subject: that more specific aspect of your subject on which you are focussing most of your attention. Secondly, determine your *attitude* toward that real subject. Think about your answers to the following kinds of questions: What do I like and what do I dislike? What do I enjoy and what do I not enjoy? What are the positive aspects and what are the negative aspects? Then consider why you take this attitude or viewpoint. Finally, you should express your subject and attitude as clearly and accurately as possible. Often a simple statement, such as, "What impresses me most about [subject] is [real subject] because [attitude]" can be helpful in this task. A sentence in which a writer presents his or her subject and attitude toward that subject is termed a *thesis statement*. After discovering what you know about a subject and your attitude toward that subject, you are ready to select and arrange this material in an outline.

The *outline* serves as your detailed "map" for proceeding from experience to expression, so that you know where you are going and how you are getting there. Your outline should be divided into three basic sections in which you (1) *introduce* your subject, (2) *develop* your subject, and (3) *conclude* your subject. The material included in an introduction should present both your subject and attitude toward that subject — a thesis statement — and also offer readers some general context, or orientation, to your subsequent development of your thesis. A conclusion should define the significance of your work with a genuine response to the question, "Why did I bother to write this?" Therefore, most of the material you have discovered during prewriting will be presented in the development section of your outline. This material should be arranged as several main items, or areas of concern. One practical way to organize your prewriting materials into these three basic sections of an outline is by following this five-part form:

I.   Introduction
II.A Item 1
II.B Item 2
II.C Item 3
III.   Conclusion

This model outline may be used for writing a simple paragraph, a short three-paragraph essay (sections 1, 2, and 3), a longer five-paragraph essay (sections I, II.A, II.B, II.C, III), and a full-length essay, report, or research paper (sections I, II.A, II.B, II.C, III further subdivided into paragraphs). This model can also be readily adapted to your material and writing techniques, especially as you gain experience in writing and learn more about the practice of other writers from your reading in this book and elsewhere.

Writing

After you have completed prewriting, your first and most important step in the writing process, is essentially a step in which you closely follow the prewriting material in your outline — your map — from the introduction through the development to the conclusion. You must choose your words and phrases carefully as you proceed, and you should present them to your readers in clear, effective, and correct sentences. In turn, your sentences should relate to one another in a unified, well-developed, and coherent pattern of expression — a paragraph. You may discover new ideas and experiences along the way, make more detailed observations, or even find shortcuts you can take in your outline, but you must try hard not to get lost. If you do encounter problems, remember that you still have one more step to take in the writing process of going from experience to expression.

Rewriting

Rewriting is your opportunity to revise your work. Slowly read what you have written. Decide what changes are either necessary or desirable. Pay special attention to your initial choices of words and phrases, sentence structure, the development of each paragraph, and the overall unity and coherence of your writing. Your spelling and punctuation should also be checked for possible errors. Repeat this rewriting step several times. Reading your work aloud is also an effective post writing technique.

During the writing process, at the writing as well as at the rewriting step, some people experience great difficulty with using an adequate vocabulary, constructing grammatically correct sentences, or maintaining general coherence in paragraphs. Some may also make notable errors in verb forms and tenses or frequently misspell basic vocabulary words. These writing problems result from poorly developed basic structures in written expression and, consequently, cannot be dealt with adequately through writing and rewriting. Supplementary instructional and exercise material presented in a good writing handbook, workbook, tutorial or writing lab are crucial in developing appropriate skills.

WRITING PATTERNS

Although writing is a process of working our way from experience to expression, a writer should take the steps in this process with an understanding of some useful patterns of thought common to both our experience and our expression. At the prewriting step, these patterns offer you many different ways of thinking about a subject. Then, when you are making an outline, these patterns will help you organize what you have discovered; each one can be used in our five-part model outline. They are also important for developing effective paragraphs and even sentences when you are writing and rewriting.

As you study the theory and practice of the following eight rhetorical patterns in this book, you will learn more about how they can be used to develop possibilities for making meaningful relations between experience and expression in your own writing.

A *description* is a presentation of detailed perceptual images to show a single dominant impression of a person, a place, an object, or an event.

A *narration* is an arrangement of actions or events in a meaningful, often chronological, sequence to show what happened.

Illustration provides specific examples, instances, or cases to support, clarify, and develop general ideas.

Comparison and *contrast* show the relations between two subjects: a comparison deals with their similarities whereas a contrast emphasizes their differences.

An analysis divides a whole subject into constituent parts: *classification analysis* divides a subject into categories, classes, or kinds; *process analysis* divides an operation into stages and steps; and, *causal analysis* divides a subject in terms of relations between causes and effects.

An *argument* is a presentation of a claim or belief about a subject by means of appeals to reason, emotion, and ethical character that attempt to demonstrate its validity.

WRITING PURPOSES

Throughout the steps in the writing process, a writer must be conscious of his or her purpose. A writer's purpose is important because it influences many of the possibilities and limitations of the choices that need to be made with each step: subjects, details, words and phrases, writing patterns, and many more. In making relations between experience and expression, a writer must consider such choices carefully in the light of the main focus in a piece of writing: the writer, the subject, or the reader. If a writer's purpose is to express personal thoughts, observations, or experiences, such as we read in diaries, journals, personal letters, and autobiographies, then the purpose may be termed *expressive*. However, if a writer wants to present information or instructions about a subject, such as we encounter in newspaper and magazine articles, textbooks, reports, and biographies, then the purpose may be termed *informative*. When a writer tries to convince readers to accept or adopt his or her own view of a subject in an essay, an editorial, a review, a letter of recommendation and so forth, the writer's purpose may be termed *persuasive*.

How are expressive, informative, and persuasive writing related to what kinds of writing patterns (description, narration, etc.) are most appropriate for you to choose for a piece of writing? In general, an expressive purpose is well served by either description or narration. An informative purpose is usually best handled in a mode of exposition (illustration, comparison-contrast, classification analysis, process analysis, or causal analysis). A persuasive purpose requires the use of argument.

How are your choices of subjects, words, or phrases related to these purposes? A writer's purpose reflects his or her awareness of the *audience* for a piece of writing. Regardless of a writer's main focus—the writer, the subject, or the reader—the task of communicating with one's readers is crucial to the effectiveness of expressive, informative, and persuasive writing. Readers' interests, needs, and attitudes should be addressed throughout the writing process by your answering the following questions: Who are my readers? What do they already know about my subject? What do they need to know? How will they respond to this thesis, this general idea, this specific example, this word, or this phrase?

A writer's successful fulfilment of his or her purpose may require *research*, particularly in informative and persuasive writing. By supplementing and developing one's personal experience with other people's knowledge, a writer can express a more authoritative understanding of a subject through his or her experience with books, journals, magazines, newspapers, documents, and interviews. A writer must often consult such research sources for background information and evidence that will contribute to a piece of writing's accuracy, comprehensiveness, and interest. Although the procedures for selecting, integrating, and documenting research sources for your writing will require the addition of special skills and concerns to each stage in the writing process, you will find the results rewarding.

EXPERIENCE AND EXPRESSION

Finally, when you are working on your own essays in the light of your reading in the theory and practice of effective writing found in this book and elsewhere, always keep in mind this advice offered by Henry James: "Write from experience and experience only," and "try to be one of the people on whom nothing is lost!" The prose selections and instructional material in this book suggest how you can relate experience and expression in a variety of ways for different purposes appropriate to common writing situations, and do so in a meaningful and significant manner. Northrop Frye writes: "Too often the study of literature, or even the study of language, is thought of as a kind of elegant accomplishment, a matter of talking good grammar or keeping up with one's reading. I'm trying to show that the subject is a little more serious than that. I don't see how the study of language and literature can be separated from the question of free speech, which we all know is fundamental to our society . . . . You see, freedom has nothing to do with lack of training; it can only be the product of training. You're not free to move unless you've learned to walk, and not free to play the piano unless you practise. Nobody is capable of free speech unless he knows how to use the language, and such knowledge is not a gift: it has to be learned and worked at."

CHAPTER 1

"You'd never guess it was a cemetery.
Death had not spoiled it at all."

DESCRIPTION

We live in a world where a common feature of our experience is the pictures created for us by others through television, movies, paintings, and photographs. A description is also a kind of picture, one painted in words by a writer to show readers a single dominant impression of a person, a place, an object, or an event. In descriptive writing, writers use words to make images that appeal to our senses of perception: sight, hearing, touch, smell, and taste. These images are arranged so that the subject is developed from one detailed perception to another until a clear and well-focussed picture results. The authors of the descriptions you will read in this chapter — Traill, Thoreau, Carr, Robertson, and Dryden — demonstrate how effectively we can use language to create such pictures in order to express ourselves or to inform others about our experiences.

The general *subject* of a writer's description is best chosen from among people, places, objects, and events most familiar from personal experience. The descriptions in this chapter are based on writers' thoughtful observations of the world around them: a picturesque pond, crosses in an Indian graveyard, a rural shopping night, a sleigh ride, and the experiences of a hockey goalie. Writing down your own day-to-day observations in freewriting, lists, and journal entries will provide a good way for you to choose an interesting and meaningful subject for a description from a wide range of possible subjects.

After a general subject has been selected, a writer must focus on a more specific aspect of this subject to define the description's single dominant impression. A writer should ask two questions: first, "What is my *real* subject?" and, secondly, "What is my *attitude* toward my real subject?" The writer's attitude toward a subject reflects the *purpose* of the description. Is it *expressive*, focussing primarily on the writer's own experience of the subject, as in Traill's account of "A Sleigh Ride"? Or is it *informative*, stressing the subject itself, as in Robertson's "Sale Night"? The answers which define both a writer's real subject and his or her attitude toward that real subject are usually expressible in the form of a single statement, such as the following one: "What impresses me most about [general subject] is [real subject] because [attitude]." For example: ["What impresses me most about my hometown is the old brick buildings because they stand in defiance of so many recent changes."] This kind of statement, a *thesis statement*, may be *explicit* (included in the description) or *implicit* (withheld from the description).

A writer's conscious awareness of both subject and purpose helps to determine what content, structure, and techniques are most appropriate to the *development* of a description. During the prewriting step, writers must recall how a subject affected them in their own personal experience, and then find the most accurate words and phrases to communicate those sensations to others. This task requires the selection of *concrete* words;

that is, words that refer to what we perceive with our senses, such as "sleighbells," "trees," "headlights," and "bruises." Many words are *abstract*, and refer to ideas removed from immediate sense experience: "beauty," "death," "religious," and "fun." Although such words may be used sparingly in a description (for instance, in a thesis statement), most of the words should be not only concrete but also *specific*; that is, be particular and definite. Consider, for example, the movement from abstract to concrete to particular in Catharine Parr Traill's sentence: "Nothing can surpass the loveliness [abstract] of the woods after a snowstorm [concrete] has loaded every bough and sprig with its feathery deposit [specific]." Instead of merely using words that tell readers about their subject, writers must carefully choose concrete words to create specific and detailed images which readers can perceive for themselves; words and phrases that appeal to the five senses create images for us to see, hear, touch, smell, and taste in our own minds. When you are working on a description of your own at the prewriting step, you might want to try the following exercise: write five sentences to support your thesis statement so that each sentence appeals to a different sense of perception.

Thesis statement: What impresses me most about [general subject] is [real subject] because [attitude].

1. Sight:
2. Hearing
3. Touch:
4. Taste:
5. Smell:

Throughout the process of writing an effective description, a writer must be concerned with the language of description: words and phrases that actually show readers the subject in a vivid, clear, and precise way.

After a writer has explored the images associated with a subject at the prewriting stage, he or she must then select several main images that will contribute to a description's single dominant impression. These images should be arranged in an outline so that they follow one predominant pattern of perception:

I.   Introduction
II. A   Image 1
II. B   Image 2
II. C   Image 3
III.   Conclusion

A writer may adopt a *spatial* arrangement, ordering these images in the way our eyes would follow them when we are observing a place. Alternatively, a writer may decide on a *temporal* arrangement, presenting the images as we would encounter them in time. A more complex, imaginative arrangement of images may be developed to emphasize their *dramatic* relations.

The writer should also establish the *position* from which these images are being perceived; usually one may work from either a *fixed* position, from which the images can be presented as several related features of the subject, or a *moving position*, whereby the images are recorded as a sequence of observations.

For readers and writers alike, descriptions offer detailed perceptions of ourselves and our world. Descriptions reveal discoveries, novelty, and awarenesses in our sensory experience of the ordinary as well as the extraordinary in life. The images and patterns of that experience require careful and thoughtful attention; they are the raw materials out of which we form our ideas and our lives.

Spatial description of objects.

CATHARINE PARR TRAILL

When Catharine Parr Traill (1802-1899) immigrated to Canada from England in 1832 shortly after marrying Lieutenant Thomas Traill, she had already published more than a half dozen children's books, including The Young Emigrants; or, Pictures of Life in Canada: Calculated to Amuse and Instruct the Minds of Youth *(1826). Traill presented practical advice and keen observations in two well-known instructional and informative guidebooks:* The Backwoods of Canada *(1836) and* The Female Emigrant's Guide, and Hints on Canadian Housekeeping *(1854). These books were based on her experiences as a pioneer and a settler in Upper Canada (in Lakefield, Peterborough, and Rice Lake, Ontario). She also wrote several more children's books, numerous magazine articles, and three books on the plants and animals of Ontario. Traill's best writing is characterized by the clear images, detailed observations, and optimistic attitude of this account from* The Backwoods of Canada, *of a winter sleigh ride with her younger sister, Susanna Moodie, also a well-known writer. "A Sleigh Ride" offers you a model of fine journal writing, a popular nineteenth-century form of expressive writing which many writers today continue to use as an invaluable prewriting technique. Although Traill's style and language differ from your own, consider what features of her content and technique could be effectively adapted to your expressive writing.*

A SLEIGH RIDE

1   I left the dear children all soundly sleeping and accompanied my sister Susan home in the ox-sleigh; we made a merry party comfortably nested in our rude vehicle, with a bed of clean straw, and a nice blanket over it, with pillows to lean against; well wrapped up in our Scotch plaids, we defied the cold and chatted merrily away, not a whit less happy than if we had been rolling along in a carriage with a splendid pair of bays, instead of crawling along at a funeral pace, in the rudest of all vehicles with the most ungraceful of all steeds; our canopy, the snow-laden branches of pine, hemlock, and cedar, the dark forest around us, and our lamps the pale stars and watery moon struggling through "wrack and mist" and silver-tinged snow-clouds. Here then were we breaking the deep silence of the deep woods with the hum of cheerful voices and the wild mirth that bursts from the lighthearted children. No other sound was there except the heavy tread of the oxen and the lumbering sound of the sleigh as it jolted over the fallen sticks and logs that lay beneath the snow.

2   "Nothing can surpass the loveliness of the woods after a snowstorm has loaded every bough and sprig with its feathery deposit. The face of the ground, so rough and tangled with a mass of uptorn trees, broken boughs, and timbers in every stage of decay, seems by the touch of some powerful magician's wand to have changed its character. Unrivalled purity, softness, and brilliancy, has taken the place of confusion and vegetable corruption. It is one of the greatest treats this country affords me, to journey through the thick woods after a heavy snowfall —whether it be by the brilliant light of the noonday sun in the cloudless azure sky, giving a brightness to every glittering particle that clothes the trees or surface of the ground, or hangs in heavy masses on the evergreens, converting their fan-shaped boughs into foliage of feathery whiteness and most fantastic forms— or by the light of a full moon and frosty stars looking down through the snowy tops of the forest trees —sometimes shining through a veil of haze, which the frost converts into a sparkling rime that encases every spray and twig with crystals. The silent fall of the lighter particles of snow, which the gentlest motion of the air shakes down, is the only motion the still scene affords —with the merry jingle of our sleighbells.

— CONTRAST   alliteration

Questions on Content

1   What is the subject of Traill's description? What is her attitude toward that subject?

2   What is Traill's thesis statement? Is this thesis explicit or implicit in her description?

3   What major images support Traill's thesis?

4   What significance do these images seem to hold for Traill?

Questions on Structure and Technique

1   What specific words appeal to the reader's senses?

2   Are the images arranged in a predominantly spatial, temporal, or dramatic pattern? Explain how.

3   What specific words and phrases does Traill choose in order to emphasize this pattern?

4   What words exemplify Traill's nineteenth-century vocabulary and style? What words would you choose instead?

5   Is Traill's purpose primarily expressive or informative? Why? Of what value do you think this purpose would be for Traill? For you?

Suggestions for Writing

1   Based on details from your own personal experience, write a description in which you support Traill's view that "Nothing can surpass the loveliness of the woods after a snowstorm . . . ."

2   Describe your experience of city streets after a snowstorm.

3   Describe a scene or an event in which difficult circumstances are made pleasurable.

HENRY DAVID THOREAU

Henry David Thoreau (1817-1862) was born in Concord, Massachusetts, and lived there almost all of his life. Thoreau was educated at Harvard College and lived an unconventional life reading classical and Hindu literature, writing in his journal, studying nature, occasionally teaching, often lecturing, and visiting with friends and acquaintances who included many of the best-known writers of the time: Ralph Waldo Emerson, Nathaniel Hawthorne, Margaret Fuller, Ellery Channing, and Bronson Alcott. In "Walden Pond," a brief selection from his most popular work, Walden *(1854), Thoreau's skills as a journal writer are applied in this description of the place near Concord where he lived relatively alone for two years (1845 to 1847). Thoreau's abstract language in the first sentence is developed through his use of concrete words and phrases which appeal to our senses of perception. The resulting images become even more refined and clear as Thoreau adds increasingly specific details. Throughout the description Thoreau not only shows us his subject, the pond; he also involves us in his process of perceiving that subject. Thoreau's other important works include* A Week on the Concord and Merrimack Rivers *(1849), essays on the abolition of slavery, and "Resistance to Civil Government," an essay on civil disobedience and human rights.*

WALDEN POND

1   The scenery of Walden is on a humble scale, and, though very beautiful, does not approach to grandeur, nor can it much concern one who has not long frequented it or lived by its shore; yet this pond is so remarkable for its depth and purity as to merit a particular description. It is a clear and deep green well, half a mile long and a mile and three quarters in circumference, and contains about sixty-one and a half acres; a perennial spring in the midst of pine and oak woods, without any visible inlet or outlet except by the clouds and evaporation. The surrounding hills rise abruptly from the water to the height of forty to eighty feet, though on the southeast and east they attain to about one hundred and one hundred and fifty feet respectively, within a quarter and a third of a mile. They are exclusively woodland. All our Concord waters have two colors at least; one when viewed at a distance, and another, more proper, close at hand. The first depends more on the light, and follows the sky. In clear weather, in summer, they appear blue at a little distance, especially if agitated, and at a great distance all appear alike. In stormy weather they are some-

times of a dark slate-color. The sea, however, is said to be blue one day and green another without any perceptible change in the atmosphere. I have seen our river, when, the landscape being covered with snow, both water and ice were almost as green as grass. Some consider blue "to be the color of pure water, whether liquid or solid." But, looking directly down into our waters from a boat, they are seen to be of very different colors. Walden is blue at one time and green at another, even from the same point of view. Lying between the earth and the heavens, it partakes of the color of both. Viewed from a hilltop it reflects the color of the sky; but near at hand it is of a yellowish tint next the shore where you can see the sand, then a light green, which gradually deepens to a uniform dark green in the body of the pond. In some lights, viewed even from a hilltop, it is of a vivid green next the shore. Some have referred this to the reflection of the verdure; but it is equally green there against the railroad sandbank, and in the spring, before the leaves are expanded, and it may be simply the result of the prevailing blue mixed with the yellow of the sand. Such is the color of its iris. This is that portion, also, where in the spring, the ice being warmed by the heat of the sun reflected from the bottom, and also transmitted through the earth, melts first and forms a narrow canal about the still frozen middle. Like the rest of our waters, when much agitated, in clear weather, so that the surface of the waves may reflect the sky at the right angle, or because there is more light mixed with it, it appears at a little distance of a darker blue than the sky itself; and at such a time, being on its surface, and looking with divided vision, so as to see the reflection, I have discerned a matchless and indescribable light blue, such as watered or changeable silks and sword blades suggest, more cerulean than the sky itself, alternating with the original dark green on the opposite sides of the waves, which last appeared but muddy in comparison. It is a vitreous greenish blue, as I remember it, like those patches of the winter sky seen through cloud vistas in the west before sundown. Yet a single glass of its water held up to the light is as colorless as an equal quantity of air. It is well known that a large plate of glass will have a green tint, owing, as the makers say, to its "body," but a small piece of the same will be colorless. How large a body of Walden water would be required to reflect a green tint I have never proved. The water of our river is black or a very dark brown to one looking directly down on it, and, like that of most ponds, imparts to the body of one bathing in it a yellowish tinge; but this water is of such crystalline purity that the body of the bather appears of an alabaster whiteness, still more unnatural, which, as the limbs are magnified and distorted withal, produces a monstrous effect, making fit studies for a Michael Angelo.

Questions on Content

1   What is Thoreau's subject? What is Thoreau's attitude toward this subject? What sentence defines his subject and attitude most clearly?

2   How does Thoreau's use of images support that thesis?

3   What significance does Walden Pond seem to hold for Thoreau?

4   What effects does the final image of "the bather" have on the description as a whole?

Questions on Structure and Technique

1   What sense does Thoreau's use of concrete language primarily appeal to? Do his words and phrases appeal to any other senses? How does this appeal to the reader's perceptions support Thoreau's thesis?

2   What comparisons does Thoreau draw in his description? What contrasts?

3   Is Thoreau's arrangement of details predominantly spatial, temporal, or dramatic? What other techniques are important to this arrangement?

4   What is Thoreau's position as an observer? What effects does Thoreau achieve by using this position to arrange his details? How does this technique support Thoreau's thesis?

Suggestions for Writing

1   Write a detailed description of a place that you have studied very carefully, emphasizing its shifting and changing qualities.

2   Describe a place from several different viewpoints, noting the similarities and differences that you observe from each perspective.

3   Select a landscape painting and write a description of the scene in which you pay particular attention to the play of light and colour you perceive.

EMILY CARR

Emily Carr (1871-1945) was born in Victoria, B.C. and studied painting in San Francisco, England, and Paris. From 1898 to the 1930s she engaged her artistic talent and creativity in paintings of the Indian culture and West coast landscapes she came to know so well. Later in her career she developed her ability to work with these fascinating images and impressions as a writer in several autobiographical books: Klee Wyck *(1941),* The Book of Small *(1942), and* The House of All Sorts *(1944). Several other books and collections of her prose were published after her death. "Century Time" is a chapter from her first book,* Klee Wyck, *which won a Governor General's Award. Carr's controlled use of details and images in this description develops several important contrasts which invite the reader to "see" the experience of one's place and time in novel, meaningful ways.*

CENTURY TIME

1   You would never guess it was a cemetery. Death had not spoiled it at all.

2   It was full of trees and bushes except in one corner where the graves were. Even they were fast being covered with greenery.

3   Bushes almost hid the raw, split-log fence and the gate of cedar strips with a cross above it, which told you that the enclosed space belonged to the dead. The land about the cemetery might change owners, but the ownership of the cemetery would not change. It belonged to the dead for all time.

4   Persistent growth pushed up through the earth of it — on and on eternally — growth that was the richer for men's bodies helping to build it.

5   The Indian settlement was small. Not many new graves were required each year. The Indians only cleared a small bit of ground at a time. When that was full they cleared more. Just as soon as the grave boxes were covered with earth, vines and brambles began to creep over the mounds. Nobody cut them away. It was no time at all before life spread a green blanket over the Indian dead.

6   It was a quiet place this Indian cemetery, lying a little aloof from the village. A big stump field, swampy and green, separated them. Birds called across the field and flew into the quiet tangle of the cemetery bushes and nested there among foliage so newly created that it did not know anything about time. There was no road into the cemetery to be worn dusty by feet, or stirred into gritty clouds by hearse

wheels. The village had no hearse. The dead were carried by friendly hands across the stump field.

7   The wooded part of the cemetery dropped steeply to a lake. You could not see the water of the lake because of the trees, but you could feel the space between the cemetery and the purple-topped mountain beyond.

8   In the late afternoon a great shadow-mountain stepped across the lake and brooded over the cemetery. It had done this at the end of every sunny day for centuries, long, long before that piece of land was a cemetery. Dark came and held the shadow-mountain there all night, but when morning broke, it was back again inside its mountain, which pushed its grand purple dome up into the sky and dared the pines swarming around its base to creep higher than half-way up its bare rocky sides.

9   Indians do not hinder the progress of their dead by embalming or tight coffining. When the spirit has gone they give the body back to the earth. The earth welcomes the body—coaxes new life and beauty from it, hurries over what men shudder at. Lovely tender herbage bursts from the graves, swiftly, exulting over corruption.

10   Opening the gate I entered and walked among the graves. Pushing aside the wild roses, bramble blossoms and scarlet honeysuckle which hugged the crude wooden crosses, I read the lettering on them—

SACRED OF KATIE — IPOO
SAM BOYAN HE DIDE — IPOO
RIP JULIE YECTON — IPOO
JOSEPH'S ROSIE DI — IPOO

11   Even these scant words were an innovation — white men's ways; in the old days totem signs would have told you who lay there. The Indian tongue had no written words. In place of the crosses the things belonging to the dead would have been heaped on the grave: all his dear treasures, clothes, pots and pans, bracelets — so that everyone might see what life had given to him in things of his own.

12   "IPOO" was common to almost every grave. I wrote the four-lettered word on a piece of paper and took it to a woman in the village.

"What does this mean? It is on the graves."

"Mean die time."

"Die time?"

"Uh huh. Tell when he die."

"But all the graves tell the same."

"Uh huh. Four this kind," (she pointed separately to each of the four letters, IPOO) "tell now time."

13   "But everybody did not die at the same time. Some died long ago and some die now?"

14   "Uh huh. Maybe some year just one man die — one baby. Maybe influenza come — he come two time — one time long far, one time close. He make lots, lots Injun die."

15   "But, if it means the time people died, why do they put 'IPOO' on the old graves as well as on the new?"

16   Difficult English thoughts furrowed her still forehead. Hard English words came from her slow tongue in abrupt jerks. Her brown finger touched the I and the P. "He know," she said, "he tell it. This one and this one" (pointing to the two O's) "small — he no matter. He changes every year. Just this one and this matter" (pointing again to I and P). "He tell it."

17   Time was marked by centuries in this cemetery. Years — little years — what are they? As significant as the fact that reversing the figure nine turns it into the letter P.

Questions on Content

1   How does Carr clarify her statement that "death had not spoiled" the Indian cemetery?

X 2   What contrasts are implicit in Carr's description of the Indian cemetery? What specific details develop these contrasts?

X 3   Where are these contrasts made explicit? What major image enables the reader to visualize these contrasts?

4   What is Carr's real subject in this description? What attitude toward her subject does this description embody?

Questions on Structure and Technique

X 1   Is Carr's arrangement of images predominantly spatial? Temporal? Dramatic?

2   What effects does Carr achieve by using this technique?

3   Does Carr adopt a fixed or a moving position for her description? Why?

4   How does Carr's treatment of specific images support her thesis? Is her purpose primarily expressive or informative? Explain.

Suggestions for Writing

1   Describe a cemetery that you have visited, showing how its appearance reveals a general concept of life and death.

2   Write a description of a scene or an event where something significant that you did not understand was explained to you so that the whole
experience became more meaningful.

3   Write a description of a place that holds significant meaning for you,
showing your readers why it has that significance through your use of specific details and images.

HEATHER ROBERTSON

Freelance author Heather Robertson (b. 1942) vividly describes her experience of "Sale Night" in a small farming community where traditional values seem at odds with contemporary life. Robertson uses detailed images to present a vivid picture of a common scene throughout this country, emphasizing the complex and contradictory qualities that bring these people and this place to life. Born and educated in Winnipeg, and now living in Toronto, Robertson has written many books on Canadian society and history, one of her latest being Willie: A Romance *(1983) about William Lyon MacKenzie King's private life.*

SALE NIGHT

Honk if you Love Jesus!
(Bumper sticker, Winkler, Manitoba)

1   It's a bad night for a sale, but the flyers have been out for days now, stuffed into 20,000 mailboxes in Winkler, Morden, Horndean, Rosenfeld, St. Jean, Gretna, Altona, Manitou, and Plum Coulee. In fact, just about every household in southern Manitoba has received a fat flyer announcing Winkler's second January

MOONLIGHT SALE!
Open Til 11 p.m.!   First Come First Served!
Keep your eyes open to get the
FANTASTIC BUYS
BACON ENDS!   BANANAS!
19¢ lb.   9¢ lb. (6 p.m. to 9 p.m.)
Check These Hourly Specials!
Starting at 10 p.m. to 11 p.m.
Wide Angle
DUST PANS!
15 inches   Reg. 98¢
39¢ ea.
ALL ITEMS ARE AS STOCK LASTS!
The Moonlight Sale will be opened by a
Torchlight Parade of Snowmobiles
Down Winkler's Main Street at 7:00 p.m.
THURS. JAN. 20th
(Prices Good Only at Time Listed)

The temperature in Winkler at 7 p.m. on Thursday, January 20, 1972, is 35 below zero and dropping. The air is frozen into little slivers of glass which pierce the lungs. The light from the full moon reflected in the crystallized air makes the night fluorescent. People scurry through the neon streets beneath small white clouds of congealed breath like the balloons in comic strips. Tears run down their cheeks. The cold freezes hands and feet to blocks of wood. It hurts to walk more than a few feet; even the cars scream and groan. The snowmobile parade has been cancelled because there's no snow.

2   Hundreds of cars begin to pour into Winkler just after suppertime, drawn like maggots to the smell of 20 per cent off. They come from all directions, strung out in long cavalcades, their lights visible on the highways for miles around, an encircling army on the march. Before 7 p.m. every parking space in Winkler is taken, not only on Main Street but on all the side streets for three and four blocks in every direction. All the church parking lots are full. The streets are choked with cars going round and round in hopeless circles, sending up blinding plumes of frozen exhaust which glow hellfire red from the brake lights. All the cars converge on the corner of Main Street and Mountain Avenue, Winkler's principal intersection, and create a monumental traffic jam, since Winkler's principal intersection, like all its other intersections, lacks a traffic light — a source of great humiliation to Winkler. Every car disgorges a horde of people swaddled in scarves, who run for the nearest store. They have waited a year for Winkler's Moonlight Sale and they're not going to miss it.

3   The stores are jammed. Knots of people spill out onto the sidewalks. They saunter casually from store to store as if it were a hot day in July and poke their heads in the windows of parked cars to say hello to the old women in babushkas huddled inside. Main Street is sunny, bathed in yellow lamplight streaming from the store windows; the headlights on the stalled cars make the street as bright as noon. The music store is piping cheerful accordion music into the street to entice people in towards the electric organs and color TVs. Even the Bible bookstore, which sells evangelical bumper stickers ("Have a Nice Eternity!"), is doing a thumping trade in sacred records and religious tracts.

4   The centre of excitement, and really the only reason for coming to Winkler, is Gladstone's store, a fabulous emporium of goods rescued from fire sales and bankruptcies across western Canada which takes up almost a full block on Main Street. Tension increases as 7:30 p.m. approaches, because that's the time of Gladstone's first Treasure Spot. The person standing closest to the hidden Treasure Spot receives his choice of any dress in the store for $1; if he has a Gladstone's sales slip for January 20, he gets another $25 worth of merchandise for another $1. The crowd in Gladstone's at 7:30 p.m. is so dense it's impossible to see who wins the Treasure Spot. The name of the winner is announced over the loud speaker; it's a man from a town 65 miles away.

5   People come at 7 p.m., because that's when apples go on sale for $2.09 a bushel and the Co-op has girls' blouses for 77 cents. But the featured items are cunningly spaced out to ensure that customers will spend as many hours as possible in Winkler. Pantyhose is 25 cents a pair at 8 p.m., but the orange juice doesn't go on sale until 9 p.m., and butter is cheap at 10 p.m. To save on all the specials a family has to spend between four and five hours in Winkler, and during that time, of course, they buy a whole lot of other stuff. The entrance-ways to the store are crammed with people standing guard over mounds of flour (100 pounds for $5.99), toilet paper, and tin cans. Waiting.

6   Eventually the crush pushes them out into the street, because in Winkler there's nowhere else to go. Winkler has a beer parlor, a dingy place in the old hotel still restricted to men only, and the Harvest Inn, a spartan arborite coffee shop. That's all. Squeezed out of the popular bargain basement stores, shoppers are forced to take refuge in the empty, higher-priced stores, much to the delight of the busi-nessmen who are able to turn a 30-cent saving on a bag of bananas into an $800 three-room group.

7   The sale is joyless. Women paw desultorily through piles of cheap chiffon scarves and odd shoes and, frowning, burrow among the bruised tomatoes and the wilted lettuce. There is no shoving or push-ing, no screaming or snatching or clawing, no bellows of anger or shrill arguments over merchandise. No laughter. Everyone is polite. People speak quietly in low voices, almost whispers. They stand patiently to be waited on, oblivious of the mob. In Penner's Dry Goods Store, where women have come for flannelette, the silence is almost reverent. It's a while before the low dull roar becomes noticeable. It's the steady oppressive sound of a million grasshoppers munching. Unsmiling, expressionless, methodical, the swarm of customers grinds its way through the store; they pick the shelves clean and devastate the fruit and vegetables. Some people have backed their cars and trucks up to the front door of Gladstone's grocery store; bent double like ants, they lug out bags of flour, cases of apples, and dozens of paper cartons full of groceries. They work with concentration, with passionate, single-minded intensity. Shopping in Winkler is taken very seriously. There is nothing else to do. Winkler has no movies (mov-ies are evil), no bars, no bowling alley, no clubs or lodges or frater-nal organizations (except the Chamber of Commerce). Dancing is forbidden. Drinking is disapproved of. Sex is frowned upon. Shop-ping is recreation, an acceptable orgy. Women often apologize after-wards, saying, "Oh, I didn't really need anything, I just went for the outing."

8   Winkler is the Shopping Centre of Southern Manitoba. It's also one of the most religious towns in the province.

Questions on Content

1   What is Robertson's attitude toward "Sale Night" in Winkler?

2   Robertson's thesis is implicit in her description, but what might that statement be if it were to be made explicit? Why is it not made explicit?

3   What do you most admire about these people's lifestyle? What do you least admire? How do you account for your view?

4   Is it necessary or unnecessary for Robertson to conclude by emphasizing that Winkler is "one of the most religious towns in the province" for the purpose of her description? Why? Why not?

Questions on Structure and Technique

1   In what ways do Robertson's choices of words and phrases emphasize her attitude towards "Sale Night"? What metaphors does she use in her descriptions? Can you account for her choices of these metaphors?

2   What senses do Robertson's images appeal to?

3   Is Robertson's arrangement of images predominantly spatial, temporal, or dramatic? Why is this pattern appropriate? Does she choose a "fixed" or a "moving" position?

4   Is the purpose of Robertson's description primarily expressive or informative? How is this purpose established? In what ways does Robertson's sentence structure contribute to this purpose?

Suggestions for Writing

1   Describe "Sale Night" at a place where you go shopping.

2   Describe an event in your city or town, showing how it embodies an apparent contradiction in people's values or beliefs.

3   Write a description of a popular event that you have experienced in which you illustrate the reasons for its success.

KEN DRYDEN

Former hockey goaltender, Ken Dryden (b. 1947), describes his experiences as a goalie by developing several different but related images that reveal the complexity of his thoughts and feelings about the role of a goalie. Dryden, now a lawyer who lives in Toronto with his family, played goal for ten years during the 1970s for the Montreal Canadiens, and for Team Canada in a series against the U.S.S.R. Dryden's autobiographical book, The Game (1983), is a fascinating discussion of professional hockey as this selection demonstrates.

THE GOALIE

1   I have always been a goalie. I became one long enough ago, before others' memories and reasons intruded on my own, that I can no longer remember why I did, but if I had to guess, it was because of Dave. Almost six years older, he started playing goal before I was old enough to play any position, so by the time I was six and ready to play, there was a set of used and discarded equipment that awaited me — that and an older brother I always tried to emulate.

2   I have mostly vague recollections of being a goalie at that time. I remember the spectacular feeling of splitting and sprawling on pavement or ice, and feeling that there was something somehow noble and sympathetic about having bruises and occasional cuts, especially if they came, as they did, from only a tennis ball. But if I have one clear image that remains, it is that of a goalie, his right knee on the ice, his left leg extended in a half splits, his left arm stretching for the top corner, and, resting indifferently in his catching glove, a round black puck.

3   It was the posed position of NHL goalies for promotional photos and hockey cards at the time and it was a position we tried to re-enact as often as we could in backyard games. There was something that looked and felt distinctly major league about a shot "raised" that high, and about a clean, precise movement into space to intercept it. Coming as it did without rebound, it allowed us to freeze the position as if in a photo, extending the movement, letting our feelings catch up to the play, giving us time to step outside ourselves and see what we had done. In school, or at home, with pencil and paper, sometimes thinking of what I was doing, more often just mindlessly doodling, I would draw pictures of goalies, not much more than stick figures really, but fleshed out with parallel lines, and always in that

same catching position. Each year when my father arranged for a photographer to take pictures for our family's Christmas card, as Dave and I readied ourselves in our nets, the shooter was told to shoot high to the glove side, that we had rehearsed the rest.

4   To catch a puck or a ball — it was the great joy of being a goalie. Like a young ballplayer, too young to hit for much enjoyment but old enough to catch and throw, it was something I could do before I was big enough to do the rest. But mostly it was the feeling it gave me. Even now, watching TV or reading a newspaper, I like to have a ball in my hands, fingering its laces, its seams, its nubby surface, until my fingertips are so alive and alert that the ball and I seem drawn to each other. I like to spin it, bounce it, flip it from hand to hand, throw it against a wall or a ceiling, and catch it over and over again. There is something quite magical about a hand that can follow a ball and find it so crisply and tidily every time, something solid and wonderfully reassuring about its muscular certainty and control. So, if it was because of Dave that I became a goalie, it was the feeling of catching a puck or a ball that kept me one. The irony, of course, would be that later, when I finally became a real goalie instead of a kid with a good glove hand, when I learned to use the other parts of a goaltender's equipment — skates, pads, blocker, stick — it could only be at the expense of what had been until then my greatest joy as a goalie.

5   I was nineteen at the time. It surely had been happening before then, just as it must before any watershed moment, but the time I remember was the warm-up for the 1967 NCAA final against Boston University. For the first few minutes, I remember only feeling good: a shot, a save, a shot, a save; loose, easy, the burn of nerves turning slowly to a burn of exhilaration. For a shot to my right, my right arm went up and I stopped it with my blocker; another, low to the corner, I kicked away with my pad; along the ice to the other side, my skate; high to the left, my catching glove. Again and again: a pad, a catching glove, a skate, a stick, a blocker, whatever was closest moved, and the puck stopped. For someone who had scooped up ice-skimming shots like a shortstop, who had twisted his body to make backhanded catches on shots for the top right corner, it was a moment of great personal triumph. I had come of age. As the warm-up was ending, I could feel myself becoming a goalie.

6   Goaltending is often described as the most dangerous position in sports. It is not. Race drivers die from racing cars, jockeys die, so do football players. Goalies do not die from being goalies. Nor do they suffer the frequent facial cuts, the knee and shoulder injuries, that forwards and defensemen often suffer. They stand as obstacles to a hard rubber disc, frequently shot at a lethal speed, sometimes unseen,

sometimes deflected; the danger to them is obvious, but it is exaggerated — even the unthinkable: a goalie diving anxiously out of the way of a 100 m.p.h. slap shot, the shooter panicking at his own recklessness, the fans "ah"-ing at the near miss. Except for that one, feared time, the time it doesn't happen that way, when the puck moves too fast and the goalie too slow, and, hit in the head, he falls frighteningly to the ice. Moments later, up again, he shakes his head, smiling as others slowly do the same, again reminded that he wears a mask which at other times he sees through and forgets. The danger of playing goal is a *potential* danger, but equipment technology, like a net below a trapeze act, has made serious injury extremely unlikely.

7   From the time I was six years old, until as a freshman at Cornell I was required to wear a mask, I received fifteen stitches. Since then I have had only four — from a Dennis Hull slap shot that rebounded off my chest, hitting under my chin, in my first playoff year. I have pulled groins and hamstrings, stretched, twisted, and bruised uncounted times various other things, sent my back into spasm twice, broken a toe, and torn the cartilage in one knee. In almost eight years, after more than 400 games and 1000 practices, that's not much.

8   Yet, I am often afraid. For while I am well protected, and know I'm unlikely to suffer more than a bruise from any shot that is taken, the puck hurts, constantly and cumulatively: through the pillow-thick leg pads I wear, where straps pulled tight around their shins squeeze much of the padding away; through armor-shelled skate boots; through a catching glove compromised too far for its flexibility; with a dull, aching nausea from stomach to throat when my jock slams back against my testes; and most often, on my arms, on wrists and forearms especially, where padding is light and often out of place, where a shot hits and spreads its ache, up an arm and through a body, until both go limp and feel lifeless. Through a season, a puck hurts like a long, slow battering from a skillful boxer, almost unnoticed in the beginning, but gradually wearing me down, until two or three times a year, I wake up in the morning sore, aching, laughing/moaning with each move I make, and feel a hundred years old. It is in those days and others that when practice comes, I shy away.

9   The puck on his stick, a player skates for the net. Deep in my crouch, intent, ready, to anyone watching I look the same as I always do. But, like a batter who has been knocked down too many times before, when I see a player draw back his stick to shoot, at the critical moment when concentration must turn to commitment, my body stiffens, my eyes widen and go sightless, my head lifts in the air, turning imperceptibly to the right, as if away from the puck — I bail out, leaving only an empty body behind to cover the net. I yell at myself as others might ("you chicken"). I tell myself reasonably, rationally, that lifting my head, blanking my eyes, can only put me in greater danger;

but I don't listen. In a game, each shot controlled by a harassing defense, with something else to think about I can usually put away fear and just play. But in practice, without the distraction of a game, seeing Tremblay or Lambert, Risebrough, Chartraw, or Lupien, dangerous, uncontrolled shooters as likely to hit my arms as a corner of the net, I cannot. In time the fear gradually shrinks back, manageable again, but it never quite goes away.

10   I have thought more about fear, I have been afraid more often, the last few years. For the first time this year, I have realized that I've only rarely been hurt in my career. I have noticed that unlike many, so far as I know, I carry with me no permanent injury. And now that I know I will retire at the end of the season, more and more I find myself thinking — *I've lasted this long: please let me get out in one piece.* For while I know I am well protected, while I know it's unlikely I will suffer any serious injury, like every other goalie I carry with me the fear of the *one big hurt* that never comes. Recently, I read of the retirement of a race-car driver. Explaining his decision to quit, he said that after his many years of racing, after the deaths of close friends and colleagues, after his own near misses, he simply "knew too much." I feel a little differently. I feel I have known all along what I know now. It's just that I can't forget it as easily as I once did.

11   Playing goal is not fun. Behind a mask, there are no smiling faces, no timely sweaty grins of satisfaction. It is a grim, humorless position, largely uncreative, requiring little physical movement, giving little physical pleasure in return. A goalie is simply there, tied to a net and to a game; the game acts, a goalie reacts. How he reacts, how often, a hundred shots or no shots, is not up to him. Unable to initiate a game's action, unable to focus its direction, he can only do what he's given to do, what the game demands of him, and that he must do. It is his job, a job that cannot be done one minute in every three, one that will not await rare moments of genius, one that ends when the game ends, and only then. For while a goal goes up in lights, a permanent record for the goal-scorer and the game, a save is ephemeral, important at the time, occasionally when a game is over, but able to be wiped away, undone, with the next shot. It is only when a game ends and the mask comes off, when the immense challenge of the job turns abruptly to immense satisfaction or despair, that the unsmiling grimness lifts and goes away.

Questions on Content

1   What aspects of being a goalie does Dryden enjoy? What aspects does he dread?

2   What major images illustrate his feelings of enjoyment? What major images illustrate his feelings of dread?

3   In what sense does the description in the final paragraph take on metaphorical significance? What aspects of the description in previous paragraphs contribute to this significance?

4   What is Dryden's thesis? Is this thesis implicit or explicit? Why?

Questions on Structure and Technique

1   Is Dryden's arrangement of images predominantly temporal or dramatic? What contrasts does Dryden exemplify within this pattern? Why are these contrasts significant to Dryden's thesis?

2   What senses do Dryden's images appeal to? Find examples of particularly effective words and phrases that intensify your involvement in Dryden's description.

3   Is Dryden's purpose primarily expressive or informative? Explain?

4   What paragraphs in Dryden's description are most objective? What paragraphs are most subjective? What differences do you find in Dryden's use of language when you contrast these paragraphs? What effects do these differences have on the description as a whole?

Suggestions for Writing

1   Write a description of yourself in which you deal with pleasurable as well as painful aspects of your experiences.

2   Complete the statement, "I have always been a _____," and then write a detailed description in which you show your readers your implicit attitude toward that subject.

3   Describe your experiences as a participant in a sport or game, developing that description in informative (objective) as well as expressive (subjective) terms. Be sure that your primary purpose is clearly established.

CHAPTER 2

"The wind was overweening; it was unmannerly; it roused resentment."

NARRATION

We all tell stories about others and about ourselves. Our stories give a sense of order and meaning to actions and events that our experiences themselves seldom possess. Narration is storytelling. In a narration, a writer selects and arranges a succession of actions or events in a meaningful, often chronological, sequence to show readers *what happened*. Any simple account of a series of actions or events is a narrative, but writers develop basic expressions of what happened into more complex forms: autobiography, biography, history, news stories, sports reports, case histories, and fictional short stories and novels. In all of these forms, writers organize experiences into sequences of actions and events taking place in time. As the narratives included in this chapter show, however, a writer's careful attention to the manner of expression — *how* a writer expresses what happened — is especially important in narration.

What happened? Every day we answer this question so frequently and easily that we have become accustomed to thinking about our experiences as sequences of actions and events which have occurred in our lives. In giving our responses, we do not usually stop to consider *how* we are selecting, arranging, and developing those sequences out of the somewhat complex, chaotic, and unrelated actions and events of our actual experiences. Throughout the process of composing an effective narrative, however, a writer must make conscious choices about the sequence of events he or she wishes to present.

When you are deciding on the *subject* for a narration during the prewriting step, for instance, choose from among those actions or events which are not only of considerable personal interest and significance for you but are also those you know best from your own experience. By doing so, that familiarity with your subject will expand the range of possibilities for its treatment in your narrative. In the narratives you will be reading here, the authors' authority on their chosen subjects, grounded in their own experiences, also gives the quality of authenticity to their writing: Charles G. D. Roberts' narrative account of a fight between a snake and a mouse exemplifies his knowledge of animal behaviour; Nellie McClung's narration of events during one of her family's Christmas gatherings illustrates her early concern with minority rights issues.

After you have carefully chosen the subject for a narrative, you must then decide which actions or events are the most important ones to develop among the possibilities offered you by the experience itself. When you are selecting these actions or events, think about how your choices reflect your *attitude* toward your experience. In the narratives you will be reading, the authors' attitudes toward events are reflected through *conflicts* between people, places, or things. These conflicts are not imposed on the actions or events, but they are usually highlighted in a narrative. An implicit or explicit thesis statement should be written to define such a conflict. A basic outline of the main actions or events may then be sketched, as follows:

I.   Introduction
II. A Event 1
II. B Event 2
II. C Event 3
III.   Conclusion

However, these main actions or events must be further arranged into a meaningful sequence that makes clear and effective relations between them. By definition, a narrative relates events in time, so you must determine their beginning and ending as well as their relative duration. In your reading, you will see how writers compress, extend, and even reorder the main actions and events in narrative time in order to suit their purposes while maintaining a clear general sense of a narrative's overall direction. You will also notice how writers use their sentences to control time sequences, and how they purposefully shift verb tenses in their sentences to indicate relations between past, present, and future.

The *development* of the fundamental question — "what happened?" — must answer several other related questions: who, where, when, why, and how. A writer's responses should lead to the selection of specific details and images, concrete words and phrases, appealing to readers' senses of perception. In narration as well as in description, a writer must strive to show rather than tell their readers about the subject. A writer's narrative shows readers what happened, but readers' perceptions are not only determined by a writer's selection, arrangement, and development of actions or events. A writer must also establish the narrative *point of view* from which events are presented. That point of view may or may not be the same as the writer's own current perspective. The narrator who shows readers what happened may be either an "I" who participates directly or indirectly in events (first-person narration), as in Nellie McClung's "Christmas in Manitoba," or an observer who stands back from the events recording his or her perceptions (third-person narration), as in Charles G. D. Roberts' "In the Deep Grass." In adopting either approach, the writer must try to ensure that the narrator's voice uses language in a consistent and appropriate manner in keeping with his or her perspective on the events as they unfold. If the writer introduces the dialogue of a first-person narrator and other speakers into the narrative, this should be done purposefully and naturally.

Just as a meaningful experience is as much how it happens as what happens, an effective narrative results from a writer's attention to how an experience is expressed as well as to what is expressed. In this process of recreation, a writer may discover new possibilities for order and meaning in actions and events in experience as in expression.

CHARLES G. D. ROBERTS

*Sir Charles G. D. Roberts (1860-1943), born and educated in New Bruns-
wick, enjoyed a long, prolific, and acclaimed career as an author and has
been called "the father of Canadian literature." Roberts published nine
books of poetry, a dozen fictional romances, and nearly two dozen collections of animal stories. From* The Watchers of the Trails, *"In the Deep Grass"
is typical of Roberts' best prose found in his animal stories, stories where
a dynamic, natural tension between destruction and survival is enacted
that, Roberts says, "helps us to return to nature, without requiring that
we . . . return to barbarism." Roberts' use of detailed images shows how
effectively and purposefully writers may incorporate description into a
narrative pattern of development.*

IN THE DEEP GRASS

1   Misty gray green, washed with tints of the palest violet, spotted with
red clover-blooms, white oxeyes, and hot orange Canada lilies, the
deep-grassed levels basked under the July sun. A drowsy hum of bees
and flies seemed to distil, with warm aromatic scents, from the sun-
steeped blooms and grass-tops. The broad, blooming, tranquil expanse, shimmering and softly radiant in the heat, seemed the very
epitome of summer. Now and again a small cloud-shadow sailed
across it. Now and again a little wind, swooping down upon it gently,
bent the grass-tops all one way, and spread a sudden silvery pallor.
Save for the droning bees and flies there seemed to be but one live
creature astir between the grass and the blue. A solitary marsh-hawk,
far over by the rail fence, was winnowing slowly, slowly, hither and
thither, lazily hunting.

2   All this was in the world above the grass-tops. But below the grass-
tops was a very different world — a dense, tangled world of dim green
shade, shot with piercing shafts of sun, and populous with small,
furtive life. Here, among the brown and white roots, the crowded
green stems, and the mottled stalks, the little earth kindreds went
busily about their affairs and their desires, giving scant thought to
the aerial world above them. All that made life significant to them
was here in the warm green gloom; and when anything chanced to
part the grass to its depths they would scurry away in unanimous
indignation.

3   On a small stone, over which the green closed so thickly that, when he chanced to look upward, he caught but the scantiest shreds of sky, sat a half-grown field-mouse, washing his whiskers with his dainty claws. His tiny, bead-like eyes kept ceaseless watch, peering through the shadowy tangle for whatever might come near in the shape of foe or prey. Presently two or three stems above his head were beaten down, and a big green grasshopper, alighting clumsily from one of his blind leaps, fell sprawling on the stone. Before he could struggle to his long legs and climb back to the safer region of the grass-tops, the little mouse was upon him. Sharp, white teeth pierced his green mail, his legs kicked convulsively twice or thrice, and the faint iridescence faded out of his big, blank, foolish eyes. The mouse made his meal with relish, daintily discarding the dry legs and wing-cases. Then amid the green debris scattered upon the stone, he sat up, and once more went through his fastidious toilet.

4   But life for the little mouse in his grass-world was not quite all watching and hunting. When the toilet was complete, and he had amiably let a large black cricket crawl by unmolested, he suddenly began to whirl round on the stone, chasing his own tail. As he was amusing himself with this foolish play, another mouse, about the same size as himself, and probably of the same litter, jumped upon the stone, and knocked him off. He promptly retorted in kind; and for several minutes, as if the game were a well-understood one, the two kept it up, squeaking soft merriment, and apparently forgetful of all peril. The grass-tops above this play rocked and rustled in a way that would certainly have attracted attention had there been any eyes to see. But the marsh-hawk was still hunting lazily at the other side of the field, and no tragedy followed the childishness.

5   Both seemed to tire of the sport at the same instant; for suddenly they stopped, and hurried away through the grass on opposite sides of the stone, as if remembered business had just called to them. Whatever the business was, the first mouse seemed to forget it very speedily, for in a half minute he was back upon the stone again, combing his fine whiskers and scratching his ears. This done to his satisfaction, he dropped like a flash from his seat, and disappeared into a small hollow beneath it. As he did so, a hairy black spider darted out, and ran away among the roots.

6   A minute or two after the disappearance of the mouse, a creature came along which appeared gigantic in the diminutive world of the grass folk. It was nearly three feet long, and of the thickness of a man's finger. Of a steely gray-black, striped and reticulated in a mysterious pattern with a clear whitish yellow, it was an ominous shape indeed, as it glided smoothly and swiftly, in graceful curves, through the close green tangle. The cool shadows and thin lights touched it flickeringly as it went, and never a grass-top stirred to mark its sinis-

ter approach. Without a sound of warning it came straight up to the stone, and darted its narrow, cruel head into the hole.

7   There was a sharp squeak, and instantly the narrow head came out again, ejected by the force of the mouse's agonized spring. But the snake's teeth were fastened in the little animal's neck. The doom of the green world had come upon him while he slept.

8   But doomed though he was, the mouse was game. He knew there was no poison in those fangs that gripped him, and he struggled desperately to break free. His powerful hind legs kicked the ground with a force which the snake, hampered at first by the fact of its length being partly trailed out through the tangle, was unable to quite control. With unerring instinct — though this was the first snake he had ever encountered — the mouse strove to reach its enemy's back and sever the bone with the fine chisels of his teeth. But it was just this that the snake was watchful to prevent. Three times in his convulsive leaps the mouse succeeded in touching the snake's body — but with his feet only, never once with those destructive little teeth. The snake held him inexorably, with a steady, elastic pressure which yielded just so far, and never quite far enough. And in a minute or two the mouse's brave struggles grew more feeble.

9   All this, however, — the lashing and the wriggling and the jumping — had not gone on without much disturbance to the grass-tops. Timothy head and clover-bloom, oxeye, and feathery plume-grass, they had bowed and swayed and shivered till the commotion, very conspicuous to one looking down upon the tranquil, flowery sea of green, caught the attention of the marsh-hawk, which at that moment chanced to be perching on a high fence stake. The lean-headed, fierce-eyed, trim-feathered bird shot from his perch, and sailed on long wings over the grass to see what was happening. As the swift shadow hovered over the grass-tops, the snake looked up. Well he understood the significance of that sudden shade. Jerking back his fangs with difficulty from the mouse's neck, he started to glide off under the thickest matting of the roots. But lightning-quick though he was, he was not quite quick enough. Just as his narrow head darted under the roots, the hawk, with wings held straight up, and talons reaching down, dropped upon him, and clutched the middle of his back in a grip of steel. The next moment he was jerked into the air, writhing and coiling, and striking in vain frenzy at his captor's mail of hard feathers. The hawk flew off with him over the sea of green to the top of the fence stake, there to devour him at leisure. The mouse, sore wounded but not past recovery, dragged himself back to the hollow under the stone. And over the stone the grass-tops, once more still, hummed with flies, and breathed warm perfumes in the distilling heat.

Questions on Content

1   What major events are recorded in this narrative?

2   What major conflict do these events show us?

3   How do the first and last paragraphs suggest the writer's attitude toward these events? What attitude does Roberts convey?

4   What questions does Roberts' narrative raise about the natural world?

5   Does Roberts' narrative have a moral meaning and purpose? If so, what is the moral of the story? If not, what is Roberts' purpose in his narrative?

Questions on Structure and Technique

1   What specific details in the first paragraph appeal to the reader's senses of perception?

2   In what paragraph does Roberts' use of a narrative rather than a descriptive mode of expression become apparent? How does Roberts' use of language establish the narrative in this paragraph? What examples of a similar use of language can you find in subsequent paragraphs?

3   In addition to showing the reader what happened, what answers does Roberts provide to other questions of who, where, when, why, and how?

4   What examples can you find in the narrative where time duration is compressed? What examples can you find where time is extended? What effects do Roberts' handling of time have on the reader's perception of events?

5   What point of view does Roberts choose for presenting this narrative? Why?

Suggestions for Writing

1   Rewrite an assignment on description as a detailed narration of events taking place in time.

2   Observe carefully the actions of several animals in a natural setting (or a zoo), and then write a narrative in which specific details and images are used to show the reader events that occurred.

3   Write a detailed narrative account of a struggle or conflict between two people in which you show the reader clearly not only what happened, but also answer questions about who, where, when, why, and how.

NELLIE McCLUNG

Nellie McClung (1873-1951) was a teacher, a social and political activist for women's legal and political rights, a member of the Alberta legislature (1921 to 1926), a popular lecturer, and a prolific writer. "Christmas in Manitoba" is McClung's bold and thoughtful narrative account of one significant incident in her childhood. Her use of dialogue is especially effective in showing readers the basic conflict involved in the situation. Thus, this selection from the first of McClung's two autobiographical books, Clearing in the West *(1935) and* The Stream Runs Fast *(1945), clearly shows rather than tells us her intense personal response to the particular events and issues of the Riel Rebellion. However, her views on the rights of women and minorities that became so important to her as an adult are still relevant to our lives today. McClung's dedicated and influential public defence of women and minorities also provided the basis for six novels.*

CHRISTMAS IN MANITOBA

1   Christmas Day has always been flavored to me with the pound cake and apple-jelly tarts of those first days in Manitoba.

2   The front-room always got a new coat of white-wash on the log walls at Christmas, and everything was scoured as white as sand or soap could make it. The hand-knit lace curtains, brought from Ontario, were washed and starched and stretched on home-made frames, so they would hang straight and reach the floor. Short curtains were considered slightly indecent. The two long widths of rag carpet in bright stripes with orange warp were brought out and laid on the white floor, with the good mats, one hooked and one braided. The homemade lounge had a covering of dark maroon canton flannel and was well supplied with patch-work cushions, crazy pattern of silks and satins and two log cabins, one made of "stuff pieces", the other one of prints. There were two bookcases made with spools, painted black, and set with shelves and a "what-not" of five shelves, on which stood china ornaments, a shell box, with a green plush pin-cushion on the top, apples filled with cloves, and cups and saucers (honorably retired from active service because of cracks, or missing handles, but with these defects tactfully concealed in the way they were placed), colored glass mugs, and on the top, a bouquet of prairie grasses, set in a frosted glass vase, a lace pattern on deep blue. I remember it well, for I broke it years later, when bouncing a ball, on the floor. Who would have thought a yarn ball would bounce so high?

3   When the weather got cold, the kitchen stove had to be brought into the big room, and it was a family grief when this change had to be made. If the weather did not come down too hard, the stove was kept out until after Christmas. Later when the storm doors and windows were added, and a bigger heater bought, a fine big barrel of a stove, with a row of mica windows around its middle, through which the coals glowed with all the colors of a sunset, the kitchen stove remained in the kitchen all winter.

4   But even when the kitchen stove was in the middle of the big room, there was a cheerful roominess about it. The wood-box papered with pictures of the Ice Palace, in Montreal (*Family Herald Supplement*), when covered with two boards over which a quilt was spread made a nice warm seat and when we got the hanging lamp from Brandon, with a pale pink shade, on which a brown deer poised for a leap across a chasm, through which a green stream dashed in foam on the rocks, the effect was magical and in the pink light the white-washed walls were softened into alabaster.

5   We had two new pictures now, enlarged photographs of father and mother in heavy oak frames with a gilt edge, done by a travelling artist, who drove a team of mules and carried a few lines of tinware. Every family in the neighbourhood had taken advantage of his easy plan to secure a lasting work of art. You paid only for the frame and received the picture entirely free though this offer might be withdrawn any minute for he was doing this merely to get his work known. He said there was no nicer way to give one's parents a pleasant surprise, and the pictures would be delivered in time for Christmas. When they came, we all had a surprise. We had thought that the seven dollars and thirty-five cents paid for both frames but we were wrong. Each one cost that amount and even at that the artist was losing money. The pictures were accepted and hung on the log walls, and in the declivities behind them were kept tissue paper patterns, newspaper clippings, and other semi-precious documents, thus relieving the congestion in the real archives, lodged in the lower regions of the clock, where notes, grain-tickets, tax receipts were kept.

6   After the Christmas dinner of turkey and plum pudding, the men sat and talked of the trouble Louis Riel was causing. He had come back from Montana, where he had been teaching school, and was now in Saskatchewan, stirring up the half-breeds and Indians and inciting them to make raids on the white settlers.

7   "Why don't they arrest him now, and get him safely in jail before someone is killed?" Mother was greatly disturbed over the situation. "I can't sleep," she said, "thinking of the poor women there, frightened to go to sleep at night. They say he has given guns to the Indians and there will be another massacre like there was in Minnesota."

8   Frank Burnett was indignant that the Government had not sent an armed force, just as soon as the trouble began.

9   "Uniforms would settle the trouble," he said; "the red coats and the flash of steel, a few guns fired and the half-breeds and Indians would know there was law in the country. Riel should be hanged anyway for the murder of Thos. Scott."

10   I wanted to talk. Mr. Schultz had told us about it in school. The half-breeds and Indians had a grievance, a real one. The settlers were crowding in on them, their land was being surveyed over again, and divided into squares like ours. They had long narrow lots, as they had along the Red and Assiniboine, so they could live side by side, and now a new arrangement of land was being made and they were afraid their land was going to be taken from them. When they sent letters to Ottawa, they got no replies.

11   I knew how they felt. I had often asked for explanations and got the prescribed 19th century dusty answer, "because I say so — that's all the reason you need." How I hated it! And how unfair I felt it to be! The Government officials were treating the Indians the same way.

12   I knew the government was to blame but I would not be allowed to say it, and if I did get it said, I might get Mr. Schultz into trouble. Mother would feel he was undermining our respect for authority.

But much to my delight, Hannah came forward and defended the half-breeds. Hannah was always listened to when she spoke. She had what I lacked, a quiet and dignified way of expression.

13   "The country belonged to the Indians and half-breeds," she said in her even voice. "We must not forget that. I know they have made little use of it and must yield it to white settlers, in time, but there's enough territory for everyone if it is handled right, and they could be easily appeased and satisfied."

14   She told about the new survey, about the delay in getting the patents out for the land of the half-breeds had proved-up on, about the slaughter of the buffalo, the Indian's source of food and clothing.

15   Hannah was fifteen then, with a fine presence, fair skin, a round face, and fine large greenish-eyes, and abundant bright brown hair, inclined to curl. She had been wiping dishes behind the stove and came out with a plate in one hand, and a flour-sack tea towel in the other. Her face was flushed and her eyes bright and to me she looked like Joan of Arc. I was very proud of her, but I knew there was a sudden tightening of the atmosphere. Even now, men do not like to be taught by women, but at that time for a girl of fifteen to presume to have an opinion, was against all tradition. However, Hannah had a prestige all her own.

16   She went on. "It is not the Catholic church, and it is not Louis Riel, who is causing the trouble — it is the stupidity of the Govern-

ment at Ottawa, and if settlers are killed by the Indians theirs will be the guilt. A few words of explanation, a few concessions and peace could be restored."

17 "My God!" exclaimed Frank Burnett in real concern, "that's hot talk, Hannah, you've said enough to hang you in some countries. If you were in Russia, you would be shot for a Nihilist, my girl."

18 My mother was too much amazed to speak. If I had said half of what Hannah had, she would know what to do with me, but Hannah, quiet, dignified Hannah, the image of her own mother, Margaret Fullerton McCurdy, could not be sent upstairs in disgrace.

19 Hannah went on wiping the dishes with great composure. She had said what she wanted to say and now withdrew from the conversation. Her hearers had heard the truth, and they could take it or leave it. Responsibility had passed from her to them.

20 Mr. Burnett continued the argument. "I am afraid there is bad work going on at Northfield School," he said. "I gather that is where Hannah gets her ideas. This man Schultz is a German; he has no love for British institutions and is using his position as a teacher to undermine the children's respect for authority. We'll have to look into this. We'll have to call a meeting of the trustees."

21 My heart stood still. Had we involved our teacher in some trouble that might lead to his losing a job?

22 They all began to talk; and I could feel a hostile tide of opinion gathering and sweeping ahead of it all good sense and reason and it seemed to me I would have to speak, no matter what happened. Will would listen to me anyway. I went over and stood before him.

23 "Will," I said, "I want to talk, make them keep quiet."

24 "Nellie has something on her mind," Will called out in his good humoured way. "It is not often this poor tongue-tied child wants to talk, and she should get her chance on Christmas day, of all times."

25 Mother rose up to protest, but Will waved her back.

26 "Let the kid talk," he said, "talk won't hurt anyone. It's the things we don't say that hurt us, I know."

27 Then came the ordeal, when the silence fell on the room. I have faced audiences who were hostile since then and encountered unfriendly glances, but the antagonism here was more terrible, being directed, not as much against what I had to say, as against the fact that I dared to say anything.

28 I addressed Will, as people air their views in letters addressed to the Editor. "The Government is like the Machine Company, Will," I said. "The half-breeds are dissatisfied with the way they are treated, they are afraid they are going to be put off their farms, just as we were afraid when the tongue of the binder broke, and we saw we were going to lose our crop. The half-breeds have written letters, and sent people to see the Government and asked them to send out

someone to straighten out their troubles, just as you, Will, wrote letters to the Company and asked them to send an expert, who would put the binder in good shape. The Government won't answer the half-breeds, won't notice them, won't talk to them — and the only word they send them is a saucy word — 'what we will send you will be an army; we'll put you in your place.' Just as the Machine Company wrote us a saucy letter saying that it was our own fault if the binders broke, and they couldn't supply us with brains. It's the same spirit. We should understand how the half-breeds feel. That's all I want to say," and before anyone could say a word, I left the room, glad to get away.

Questions on Content

1   What sequence of events does McClung record in this narrative?

2   What conflicts emerge during the course of McClung's account? Is one of these conflicts more central to the narrative than the others and, if so, which one?

3   What significant relations do you notice between the introductory descriptive paragraphs (paragraphs one through five) and the subsequent narrative?

4   What important similarities and differences do you see between the respective arguments presented by Hannah and Nellie? Which argument do you find more convincing? Why?

5   What conflicts are resolved by the conclusion of the narrative? What conflicts remain unresolved? Why?

Questions on Structure and Technique

1   In what ways is the presentation of specific details in the opening descriptive paragraphs a technique similar to the subsequent use of dialogue in McClung's account?

2   McClung's use of dialogue affects her handling of narrative time duration. Find examples where time is compressed, expanded, and reordered, and consider why.

3   What differences in the language of each speaker do you notice in the dialogue? How are these differences consistent and appropriate to each speaker?

4   What is the difference between Nellie's use of language in her concluding argument and that of the other speakers?

5   What does McClung's use of the first person, "I", throughout her narrative contribute to the effectiveness of the point of view she expresses in her argument?

Suggestions for Writing

1   Write a detailed narrative account of a holiday gathering that you have attended.

2   Recall a memorable experience from your childhood, and write a narrative in which you show your readers its significance for you.

3   Write a narrative account of an argument in which you have been a participant, using dialogue carefully to show your readers what issues, conflicts, and resolutions were involved in the experience.

A. Y. JACKSON

Alexander Young Jackson (1882-1974), among Canada's most famous painters, worked and exhibited with the Group of Seven: J. E. H. Mac-Donald, Lawren Harris, Arthur Lismer, Frederick Varley, Frank Carmichael, Frank Johnston, and Jackson. Born in Montreal, A. Y. Jackson left school at the age of twelve to work in a lithographing company before he formally studied art in Montreal, Paris, and Chicago. While studying and travelling in Europe several times between 1905 and 1912, Jackson was strongly influenced by French Impressionist painting. In the following narrative selection from his autobiography, A Painter's Country *(1958), Jackson has purposely chosen events from among many which occurred in 1920 when he returned to Toronto after a serene winter of painting around Georgian Bay. Consider why he selects these particular events. Despite the initially adverse judgments of the Group of Seven's first exhibits, when Jackson's work and others' was criticized for its unconventional qualities, Jackson travelled throughout every part of Canada during the years to follow, painting his experience of its landscape in works that have found a prominent, undisputed place in Canadian art and culture.*

THE GROUP OF SEVEN

1 Towards the end of April the ice got honeycombed, turned almost black and suddenly disappeared. I went by boat into Penetang, and from there to Toronto. The first thing I heard when I reached that city was that the Group of Seven had been formed, and that I was a member of it. Had it not been for the war, the Group would have been formed several years earlier and it would have included Thomson. Even before the war, we had attempted to interpret Canada and to express, in paint, the spirit of our country. The men who formed the first Group, dedicated to this purpose, and who turned their backs on the European tradition, were Lawren Harris, Arthur Lismer, J. E. H. MacDonald, Fred Varley, Frank Johnston, Frank Carmichael and myself. The organization was a loose one; it had a name and a purpose but it had no officers, no bylaws and no fees.

2 It must not be thought that the movement was a local one, confined to Toronto only. About the same time an effort was made to establish a similar group in Montreal. It was named the Beaver Hall Group as its members rented a house on that street. It brought a number of talented young artists together but financially it was a failure.

3   Our first exhibition had a very poor reception. In addition to the work of the members of the Group, there were canvases from three invited contributors, R. S. Hewton, Robert Pilot, and Albert Robinson, all of Montreal. Among the paintings exhibited were J. E. H. MacDonald's "Wild River" and "The Beaver Dam," some of Harris' old Toronto houses, a number of canvases that Lismer had painted while he was living in Nova Scotia, and some lyrical paintings of trees by Frank Carmichael. My own canvas was "*Terre Savage*," perhaps the most radical painting in the show.

4   Some people who saw the exhibition were amused, and some indignant. Some members threatened to resign from the Art Gallery of Toronto. In the catalogue it was announced that "the artists invite adverse criticism. Indifference is the greatest evil they have to contend with." There was plenty of adverse criticism, little of it intelligent. A great deal of it was mere abuse, much of it from people who had not even seen the exhibition. It came not only from laymen but from artists as well. "Products of a deranged mind," "art gone mad," "the cult of ugliness," these were some of the terms used to describe paintings which, whatever their faults, attempted to depict the Canadian scene sincerely and honestly.

5   The only possible explanation for the uproar caused by that first exhibition is that we, in Canada, had become so accustomed to seeing paintings that were made according to a European formula that a simple portrayal of a Canadian subject was incomprehensible to us.

6   Looking back after thirty-eight years it is difficult to know now what all the shouting was about. Paintings that were in the first exhibition are now in our National Gallery, in Hart House, the Art Gallery of Toronto, and in private collections all over Canada. Nowadays they are considered "sound and sane art," to use the expression that one of our most virulent critics employed to praise dull academic pictures.

7   One result of the opposition was that we were confirmed in our resolution to carry on. While the bad publicity received did not bother us, it did have an immediate consequence: Frank Johnston resigned from the Group. From the economic standpoint he had difficulty in earning a living from his painting. People were afraid to buy pictures that were the subject of ridicule.

8   The second exhibition of the Group of Seven showed that we were far from being deflated by our experience. A note in the catalogue said:

> A word as to Canada; these pictures have all been executed in
> Canada during the past year. They express Canadian experience
> in the onlooker. These are still pioneer days for artists and after
> the fashion of pioneers we believe wholeheartedly in the land.
> Some day we think that the land will return the compliment and
> believe in the artist not as a nuisance nor as a luxury, but as a real,
> civilizing factor in the national life.

9   Harris and I made the sets for the first plays at Hart House; we were friends of Roy Mitchell, the first director of Hart House Theatre. My set was for "The Queen's Enemies." I went to the Royal Ontario Museum to find some Egyptian costumes to serve as models. Later, at the production, Dr. Currelly, the Director of the Museum, was shocked to see slaves wearing headgear that was reserved for royalty. Harris' set was for "Patelin." Partly because we knew so little about it, we made some very unconventional settings for plays. Later on, Lismer took over the job as experimental work for his students at the Ontario College of Art.

10   Meanwhile, there remained the bothersome business of earning a living. We made a series of Christmas cards that were most successful. They were sold not only in Canada; orders came from New York, and even from Liberty's in London. Most of the Group depended on teaching, or commercial art. I did an occasional commercial job.

11   I was approached by Watson McClain of the Kent-McClain Company, who made showcases, to undertake a commission. His company was having its offices redecorated and there was a space between the cornice and the ceiling which was covered with a very commonplace stencilled ornament. If the stencil had to be done over it would cost two hundred dollars. Could I, for the same sum, paint something, a simple landscape or anything else, to replace the stencil? Two hundred dollars was a lot of money to me at that time, so I accepted the commission. I roughed out a northern Ontario landscape in four colours, with hills, lakes, creeks, rivers, all in a hundred and fifty feet. It was great fun. The men from the factory would drop in to watch my progress, and their comments pleased me. "There should be fish in that lake," they would say, or, "I bet you that is good hunting country." An old gunner said there was fine cover for guns back of that hill. When I was finished, Watson McClain said, "You know, when I asked you to paint something in place of that old stencil I did not expect to have two hundred miles of Northern Ontario in our office. I have made out the cheque for three hundred dollars. I hope you don't mind." My feelings were not hurt.

12   Another job proved less satisfying. Clarence Gagnon had a book of essays by Adjutor Rivard which he greatly admired; he thought an English edition of the book should be brought out. After reading the essays I agreed with him. I suggested to a Toronto publisher that his house should publish the book and he agreed on condition that W. H. Blake would undertake the translation. Blake was very happy to do so and I was asked to make, as illustrations, a series of chapter headings. I made them while in Baie St. Paul and sent them to the publisher but received no acknowledgement from him. I wrote to Jim MacDonald, who went to the publisher's to inquire after them, and was told that the drawings were no good. Jim told the publisher

he did not know good work when he saw it. When I returned, I saw the man in charge of production. He had an edition of *Maria Chapdelaine* with drawings by Suzor-Côté. "Why can't you do something like that?" he asked me. I said because I wasn't Suzor-Côté. He objected to the title, *Chez Nous*. No one in Ontario, he said, would know what it meant. I replied, "Just the sound of it is lovely; they do not have to know what it means." He went over my drawings and pronounced them poor. When the book finally came out, only a few of the drawings were used, not as chapter headings but on blank pages as illustrations. In spite of his misguided efforts, the book was a real success. Many of the drawings were reproduced in a review of *Chez Nous* in the *New York Tribune*.

13   About the same time, MacDonald undertook a commission to decorate St. Anne's Church in Toronto. This was one of the first efforts to introduce more modern ideas into church decoration. There was not much money available, but with the help of several other artists he got away from the kind of stock and machine-made ornament with which most of our churches were embellished. His work at St. Anne's was perhaps a mild assertion of the belief that a place of worship should be beautiful.

14   MacDonald was growing more confident of his abilities. Everything he undertook now bore a mark of distinction; but there was never enough work for him and the returns from it were inadequate for him to live on. He turned his hand to all kinds of things: book covers, illuminated addresses, posters. He had a sound knowledge of historical ornament and his lettering was quite distinguished.

15   Among my critics were my aunts in Berlin, which had changed its name to Kitchener during the war. My Aunt Geneva took pride in any success that came my way, as when the Tate Gallery acquired one of my paintings, but she had no sympathy with radical movements and I had to submit to many a tongue-lashing from her about painting pictures no sane person could understand. Living on incomes that remained stationary, while expenses went up year after year, was difficult for the aunts. They expected their servants to know their place as they did in the days of dear Queen Victoria. To one maid my aunt said, "Mary, I'll tell you what I want for dessert," and went into a full description of the dainty she expected.

16   "All right, Miss Jackson," said Mary. "Now I'll tell you what you are going to get."

17   Aunt Geneva liked to go sketching though she was not very successful at it; she niggled with small brushes while I tried vainly to get her to paint with more breadth. She was always making things for bazaars, among other items tea cozies of coloured felt which were most attractive in design. I told her that the next time she went sketching she should leave her paints at home and take her coloured felts along.

18   When my work was finally acquired by various public galleries, she rather reluctantly admitted there must be some virtue in it. She was very fond of me in spite of my lack of respect for her many cherished traditions.

Questions on Content

1   What succession of events does Jackson recount?

2   Throughout Jackson's narration of these events, what subject and attitude toward that subject is maintained? Where does Jackson state this thesis most concisely?

3   What problems do Jackson and other members of the Group of Seven encounter?

4   What successes do they enjoy?

5   In what ways is Jackson's final anecdote about his aunts an appropriate and significant conclusion for his narrative?

Questions on Structure and Technique

1   To what extent is Jackson's narrative time arranged in a chronological sequence of events?

2   In what ways other than chronology does Jackson maintain a meaningful narrative arrangement and development of events?

3   Why does Jackson include the "note" from the catalogue for the Group of Seven's second exhibition?

4   For what purposes does Jackson include dialogue in his narrative?

5   What details and events does Jackson include in this first-person narrative that would be inappropriate and excluded from a third-person narrative? What kinds of details and events does Jackson exclude from his narrative that would likely be included in a third-person narrative about the Group of Seven? What details and events does Jackson include that might also be appropriate for a third-person narrative account?

Suggestions for Writing

1   Write a narration of an experience in which someone else believed that you exhibited a "lack of respect for . . . cherished traditions."

2   Narrate the events surrounding your involvement in a group in which you are a member.

3   Recall an experience when a member of your family or a friend, who had no sympathy for an activity or work that you found rewarding, "reluctantly admitted there must be some virtue in it." Write a narration of events leading up to this change in that person's judgment.

MAX FERGUSON

CBC radio personality and satirist Max Ferguson (b. 1924) became syn-
onymous with "Old Rawhide," whose accidental conception in 1946 is
recounted in this humorous selection from Ferguson's And Now . . . Here's
Max (1968). As a result of Ferguson's skill in showing people the more
ridiculous aspects of their experience, this book won the Stephen Leacock
Medal for Humour. However, Ferguson's popularity spanned his radio
career of over thirty years on "The Max Ferguson Show." In 1976, Ferguson
retired to his home on Cape Breton Island.

THE BIRTH OF RAWHIDE

1   It was somewhere in the dying weeks of December, 1946, that Old
Rawhide was born and rose, more like a Quasimodo than a Phoenix, from the ashes of the old year. As the newest addition to the
announcer staff of CBC Halifax, I took my turn at all the various
assignments in the normal program day—newscaster, host of record
shows, farm broadcast announcer, wet nurse to women commenta-
tors and, of course, surf and gull man on Harmony Harbour. At the
end of my second week, I reported for duty on a Saturday morning,
checked my schedule of duties and found to my horror that they
included a half hour of cowboy records called *After Breakfast Breakdown*. With the exception of a very few legitimate songs which were
actually sung by cowboys and have come down to us from the old
frontier days of the American west, I loathe the entire field of Tin
Pan Alley hokum loosely termed "cowboy music". Moreover, at
twenty-one I was a good bit more impressionable than I am now and
being a fully fledged CBC announcer was to me, at least in those
days, only a rank or two below beatification. I had already blabbed
all over Halifax to any who would listen the long list of vital and
indispensable duties with which I had been entrusted by the CBC.
What on earth would these people think now if they should hear me
feigning an enthusiastic introduction to some guitar-twanging drug-
store cowboy singing, "I Rapped On the Hearse Window, Granny,
But You Did Not Look Out", or something of similar inspiration.

2   With a desperation born of despair and with just twenty seconds
to air time, I hit on the idea of disguising my voice by dropping the
register, thrusting out my jaw, and clamping my back teeth together.
As I pushed down the microphone switch, out came the words,
"Howdy! Welcome to *After Breakfast Breakdown*," in a low, aged,
hard, flat, sloppily sibilant voice that surprised even myself. "This is

your old pal Rawhide," I continued, pulling the name out of the air on the spur of the moment, although I'd heard it used once or twice in my life to denote a type of tough, untanned leather. I then proceeded for the next half hour to introduce each cowboy record in the most insulting fashion I could devise, popping in at the close of each song to thank the artist and bid him farewell as he "mosied off down the canyon, headin' tall in the saddle into the flaming sunset, whose glare would no doubt prevent him from seeing in time that 400-foot sheer drop into the chasm below waiting to claim him for that great Studio in the Sky . . . and not a moment too soon."

3   The names of the various cowboy singers were all strange to my ears (as were the voices) and so, when I cued up the second last record that morning and noticed that the performer was billed as the Yodelling Ranger, I didn't think it would be too indiscreet to good-naturedly change this in my introduction to the Yodelling Idiot. The record finished, and I thanked him, sending him on his way to the Great Studio in the Sky via the 400-foot chasm I'd so felicitously invented. Suddenly the studio door opened slightly, and there was Syd Kennedy's panic-stricken face mouthing some message which, though I couldn't decipher it, nevertheless seemed quite urgent. The thought crossed my mind as I was trying to lip-read Syd and at the same time verbally despatch the Yodelling Idiot over the cliff, released the last record of the program without any introduction, and cut my microphone.

4   At last I was able to ask Syd what the problem was. He took two full minutes to babble out his message, but when I'd mentally pruned all the extraneous and profane prefixes and suffixes it was reduced to a rather concise skeletal form—"The Yodelling Ranger is not only a local Halifax boy but also the most popular idol in the Maritimes." Syd further advised that, to avoid being lynched the moment I stepped out onto Sackville Street, I should hastily make the most abject apology I could think of. There wasn't much program time left, so I faded down the record that was playing, opened my microphone, and said, still in the Rawhide voice, "I just made a very unfortunate mistake in calling that previous singer the Yodelling Idiot. I certainly didn't mean to be disparaging and was obviously confusing him with *another* Yodelling Idiot I once knew in Upper Canada. This is the Canadian Broadcasting Corporation."

5   Kennedy showed great restraint, waiting till the very last word of the corporation cue was finished and the microphone cut before he clasped both hands to his head, emitted an anguished groan, and vanished from the studio. His fears were quite unfounded. It must have been my juxtaposition of the words "idiot" and "Upper Canada" which appeased the aficionados of the cowboy idiom in Halifax. At any rate the apology was accepted as a complete and penitent

catharsis, and I was to reach my little rented room that day without being set upon by an unruly mob.

6 The chief danger to my well-being was to come a few days later from a different and totally unexpected source, S. R. Kennedy. I was called into his office at the beginning of the following week to face what I presumed would be nothing more than a mild lecture on the importance of being kind to local cowboy singers. However, it turned out that Syd had completely forgotten my faux pas in the excitement of a brilliant idea he'd conceived over the weekend and which was now beginning to spring fully formed, mirabile dictu, from his mouth. "I like the idea of using that old guy's voice. Starting next Monday, we're scheduling a half hour of cowboy music, six mornings a week, to the Maritime network with you as host doing the old guy's voice!"

7 I can remember, once my speech returned, trying to reason with Syd. I was being quite serious when I offered to do extra announce shifts and even give the CBC one night a week janitorial service if he'd only abandon this insane idea. But it was like asking a mother to abandon her first-born, and though I continued to plead and protest, Syd merely sat, smiling smugly like a balding Mona Lisa, gazing out through his office window at his favourite landmark, the red funnels of the old *Aquitania* thrusting up from the harbour. The following Monday I reluctantly launched the first program in a series that was to run for seventeen consecutive years.

8 Whereas most broadcasters strive either to entertain or inform, my motivation during those early weeks of incarceration on the Devil's Island to which Kennedy had sent me was considerably more selfish. It was simply to make that half hour of cowboy music each morning pass as quickly and painlessly as possible. Not knowing or caring who might be listening and strictly for my own amusement, I brought into the studio with me each morning a little sound-effects door. Between cowboy records I would open and close this door to signal the arrival of mythical characters and, one by one, I would people my little cell with quite an assortment of warped figments of my imagination to keep me company.

9 There was Granny, her sweet little eggshell voice giving no indication of the thoroughly rotten, corrupt, and malicious personality which lurked behind it. There was Marvin Mellobell, a sickeningly irritating embodiment of all the adenoids, pomposity, and self-adulation that the world of show-biz had to offer. Then there was my favourite, the unnamed pest and constant thorn in Marvin Mellobell's flesh, whose wild, semi-literate speech poured out in the raucous voice of Doug Trowell's old Scott C. Mulsion. He was a sort of Rousseau's natural man carried to the extreme, unfettered by even the thinnest veneer of social decorum. What he lacked in polish and mentality he made up for in enthusiasm and in his time played all the major roles

in the Rawhide Little Theatre Company. From Tarzan of the Apes to the brooding Prince of Denmark, they all rolled out with the same raw gusto and paucity of dramatic insight.

10   There were also the Goomer Brothers, rural entrepreneurs who operated an illicit hard-cider operation in the Gaspereau district of Nova Scotia's lovely Annapolis Valley. They hated the RCMP and were constantly and angrily campaigning on the program to get the CBC to include, along with road and weather reports, Mountie Reports designed to keep the little man in their particular field posted on the latest whereabouts of the federal law. They also purveyed as a sideline 155 ever-proof eggs derived from a flock of semi-stoned White Leghorns which they fed on fermenting apple mash. Their steady customers included world famous personalities who unwittingly bit into the free trial samples which the Goomer Brothers mailed out all over the world and became hopelessly hooked. The only sample egg ever to be returned unopened was the one they sent Princess Margaret Rose, and she was immediately lumped in with the RCMP as their favourite objects of scorn and dislike.

11   Rawhide often feigned horror at some of the things all these characters came out with, but secretly he, and certainly his creator, welcomed these morning visits and prolonged them, knowing full well they were eating up valuable time which otherwise would have to be devoted to the cowboy records. Although these little interludes with character voices served as welcome and selfishly devised breaks in the monotony, I never for a moment lost sight of my main objective in those early weeks. I continued to wait patiently for the opportunity to get myself taken off the air.

12   It was a good six weeks before the golden moment arrived in the form of a nasty letter from some lady in New Brunswick who was taking violent umbrage at what she alleged was my blatant partiality toward Wilf Carter and the shameful neglect of Hank Snow. These men were the two top favourites in the Maritimes in the field of cowboy music. Like a mother striving to avoid sibling rivalry, I meticulously played one record of each singer every single morning, except on one occasion while possibly wool-gathering, when I allowed a second Wilf Carter aria to slip in at the expense of Hank Snow. It was this occasion to which she was referring in her letter. I read the letter through to myself twice, scarcely able to believe, from the strength of the language, that it had been penned by one of the weaker sex. However, for what I had in mind she'd do nicely. Dreyfus had found his Zola.

13   The very next morning, instead of opening with the usual camaraderie, I asked the operator in the control room to play a particularly heartrending version of *Hearts and Flowers*. Then I came in over this as Rawhide, with much sniffling and noseblowing, to say in a

shaken voice, "In the short time I've been living in these parts, I've come to look upon Marimtiders as a friendly, warm-hearted bunch, and it saddens my old heart this morning to realize there's one among you who is trying to cut my throat behind my back." I then read the letter verbatim (omitting only the pungent parts) and ended with the writer's name, street address, and home town. Then I went on to, "You realize, of course, Mrs. _____, of _____ Street in _____, New Brunswick, that I would be quite within my rights to say something nasty to you in return. But somehow, deep down inside, I'm . . . well . . . I'm just not built that way. Instead, I'm merely going to turn the other cheek and ask you, in the spirit of true Christian friendship to (there I paused for dramatic effect) . . . *drop dead*!"

14   The expression in those days was just coming into vogue and had not yet lost its freshness and shock value through later overuse. It must have sounded particularly fresh when boomed over a 50,000-watt transmitter to a CBC customer who at the time was no doubt paying her $2.50 licence fee to help keep the likes of me on the air. There was no doubt in my mind that she would be justifiably outraged and would contact her local MP in Ottawa who, in turn, would contact the Minister of Transport. Next in the chain of command would be A. Davidson Dunton, then chairman of the CBC Board of Governors, who would call W.E.S. Briggs, who would take me off the program. Like the old lady's cow, I'd be over the stile and home free. Two days later my house of cards collapsed when the woman wrote me again to say, "Well, Rawhide, old pal, you sure gave it to me over the air the other day and by golly I asked for it. No hard feelings."

15   Along about this time the Rawhide program had begun to bring in a rather steady flow of mail from all over the Atlantic provinces. From these letters I began to realize that there was an encouraging percentage of the audience who were listening for the skits I was doing and not the cowboy records. My morale picked up. Earlier, the mail had consisted almost entirely of requests for cowboy songs, usually of the more morbid variety. One lady, writing with soft pencil in a most laborious and semi-legible hand, had requested *We Shall Gather By the River* sung by the Carter Family, "in memory of my daughter that was drowned there six years ago."

16   The mail each day would invariably bring several parcels, sometimes chocolates or home-made cookies, but most often sturdy knitted mittens or tuques from Newfoundland. Among the many pairs of heavy-duty white wool socks that were knitted and sent in by ladies in Newfoundland was one pair which came with the instructions, "Wear these over your shoes to save the leather." On my CBC salary of nineteen hundred dollars a year I can assure you that none of these gifts was sneezed at.

Questions on Content

1 How is it that "Old Rawhide was born and rose more like a Quasimodo than a Phoenix, from the ashes"? In what sense was Rawhide "born"?

2 What is Ferguson's attitude toward working on the "After Breakfast Breakdown" radio program? How does his attitude change, and why?

3 What details does Ferguson include in his narrative that account for the continuing success of Rawhide?

4 What conflicts does Ferguson establish and develop in his narrative?

5 How are these conflicts resolved? How does Ferguson's concluding statement, "I can assure you that none of these gifts was sneezed at," emphasize this resolution?

Questions on Structure and Technique

1 What words and phrases does Ferguson use in paragraph one to establish his humorous tone? What subsequent examples of Ferguson's choices of details and anecdotes that maintain this tone can you find?

2 What examples can you find where Ferguson extends his narrative's time duration? What examples show his compression of time? What effects does Ferguson achieve by using these techniques of handling narrative time?

3 What details is Ferguson appropriately able to include in his narrative by choosing a first-person point of view? What do these details contribute to the effectiveness of Ferguson's writing?

4 What details about the character of Rawhide does Ferguson show his readers? What aspects of his own character does Ferguson reveal in his writing?

5 What details about his radio audience does Ferguson emphasize? Why are these details important to his development of this writing?

Suggestions for Writing

1 Write a humorous narrative account of events which occurred during your first work experience.

2 Recall a personal experience when a surprising change took place in your life. Write a narration of the experience, showing your readers what happened and why it is important to you.

3 Narrate an actual (or perhaps imagined) experience where circumstances made it necessary for you to be involved in a particular activity that you had always loathed.

FREDERICK PHILIP GROVE

*Born in Russia, raised in Hamburg, and educated at universities in Bonn
and Munich, Frederick Philip Grove (1879-1948) was the name taken
shortly after 1909 by Felix Paul Greve when he moved to North America.
This followed his erratic but productive career as a poet, playwright, novelist, literary critic, and translator in Europe. Grove settled in rural Manitoba in 1912 where he taught school until 1923. His first two books in
English,* Over Prairie Trails *(1922) and* The Turn of the Year *(1923), are
autobiographical accounts of his observations and experiences of day-to-
day life on the prairies during those years. In "A Storm in July," an essay
from* The Turn of the Year, *Grove narrates a sequence of events from his
experience of a violent summer storm by incorporating starkly detailed,
epic descriptions. In 1923, Grove devoted himself to a full-time career as
an author. His works include a half dozen novels, beginning with* Settlers
of the Marsh *(1925).*

A STORM IN JULY

1   For three days in succession the wind has been blowing from the
south—a loud, boisterous, rollicking wind, at first very nearly refresh-
ing: a wind that made the leaves flutter, the twigs sway, and the boles
bend.

2   The first day it died down towards evening; and we had had a
quiet night; but the second morning it had sprung up again, bringing
with it thin waves of vapor and a suggestion of smoke in the air which
grew stronger as the day advanced; till at last towards noon the wind
seemed to blow from a huge conflagration in the south. Down there
the big marsh which stretches north of the open prairie was on fire as
it often is. The speed of the wind was increasing, too, on this second
day. The leaves strained at their stalks; the small aspens stood vibrating
at an angle; the large black poplars huddled their tops together on
the north side of their trunks; while the wind pulled and snatched at
the edges of their green garments. A rag tied to a pole to mark off a
neighboring homestead claim cracked and crackled with the slight
changes in the direction of the blast; and in the kitchen-garden behind
the house the cucumber vines were lying helpless, belly up, with their
foliage ragged and dusty and worn by the sand which even in this
country of the northern bush began to blow.

3   The wind was overweening; it was unmannerly; it roused resentment. When, for some reason or other, I had to step down into the
ditch along the road, it threw the sand and gravel into my face by the

handful. Besides, it was hot, it was oppressive and sultry. There was that in the air which made me lose my temper when the wind threw my hat down: it was such a mean and contemptible trick to make me exert myself in recovering it on a day like this; and there was also that which made me sit down on an inverted candy pail in the lee and the shade of the house, back against wall, hat pushed down my neck, handkerchief in limp sweaty hands, ready to wipe the clammy brow and to resign myself with a sigh. What could one do but resign oneself?

4   I have said nothing about the sun. I did not care about him. It was not he who ruled the world or the landscape. His Titan-son Wind was having his fling and tyrannizing and lording it over the lower realms. Father Sun stood high up — when you did look for him; somewhat coppery and red in the face, but distant and critical, as though he were saying, "I wonder what all this tomfoolery will lead to in the end. No doubt I shall have to go bail for the boy at last." But if one did not simply forget about him, one might even have dared to look straight at him without blinking. His Majesty was eclipsed and jostled into the background.

5   The second night the wind persisted; there was not even the usual let-up at sundown. A smell of smoke filled the little house in the bush and gave its inmates a headache. The whistling and rustling noise kept us from sleeping; even the little child tossed about in her bed, hard as it otherwise was to disturb her. We felt nervous, expectant. Dust drifted in through the crack of the slightly raised window. A mosquito sang in the bedroom; expertly it had squeezed in through a mesh of the screen; and every now and then, when it approached my ear, its strident song seemed to assume the tone-volume of a trumpet blast, so that I started up from my troubled half-sleep and struck viciously but ineffectively at my ear which felt gritty with dust and which now began to smart with a burning irritation.

6   The last I remember before I finally fell asleep for a few short hours was a lull in the general din. It seemed five minutes later when the alarm clock rang; and at the same moment I heard the wind again. I had to rise and go about my chores, for I did a little farming during the holidays, between teaching; but I felt fagged out, morose, and evil-humoured from the start.

7   Somehow I got into my clothes and, holding on to shirt and hat, went out. Had I considered the question the day before, I should have thought it impossible for a further climax in discomfort to outtop the one then present. Yet, on this third morning of the windstorm — there it is. Possibly it consists in nothing more than the cumulative effect of the two preceding days; but to me it seems nearly unreal, like an exaggeration stretched to the breaking point.

8   Nature seems to lie prostrate. In passing, on my way to the stable, along the kitchen-garden, I notice the large canes of sweet corn, blowing north like tattered streamers, weary and resigned. I look at the

young boles of white poplar — resistance is useless now; they have given in; there is nothing else to do. Not the slightest attempt is made any longer to raise their thin and mobile leaf-stalks and to lift their blades into the path of the light. Wearily I fix my smarting eyes upon the sun. He looks like the moon: wan, pale, resigned like the rest of nature.

9 Had he given up entirely, too — he, the lord of the world — given in to his rebel son who henceforth is to rule all things, a tyrant, resistless wielder of brutal might usurped? Ceaseless monotony holding sway over the universe?

10 I linger over the horses while I brush them; their coats are damp, ready to break into dripping beads. I stand for a while in the stable-door, looking out at the sky where impalpable waves of vapor are still scudding north. I think of the chickens and find them on the lee-side of the stable, lying in the dust, mouths agape, hardly thinking it worth their while to get up in expectation of a feeding.

11 And suddenly it strikes me that there is not a bird, not a fly, not a gnat on the wing!

12 I do not put the harness on the horses as I had meant to do. Instead, I turn them loose into the lot and go back to the house to get my breakfast. There the little girl babbles away, cheerfully, and shames her elders into controlling their lack of good humor.

13. Shortly before the noon-hour there is a sudden strange sensation borne in upon me — something profoundly disquieting — and I look through the window, across the grade, towards the giant spruce tree that has escaped the early fellers in the bush — it has found a friendly homestead master who left it there, a corner-pillar of his yard, to dominate the landscape for six miles around.

14 "The wind has stopped," I say to my wife. "I suppose I had better go and draw some hay."

15 But I am not revived although the little girl comes running along, in anticipation of a ride. When I reach the stable, I just feed the horses and let it go at that.

16 It is immensely hot; the sun begins to shine more actively while the vapors lift: a bright, aggressive, nearly cruel blue appears in the sky. There is a sting to the rays of the sun. The back of my hand is dotted with little drops, and, as I lift it, the rays of the sun feel like the points of little glowing wires just grazing tormentingly along the skin.

17 I return to the house. My wife does not remark upon the fact that I have not gone; things are self-evident and self-explanatory; no need for futile words. I sink back into my easy-chair.

18 Then — a sudden chill through the open window — a swirl of dust across the grade in front of the yard: it came from the north! A rattling din! I get up and go out on the porch to look about, the little girl preceding me. A squall of wind has blown the lid off the rainwater

tank at the corner of the house. But already a deadly calm has returned.

19   A wall of black cloud has arisen in the northwest — black, with a strangely undefinable, livid tinge to it. The sky overhead is more aggressively, more cruelly blue than ever before.

20   "I think I had better do my chores," I say to myself; and as I look at my watch, it is two o'clock.

21   "I suppose we are going to have a storm," I say into the open window of the little house.

22   "I suppose so," the answer comes back as I stride over to the woodpile and load up my arms; the little girl, too, carries a stick. "Look, daddy," she says, "How much I can take!"

23   After a while I put the lid back on the water tank and place a stout cordwood stick on top to weigh it down.

24   The wall of cloud has risen now. It covers the sky in the northwest to an angular height of thirty degrees. It has taken on a ragged edge, with rounded bulwarks thrown out whose margin is ghostly white. All tints of gray shade into each other, down to that dark, bluish gray which in clouds we call black.

25   And suddenly, while I stand watching on the porch, nerved up, refreshed already in anticipation, the wind breaks loose again, this time from the northwest, however — like a wild beast of the cat-tribe that springs up, confronts, and snarls at you. Instantly the grade is swept bare of dust; fragments of bark, old leaves, rags, bits of paper, start a unanimous march to the southeast, as if at a word of command. Out of the corner of my eye I notice something moving on the siding of the porch. I turn for a moment, for the moving speck seems to irritate me. A fly is holding on, there, with six strained feet, wings a-flutter, trying to crawl, against the wind, behind the shelter of the jutting corner-plate. Doors slam; whatever can rattle, rattles. I brace myself and stand and look; I am as if I could not move.

26   The wind plays strange antics. It reminds me now of a dog that pulls at something and jumps around it, snarling the while and baring his teeth in the determination to get whatever he pulls at, a rag maybe. The woodpile is southeast of a building, exactly in its lee. A cordwood stick topples over from its western edge — not to the south or east, in the direction of the wind, but to the west, against that direction. A counter-swirl is set up there: suction pulls towards the wall and upward, whirling; a bit of paper which first has been blown into the lee of both pile and building gets caught, rises, rushes over the woodpile, towards the wall, and upward; and as it reaches the height of the eaves, it starts back at an angle, downward and southward, enveloped at last in the main current of the leaping careering wind.

27   This wind runs in waves; the wires of the fence vibrate and hum; the house shakes; the trees sway; but the giant spruce tree merely nods.

28   While I am taking all this in, the wall of clouds has risen in front to the height of sixty degrees. My wife has stepped out of the screen door behind; but I do not turn. We both look forward, eyes wide, and watch. The little girl calls from the window, unconscious of whatever may be preparing.

29   Right in front, a light, grayish mass detaches itself from the darker background of cloud. There is an eddying movement in it, downward, outward—a movement incredibly swift for the bulk involved, incredibly sure and determined. The light gray mass assumes the form of a funnel with ragged edges, mouth downward; or that of an inverted, huge, ghostly flower with trumpet-shaped cup, the short stalk springing from the clouds above. A circular wind, independent of the mad roaring rush which envelops the rest of the world, seems to sweep around it; and where it touches the ragged edges of the funnel, these edges seem to dissolve, to melt away, to disappear.

30   Low rumblings are heard high up in that wall of clouds, away in the west, as if some master were coming, scolding from afar—coming as a deputy of Father Sun to settle all this foolishness of South Wind and North Wind in rebellion. But already we know, mere rumbling and scolding will not do it. Sterner things are on their way. And everything around us knows: for everything around us is in flight.

31   Look at the trees: how they are running, their shoulders humped!

32   But the sun still shines. He superintends the preparations.

33   And while we look, that gray inverted funnel or flower seems, of a sudden, to spread out, to expand into a second wall or veil in front of the dark main wall of clouds. Both are rising fast.

34   Then the sun blows out like a candle. His deputy is in charge and well able to see to it that things are done properly and duly restored; and so He himself retires.

35   My eye fastens on to the bluff of balm poplars, a quarter of a mile away, right in front of me, across the big meadow. A strange thing happens there; the bluff becomes so dim; it gets blurred; and suddenly it is blotted out entirely, swallowed by that light gray veil which arose out of the funnel and which now shuts us off from the world farther west.

36   At the same time a few heavy drops come slantways down and rap at my body like knuckles, striking right through my clothes, straight to the skin. The pitter-patter of the rain begins to drown out the roar and swish of the wind; but more imperiously now does the rumbing overhead dominate the enveloping gloom. It is no longer a rumbling; it is the growling of a beast caught in a cage and trying to break out.

37   The rain comes down in streaks, ever increasing. The wind, which is no longer audible above the noise of falling water, blows it into waves or sheets. Like streamers of gray in gray they follow each other, hurrying, scurrying, pitter-patter-fashion, louder and louder, till the

impact on leaves and roofs and ground becomes like the roar of a swollen river falling in a chasm between rocks. Wave after wave, ten inches to three feet apart, hurtles by; and in each wave, drops and darts of water hurry down.

38 It blots out all creation around. None of the buildings is visible any longer. Not even the woodpile, scarce fifty feet away, shows anything beyond a mere outline. I myself stand in a small murky dome of visibility — beyond it is chaos.

39 And then I look down at the gravelled ground in front of the house, at the floor of the porch. In streaky waves the rain reverberates there, the base lines of the upward jumping streaks slightly behind the base lines of the incident rain-waves, retarded and at an angle to them, making a crisscross pattern on ground and floor. And while I look, a transformation seems to take place. Somewhere, sometime, I have seen a tiny marmoset monkey in a rage, beside himself with fury, dancing about, upright, swinging his arms and gnashing his teeth, and chattering in senseless raving. And what I see in front of myself on the ground, on the floor of the porch, transforms itself into myriads of such little monkeys, close to each other, crowding each other, and jumping and dancing and fuming with inexplicable rage — that is the rebound of the rain.

40 And then there comes the first great burst of light — a bluish flash; and, half sheltered, half soaked on the open but roofed-over porch, I raise my head and count. I get as far as five. Then a short bellowing bark, and a growl so fierce that it sets my hair a-tingle. And somehow, incomprehensibly, the rain redoubles, as if spurred and lashed on to a supreme effort of "do-or-die" — and while I still marvel at it, in spite of the noise, of the roar that surrounds me, a feeling comes over me as if everything were suddenly hushed. My mind gropes about for a moment; and then the impression crystallizes.

41 That master above who was coming to set the world to order again steps right over me and, standing astride above me, seems to stop for an impalpable second before he empties out the bag of his wrath. And then he does it.

42 A burst, a cataract, a convulsion, a spasm of light breaks loose. I feel the grip of a hand on my arm. I wince, catch a gasping breath, and close my eyes, but it was too late. That searching light looked into the basement, under the staircase, into the closet, into the oven, and into every nook and crack and cranny on earth — and maybe into my innermost thought and heart.

43 And instantaneously, before I even have had time to realize what has happened, a thunderclap follows, short, rattling: a blasphemy and an abomination of sound — making the house jump, tearing into my sense of hearing like a knife into a raw wound, leaving me knock-kneed and trembling, an atom, a nothing in a world of higher significances.

44   On strides the master. I hear him bark again, once or twice — then he growls; and at last he rumbles, while in the west the sun breaks through and around us plays at rainbows on every leaf.

     The little girl comes out, barefooted, to splash in the pools.

45   I had not noticed that the rain subsided and the wind died down. Like a desert of barren snow is my mind, a white blank, stunned into unconsciousness of all things about me. But like a scarlet patch of blood shed on a real snowfield there lies on the white impassive background of my vision the memory of that frightful clap of wrath.

46   When at last, in the evening, I go to the stable, I draw gratefully in through my nostrils the strong and fertile smell of Mother Earth.

Questions on Content

1   Grove's very detailed narrative account of this storm presents a succession of many related events, but what happens leads to one major event that provides a sense of direction and purpose to the narrative. What is this event? How do preceding events relate to this event?

2   What conflicts are developed by Grove in his narrative? How are these conflicts resolved?

3   What role does the little girl play in the narrative?

4   Based on this narrative, what general view of human experience does Grove seem to take? Do you agree or disagree with that view? Why?

5   In what ways does Grove suggest that a spiritual experience has taken place?

Questions on Structure and Technique

1   Grove's narrative opens with a clear, well-organized sequence of events in paragraphs one through seven. On what basis does Grove organize the beginning of his narrative? How does Grove use verb tense in paragraphs seven and eight to change this pattern of organization? Why do you think Grove makes this change?

2   Why is Grove's use of a first person narrative point of view appropriate in this narrative? How would the narrative have been fundamentally different had he used third person?

3   Grove uses personification when he attributes human qualities to nature, animals, and things. What are the most significant examples of personification in this narrative? Why is personification particularly appropriate to Grove's general view of human experience in this narrative?

4   Grove's use of description in this narrative often develops startling images by indirect and direct comparisons (similes and metaphors) other than personification. What examples of such images seem most effective?

5   Look up the meanings of the word "stable" in a dictionary. Why is Grove's choice of this word in his final sentence significant and appropriate for his account?

Suggestions for Writing

1   Write a first-person narration about a storm that you have experienced, emphasizing not only the details of what happened but also your responses to the experience.

2   Write a first-person narrative account of an experience in which you felt helpless, providing a detailed treatment of those aspects of the experience that seemed particularly uncontrollable.

3   Write a narrative account of an unpleasant or a pleasant experience that seemed, at the time, to be continuing on forever. Provide specific details about the events that took place, but carefully organize and develop those details in a sequence by compressing and expanding the narrative time duration in order to maintain your readers' interest.

VIRGINIA WOOLF

English author Virginia Woolf (1882-1941) was born in London and privately educated herself in the library of her father, Leslie Stephen, a Victorian scholar and philosopher. She became a prominent member of the "Bloomsbury Group" of writers, artists, and thinkers. Virginia Woolf's novels include Mrs. Dalloway *(1925),* To the Lighthouse *(1927),* Orlando *(1928), and* The Waves *(1931), and her essays have been collected in* The Common Reader *(1925),* A Room of One's Own *(1929), and* "The Death of the Moth" and other Essays *(1949). In "The Death of the Moth," Woolf narrates her detailed observations of a moth in order to develop her expression of fundamental ideas about the experience of life and death. Woolf's own life was marked by periods of nervous depression and ended in suicide.*

THE DEATH OF THE MOTH

1   Moths that fly by day are not properly to be called moths; they do not excite that pleasant sense of dark autumn nights and ivy-blossom which the commonest yellow-underwing asleep in the shadow of the curtain never fails to rouse in us. They are hybrid creatures, neither gay like butterflies nor sombre like their own species. Nevertheless the present specimen, with his narrow hay-coloured wings, fringed with a tassel of the same colour, seemed to be content with life. It was a pleasant morning, mid-September, mild, benignant, yet with a keener breath than that of the summer months. The plough was already scoring the field opposite the window, and where the share had been, the earth was pressed flat and gleamed with moisture. Such vigour came rolling in from the fields and the down beyond that it was difficult to keep the eyes strictly turned upon the book. The rooks too were keeping one of their annual festivities; soaring round the tree tops until it looked as if a vast net with thousands of black knots in it had been cast up into the air; which, after a few moments sank slowly down upon the trees until every twig seemed to have a knot at the end of it. Then, suddenly, the net would be thrown into the air again in a wider circle this time, with the utmost clamour and vociferation, as though to be thrown into the air and settle slowly down upon the tree tops were a tremendously exciting experience.

2   The same energy which inspired the rooks, the ploughmen, the horses, and even, it seemed, the lean bare-backed downs, sent the moth fluttering from side to side of his square of the window-pane. One could not help watching him. One was, indeed, conscious of a queer feeling of pity for him. The possibilities of pleasure seemed that morning so enormous and so various that to have only a moth's

part in life, and a day moth's at that, appeared a hard fate, and his zest in enjoying his meagre opportunities to the full, pathetic. He flew vigorously to one corner of his compartment, and, after waiting there a second, flew across to the other. What remained for him but to fly to a third corner and then to a fourth? That was all he could do, in spite of the size of the downs, the width of the sky, the far-off smoke of houses, and the romantic voice, now and then, of a steamer out at sea. What he could do he did. Watching him, it seemed as if a fibre, very thin but pure, of the enormous energy of the world had been thrust into his frail and diminutive body. As often as he crossed the pane, I could fancy that a thread of vital light became visible. He was little or nothing but life.

3   Yet, because he was so small, and so simple a form of the energy that was rolling in at the open window and driving its way through so many narrow and intricate corridors in my own brain and in those of other human beings, there was something marvellous as well as pathetic about him. It was as if someone had taken a tiny bead of pure life and decking it as lightly as possible with down and feathers, had set it dancing and zig-zagging to show us the true nature of life. Thus displayed one could not get over the strangeness of it. One is apt to forget all about life, seeing it humped and bossed and garnished and cumbered so that it has to move with the greatest circumspection and dignity. Again, the thought of all that life might have been had he been born in any other shape caused one to view his simple activities with a kind of pity.

4   After a time, tired by his dancing apparently, he settled on the window ledge in the sun, and, the queer spectacle being at an end, I forgot about him. Then, looking up, my eye was caught by him. He was trying to resume his dancing, but seemed either so stiff or so awkward that he could only flutter to the bottom of the window-pane; and when he tried to fly across it he failed. Being intent on other matters I watched these futile attempts for a time without thinking, unconsciously waiting for him to resume his flight, as one waits for a machine, that has stopped momentarily, to start again without considering the reason of its failure. After perhaps a seventh attempt he slipped from the wooden ledge and fell, fluttering his wings, on to his back on the window sill. The helplessness of his attitude roused me. It flashed upon me that he was in difficulties; he could no longer raise himself; his legs struggled vainly. But, as I stretched out a pencil, meaning to help him to right himself, it came over me that the failure and awkwardness were the approach of death. I laid the pencil down again.

5   The legs agitated themselves once more. I looked as if for the enemy against which he struggled. I looked out of doors. What had happened there? Presumably it was midday, and work in the fields had

stopped. Stillness and quiet had replaced the previous animation. The birds had taken themselves off to feed in the brooks. The horses stood still. Yet the power was there all the same, massed outside indifferent, impersonal, not attending to anything in particular. Somehow it was opposed to the little hay-coloured moth. It was useless to try to do anything. One could only watch the extraordinary efforts made by those tiny legs against an oncoming doom which could, had it chosen, have submerged an entire city, not merely a city, but masses of human beings; nothing, I knew, had any chance against death. Nevertheless after a pause of exhaustion the legs fluttered again. It was superb this last protest, and so frantic that he succeeded at last in righting himself. One's sympathies, of course, were all on the side of life. Also, when there was nobody to care or to know, this gigantic effort on the part of an insignificant little moth, against a power of such magnitude, to retain what no one else valued or desired to keep, moved one strangely. Again, somehow, one saw life, a pure bead. I lifted the pencil again, useless though I knew it to be. But even as I did so, the unmistakable tokens of death showed themselves. The body relaxed, and instantly grew stiff. The struggle was over. The insignificant little creature now knew death. As I looked at the dead moth, this minute wayside triumph of so great a force over so mean an antagonist filled me with wonder. Just as life had been strange a few minutes before, so death was now as strange. The moth having righted himself now lay most decently and uncomplainingly composed. O yes, he seemed to say, death is stronger than I am.

Questions on Content

1   Although Woolf's specific subject is the death of a moth, what other, more general, subject does Woolf develop in her narrative?

2   What ideas and images does Woolf develop in the description of her observations of the moth in the first three paragraphs? Why is this description important to the narration of the death of the moth in subsequent paragraphs?

3   What major conflict does Woolf develop in her narrative. Where is this conflict most clearly shown through her presentations of a specific image? Where is this conflict most succinctly stated in general, abstract terms?

4   What meaning does Woolf's observation of the death of the moth hold for her?

5   In what ways is Woolf's narrative account of the death of a moth relevant to the human experience of life and death? What moral does Woolf develop for her readers in this narrative?

Questions on Structure and Technique

1   What main images does Woolf present in paragraph one? In what ways do these images contrast with the image of the moth in paragraph two? In what ways are these images similar?

2   What is the purpose of paragraph three?

3   What words and phrases does Woolf use in paragraph four to emphasize a narrative sequence of events? What similar words and phrases are used in paragraph five?

4   Why is Woolf's use of a first-person narrative point of view important in contributing to the effectiveness of this writing? Is Woolf's point of view strictly limited to her own observations? Explain.

5   Reconsider the classification of Woolf's essay as narration. Why should this writing be classified as narration rather than as description?

Suggestions for Writing

1   Write a narrative of your experience of the death of an animal, using specific details to show your readers why this death was significant to you.

2   Narrate the specific events of an experience from which you learned that "death is stronger than I am."

3   Write a narration about your experience with a person or an animal whose actions you have observed carefully, using a first-person point of view to present not only your own observations of your subject but also the details of that subject's experiences as you have sympathetically understood and interpreted them. Be sure to study Woolf's handling of narrative of view but also consider the similar (third-person) narrative technique used by Roberts in "In the Deep Grass."

CHAPTER 3

*"It is difficult to describe the absolute
dreariness and hopelessness of this
kind of job."*

LLUSTRATION

Illustration is the most basic way writers show rather than simply tell readers about their subject. A writer's illustrations provide relevant examples, instances, and cases that support, clarify, and develop general thoughts or abstract ideas in specific and concrete terms. A detailed description or narration serves as a single extended illustration of a writer's subject and attitude, as we have seen, but a writer's illustrations need not be limited to a single sequence of images or events. A writer may select several different examples from one or more sources to illustrate the same idea or thesis. The reading selections in this chapter show how writers use such multiple illustrations as a primary method for developing their ideas.

In an illustrative essay, the writer's subject and attitude toward that subject, a thesis, must be clearly stated, or at least strongly implied, so that the main unifying thought or idea common to the writer's particular experience and knowledge is firmly established. For instance, Edward McCourt's three different (and seemingly insignificant) observations selected from his own experiences while travelling serve to illustrate his thesis in "The Little Things," that "the chief pleasure of travel is the sum of little things that happen or are seen and heard along the way." Without such a stated (or an implied) thesis, a writer's illustrations may seem unrelated and purposeless to readers. In some illustrative essays, such as McCourt's and George Bowering's "Between the Lines," writers emphasize the specific examples themselves rather than the general idea being illustrated, but often writers develop other related or supporting ideas, using illustrations to give substance to their general statements in a phrase, a sentence, several sentences, or a paragraph. The essays by Pierre Berton, Hugh MacLennan, and William James are fine examples of this use of multiple illustrations.

All of these essays show the importance of writers' thoughtful selection and arrangement of their illustrations. A writer's own particular personal experiences are a good starting point for selecting illustrations, as in McCourt's description of some memorable moments that took place on his trip to the Yukon, and in Pierre Berton's discussion of "The Religion of Work . . ." in which he provides descriptive as well as narrative illustrations from his summer job experiences working in a northern mining camp. However, George Bowering's short essay, "Between the Lines," presents a series of examples from his reading on contemporary literature as well as "from personal experience and talking with other writers." Similarly, Hugh MacLennan begins "But Shaw Was a Playwright" with a personal narrative account and several brief examples from his own experience, and then he too introduces illustrations from his reading, drawing on his extensive knowledge of literary and cultural history to support his thesis. Contemporary politics, mass media, and popular culture are also among the wide variety of a writer's possible sources for illustrations suitable to his or her

ILLUSTRATION   67

subject and attitude. The writer's arrangement of illustrations must support, clarify, and develop the thesis and any related ideas. Therefore, the writer need not necessarily establish a spatial or temporal pattern of organization (as in description and narration), but some appropriate pattern or principle should be followed.

I.   Introduction
II. A   Illustration 1
II. B   Illustration 2
II. C   Illustration 3
III.   Conclusion

When writers such as McCourt and Bowering use multiple illustrations to support a single thesis or idea, they usually place their most important and effective illustrations toward the beginning and the end. This same pattern is sometimes chosen when a writer such as Pierre Berton is concerned with arranging several related ideas, in which case the illustrations are placed in support of each point as it is introduced. Hugh MacLennan further arranges his ideas and illustrations into several types or kinds, by using principles that we will be exploring further, such as classification, comparison and contrast, and cause and effect.

Illustrations show readers some of the particular things that a writer has in mind when he or she makes a general or abstract statement. By carefully selecting and then arranging multiple illustrations rather than developing a single extended illustration in a description or a narration, a writer can communicate thoughts and ideas with substance and form. Whether a writer's subject is the pleasures of travel or philosophical principles, illustrations are basic requirements for expressing our experiences and our knowledge effectively.

EDWARD McCOURT

Edward McCourt (1907–1972) was an author and a university English professor at the University of Saskatchewan at Saskatoon. He wrote five novels, among them Music at the Close *(1947), three historical adventure books for young people, an important literary study on* The Canadian West in Fiction *(1949), and three travel books. "The Little Things" is an effective illustrative essay from one of these travel books,* The Yukon and the Northwest *(1969), and it offers us a good example of basic essay organization and development: an explicitly-stated thesis in paragraph one, three interesting illustrations in the "body" paragraph, and, a unifying (and somewhat bizarre) conclusion in the final paragraph.*

THE LITTLE THINGS

1   The pleasures of travel are rarely confined to scenery and contacts with people. Indeed I would go so far as to say that the chief pleasure of travel is the sum of little things that happen or are seen and heard along the way — little things that linger in the memory long after the impact of big things like a twenty-thousand-foot mountain or a meeting with a great man has weakened almost to extinction.

2   In Watson Lake, for instance, I came across a peculiar treasure — a brochure advertising the merits of a motel association in prose that belongs to the ages. Grading of the member units began with "excellent" — nothing lower — and progressed upwards through "exceptional" to "extraordinary". And the description of the attractions of one western member of the association is something I'm sure I will cherish all the days of my life: "Air conditioning and double sound-proof walls, plus a welcome as big as the surrounding Cariboo country — vast and rugged — and hospitality as western as any cowboy ballad . . . Elizabethan decor . . ." It seems superfluous to add that this motel rates "extraordinary".

3   And what of the attraction, indeed the awful fascination, of the word spoken but uncomprehended, the phrase snatched from a vagrant breeze, the sentence isolated from its fellows that brands itself upon the brain for no other reason than the sure knowledge that being in transit you will never know what went before or came after. Thus, strolling down the main street of Watson Lake I saw approaching me through the dust-haze the two mini-skirted Alaska-bound California girls in the company of a handsome white-haired elderly gentleman wearing a flaming red shirt. The girls had been our road

ILLUSTRATION   69

companions for several days now and I bared my teeth in anticipation of a brisk exchange of social pleasantries, but they never so much as glanced my way. All their attention was fixed on the white-haired gentleman. "And then," I heard him say as we drew abreast, "I was bitten by a seal. At thirteen thousand feet."

4   And that was all. They went their way, the girls playing duplicate Desdemonas to the white-haired gentleman's Othello ("They loved me for the dangers I had pass'd"), and I went mine: they no doubt light-hearted, not a care in the world, and I with a phrase snatched out of a passing stranger's mouth that assured me many a sleepless tortured hour. How in God's name could a man be bitten by a seal at thirteen thousand feet? Of course there was Richthofen's World War I Flying Circus but I don't think any seals belonged.

5   The little things. Printed words. Spoken words. And tangible objects which in ordinary circumstances would not arouse the faintest curiosity but in the extraordinary circumstances under which I so often find them in the course of my wanderings serve to oppress me with the awful burden of the unsolved riddles of existence.

6   For instance, the false teeth.

7   We found them in a deserted cabin which stood on the bank of a nearly dry Klondike creek. They sat in the middle of the cabin floor and grinned up at us. They were surrounded by dust and debris and they posed the fearful question — *where was the rest of the man?* Was he the dust in which they sat? Had he, being a careful man not wishing to destroy an expensive set, removed the plates before putting the muzzle of the gun into his mouth and blowing his head off? I will never know.

8   The teeth are just one more addition to the sum of unanswered questions that hurried journeys pose. Like Ulysses, but for different reasons, I cannot rest from travel. Particularly around 4 a.m. when I'm home and in bed and a seal starts biting me with his false teeth.

Questions on Content

1   McCourt's thesis is stated in paragraph one, as follows: "The chief pleasure of travel is the sum of little things that happen or are seen and heard along the way." Why is this thesis appropriate for an illustrative essay? In what way does McCourt's statement anticipate his conclusion in the final paragraph?

2   What is "peculiar" about the advertising brochure described by McCourt in paragraph two?

3   McCourt's second illustration of his thesis in paragraphs three and four emphasizes several incongruities. What are they?

4   Paragraph five is a transitional paragraph. What relations do you notice between McCourt's general statements in this paragraph and his specific illustrations that precede and follow it?

5   McCourt's third illustration in paragraphs six and seven is introduced as an example of "the unsolved riddles of existence." Why is McCourt's illustration of this idea effective?

Questions on Structure and Technique

1   Sketch the basic outline of McCourt's essay. On what basis does McCourt divide the essay into paragraphs?

2   What brief illustrations does McCourt use in paragraph one? What is their purpose?

3   What words and phrases does McCourt use to introduce his illustrations? What other words or phrases might he have chosen?

4   What descriptive and narrative techniques do you notice in McCourt's essay? What main images are developed?

5   Why is McCourt's final paragraph such an effective conclusion for his essay?

Suggestions for Writing

1   Write a well-organized essay in which you present three different illustrations selected from your own experiences that support and develop McCourt's thesis that "the chief pleasure of travel is the sum of little things that happen or are seen and heard along the way."

2   Select three different personal experiences that reveal the same general idea to you. Write a well-organized essay in which you state that idea as a clear and concise thesis statement in your first paragraph, illustrate that thesis in specific detail using descriptive and narrative techniques in three subsequent paragraphs, and bring the essay to an effective conclusion in the final paragraph.

3   Write a well-organized and well-developed illustrative essay in which you discuss "the awful burden of the unsolved riddles of existence." Be sure to support and clarify your ideas with specific details and effective examples.

ILLUSTRATION   71

GEORGE BOWERING

George Bowering (b. 1935) is a novelist, poet, literary critic, editor, and university professor at Simon Fraser University. Influenced by American poets such as William Carlos Williams, Robert Duncan, Robert Creeley, and Charles Olson, Bowering published his first of almost forty books of poetry, Sticks and Stones *(1963), as a graduate student in English at the University of British Columbia. Bowering won Governor General's Awards for one of his books of poetry,* The Gangs of Kosmos *(1969), and for his novel about George Vancouver,* Burning Water *(1980). A prolific and innovative author, Bowering's writings include two other novels, collections of short stories, and several books of literary criticism. "Between the Lines" is a magazine article in which Bowering discusses one overlooked, practical side of a writer's craft.*

BETWEEN THE LINES

1   This is a true story: yesterday an English professor asked me how I decided on the length of the lines in my poems. I said that it depended on two things — how I hear what's being said, and what size paper I'm writing on.

2   In all the years I have devoted to writing and reading literature, I have read only one discussion of the effect of the writing surface on the writing. That was the transcript of a discussion between Allen Ginsberg and Robert Creeley at the 1963 summer poetry extravaganza at the University of British Columbia. But I know from personal experience and talking with the other writers that critics seldom consider such mundane things as whether the author wrote his novel in a stenographer's pad or on custom-made vellum.

3   William Carlos Williams has been called everything from a social realist to a post-modernist grandpa. Yet it is no secret that he scribbled lots of his poems on prescription forms while the next patient was putting down the magazine in the waiting room and entering his office. That could explain two things: (1) why a thousand of Dr. Williams's poems are half a page long; (2) that the poems are generally recognized as good for what ails you.

4   When it comes to manuscripts, Robert Creeley is an interesting case. Creeley doesn't like to scratch revisions on his work in progress. If he makes a mistake, or gets a better idea, he throws away the page and starts over. It has something to do with getting into the right rhythm or head-space. He does the same thing with prose. When

the U.S. Library of Congress acquired the working typescript of his novel, *The Island*, they got the same thing his publisher, Scribner's, got — 300 pages of perfect copy. — u

5   Allen Ginsberg, on the other hand, writes everything in notebooks he carries with him, on airplanes, in the front seat of a Volkswagen bus, in a cafeteria in Marrakesh. Every few years, when he gets a prod from his publisher, City Lights, he goes through the notebook scribblings and extracts 100 pages of poetry. — R

6   I know a man who cannot write on anything but cheap yellow carbon-copy paper, with a 4H pencil. I know a composer who would be lost without her ancient typewriter, a machine so old and funny-looking that the keys are laid out in alphabetical order.

7   The Vancouver novelist Audrey Thomas sits and writes in ink on the ruled lines of yellow legal-sized foolscap. Her work, as many critics have noticed, is animated by a meticulous memory. When Thomas started writing her stories and novels, she was a housewife and college student, with a house full of children. In order to steal time for writing fiction, she would sit at her student desk, or rather table, and pretend she was writing an English assignment. That's a memory she has never forgotten. It might also explain why her books are so inviting for students who know how to handle them as English assignments.

8   Thomas still hires somebody to type her work from that hand-writing. I have been trying for years to shame her into learning to type. But she knows how her imagination works, and she knows that the conversations her characters have get a little more room on that long page. She gave me an oblong notebook once, and I wrote short poems with long lines in it. People are always giving me nice notebooks, and I keep them till I find a poem that will fit. The poem is always as long as the notebook. This will perhaps encourage people to slip me single sheets of hand-made paper.

9   When it comes to essays, I like to use the 12-page booklets that university students get to write their exams in. Most of my essays extend to 36 or 48 pages of double-spaced handwriting. Despite what you may have heard, I take more than three hours to write them. I usually write short stories the same way.

10   But when you are planning to write a novel you know you are in for a routine that will dominate your days for a year or two. With novels I like to set myself a routine I haven't learned before. Maybe I think that will make it impossible to write the same book over and over.

11   My first novel I just sat and typed with a manual typewriter on the kitchen table. When I was ready to do a novel about Captain Vancouver I took my index-card notes, bought three beautiful bound

ILLUSTRATION 73

notebooks in Chinatown, and 10 of my favourite German felt pens, and flew to Trieste. There I sat every day and wrote a 1,000-word chapter, or as I like to think of it, 10 pages of ink. My next one I did at home, on the same black no-nonsense hardback scribblers I do my diary in. Then I typed it up on my new word processor.

12   Last year I decided to write the novel I have been thinking of for seven years— a western that takes place in the Thompson Valley of British Columbia in 1889. Again I stayed home, but for a reason the reviewers will never bother to think of. I wrote it right on the computer screen. Now I am shopping for a little portable computer: The next novel is going to be written on the road somewhere. Maybe I can take it to the ball-park with me.

Questions on Content

1   What is Bowering's thesis? Is this thesis stated implicitly or explicitly? What sentence or sentences, if any, contain this statement?

2   What attitudes of writers toward their writing do Bowering's illustrations exemplify? What attitudes of readers toward writers and their writing does Bowering encourage through his illustrations?

3   How does Bowering's detailed discussion of what "I know from personal experience and talking with other writers" contribute to the effectiveness of his essay? What details do you find most interesting?

4   Does Bowering's concluding illustration of his writing novels on a computer screen support or modify his thesis?

5   Why is his last sentence, "Maybe I can take it to the ballpark with me," an appropriate concluding statement?

Questions on Structure and Technique

1   What is the purpose of Bowering's "true story" in paragraph one? What is the relation between paragraph one and paragraph two?

2   On what basis does Bowering divide the rest of the essay into paragraphs? What variations in this organization do you notice? Why are these variations appropriate?

3   What three main groups does Bowering divide his illustrations into?

4   How many of Bowering's sentences contain general statements? What examples of sentences with very specific details can you find? What is the effect of these sentences?

5   Why is illustration a more appropriate mode for Bowering to choose for his overall development of his subject than either description or narration? Where are descriptive and narrative techniques important?

Suggestions for Writing

1   Write a well-organized illustrative essay in which you discuss, in very specific detail, your own methods of writing. Consider not only the writing materials that you use but also the different situations, the different kinds of writing, and their relations to one another.

2   Choose any ordinary, daily activity that you perform, such as reading, walking, sleeping, or eating, and write a well-organized and detailed illustrative essay in which you discuss several different ways you have found to perform that activity.

3   Read some poetry written by William Carlos Williams, Robert Creeley, Allen Ginsberg, or George Bowering. Then write an illustrative essay in which you discuss what you believe makes the author's poetry effective. Be sure to support your ideas with specific details and examples.

ILLUSTRATION   75

PIERRE BERTON

Author, journalist, and radio and television personality, Pierre Berton (b. 1920), was born in Dawson City in the Yukon. He attended the University of British Columbia and in 1942 began his career in journalism at the Vancouver News-Herald. *For the next twenty years, Berton worked as a writer and editor for the Vancouver* Sun, Maclean's *magazine, and the* Toronto Star. *Among several books he wrote during these years are* The Mysterious North *(1956) and* Klondike: The Life and Death of the Last Great Goldrush *(1958), both of which won Governor General's Awards and* Just Add Water and Stir *(1959), which won the Leacock Medal for Humour. By the early 1960s, Berton had begun his broadcasting career that included several television series:* Front Page Challenge, The Pierre Berton Show, The Great Debate, *and* My Country. *Berton's two-volume narrative history of the Canadian Pacific Railway,* The National Dream *(1970) and another Governor General's Award winner* The Last Spike *(1971), are two examples of his many books on Canadian history and culture. His other books include* The Smug Minority *(1968), an irreverent critique of the Canadian establishment from which this essay on the "Religion of Work . . ." has been selected. Berton's use of description and narration to illustrate ideas formulated from his own personal experiences makes this writing both interesting and intellectually challenging.*

Author's - attitude   *class discussion*
- point of view

THE RELIGION OF WORK AND THE DIRTIEST JOB IN THE WORLD

4.2 are intro

1   On my seventeenth birthday, which fell on July 12, 1937, one of the worst years of the Depression, I went to work for pay and there was jubilation among my friends and relatives. In an era when jobs were scarce I had a job; and having a job was the goal of everyone in those days. Having a job in the Thirties was a bit like having a swimming pool in the Sixties; it conferred status. It didn't really matter what the job was. It could be rewarding, mindless, foolish, unproductive, even degrading—no matter: it set you apart as a paying member of a society whose creed was that everyone must work at something, and the harder the better, too.

2   My job was in a mining camp in the Yukon some 1,500 miles from my home in Victoria, B.C. I worked ten hours a day, seven days a

week, and I was paid $4.50 a day plus my board. Almost everybody who learned about my job had the same thing to say about it: 'It will make a man out of you!' And when the job came to an end at the start of my university term, almost every adult I knew examined my hands to note with satisfaction the heavy calluses. Back-breaking work was considered to be a high form of human endeavour. A man who worked hard couldn't be all bad, whether he was a convict breaking rocks in a prison yard or an executive neglecting his family by toiling weekends at the office.

3   I worked for three summer seasons at that same job and it was commonly held that I was 'working my way through college', another laudable endeavour in a society which believed, and still believes, that every individual must pay his own way regardless of position, health, mental ability, or physical condition.

4   The first year I worked on a construction gang; the following years I worked on the thawing crew, engaged in preparing the ground for the actual gold mining that was to follow. Thawing permafrost with cold water is a fascinating process to almost everyone except those actually employed in it. As far as I know, it is the world's muddiest job, involving as it does the pumping of millions of gallons of cold water into the bowels of the earth.

5   And so we toiled away, up to our ankles, our knees, and sometimes even our hips in a pulsating gruel of mud and ice-water. The men who drove those points into the rock-like soil were soaking wet most of the time, for it was difficult to add extension or withdraw a point without water spurting in all directions. All day long they laboured, with their fingers curled around the handles of their slide hammers, their torsos rising and falling as they drove each pipe inch by inch into the earth. When a point became plugged it had to be hauled up and unplugged while the ice-water squirted in their faces. Each man was logged on the amount of footage he had driven in a day, and if that footage was seen to be too low he could expect to draw his time slip that evening. There was a story current in my day that the general manager had come out from Dawson on a tour of inspection and seen a man standing immobile in the distance. 'Fire that man!' he cried. 'I've been watching him and he hasn't moved for half an hour.' Later it was discovered that he *couldn't* move; he was up to his hips in mud.

6   When you work for ten hours at hard labour, whether you are seventeen or fifty-seven, there is precious little time or energy left for anything else. We rose at six, performed our swift ablutions, wolfed an enormous breakfast, and headed off for the job which had to begin at seven. At noon we started back up the valley slopes through the mud to the messhall, wolfed another vast meal, and finished it just in time to head back once more. At six we were finished, in more ways

than one. I have seen men so tired they could not eat the final me. the day which was always consumed in silence and at top speed. was said that any man who stumbled on the messhall steps on the way in found himself trampled by the rush coming out.) When this was over, large numbers of men of varying ages simply lay down on their bunks utterly fagged out, and slept. There was nothing else to do anyway: no library, no recreation hall, no lounge, no radio or films — nothing but a roadhouse five miles distant where you could buy bootleg rum. Civilization was represented by Dawson, forty miles away; we never visited it. We were like men in a prison camp, except that we worked much harder.

Under such conditions any kind of creative act or thought is difficult. I remember one man, a German immigrant, who was trying to learn to draw by correspondence. He had some talent but in the end he had to give it up. He was too tired to draw. I had brought along a pile of books required in my university course for summer reading, but most of the time I found I was too tired to read. Those who did not immediately go to sleep after supper spent their spare time washing their work clothes or lying in their bunks indulging in verbal sexual fantasies. I often wondered if this was what the adults meant when they said that mining camp life would make a man of me. Certainly I learned a great deal more from these sexual bull sessions than I had at my mother's knee. It was not until many years later that I discovered most of it was wrong.

It is difficult to describe the absolute dreariness and hopelessness of this kind of job. The worst thing about it was that there was no respite, since — in a seven-day-a-week job — there were no breaks of any kind to look forward to until the coming of winter rendered further toil impossible. There was one wit among us who used to leap from his bunk once a week, when the bull cook banged the triangle at 6:00 a.m., crying jubilantly: 'Thank God, it's Sunday!' This always provoked a bitter laugh. Without any change of pace, time moves sluggishly; without any break in the routine, a kind of lethargy steals over the mind. The blessed winter seemed eons away to all of us.

Yet for me, in my late teens, life in this mining camp was immeasurably easier than it was for the others. There were men here in their sixties who had lived this way all their lives. There were men in their prime with wives and children to support — families they did not see for half of every year. There were all kinds of men here and few who were really stupid. I worked with immigrants from Austria, Germany, Switzerland, Italy, Sweden, Norway, and Denmark, as well as with Canadians. Most were intelligent and a great many were extremely sharp and able. All were industrious. Each had displayed enough courage and independence to somehow make his way several thousand miles to the one corner of North America where a job of sorts was comparatively easy to get. But all had one thing in common: according to my observation, none had been educated up to his ability.

10   There were many men in that mining camp easily capable of obtaining a university degree; and there were many more who might have completed high school and then gone on to technical school. I saw them each evening, lying on their bunks and trying to force their hands open — hands that had been curled into almost permanent positions around cold pipes; I saw them each morning, shambling down to that grotesque mudpie of a valley; during the day I saw them — scores of ant-like figures, bend double over their slide hammers, struggling in the gumbo, striving and groaning; and the thought that came to my mind was ever the same: 'What a waste of human resources!'

11   For this 'job', which everybody had congratulated me upon getting, which was supposed to be so ennobling, which was to make a man of me, was actually degrading, destructive, and above all useless. It was degrading because it reduced men to the status of beasts. There was one wag who went around with his zipper purposely undone and his genitals exposed. 'If I'm working like a horse, I might as well look like one,' he'd say. It was destructive because it reduced a glorious setting to a black obscenity. And it was useless because the gold, which was mined at such expense and human cost, was melted into bars and shipped to Fort Knox in the United States where it was once again confined below ground. Every manjack of us knew this; it was the subject of much bitter banter and wisecracking; each of us, I think, was disturbed by the fact that we were engaged in an operation which was essentially unproductive. If we'd been growing wheat, we would at least have had the satisfaction of knowing our labours were useful. The whole, vast, complicated operation seemed to me to be pointless: even the stockholders failed to profit by it greatly; for years the company was forced to pass its dividends. Would we or the nation have been worse off if we had stayed drunk all summer?

12   The one valuable asset that I recovered from my mining camp experience was status. It allows me to use a line in my official biography which I notice is seized upon joyfully by those who have to introduce me when I make after-dinner speeches: 'During the Thirties, he worked in Yukon mining camps to help put himself through university.' When that line is uttered the audience is prepared to forgive me almost anything: outlandishly radical opinions, dangerous views on matters sexual, alarming attitudes toward religion. I am pronounced worthy because, in that one sentence, is summed up the great Canadian myth: that work — *any* work — is the most important thing in life, and that anybody who is willing to work hard enough can by his own initiative get as far as he wants.

ILLUSTRATION 79

Questions on Content

1   What is the subject of Berton's first paragraph? What attitude toward this subject does Berton discuss? Does he share this attitude? What words and phrases convey his own view of the subject?

2   What further relevant ideas does Berton present in paragraphs two and three? What is Berton's thesis statement?

3   What are the main ideas that support and develop Berton's thesis in the subsequent paragraphs?

4   What are the main targets of Berton's criticism in this essay?

5   Do you agree or disagree with Berton's concluding definition of "the great Canadian myth"? Why? What does Berton mean by the word "myth"?

Questions on Structure and Technique

1   Berton's introductory paragraphs one through three provide a thesis and some background context for his subsequent discussion. What general statements establish his thesis? What specific details support this thesis? What other information does Berton include in these paragraphs?

2   What are the purposes of paragraphs four and five?

3   In paragraphs six through eleven, what sentences state Berton's main ideas in general terms? Where are these sentences located in the paragraphs? Why?

4   What humorous examples and details does Berton present to support these statements? What serious ones? What does the writer achieve by using both humorous and serious illustrations?

5   What is the purpose of Berton's final sentence in the concluding paragraph? Why is this statement not made more explicit in paragraphs one through three? Why is it effective in the concluding paragraph?

Suggestions for Writing

1   Write an illustrative essay in which you discuss either the beneficial or the detrimental aspects of your own summer work experience.

2   In an illustrative essay, discuss an opinion or a belief that you hold as a result of your own experiences, presenting three or four different examples to illustrate your view.

3   Consider other activities, ideas, or beliefs that might be viewed as "the great Canadian myth." Write a well-organized and well-developed illustrative essay in which you discuss that "myth" in both general and specific terms, using details and examples from your own experience to support your view.

HUGH MACLENNAN

Hugh MacLennan (b. 1907) was born in Glace Bay, Nova Scotia and grew up in Halifax. He was educated at Dalhousie University, was a Rhodes Scholar at Oxford, and then took his doctorate in classical studies at Princeton in 1935. For most of his career as an author, MacLennan held academic teaching positions in Montreal, first at Lower Canada College and then at McGill University until his retirement in 1979. After writing a successful first novel, Barometer Rising *(1941), based on his childhood experience of the 1917 Halifax explosion, MacLennan wrote three more novels that each won Governor General's Awards:* Two Solitudes *(1945),* The Precipice *(1948), and* The Watch that Ends the Night *(1959). Two collections of his essays,* Cross Country *(1949) and* Thirty and three *(1954), also won Governor General's Awards. His more recent novels are* Return of the Sphinx *(1967) and* Voices in Time *(1980). "But Shaw Was a Playwright" is an essay from* The Other Side of Hugh MacLennan *(1979), and it shows how MacLennan places his personal experiences within a broader historical and cultural context, that of the novelist's invaluable ability to "enrich our understanding of man's relationship to men."*

BUT SHAW WAS A PLAYWRIGHT

1   It was shortly after my last novel made its Canadian debut that somebody said it again. I was in the bank in the act of drawing out a small sum of money, and I mean small. The extremely pretty, competent, and vivacious teller, as she began to count out the bills, said, "It must be wonderful!"

2   I looked over my shoulder, but the man who stood behind me in line was busy talking to the man who stood behind him, so I looked back at the girl on the other side of the wicket.

3   "What must be wonderful?" I said.

4   "Being a writer."

5   She counted the bills again. "I wish I could write. Just think of never having to get up in the morning like other people!"

6   "I'm up now," I said, but as I looked at the clock it didn't sound convincing. It was half past ten.

7   She shoved the bills toward me. "Think of sitting down and writing something that everyone wants to read and then sitting back to watch the money come rolling in."

ILLUSTRATION   81

8   I looked at her sharply and wondered if she were mistaking me for the late Lloyd C. Douglas. I thought of telling her I had read only the night before that Sinclair Lewis, after one of the most spectacular writing careers in modern times, had left a mere fifteen thousand dollars, together with some real estate, when he died. But she was smiling at me as I pocketed the bills, and she really did think it was a wonderful thing to be a writer, and what was more, she thought everyone liked what I wrote. If she had been the manager of the bank it would have been the right time to ask for a loan.

9   "It's a shame to spoil such pleasant thoughts," I said. "But in the strictness of meaning I neither brew nor distil. If I did, then you could be sure that everybody would like my products and the money would really be rolling in."

10   She laughed as I made way for the man behind me. Perhaps it would occur to her later in the day to look up my file and discover the facts of my financial life. But I rather hoped she wouldn't. I could have told her the truth in unmistakable terms; by not doing so I was only living up to the tradition of my profession. Novelists move and have their living by recounting myths to the world. Our books stand or fall by their capacity or ineptness in persuading people that fictitious characters really lived and imaginary events really occurred. Who am I to explode myths concerning the arts?

11   On the other hand, people believe what they want to believe, and these myths are so well-worn and established that I doubt if any amount of evidence to the contrary will serve to explode them. What if she were to look up my bank account, which was never far from overdraft all the past winter? This charming and capable young teller would still be convinced that writing books was a fine way to watch the money come rolling in. She's seen it in the movies.

12   As a general rule, the thoughtful public believes that all poets are impractical, all painters are poor, and all novelists are rich. In a vague sort of way I thought so, too, once upon a time. But during the past twenty years I have come to know personally a number of poets and painters, as well as novelists, and I realize that of all the misconceptions generally held about artistic folk, the one which holds poets to be impractical is the silliest. Most of the poets I can think of are extremely shrewd.

13   An English poet whom I knew well at Princeton is now the head of the British Council in Italy and during the last war served in Military Intelligence in Scandinavia. One well-known poet in Canada has one of the sharpest and clearest legal minds in the country. Still another in France was an important leader in his country's underground during the war. A fourth poet friend of mine was well on his way to becoming president of a large university when he dropped dead at the age of forty-odd. In fact, I have finally reached the conclusion

that the ability to write poetry has some strange connection with the ability to administer both men and affairs.

14   When Wallace Stevens was awarded the Pulitzer Prize for poetry I decided to look up the records for my own satisfaction. Stevens is either president or managing director or something of the like of a large Hartford insurance company. Of him Louis Untermeyer has written, ". . . Stevens is a stylist of unusual delicacy. Even the least sympathetic reader must be struck by the poet's hypersensitive and ingenious imagination." So there is a man of unquestionable talent who is also practical enough to rise to heights in the management of a company with world-wide financial interests. Let's look at some of the others.

15   David — one of the most beloved poets of all time — was also the greatest soldier-king Israel ever produced. Hadrian, an excellent poet, was the second-best administrator in the long history of Imperial Rome. Aeschylus was an extremely tough infantry soldier, far prouder of having stood in the line at Marathon than of writing the famous *Agamemnon* trilogy. Sophocles at one period in his life was a general of the Athenian republic. Horace was astute enough to acquire a life-pension from Augustus, although he had previously fought against him as an officer in Brutus's army. Vergil also won a life-pension from Augustus, an accomplishment as practical as his poetry was memorable.

16   Dante played an important role in the politics of Italian city states before he was exiled. Geoffrey Chaucer, gentle poet of *The Canterbury Tales*, served his king as a foreign diplomat, as comptroller of customs on wool and hides, and as clerk of the King's works. François Villon was a celebrated (and practical) thief. Shakespeare made a fortune as a theatre manager. Sir Philip Sidney was a general. Milton served for years in Cromwell's government and was at one time his secretary. Andrew Marvell became a member of Parliament. Goethe was for ten years the principal minister of state in Weimar. In our own day, to find one more example, T. S. Eliot has not only won a Nobel Prize, which is a considerable sum of money, he has also for many years drawn an excellent salary from one of England's largest publishing houses.

17   So for every Shelley, Heine, and Dowson you can give me on the side of impracticality, I will show you six more poets who knew how to take care of themselves, and command other men into the bargain.

18   As for the myth that all painters are poor, there is some basis for it — especially in our own day. For one thing, there are so many painters. We are told that more than two million people paint pictures in the United States alone, and clearly only a few of them can earn much money from their painting. Here it is not a question of whether or not painters are practical; the myth says they are poor. Well, it is true

ILLUSTRATION   83

that many men who would have been worth large fortunes if they had possessed only a fraction of the price their pictures sell for now were poor enough while they lived. Geniuses like Cézanne and Van Gogh made little money, and Modigliani and Utrillo were always in debt. But again let's look at the record.

19   In Italy Raphael, Titian, and Michelangelo were patronized by noblemen and popes, and they could afford to live in the style of princes. In the Low Countries Rubens and Van Dyke displayed magnificence in their manner of living. Rembrandt could have lived the life of a rich Dutch burgher from the income he derived from his paintings had he not deliberately turned his back on the things of this world to search for his own private vision. In Spain Velasquez, Goya, and El Greco all rubbed shoulders with grandees and lived in fine style. Even in England, which has never been outstanding in the plastic arts, painters like Reynolds and Gainsborough fared much better financially than the most celebrated of British novelists. Today, without benefit of nobility, Picasso can sell anything he paints for an immense sum.

20   There is still a lot of hungry artists, to be sure, but we've been talking about top-flight poets and painters through time. It is the exception to find a ranking painter who went hungry, unless a bottle of wine or a tube of paint gave him more promise of pleasure than a loaf of bread.

21   But the myth which amuses me more than any of the others is the one that would have us believe that all novelists are wealthy. Where on earth did that one start? Relative to the rest of the arts, novel-writing is young, so one can't go as far back as Horace or even Titian to find examples to refute the belief. It is my own conviction that the people who hold it do so from nothing but wishful thinking. Most of them have never thought of composing music, painting a portrait or even balancing words to make a sonnet, but they are convinced that a novel would be easy to write if only they could find time to get around to it. In fact, they are *going* to write a novel some day. It's the ace in the hole that will over-balance the budget and take the whole family on a trip around the world.

22   Scott Fitzgerald did nothing to lay this ghost-belief. He was undoubtedly a victim of it himself. When the money made on his first two books came rolling in, he spent it so fast that the news of his exploits could barely keep up with him. But when he died he was some tens of thousands of dollars in debt. That's the trouble with writing for a living. As Dorothy Thompson once said, you can't take out insurance on your brains.

23   Dostoevsky's works will be considered outstanding as long as people can read. He was even famous while he lived, yet he was seldom out of the hands of the pawnbrokers. Tolstoy never lacked for money,

but he was born a nobleman and he gave a large portion of his royalties away in sponsoring a variety of impractical social schemes, including the shipment of Doukhobors to western Canada.

24   Balzac, the most prolific novelist who ever lived, wrote like a maniac to escape an appalling burden of debt incurred by his failures in the business life he portrayed so brilliantly in his books. Had he saved his earnings he would have been fairly well off; not rich as the great painters have been, but more than comfortable. Yet from his early twenties until his death Balzac was always in need of thousands of francs to raise him to the status of being worth nothing.

25   Dickens probably fared better financially than any other famous English novelist, but he was the exception which proved a rule in his outstanding nose for a dollar. It is more than likely, however, that he made more money as an actor (reading his own works) than he ever earned as a straight novelist.

26   It has been estimated by the Author's Guild that there are, at the present time in North America, scarcely a hundred men and women who can live on the income from their novels alone. Some of them are now able to afford a secretarial staff which allows them to turn out a new book a year, but the majority of novelists whom you and I know by name spend an average of three years writing each book, on which they received from ten to fifteen per cent of the retail price in royalties. And how many copies does the average full-length novel sell? About three thousand.

27   You will tell me that in the fields of painting and poetry I have used as examples not the average, but the outstanding. So I have. It is only in the realm of the novel that I can be specific in a quotation of averages. Besides, it is only in the field of novel-writing that so many people are so sure they can hit the jackpot if only they take time to try.

28   I don't know why I attempt to explode the myth which makes all novelists rich. The life of the writer is generally so quiet and solitary that he is greatly encouraged when he realizes that people who recognize him consider him quite a dog. "It must be wonderful to be a novelist and write something that everyone likes and then watch the money come rolling in." Indeed it must be.

29   Yet in another sense the life of a novelist *is* wonderful, for he is always dealing with and thinking about people. In time he even comes to understand them a little. So long as there are people about, it is hard to feel dull. Balzac's entire life was a quest for a fortune, but all his business schemes and all his negotiations were upset by his overriding fascination with human nature. Whenever he faced a new creature whom it was important to best in a deal, his genius was busy discovering how this strange man ticked. There were even occasions when he probably wilfully allowed men to cheat him in order to pro-

ILLUSTRATION   85

vide himself with knowledge of all the tricks and turns of a sharper's mind.

30   Such men as Balzac, Sinclair Lewis, Joyce Cary are not practical, in the manner of poets. They seldom make much money, but they do make good novelists and thereby enrich our understanding of man's relationship to men.

31   George Bernard Shaw? But he was a playwright . . . and that's something else again.

Questions on Content

1   What subject is raised in MacLennan's opening illustration (paragraphs one to nine)? What conflicting views of his subject does MacLennan discuss in paragraphs ten through twelve? What is MacLennan's thesis?

2   What view of poets does MacLennan illustrate?

3   What myth about painters does MacLennan attempt to refute?

4   What myth about novelists amuses MacLennan? Why? What examples does MacLennan use to support his own view?

5   What conclusion does MacLennan arrive at concerning novelists? What are the implications of this conclusion for his previous discussion of poets and painters? What is the significance of the final paragraph?

Questions on Structure and Technique

1   What contrast is illustrated by MacLennan in paragraphs one through nine? What sentences in paragraphs ten through twelve most clearly express this contrast?

2   How does MacLennan organize his numerous illustrations in this essay? What sentences in paragraphs ten through twelve emphasize this organization?

3   In what three paragraphs does MacLennan introduce these three groups of illustrations? What sentences most clearly express MacLennan's general treatment of each of these groups?

4   What are the sources for MacLennan's illustrations?

5   Why does MacLennan select many illustrations for this essay? Why doesn't MacLennan develop each illustration more fully? Why is the illustration of Balzac developed in greater detail than others?

Suggestions for Writing

1   Select an activity that you find rewarding, and write an illustrative essay in which you discuss its rewards in detailed and specific terms.

2   Consider another group of people about whom there is a common misconception. Write an illustrative essay in which you develop sufficient evidence to refute that misconception.

3   Write a well-organized and well-developed illustrative essay in which you attempt to disprove MacLennan's view of poets, painters, or novelists, drawing on your own experience and knowledge as well as reference and research material for alternative examples.

ILLUSTRATION   87

WILLIAM JAMES

*American philosopher and psychologist William James (1842–1910),
brother of novelist Henry James, was educated at Harvard University and
in Europe. He taught biology, psychology, and philosophy at Harvard from
1872 to 1907. While completing his first book on the* Principles of Psychology *(1890), William James gradually turned toward the philosophical dimensions of human experience that he would discuss in his major
works:* The Will to Believe and Other Essays *(1897),* Varieties of Religious Experience *(1902),* Pragmatism *(1907),* The Meaning of Truth
(1909), A Pluralistic Universe *(1909), and* Essays in Radical Empiricism
*(1912). In William James's following discussion of the importance of
"Habit" to human consciousness, an excerpt from* Psychology: Briefer
Course *(1892), he develops a number of illustrations to show its relevance
to an understanding of the relations between free will and determinism.*

HABIT

1   "Habit a second nature! Habit is ten times nature," the Duke of Wellington is said to have exclaimed; and the degree to which this is true
no one probably can appreciate as well as one who is a veteran soldier himself. The daily drill and the years of discipline end by fashioning a man completely over again, as to most of the possibilities of
his conduct.

2   "There is a story," says Prof. Huxley, "which is credible enough,
though it may not be true, of a practical joker who, seeing a discharged veteran carrying home his dinner, suddenly called out, 'Attention!' whereupon the man instantly brought his hands down, and
lost his mutton and potatoes in the gutter. The drill had been thorough, and its effects had become embodied in the man's nervous
structure." THESIS IMPLIED (HABIT IS DIFF TO CHANGE)

3   Riderless cavalry-horses, at many a battle, have been seen to come
together and go through their customary evolutions at the sound of
the bugle-call. Most domestic beasts seem machines almost pure and
simple, undoubtingly, unhesitatingly doing from minute to minute
the duties they have been taught, and giving no sign that the possibility of an alternative ever suggests itself to their mind. Men grown old
in prison have asked to be readmitted after being once set free. In a
railroad accident a menagerie-tiger, whose cage had broken open, is
said to have emerged, but presently crept back again, as if too much
bewildered by his new responsibilities, so that he was without difficulty secured.

4 Habit is thus the enormous fly-wheel of society, its most precious conservative agent. It alone is what keeps us all within the bounds of ordinance, and saves the children of fortune from the envious uprisings of the poor. It alone prevents the hardest and most repulsive walks of life from being deserted by those brought up to tread therein. It keeps the fisherman and the deck-hand at sea through the winter; it holds the miner in his darkness, and nails the countryman to his log-cabin and his lonely farm through all the months of snow; it protects us from invasion by the natives of the desert and the frozen zone. It dooms us all to fight out the battle of life upon the lines of our nurture or our early choice, and to make the best of a pursuit that disagrees, because there is no other for which we are fitted, and it is too late to begin again. It keeps different social strata from mixing. Already at the age of twenty-five you see the professional mannerism settling down on the young commercial traveller, on the young doctor, on the young minister, on the young counsellor-at-law. You see the little lines of cleavage running through the character, the tricks of thought, the prejudices, the ways of the "shop," in a word, from which the man can by-and-by no more escape than his coat-sleeve can suddenly fall into a new set of folds. On the whole, it is best he should not escape. It is well for the world that in most of us, by the age of thirty, the character has set like plaster, and will never soften again.

5 If the period between twenty and thirty is the critical one in the formation of intellectual and professional habits, the period below twenty is more important still for the fixing of *personal* habits, properly so called, such as vocalization and pronunciation, gesture, motion, and address. Hardly ever is a language learned after twenty spoken without a foreign accent; hardly ever can a youth transferred to the society of his betters unlearn the nasality and other vices of speech bred in him by the associations of his growing years. Hardly ever, indeed, no matter how much money there be in his pocket, can he even learn to *dress* like a gentleman-born. The merchants offer their wares as eagerly to him as to the veriest "swell," but he simply *cannot* buy the right things. An invisible law, as strong as gravitation, keeps him within his orbit, arrayed this year as he was the last; and how his better-clad acquaintances contrive to get the things they wear will be for him a mystery till his dying day.

6 The great thing, then, in all education, is to *make our nervous system our ally instead of our enemy*. It is to fund and capitalize our acquisitions, and live at ease upon the interest of the fund. For *this we must make automatic and habitual, as early as possible, as many useful actions as we can*, and guard against the growing into ways that are likely to be disadvantageous to us, as we should guard against the plague. The more of the details of our daily life we can hand over to the effortless custody of automatism, the more our higher powers

ILLUSTRATION 89

of mind will be set free for their own proper work. There is no more miserable human being than one in whom nothing is habitual but indecision, and for whom the lighting of every cigar, the drinking of every cup, the time of rising and going to bed every day, and the beginning of every bit of work, are subjects of express volitional deliberation. Full half the time of such a man goes to the deciding, or regretting, of matters which ought to be so ingrained in him as practically not to exist for his consciousness at all. If there be such daily duties not yet ingrained in any one of my readers, let him begin this very hour to set the matter right.

Questions on Content

1   What idea is illustrated by James's illustrations in paragraphs one through three? In what general statement does James most clearly express this idea?

2   What beneficial influences of "habit" does James illustrate in paragraphs four and five?

3   What unfortunate influences of habit are illustrated in paragraphs four and five?

4   What do we learn from an understanding of such influences of habit on our experiences, according to James?

5   What is the most appropriate and valuable role for habit to play in our lives according to James? What is James's thesis?

Questions on Structure and Technique

1   Why are the illustrations in paragraphs one through three an effective introduction to James's discussion?

2   In paragraph four, what examples of metaphor and simile do you find? Why is this figurative language effective? What other effective uses of language do you notice in paragraphs four and five?

3   Why does James incorporate multiple examples into his discussion rather than one or more extended illustrations?

4   In what sense are the general ideas in paragraph six supported by the examples in the preceding paragraphs?

5   What is James's main purpose in presenting those examples? Is this purpose primarily expressive, informative, or persuasive? Why?

Suggestions for Writing

1   In the light of William James's discussion, write an illustrative essay in which you consider the significance of "habit" in your own experiences.

2   In an illustrative essay, discuss the contemporary relevance of the following statement by James: "The more details of our daily life we can hand over to the effortless custody of automation, the more our higher powers of mind will be set free for their own proper work."

ILLUSTRATION   91

"CAR gave to many a slave promise of freedom. He offered escape from orders, from routine, from boredom."

COMPARISON AND CONTRAST

Using metaphore
rник si

Comparison and contrast are the related methods writers use to show their readers the relations between two subjects. A comparison presents these relations in terms of the *similarities* between two subjects. A contrast emphasizes the *differences* between them. The purpose of expressing or explaining a subject in its relation to another may clarify an image or an idea. A simple figurative comparison, such as a simile, a metaphor, an analogy, or a symbol, often serves this purpose. A *simile* states that one thing is indirectly *like* or *as* another. For instance, in "Learning to Love the Big City," Philip Marchand describes one situation where "This guy would attack some poor timorous girl . . . and stick to her *like* a horsefly," and the experience of "going into the subway at rush hour, and having people rush by you on the steps in panic, *like* a scene out of the fall of Berlin." If a statement of comparison is direct, that one thing *is* another, then the statement is termed a *metaphor*, as discussed by Allan Smith in "Metaphor and Nationality" with regard to "the American melting pot" and "the Canadian mosaic," terms which express national ideals as metaphors: "America *is* a melting pot," "Canada *is* a mosaic." An extended or applied metaphor or simile is called an *analogy*. In "The Great God Car" Arthur Lower develops a simile, " 'the country to the south' could make a new goddess as quickly as it made a new car," into a metaphor, "in making new cars, it made a new god," which in turn serves as the basis for the author's extended comparison of a car and a god in an analogy, as you will read. You will discover that the "car" serves as a concrete visual image representing something other than or more than itself; therefore, the "car" is presented as a *symbol* — a symbol of beauty, scientific progress, equality, and freedom, among other things. Although all of the selections in this chapter and others show writers' uses of these various forms of simple comparison for the purpose of clarification, the writers' main purpose in these comparison as well as contrast essays is the *extended* exploration and development of the relations between two subjects in terms of their similarities and differences.

In comparison as well as in contrast essays, the writer's thesis must establish his or her *two* subjects and an attitude toward the *relations* between them in view of their perceived similarities and differences. The thesis may be stated in the basic form used by Arthur Erickson in his contrast essay, "Ideation as a Source of Creativity": "My purpose in this essay is to point to the limitations of the single view of reality by which an architect ordinarily observes, understands, and evaluates architecture, and thus to try to open another view, because I believe that such an opening could show a way for architecture beyond what we may now envision." In whatever rhetorical mode they choose, many writers prefer to avoid references to the writing process itself. They focus our attention directly on subject and attitude in their thesis statement as Arthur Lower does in his concise introduction to "The Great God Car": "That inventive society known in Canada as 'the country to the south,' could make a new goddess as quickly as it needs a new car. But in making new cars, it made a new god." Lower's assertion of incongruous similarities between a god and a car not only states his subjects but also implies his negative attitude toward the worship of the car illustrated in the development of this thesis.

After a writer's subjects and attitude toward their relations is established in a comparison or a contrast essay, the writer's organization and development follows one of two general approaches: a subject-by-subject approach or a part-by-part approach.

In a subject-by-subject approach a writer adapts the basic mode of organizing and developing one subject to the treatment of two subjects, as in Philip Marchand's "Learning to Love the Big City." The writer first presents one subject and develops several parts, or aspects, of that subject. Then, the writer presents the second subject and develops the same or equivalent parts of this subject.

I.		Introduction
II. A		Subject 1
		Part 1
		Part 2
		Part 3
II. B		Subject 2
		Part 1
		Part 2
		Part 3
II. C		Subject 3
		Part 1
		Part 2
		Part 3
III.		Conclusion

For example, in Philip Marchand's contrast of "small towns" and "large cities," he focusses the reader's attention on one subject, life in a small town, before turning to his other subject, life in a large city. This subject-by-subject approach allows the writer to develop each subject in a detailed and comprehensive manner, giving the reader a clear picture of the subjects themselves. Note that Marchand's contrast between his two subjects is effective because the particular aspects of life in towns and then cities are identified by the same or similar terms and presented roughly in the same order. A writer can neither compare nor contrast apples and oranges unless the terms (criteria) and the procedure are well-established in that process.

Using a part-by-part (or aspect-by-aspect) method, a writer inverts the subject-by-subject approach to presenting each *part* of the subject as a main unit of organization and then treating each subject in turn.

I.   Introduction
II. A   Part 1
        Subject 1
        Subject 2
II. B   Part 2
        Subject 1
        Subject 2
II. C   Part 3
        Subject 1
        Subject 2
III.   Conclusion

This approach should be chosen if the writer wants to emphasize similarities or differences between two subjects rather than the subjects themselves. For example, in his essay on "Metaphor and Nationality," Allan Smith's first concern is defining two ideal metaphors used to symbolize two societies. He subdivides this *first part* of his subject—the ideal—by presenting the American "melting pot metaphor" first (in paragraph two) and the Canadian "mosaic metaphor" second (in paragraph three). Smith then introduces the *second part* of his subject—actual experience in these two societies (paragraph four)—and, again he subdivides this part of his subject by dealing with the American immigrant experience first (in paragraphs five and six) and the Canadian immigrant experience second (in paragraphs seven and eight).

In a part-by-part approach to a comparison *or* a contrast of two subjects, every part deals with *either* the similarities *or* the differences between the two subjects. However, a writer may want to show *both* similarities and differences, as Smith does in his essay, in which case one or more parts may be used to present similarities and others to present differences. Smith *contrasts* American and Canadian ideals in the first part of his discussion, and then he *compares* actual experiences in these societies in the second part. In his conclusion (paragraph nine) to this complex comparison *and* contrast essay, Smith asserts that the similarities of experience (part two) belie the differences in ideals (part one). A subject-by-subject approach may also be used to develop complex comparisons and contrasts. Within the presentation of each subject, a writer groups the parts together into aspects that are similar and those that are different or simply examines detailed similarities and differences for individual aspects.

A subject-by-subject or a part-by-part approach to the organization and development of either a comparison *or* a contrast essay or a comparison *and* contrast essay may thus be chosen by a writer. These choices simply depend on the writer's purpose, on whether the subjects themselves or the relations between the subjects should be emphasized, and on whether the similarities *or* the differences or the similarities *and* the differences are to be examined. The following comparison and contrast essays illustrate a variety of these ways in which the relations between two subjects can be effectively presented.

ARTHUR R. M. LOWER

Arthur R. M. Lower (b. 1889) was born in Barrie, Ontario. He studied at the University of Toronto and Harvard University, and taught history at several universities in the United States and Canada before being appointed Douglas Professor of History at Queen's University in 1947. Following several important collaborative studies in Canadian economic history with historian Harold Innis, Professor Lower wrote three major works on Canadian history: Colony to Nation: A History of Canada *(1946),* Canada: Nation and Neighbour *(1952), and* Canadians in the Making: A Social History of Canada *(1958). "The Great God Car" is an excerpt from* Canadians in the Making *in which Lower's analogy between a god and a car not only clarifies the social significance of the automobile in North America but further suggests a fundamental difference between American and Canadian societies.*

THE GREAT GOD CAR

1   That inventive society known in Canada as "the country to the south," could make a new goddess as quickly as it made a new car. But in making new cars, it made a new god. For the god, no better name could be found than simply — CAR!

2   In one of the annual reports of a great motor-car company during the mid-century years, there might be seen pictured the dignified and elegant ritual which surrounds the birth and renewal of this god — his Easter! The artist who depicts the scene has drawn a great crowd of people, of every conceivable social type, gathered about altars on which current images of the god CAR are displayed. In the upper left of his picture, there is a vast symphonic band of music, possibly a heavenly choir, its every violin bow at the ordained, precise angle. In the centre, richly but decorously dressed ladies grace a stage, beside which fountains play and from whose wings ballet dancers make appropriate obeisance. At the back of the stage, on a higher level than ladies and audience, surrounded by a nimbus of light clouds, at the point reserved in temples for the principal altar of the god, CAR is pictured midway between heaven and earth. "Lo, He comes, in clouds descending," the rapturous beholders seem to cry, as they greet the great god in his form of "The New Model for the Coming Year".

3   CAR's worship detracted even from that of Aphrodite herself (though the two were not without their intimate relationships). "Cars outshine the stars," says a popular magazine, picturing a daughter of the goddess reclining languidly, though with a second-best look, against one of the elegant new images of the god. All ranks and classes

burned incense to CAR—save a few sour intellectuals who thought to avoid the industrial revolution he symbolized by ignoring it. "Yesterday I bought a Cadillac, and realized a lifelong ambition," says one of the gentlemen reported in that anthropological study of a wealthy Toronto suburb, *Crestwood Heights*. CAR's devotees increased with the years. And no wonder. A patient, obedient god who takes you where you want to go, faster than any magic carpet. A comfortable, well-upholstered god. A god whose priests well knew how to gain new worshippers by playing on the qualities of vulgarity and ostentation. And above all, the god of power, who multiplied man's ego manifold. Yet a ruthless god, sometimes, too, who could turn on his idolater and rend him.

4   CAR brought in his company a whole host of lesser godlets (most of them born of Electra), which their worshippers called "modern conveniences" or more simply "progress"—the labour-saving devices that stood in every housewife's kitchen, and the long series of instruments of communication such as the radio, television, and the rest. What this vast upheaval would mean before it reached its logical conclusion—and what is its logical conclusion?—who was to say? We all worshipped CAR and his fellows, that is, the innumerable by-products of science, power and human ingenuity, and some of us thought we saw these gods admitting us to a cheerful, effortless heaven. Slowly it dawned on the less simple that there was not much satisfaction in that type of "progress" which eventuates in hydrogen bombs. And so we come again, by another route, to the disillusionments of the day, to that look of dread in human faces that was not there before.

5   Meanwhile, CAR and his associates changed our society out of recognition. They scattered our homesteads far beyond the cities, so that many of us became once more, after a fashion, country dwellers. Others, yielding to the logic of CAR, married themselves to him for better and for worse, moving their habitation from place to place under the hauling power that he provided. CAR threatened to turn us all into nomads, and his wheels, like Juggernaut, levelled every physical and psychical obstacle they met. They invaded every urban open space and threatened to destroy every blade of urban grass. They knocked down houses. They called imperiously for straight, wide roads to be carved out of our diminishing fertile fields. They tore up our precious peach orchards and ordained that factories for making new parts of CAR should be erected in their place.

6   More than that, CAR forced on men, far more effectively than French Revolutionary slogans could ever do, the worship of another great god, Equality (though not Fraternity), for once surrounded by his metal-and-glass turret, every man became equal to every other man, just as every metal-and-glass turret, despite the efforts of their

advertisers to the contrary, was approximately equal in value and in efficiency to every other metal-and-glass turret. But it was not a new brotherhood that our god created for us, for once inside his fortress, a man became a world in himself, proudly independent, to whom the objects shaped like his own were threats which approached and passed, forgotten as quickly as avoided. They might contain millionaires or paupers, good men or rogues: to each other as they whirled by they were just shapes.

7   Were there no good words to be used of CAR? Of course there were, many. For one thing, CAR gave to many a slave promise of freedom. He offered escape from orders, from routine, from boredom. He made, or seemed to make, the humble masters of their fate. By opening up the vistas of the roads, he brought back to life the pathfinder, the explorer, the romantic in us. He was really a kindly god if worshipped with common sense. But instead his cult often carried his faithful into ecstasy and hysteria.

8   The effects on men of CAR worship, that is of the new mechanical society, are not yet fully discernible. That society is without question one of the most remarkable in history: it is perhaps also, all its aspects considered, the most lunatic. Once again, it has not been our own creation and though Canadians are almost as ardent worshippers at these shrines as are Americans, they have not invented them. They do not resist the modern god, but he is not quite their god in the same sense as he is the Americans'. It has always been Americans who have worked up the folk-lore of this modern religion (as, for example, the stories that used to be told about the old model-T Ford such as giving a squirrel away with each one to follow it and pick up the nuts), just as it has been Americans who have supplied and taken most seriously its high priests, among them the great cardinal who did so much towards establishing it, Henry Ford himself.

Questions on Content

1   In what ways is a car similar to a god, according to Lower?

2   What is Lower's attitude toward this comparison between a car and a god? What negative qualities does Lower emphasize in his treatment of this analogy?

3   What is the main difference between Americans' and Canadians' attitudes toward the car, according to Lower? What do you think is the significance of this difference in attitude?

4   Do you agree with Lower's view of the social significance of the car? Why or why not?

Questions on Structure and Technique

1   What main image does Lower present in order to clarify his analogy

between a car and a god? Why is his comparison of the car with Aphrodite also appropriate?

2   What specific examples does Lower provide in order to support his criticism of the car as a god?

3   What words and phrases does Lower use throughout his essay in order to emphasize the analogy between a car and a god? What is the effect achieved by this use of language?

4   Is comparison, contrast, or comparison and contrast the main purpose of Lower's treatment of the analogy between a car and a god? Explain.

Suggestions for Writing

1   Consider other modern "gods" that we worship in our society. Then, write an essay in which you develop an analogy between a person or a thing and a god. Be sure to use images, details, and words and phrases that clarify and support your analogy.

2   Choose a simile or a metaphor that you believe is particularly interesting or appropriate in its expression of the similarities between two subjects. Write an essay in which you develop a full and detailed presentation of that figure of speech as an analogy.

PHILIP MARCHAND

Freelance writer Philip Marchand (b. 1946) began writing for magazines such as Saturday Night *and* Chatelaine *in 1971 after receiving B.A. and M.A. degrees in English from the University of Toronto. This lively and thoughtful essay on the differences between small-town life and city life is a good example of the "New Journalism" style of writing made popular by American writers such as Tom Wolfe and Norman Mailer. Marchand pays careful attention to the details of personal experience as a means of showing their broader social significance so that his work both entertains and informs his readers. "Learning to Love the Big City" has been selected from Marchand's book of essays,* Just Looking, Thank You *(1976).*

LEARNING TO LOVE THE BIG CITY

1   Man does not live by bread alone, but by fantasy and daydream as well. Young men and women are sitting behind desks in downtown Toronto, Montreal, and Vancouver and thinking, when I get my grubstake I'm going to leave this scene for good. I'm heading for the country. Get a place ten miles from the nearest town and only come in on weekends for supplies, like lentils and Crunchy Granola. Yes. A little homestead far from the Great Urban Maw . . . and at the same time as these visions are being entertained, the other men and women are flocking to Toronto and Montreal and Vancouver, from places like Marathon, Ont., and Gypsumville, Man., and Vanderhoof, B.C., for jobs in life-insurance offices and a comfortable nook in some monstrous high-rise. It's not the popular dream, to settle down in the big city, but there you have it — real alternatives are simply too scarce. Small-town life practically doesn't *exist* in Canada anymore. Or rather it exists, but it's fading all the time. We're in a stage (roughly analogous) to the Late Roman Republic, when poets and politicians were praising the virtues of the simple old Roman country life, sturdy farmers worshipping the household gods and taking cold-water baths, while everybody who had the chance was heading for the city for some fast money and funky entertainment.

2   For people like Lynda, eighteen years old and fresh into Toronto from a town of 5,000 in the wilds of northern Ontario, all this talk about getting out of the city is definitely puzzling. For a weekend, sure — who doesn't like the peace and quiet? But the city is fascinating. The first few weeks she was here she would spend ten minutes at

a time standing on a street corner like the Bloor-Yonge intersection, just watching. She would see, for instance, this young man with a shaved head and a saffron robe dogging passersby on the sidewalk, talking it up for the Lord Krishna. Disgusting! Nobody she had ever known in her whole life would act like such an idiot, but she had to watch. This guy would attack some poor timorous girl going back to work at a reception desk and stick to her like a horsefly, threatening her with his humbleness, his shamelessness, asking for money, asking for her name, her address, silently hinting that if she yielded a little bit he would never let up until she was there in the temple babbling insane praise to Lord Krishna for the rest of her natural life. He did this until he tried it on one guy in a business suit, who just grabbed him by his saffron robes and threw him off the sidewalk, into the traffic.

3   Well, the things you can see just standing for ten minutes at a big-city intersection. Lynda can't get over it. But, of course, she comes from a town where the main recreation is drinking. It overshadows such country sports as ice-fishing, snowmobiling, backpacking, even hockey. At school dances the Ontario Provincial Police officer is standing by the door watching fourteen- and fifteen-year-old kids reel in, and the only time he interferes is if they start attacking each other. Of course, the booze is cheap up there in the north country — you go to one of the three hotels in the town and get a bottle of beer for 50 cents, or a shot of vodka for 70 cents. It always surprised Lynda when people in Toronto would say they were going out drinking, and then they'd end up having only three shots of rye the whole evening. That was not Lynda's idea of serious drinking. She would be having her sixth or seventh vodka, and calmly watching her boyfriend knocking over chairs as he stumbled back to their table from the men's room — she would be just getting warmed up, you see, and here he was losing control of his basic motor functions after consuming the same quantity of booze.

4   But after a while Lynda began to grasp the point, which is that you don't really have to get drunk in the big city. Lynda gets drunk in Toronto, and all she wants to do is go home and sleep. That means, really, that she misses all the weird and wonderful action around her, the satin freaks in star-spangled boots, the criminal types with tattoos on their arms, pre-med students wearing sleeveless sweaters and Bulova watches, the whole urban monkey house drinking draught beer out of jugs and having their ear membranes warped from the rock music.

5   Back home there was a point to getting drunk. You could not conceive, in fact, of having a party or dance without getting ripped before 10 p.m. You'd end up rolling around on the floor, and the guys would be shouting at each other — "George, get your arms off me, you queer!"

— like a class of ten-year-olds who had just been forced to sit a whole half-hour with their feet still and their hands on top of their desks, and the girls would be giggling at the sight of their boyfriends making such utter fools of themselves. And, of course, a few party games. In this one game a person would doodle a few lines on a piece of paper and then another person who didn't know what the game was about would take a strand of hair and try to bend and twist the hair so it covered the lines on the paper, meanwhile some girl who knew Pitman shorthand would be recording his remarks on the sly. These remarks would then — surprise! — be read back to the guy later as the things he would say on his "wedding night". With half a pint of rye, rum, vodka, gin, or Zing under their belts, the kids would kill themselves laughing at remarks like "Geez, I can't keep hold of this thing." Party night for the young folks in — — , Ont.

6   But at least it was something to talk about in school on Monday, the number of bottles consumed, and what happened to so and so who was found with his head resting on the toilet, and this other couple who disappeared a little after midnight, under a bed, or some place. A few of the guys, and the girls even, would have arguments about just how much each person drank, it being a point of honour, of course, to hold your liquor and not act too foolish unless the kidneys and the lobes of the brain were actually getting soggy from alcohol. These are all, indeed, lively topics of conversation . . . but after a while it does get tiresome, Monday after Monday, the endless gossip about drinking, and sometimes about sex. Kids couldn't possibly have a little sexual adventure without everybody they met on the street knowing about it within a few days. Sometimes the people on the street even knew about things that never happened. A girl might enter the hospital to have her appendix removed and come out to discover her friends and neighbours all firmly believed she'd had an abortion.

7   But what else is there to talk about? Lynda is not an intellectual, but sometimes during conversations she tried to discuss topics of wider interest than, say, last night's alcoholic blowout — like what is the future of life in this town, for instance — and her friends started examining their fingernails and clearing their throats and after 30 seconds the conversation slid back into the old, hairy trough of local gossip. Or she used words like ("progressive") or "confrontation" in conversation, and they asked, "What's with the vocabulary?" These people are all carrying on like Leo Gorcey and his Bowery Boys. Great for nostalgia, watching Gorcey movies from the forties, but it's not so funny in real life.

8   The guys, for instance have two alternatives facing them when they leave high school. They can work in the mines or they can work in a garage somewhere. Either way, they will get married and have a

family and try to get on the graveyard shift, so they can goof off and sleep for a few hours and brag about it afterwards to their buddies in the beverage room of the hotel. They will actually do things like trade war comics with their co-workers, the kind that feature granite-jawed Marines with five o'clock shadows, blasting away at Japs on Gizo Island. They will get their greatest excitement from picking fights with guys who come in for the hockey tournament with their team, from some town a hundred miles away, and they will continue to do this until their bellies turn soft from drinking and they can't take the punishment anymore. That will be a sad day for them, incidentally, because they do like picking fights with strangers. The adrenalin wash helps clear up the brainstem and, besides, it's one of the few things they can do that girls can't, with their blue jeans and T-shirts and ability, some of them, to out-gross and out-drink even the hairiest males.

9   But this is their future, ladies and gentlemen. And their girlfriends do not exactly have it better. They will work in the bank or an insurance office after they leave school, and then they will get married and tend to the kids. Some of them will skip the high school graduation and employment part of it and get married out of Grade 11 or 12. Indeed, it is not uncommon for fourteen-year-old girls to get married in this town. These blossoming children who would prefer scar tissue to wearing something other than their blue-jean-and-T-shirt ensemble — except maybe a short skirt with lime- or raspberry-coloured nylons, for the glamorous occasions.

10   Lynda recalls that the girl she admired most in this town was a secretary who had her own apartment, her own money, her own definite views on life — she knew definitely where she was going in this world. This was a girl Lynda actually thought stood out from the crowd. This was a girl Lynda thought really had an interesting point of view, some unique statements on life to make, as opposed to the general numbness of intellect around town. If you want to know what a boy you're thinking of marrying is going to be like 20 or 30 years from now, she would say to Lynda, take a look at his father. That's what he's going to be like. Truly a sobering thought . . . and she had more, much more, to say in this vein. Well, when Lynda came back from Toronto for her first homecoming, her first Christmas visit, and met this girl again, somehow she appeared in an entirely different light. Instead of being a person of strongly held views and unique personal vision, she just seemed . . . well, opinionated, and as set in her ways as any middle-aged lady with tortoise-shell glasses and menthol cigarettes whose greatest challenge in life is deciding on what cheese dip to serve for the weekly meeting of her canasta club. Now her discussion of young men centred on whether or not they were "self-starters". That, apparently, is more important than what

their fathers are like, because she has just gotten herself engaged to a young engineer at the mines, whose father spends most of his time down in his basement with some ice water and Saltines, going over his stamp collection.

11   Had this girl changed — or had Lynda changed, in the four months she had spent away from home for the first time in her life, back there in the big city? Lynda suspects that she herself has changed. She suspects that if she had lived in Toronto before, she would never have been taken in by this secretary. One thing she has learned in Toronto is not to take people for granted. They just aren't moulded in those cast-iron, unbreakable reputations that are given to people past the age of five in small towns. In Toronto you have to find out for yourself what they're like; you have to pick up all the subtle little indicators — practically in the first few minutes you meet them.

12   With guys, for instance, Lynda now can tell how promising they look after two or three minutes. It's all based on the degree of shyness they present to you when they talk to you in your favourite bar, the Nickelodeon, say, or the Generator, or Zodiac I. At one end of this spectrum you find guys who are not shy at all. A guy like this sits down at your table and turns around and leans forward so his face is squarely in front of yours and there's an upbeat, lively tone in his voice as he starts talking about how boring this whole scene is, and what a drag so many of these girls are, they look like they're out on horse tranquillizers, and you know that before the evening's over he'll be suggesting that someone like you is obviously cut out for finer things, like going over to his apartment above an Army-Navy store on Yonge Street and shooting up. Most aren't this extreme, but if there's no *hint* of shyness in the character it often means there is a definite tilt to psychopathic lunacy here.

13   And at the other end of the spectrum there is the guy who is tormented by shyness, but obviously driven, forced, impelled to seek out contact, so he talks to you with his eyes fluttering back and forth between your own two eyes and the little pools of beer on the table-top, talking with such effort that it is obvious he must have worked himself up to come here tonight by performing unspeakable acts in front of some *Penthouse* nudes.

14   But Lynda has discovered that it isn't all that difficult to meet reasonable people somewhere in the middle of the shyness spectrum, even in bars. Curiously enough, the fact she was from a small town made it much easier, in a way, because she thought nothing of starting up a conversation with the people sitting next to her in the Nickelodeon or the Generator. Hard-bitten Torontonians do not as a rule do things like this, because they're already sure the person sitting next to them is somebody who will respond to their friendliness by putting a hand on their thigh, or quoting whole passages from the

Book of Revelations at them, or shutting them up with their Penetrating Death Stare.

15   But Lynda, as I say, came from a small town where you speak to people who sit next to you in public places, as a matter of course. And not only does she meet a lot of *nice* guys this way, but she can tell how much other girls sitting around get absolutely burned up at her for it. I mean, she knows they're carrying on as if she were Little Orphan Annie befriending the poor and the outcast, and they're just sitting by doing a pictorial spread for *Vogue*, but — well, that's not her problem. Let them wobble by on their platform shoes, with their slithery satin gowns coming down low under the shoulder blades, let them entice these young men with such obvious displays of themselves; Lynda knows that guys also appreciate a girl who can talk to them, a girl they can approach without feeling they've strayed into a walk-in refrigerator. Good conversations can be sexy, too, as Lynda knows, who comes from a place where they are nonexistent. It kills her, for instance, that Lennox there, who she met at the Nickelodeon two or three months ago and with whom she has been more or less going steadily ever since, was actually interested, in one conversation they had, in the details of how people go about ice-fishing back home in — —. Lennox, who was born in Morocco and has lived in about three different countries in Europe, interested in how Lynda's friends and neighbours ice fish! I mean! Well, Lennox, how you do it is you start cutting a hole in the ice with a pick, and . . . and this is what Lynda came to Toronto for, to meet people and *talk*, to share experiences, to learn, to — oh, Lynda doesn't know, but to — to widen her horizons a bit beyond the world of the mines and incipient alcoholism.

16   This is what makes it worthwhile for Lynda — her boyfriend Lennox, who is interested in how you go about ice-fishing, and things like the whole variety of clothing stores in the city where you can buy practically anything outrageous or elegant, and you can dress like a lady and put on the nail polish and the green eyeliner without people staring at you in the pub and your friends calling you "green eyes", and you can get your hair cut'n'curled any way you want, and you can get a decent Chinese meal and you can take long walks in the city and admire everything from the skyscrapers to odd little filigreed Victorian houses, and you can even stand at the corner of Yonge and Bloor and watch altercations between secretaries and Hare Krishna mendicants.

17   Yes, this is what makes it all worthwhile, and at times Lynda actually has to remind herself that for the first two or three months she was here she was often on the verge of packing it in and going home. For those first few months, the fascination of life in Toronto was balanced by certain of its more frightening aspects. It was just all so

unknown. Before she met Lennox, for instance, she really was dependent on some of the bars in town, the ones with the ear-warping rock music, for meeting people. But it was more than that. It was going into the subway at rush hour, and having people rush by you on the steps in panic, like a scene out of the fall of Berlin. It was the feeling of being a stranger, a foreigner almost, in your own country, riding the elevator in your apartment building every morning and hearing all these different languages, seeing black people for the first time, Sikhs, Chinese . . . I mean, Lynda is no bigot, but she was not quite ready for a lot of the cosmopolitan mix here in the city, the Detroit dudes in the peach-coloured suits, say, with matching fedoras, introducing some of that U.S.-patented pimp-flash to Toronto, looking as if any minute they would approach you on the sidewalk and say something like "Hey, honey, you so *fine*."

18   It was the feeling of having to be on your guard all the time, of riding the subway and finding yourself sitting next to some drunk talking to you at the top of his voice, asking you all these questions, like did you know about this here Bermuda Triangle, and everybody else in the car looking at you to see how you're going to handle the situation. It was the feeling of wanting to go for a walk by yourself, late in the evening perhaps, and being afraid to, because guys on the street would be eyeing you, staring hard as if you were swinging a purse and wearing a leopard skin coat and white vinyl boots. One night Lynda was eating by herself in a restaurant and a table full of men in business suits kept *looking* at her the whole time. When Lynda walked by their table on her way out she couldn't take it anymore, she was so annoyed—she said something sarcastic to them like, "Have you fellas had a good look?" and one of them stood up and started yelling at her, calling her names, telling her to get out — it was a thoroughly bad scene. But why can't she eat by herself in a restaurant without being gawked at? And why can't she go out by herself late at night, if that is her wish? It's her right, isn't it? It was certainly her right back home. But then, of course, this is the big city, and we have different rules here, lady.

19   Most disturbing of all, perhaps, was something more subtle, something Lynda found hard to put her finger on. In its more extreme forms, it was, she guessed, simple big-city rudeness. All those waitresses who never seemed to crack a smile, for instance, and rolled their eyes in exasperation when you pointed out that you ordered your fried eggs done on both sides, not sunny-side up. But even when people in the city were not rude, when they had no intention of being anything other than decent and friendly and sociable, they still seemed curiously indifferent to other people's feelings. At work, for instance, Lynda will be doing these letters, not a rush job but she can't take forever on them. Her boss will ask another typist to do something,

and that typist will say, right in front of Lynda, "Oh why can't you give it to Lynda? She never has that much to do." Or at lunch one of the girls will say to another, who is eating a full slice of rich, creamy cheesecake in spite of some obvious weight problems, "Are you sure you should be eating all that?" They don't seem to *care* about what other people think or feel, and they say these things that just cut you, things that people back home would never say.

20   But at Christmas, when Lynda went back home for the first time, she acquired a little perspective on the whole thing. She found that, yes, people in her town were friendly. Folks had a big smile for her when they met her on the street, and asked her questions — "Have you met anybody in Toronto?" — and seemed just full of concern. But after a while Lynda noticed how they kept giving her these surreptitious stares in the hotel bar when she walked in wearing a pantsuit and all this makeup. She noticed that when she talked about Toronto, especially in an enthusiastic tone of voice, the look on their faces began to get more and more quizzical, as if they couldn't figure her out, as if they were thinking — is this girl turning *strange* on us? And then she remembered all the times she felt she *had* to smile at people on the streets, greet them nicely, be careful of what she said, because, after all, this was a small town and you were going to have to live with these people whether you liked it or not. It was certainly true that she did have a definite place in this town, that her absence from it had been noted, that the merchants here never hesitated to cash one of her cheques. All this was a comfort when you thought about that big-city anonymity . . . but it hardly seemed worth it when you considered how hollow much of this recognition, this position in the community, actually was. I mean, Lynda's family happened to live in — —Heights, the most prosperous area of town and her address alone guaranteed that a cheque of hers would be cashed anywhere in town, even if the merchant or clerk didn't know her personally. But there are, of course, other areas in town that aren't so nice, areas closer to the mines where families with eight or ten kids live and the old man works as a gas station attendant. Lynda recalls that a lot of this small-town friendliness begins to evaporate when it comes to dealing with people like this, and you will never find them hanging out with the — — Heights United Church Women, for instance.

21   So all in all, Lynda finds herself voting for the big city. People who have lived in the city for a long time will no doubt continue to complain about it, and dream of the day they can settle down in the country on a farm perhaps, but for the vast majority of these people it will always be a dream. Economic pressure alone will continue to coerce people into living in the great cities. But there is something else involved. In 1806 John Loudon, in *A Treatise on Forming, Improving and Managing Country Residences*, wrote, "Such is the superi-

ority of rural occupations and pleasures, that commerce, large societies, or crowded cities, may be justly reckoned unnatural. Indeed,
the very purpose for which we engage in commerce is, that we may
one day be enabled to retire to the country, where alone we picture
to ourselves days of solid satisfaction and undisturbed happiness. It
is evident that such sentiments are natural to the human mind." Such
sentiments may indeed be natural to the human mind, but as long as
there are cities there will always be a counter-appeal, expressed in
the medieval proverb that city air breeds freedom. For the foreseea-
ble future, the city will continue to draw people like Lynda with this
lure — the freedom of lifestyle, the freedom of movement, the freedom of anonymity itself.

Questions on Content

1   What two kinds of "fantasy and daydream" does Marchand discuss
in both the first and the last paragraphs of his essay?

2   What main aspects of life in a small town are described by Marchand?
What disadvantages are emphasized?

3   What main aspects of life in a large city are described by Marchand?
What disadvantages are emphasized?

4   Why does Lynda find herself "voting for the big city"?

5   What broader social issue does Marchand concern himself with in
this essay? What is his view on this general subject? Do you agree or disagree with him? Why or why not?

Questions on Structure and Technique

1   What is the purpose of Marchand's comparison in paragraph one?
What attitude toward the relation between small towns and large cities is
illustrated in paragraph two? Why is Marchand's concluding paragraph
effective?

2   In what paragraphs does Marchand describe life in a small town? In
what paragraphs does Marchand describe life in a large city? What is the
purpose of paragraph eleven?

3   What paragraphs does Marchand develop using primarily description? Narration? Illustration? Comparison? Contrast?

4   What examples of colloquial and slang words and expressions can
you find in Marchand's essay? What examples of more formal diction can
you find?

5   What specific allusions to contemporary North American popular culture does Marchand make? What specific historical allusions are made? Why is each kind of allusion effective in this essay?

Suggestions for Writing

1   Using a subject-by-subject approach, write a contrast essay in which you discuss the differences between life in a small town and life in a large city based on your own experiences. Be sure to use specific details and examples in order to create vivid images in your readers' minds.

2   Using a subject-by-subject approach, write an essay in which you contrast a fantasy or a daydream that you have had about a person, place, object, or experience, with the "real thing" that you later experienced.

ALLAN SMITH

In this essay, Allan Smith examines the relations of metaphors we commonly use to represent experience to the nature of that experience itself; specifically, Smith contrasts the "melting-pot" and the "mosaic" as metaphors for the experience of immigrants in the United States and Canada, respectively. Smith then considers how "each of these metaphors idealizes the society to which it refers, and it idealizes the experience of the immigrant who has come to that society." Through this comparison and contrast, the author indicates the complexity of views of society often taken at face value and also illustrates the importance of using metaphors, analogies, and language in general to clarify rather than to obscure our perceptions of our experiences.

METAPHOR AND NATIONALITY

1 Canada and the United States have been peopled by immigrants. The experience that these immigrants have undergone, and the character of the society they have helped to form, has been described metaphorically in both countries. One speaks of the American melting pot and the Canadian mosaic. Each of these metaphors carries a double burden. Each is supposed to symbolize the actual nature of the society to which it is applied, and each is held to represent the ideal form which that society is attempting to realize.

2 The melting-pot metaphor conjures up a picture of peoples of diverse origins being fused in the crucible of a new environment into a group of wholly new beings. Each of these beings has severed his ties with the Old World, and each has been regenerated by his new environment. Each has become, in Crèvecoeur's classic phrase, a new man. This theme has been one of endless fascination for Americans. They have expended much time and energy elaborating the image of America as a New World, a garden, a virgin land, free from the corrupt and corrupting influences of the Old World, and capable of regenerating man. The American, and all men who come to America, are transformed.

3 In Canada the idea of creating a new man has gained nothing like the currency it has in the United States. Here the controlling metaphor has been the mosaic, a grand design consisting of many different elements, each of which retains its own character and quality while simultaneously contributing to the realization of the design as

a whole. The objective is the rendering of a composite figure, not the creation of one that is wholly new. The elements of which this composite figure, this new nation, consists will be juxtaposed in such a way as to create a new nationality, one which rests not upon a common culture, but upon its capacity to serve and protect the interests, cultural and otherwise, of its component parts. The essence of this new nationality will be found in the nature of the relationship these different elements bear to one another, and not in the fact that there will cease to be different elements. There will need to be a consensus in this national state. It will, however, be a consensus which derives not so much from a shared culture or shared values as from the belief by all its peoples that their best interests are being served by continuing association in a common political framework.

4   Each of these metaphors idealizes the society to which it refers, and it idealizes the experience of the immigrant who has come to that society. Immigrants to the United States have often retained, and have often been encouraged to retain, some measure of their ethnic consciousness . . . .

5   To the extent that the immigrant to America has, however, been required to divest himself of this ethnic identity, he has not become a wholly new man. He and his fellows have not been melted down and then recast in an entirely new mould. They have become, instead, Americanized Englishmen. The dominant social type in the United States is an Anglo-Saxon type, and it is to this type that immigrants have been expected to assimilate. The American becomes, then, not a new man, but a modification of one who is old and familiar. And so the term "anglo-conformity" has been held to describe more accurately than does the melting-pot metaphor what happens to the immigrant who comes to the United States.

6   Finally, while the immigrant to the United States might be assimilated to the prevailing culture and value system, he is not always assimilated into the agencies and institutions that operate society. His assimilation is behavioural, but not structural. It is not total, and here too, the melting-pot metaphor breaks down.

7   The mosaic concept is also an idealization of reality. A greater degree of behavioural assimilation has taken place in Canada than that concept would appear to allow for. The majority of second generation German-Canadians, Icelandic-Canadians, and even Ukrainian-Canadians speak English and not their parents' native tongue. Their Old World culture, when it is retained, is regarded as something to be brought out and dusted off, rather self-consciously, on special national occasions. It does not form a central part of Canada's cultural life, and when it is brought to the attention of Canadians at large, the tendency is to regard it as an imported exotic.

8   The mosaic further implies a social situation in which members of different ethnic communities are able to retain their ethnic identity, and yet participate to the full in the national life. Here, also, the metaphor fails to represent the reality. Positions of power, influence, and prestige have tended to go to Canadians of British descent, and continuing emphasis on ethnic origins has been judged likely to perpetuate this state of affairs.

9   Finally, a state dedicated to the proposition that all cultural groups within it have an inalienable right to flourish would be a state in which, ideally, brokerage politics would have no place. Representatives of each cultural group would know that their special interests would be looked after, and they would not, therefore, find it necessary to solicit special favours. The national interest would not demand constant adjustment of the claims of rival groups. And precisely because the interests of each group would, automatically as it were, be served, politicians would have nothing to gain by manoeuvring for the support of these groups. But this clearly is not the situation. Politicians who, as André Seigfried wrote at the beginning of the century, found it necessary to "exert themselves . . . to prevent the formation of homogeneous parties, divided according to creed or race or class" have noticed no changes in what is required of them. The different groups still feel it necessary to promote their interests, and those interests must still be reconciled with one another. It remains an essential part of politics in Canada to adjust the claims of different groups and interests and to insure as nearly as possible that none shall have undue influence and that the state shall not fragment along ethnic lines. The existence of the politician as broker indicates, not the presence of a fully functioning cultural mosaic, but its absence.

Questions on Content

1   What is Smith's definition of a "melting pot"? What images are associated with the "melting pot" metaphor?

2   What is Smith's definition of a "mosaic"? Are there any images associated with the "mosaic" metaphor?

3   Why is the "melting-pot" metaphor an idealization of experience in America, according to Smith?

4   Why is the "mosaic" metaphor an idealization of experience in Canada, according to Smith?

5   In what sense does this similarity of the mosaic ideal in Canada to the melting-pot ideal in America indicate a basic difference between these ideals, as Smith suggests in his conclusion?

Questions on Structure and Technique

1   What sentence in paragraph one presents the author's two subjects? What sentence(s) in paragraph one indicate the parts (or aspects) of these subjects to be examined by the author? In what sentence does the author express his thesis most clearly?

2   What "part" of the author's subjects is examined in paragraphs two and three? What "part" of the author's subjects is examined in paragraphs five through eight? What is the function of paragraph four?

3   Why does Smith organize and develop his essay part-by-part rather than subject-by-subject?

4   What words and phrases does Smith use to help clarify the organization and development of his essay for the reader?

5   What unfamiliar words does Smith use? Look these words up in the dictionary. What words and phrases belong to a specialized vocabulary used in the social sciences?

Suggestions for Writing

1   Write a well-organized essay in which you contrast Canada and the United States in terms of your own experiences of these two countries, choosing either a subject-by-subject or a part-by-part approach.

2   Using a subject-by-subject approach, define and illustrate an ideal that you hold, and then contrast that ideal with an experience that you have had.

ARTHUR ERICKSON

Arthur Erickson (b. 1924) was born in Vancouver, British Columbia, and studied at the University of British Columbia and then McGill University, where he received his Bachelor of Architecture degree. Erickson is principal architect for his firm, Arthur Erickson Architects, with offices in Vancouver, Toronto, and Los Angeles. He has received numerous honours and awards for his work, which includes Simon Fraser University, The MacMillan Bloedel Building, Man and the Community and Man and His Health at Expo '67 in Montreal, the Canadian Pavilion at Expo '70 in Japan, the Museum of Anthropology at the University of British Columbia, Robson Square and the Law Courts Complex in Vancouver, Roy Thompson Hall in Toronto, and many private residences. Erickson has also taught at the University of British Columbia, and his work has been featured in books and television programs. In Erickson's essay, "Ideation as a Source of Creativity," he contrasts two fundamental views of reality and then suggests that one is preferable to the other if architecture is to be satisfactorily responsive to "human needs."

IDEATION AS A SOURCE OF CREATIVITY

1   My purpose in this essay is to point to the limitations of the single view of reality by which an architect ordinarily observes, understands, and evaluates architecture, and thus to try to open another view, because I believe that such an opening could show a way for architecture beyond what we may now envision. As an architect my concern with creativity is fundamental. It is therefore hard to realize that creativity, as architects use the term, is a relatively new concept in the history of ideas, having significance only for that part of the world's population influenced by the Christian Judaic and humanist traditions. So important is this concept to the Western mind that the founding religion of its civilization represents God creating the universe out of the void, and then creating man in His own image. This belief that creation is an act of the individual will, divine in origin, became part of the "mind-set" of western culture, the source, in part, of the West's restless and zealous quest for the betterment of the human lot, as well as its unstable, indeed tumultuous history.

2   By "mind-set" I mean a set of values which, once established, controls the future development of ideas. If God, in the creation story,

created man in His own image, it follows that God is like man; a projection of man's own self-image. Thus it was that the development of the theistic concept ended with man, at the centre of the universe, replacing God.

3 Furthermore, if man reflects the acts of the creator, he must learn to create. Out of the deterioration of the classical humanism of the Renaissance grew both individualism and science, twin outgrowths of Western man's abnormal preoccupation with himself. Together they posited man standing outside nature, which he could then try to shape according to his need. This concept of creativity, requiring a separate and distinct ego over and against an entirely neutral and pliant Nature, is the invention of specifically Western culture. It is not a view of reality shared by other world cultures, which reject such a man-centred universe.

4 Most cultural patterns were not established through the creative violence fostered by an egocentric world view, but through a long process of selection and adaptation to reach solutions eminently suited to their particular environments. (Though plant and animal life are also adaptive, they modify their own vital forms to fit the environment, whereas man modifies his environment by the use of tools. His dwellings, his dress, his utensils form a screen of artifice between himself and the raw environment.) When what these anonymous village cultures produced through an endless process of trial and error had been successfully established, the methodology of artifice was codified and ritualized for the sake of preservation and continuity, and a rigorous order was elaborated from which there could be no departure. Conservation, not creation, formed the basis of the cultural dynamic of these cultures, and remains to this day the primary motivating force for a major part of the world's population.

5 The world view of the non-Western cultures pictured man as a part of nature, not set above it in a different order of reality, and nature as a subject of worship and homage. This world view saw man's life related in its most mundane details to the whole of life in an intricate pattern of relationships on every level: physical, philosophical, psychological, social. It was this whole-life pattern that must be preserved. In large parts of Africa, and Southeast Asia, this view survives, and there the art and architecture serve the ceremony of the life pattern. So the house becomes not just a shelter, but a sacred place for the celebration of birth and death and the consummation of marriage. In Shinto Japan, the most highly refined of the animist cultures, art was a vital act of worship and perpetuation. Whereas Western art and architecture has emulated the human physique in its finiteness, proportions, and physical vitality, their art centred on Nature and emulated the linearity, grace, and infinite extension of tree and plant physiognomy. This was an entirely different source of

form from ours. Nor did the advent of Buddhism alter the perspective, but deepened and enshrined it. The reality of nature in Buddhist philosophy was ceaseless change in a rhythm of creation and destruction with man, as part of nature, subject to these laws. But art and architecture sought to fix these concepts in unchanging, eternal symbols and thus, through the same period of history as our art showed dramatic development in concept, style, and technique, theirs betrayed relatively little change. Whereas art for us was an act of creation, for them it was an act of imitation, for imitation represented respect for the tradition; creativity for them rested in the perfection of known technique, in how well the precedent could be recaptured and reiterated.

6   The West has always put its sights on an unattainable paradise and thus looked idealistically to the future, discarded the past, and made progress towards that goal the criterion of moral judgement. The East tried to understand the reality of existence itself, accepting all aspects of that existence as part of reality without moral judgement. If we of the West are the idealists forever chasing a chimera, they were and are the realists, having little faith but great wisdom about life. If creation to us means a breakthrough to new frontiers, a casting-off of the old, the initiation of the new, then creation to them means a deeper insight into reality, a stronger grasp, a revelation of that which already exists. Art strove to recapture, again and again, the superb relationship, the whole-life pattern of man in nature, realized at its profoundest in the Buddhist master works.

7   If the East represents a cultural development which we can see is quite distinct from that of the West, it must be remembered that in its pre-Renaissance history, the West had not yet explicated its egocentric world view. The mystic tradition of the early church reminds us in some ways of the teachings of the Buddhist contemplatives. And in Christian culture there was a period of anonymity in art, during the Dark and early Middle Ages, when human social purpose was so subordinated to divine purpose that human creativity was not acknowledged as such. Rather, the creative act was seen simply as a celebration of the divine will. All aspects of nature were perceived not in themselves, but as earthly reflections of a heavenly order. But when men like St. Francis of Assissi began to observe and celebrate the world around them they started a process which led to the fateful observation that objects were related to one another not so much in divine hierarchy as in physical space. The interest in the physical aspect of man and nature grew until the curiosity of a Leonardo demanded to know how things were made and how they functioned. That burning curiosity was the beginning of modern science.

8   Who could have guessed the effect of the scientific awakening on the mind of Western man? Today our thought processes have become so conditioned by scientific materialism that we are incapable of holistic perception. Committed to the observation of how things are constituted and how they perform, we cannot perceive phenomena except in a fragmented, functional way, defining them as a sum of interdependent parts, not as a whole with a larger significance. Such a mind-set was the genesis of our invention of machines — machines aped the observed performance of nature — and has completely taken control of our perceived world. It has also formed our view of architecture as the art of individual buildings; of a building as an arrangement of spaces for different uses; of cities as an agglomeration of functionally separate zones; of human knowledge as the accumulation of different fields of study; of the body as a functioning system of individual organs; of a tree as a system of roots, trunks, leaves, cells, and protoplasmic fluids.

9   Where in all this, is the reality we seek? As our foremost scientists now admit, reality perpetually evades analysis; yet the analytical approach remains our cultural commitment, blinding us to reality as much as paganism, witchcraft, or alchemy once blinded others. In our history's sequence of rationalizations attempting to resolve reality, but capturing only a part of it, we are inevitably caught in the dangerous fiction that was ours, after all, is the only rational approach to reality.

10   What is the result? In architecture, the machine ethic is so basic to our perception that functionalism remains the dominant ordering principle. For over forty years now architecture has been mechanistic. There have been aberrations, of course, but these are consistent with the cerebral preoccupations of our culture. Though cerebration quells the emotions, and its inherent scepticism vitiates belief, it provides fertile ground for imagination and sensation. Thus, along with the mechanistic purists are those who revel in the sensual aspect of the machine ethic or those who find a mechanistic analogy to natural form in so-called "organic" architecture.

11   Lacking the comprehensiveness of the whole-life pattern, we excel in all areas of mechanical proficiency. The last one hundred years of architecture have been a history of increasing prowess in techniques of construction, environmental control, equipment development, until in fact we can "do anything," except that we hardly know what to do. Our preoccupation with technique as an end in itself has stifled the soul in our art.

12   The mechanistic bias coloured our view even of the history of architecture, where too often a change of style has been credited to a breakthrough in technique when, in fact, up until the eighteenth century all techniques have been known since at least the beginning of the

Christian era, even long before. If the human race is to survive this century, the technological bias, and the materialism which supports it, will have to find other goals for humanity than mere physical well-being.

13   My point is that Western ideation, which in the Renaissance and early scientific era had greater creative power, has established a cultural wilderness in which art and architecture stand as alien witnesses. I have described the non-creative and non-ideational source of artistic development revealed in the experience of other cultures remote from the West. Are they also remote in spirit, or can they show us the way to a redefinition of creativity at a deeper level than any form of ideation that has yet occurred to us?

14   Surely most architects would agree that ideation cannot be a goal in itself, even when it serves a creative process. We all know that one source of ideation, the human imagination, is boundless but seldom relevant. The pursuit of inventiveness alone produces nothing but a vast desert of applications at the patent office. For an action to be creative its results must contribute to the cultural context in which it has emerged. That context is vital, as can be proven by the fact that both steam power and gunpowder were known in ancient China, but were used for toys and amusement and harnessed for power and destruction only centuries later in the different cultural context of the West. When we confuse creativity with mere invention and novelty we are falling into the mechanistic trap of isolating process from the context in which it exists. We take a similar attitude to the creative process itself, trying to understand it by analyzing and finding rational answers to its essentially non-rational nature. In his admirable book, *The Creative Imagination*, Arthur Koestler describes creativity as an anti-logical process involving a breakthrough from one thought plane, or matrix, to another; in other words, a fusion of two formerly unconnected matrices achieving a new synthesis. Koestler calls this process "bisociation." The revelation of new truth is accompanied by an emotional catharsis that is the experience of beauty. No amount of thought can lead to this moment of truth — on the contrary, it requires a suspension of rational thought — a floating, unselective frame of mind in which we free ourselves in order to receive information from all sources unconditionally. It is when we are without preconceptions of any kind that we can respond with sensitivity and perception to the real demands of the moment. In Zen terms, the artist should be like an empty vessel, for it is only the empty vessel that can be filled. Or in Picasso's words: "I do not seek — I find."

15   Whereas artists are constantly defensive about their creative methods and try to rationalize the act of creation into logical procedures, in the logical areas of research like physics and mathematics the scientists recognize their dependence on intuition. Koestler quotes Dirac

upbraiding his fellow physicists with the observation: "It's more important to have beauty in one's equations than to have them fit the experiment."

16   Architects on the other hand are obsessed by scientific and pseudo-scientific theories for how and why they do things, for example, Le Corbusier's modular. But logic and reason subvert the very nature of creativity, for they demand consistency within a certain plane of thought while creativity demands superseding and breaking through the boundaries of that plane.

17   In this condition of non-thought, the supra-conscious intelligence comes into play, providing a basis of judgement superior to conscious thought. On this unconscious level we are open, antenna-like to peripheral stimuli, and this much wider range of information is absorbed without our knowing it to become part of our intuitive perception. It is only then that we are capable of perceiving what is culturally significant, because we are then at the level of the "collective unconscious." Thus similar creative breakthroughs occur simultaneously in different parts of the world without apparent connection.

18   The creative process, as described by Koestler, cannot be regarded as having an ideational source. First, it does not involve rational thought — or even conscious awareness — and second, it requires that the mind's condition of free-floating perceptiveness becomes focussed on some real cultural need that has a context in space and time.

19   It is clear that such a description of creativity is not the creativity of the Old Testament — or of Western man in the post-Renaissance period — which demands the production of something out of nothing. Rather it presents creativity as the discovery of a relatedness between separate things. The role of the architect is to discover, amid the confusion of our surroundings, the spaces that have significance, and to bring coherence and meaning to our fractured environment. In architecture, it is not mere variation on the forms that is our concern, but the restatement of the subsistent forms, the archetypes, in a form meaningful to our time.

20   The redefinition of creativity by Koestler and others, relating the artist and architect to springs and sources of being known to the ancients and to other cultures, carries with it a set of mandates. Architects can do little more than be the most keenly tuned sensors and perceptors of our culture. They are not here to make new shapes, find new techniques, or build monuments, but to point directions and to provide meaning, signposts for this perplexing contemporary world. In the past it was important that such signposts be individual masterworks, as in the time of the great churches. But the future approaches when the individual work will be of little significance. The pressures of our planet are forcing us into various forms of

collectivism in which Western individual creativity may lose its meaning. The curve of history is taking us back into an age of anonymity, slowly but irrevocably, where, as in the medieval hilltown, no single entity can be separated from the context of the whole. We are learning slowly but inevitably that just as individuals cannot act, nor even create, alone, nothing can be divorced from its environment, for that is to isolate it from reality.

21   Therefore, the most pressing need in architecture today, I am convinced, is to be sensitive to context — context in the profoundest cultural and intellectual sense and in the physical sense of the environment itself.

22   In the earlier period of the architecture of this century, function in the purely mechanistic and physical sense was the source of ideation, along with the spatial aesthetic of the cubists. But all were exercises in isolation, taking no account of, in fact defying, their surroundings. Since that time architectural skills and knowledge of human need have expanded profoundly. The physical aspect of human need, for shelter, warmth and light, is now subordinated to cultural determinants. In the Americas, and I would suspect in most of the world, the symbolic aspect of shelter is as important as the fact of shelter itself.

23   Yet architects tend to interpret human needs in Africa, in China, in Mexico, in Iran in the light of their own experience, which may not apply at all. So far architecture has ignored culture, just as it has largely ignored the aesthetic and psychic effect of climate, and in doing so has ignored the roots of human need. Ignorance of the vital facts of life experienced in the particularities of a given physical and cultural context is the worst aspect of contemporary architecture, and persists at a time when sensitivity to human need in relation to context should be architecture's most welcome source of ideation.

24   Human needs cannot be divorced from context, for they are as inseparable as an individual is inseparable from his culture, or as a culture from its history, or as a country from its climate and geography. Human need in its context — the context of time and place, culture and history — and these in relation to the rest of human culture, should be the source of ideation. Since the relationship of need to context is in perpetual flux, the result can only be innovative, yet always pertinent, always relevant, and always meaningful to the life in the culture.

Questions on Content

1   Why does "the Western mind" place so much value on the concept of "creativity," according to Erickson? What view of reality results?

2   What concept does "the world view of non-Western cultures" value? Why?

3   What is the result of the Western concept of creativity in modern architecture?

4   What alternative approach to the creative process does Erickson propose for architecture?

5   Why would this approach be preferable, according to Erickson? Do you agree or disagree? Why?

Questions on Structure and Technique

1   Is Erickson's approach to the organization and development of this contrast essay subject-by-subject or part-by-part?

2   What main parts, or aspects, of each subject does Erickson contrast?

3   What details and illustrations did you find most effective in Erickson's essay? What purposes do they serve?

4   What references to specific people does Erickson make? What are the purposes of these references?

5   What does the word "ideation" mean? Why is "ideation" an appropriate word for Erickson to choose for his discussion?

Suggestions for Writing

1   Consider two different buildings with which you are familiar in terms of their responsiveness to "human need" as discussed by Erickson. Write an essay contrasting several aspects of these two buildings in order to show which one demonstrates greater "sensitivity to human need in relation to content."

2   Study an example of Erickson's architectural work, and then write an essay using either a part-by-part or a subject-by-subject approach to contrast his work with another building of a similar kind.

PLATO

The Greek philosopher Plato (ca. 429-347 B.C.) used "Dialogues" such as the Apology, Euthyphro, Phaedo, Republic, *and* Timaeus, *in order to express his imaginative philosophical vision of human existence. In the following dialogue between Socrates and Glaucon in Book VII of Plato's* Republic, *Socrates provides a complex comparison in the form of an allegory of a cave — a figurative representation of the human condition — as the concrete basis for his more abstract philosophical discussion of the limits of human knowledge and the nature of goodness, beauty, and truth.*

THE ALLEGORY OF THE CAVE

1   And now, I [Socrates] said, let me show in a figure how far our nature is enlightened or unenlightened: — Behold! human beings living in an underground den, which has a mouth open towards the light and reaching all along the den; here they have been from their childhood, and have their legs and necks chained so they cannot move, and can only see before them, being prevented by the chains from turning round their heads. Above and behind them a fire is blazing at a distance, and between the fire and the prisoners there is a raised way; and you will see, if you look, a low wall built along the way, like the screen which marionette players have in front of them, over which they show the puppets.

2   I [Glaucon] see.

3   And do you see, I said, men passing along the wall carrying all sorts of vessels, and statues and figures of animals made of wood and stone and various materials, which appear over the wall? Some of them are talking, others silent.

4   You have shown me a strange image, and they are strange prisoners.

5   Like ourselves, I replied; and they see only their own shadows, or the shadows of one another, which the fire throws on the opposite wall of the cave?

6   True, he said; how could they see anything but the shadows if they were never allowed to move their heads?

7   And of the objects which are being carried in like manner they would only see the shadows?

8   Yes, he said.

9   And if they were able to converse with one another, would they not suppose that they were naming what was actually before them?

10   Very true.

11   And suppose further that the prison had an echo which came from the other side, would they not be sure to fancy when one of the passers-by spoke that the voice which they heard came from the passing shadow?

12   No question, he replied.

13   To them, I said, the truth would be literally nothing but the shadows of the images.

14   That is certain.

15   And now look again, and see what will naturally follow if the prisoners are released and disabused of their error. At first, when any of them is liberated and compelled suddenly to stand up and turn his neck round and walk and look towards the light, he will suffer sharp pains; the glare will distress him, and he will be unable to see the realities of which in his former state he had seen the shadows; and then conceive some one saying to him, that what he saw before was an illusion, but that now, when he is approaching nearer to being and his eye is turned towards more real existence, he has a clearer vision, — what will be his reply? And you may further imagine that his instructor is pointing to the objects as they pass and requiring him to name them, — will he not be perplexed? Will he not fancy that the shadows which he formerly saw are truer than the objects which are now shown to him?

16   Far truer.

17   And if he is compelled to look straight at the light, will he not have a pain in his eyes which will make him turn away to take refuge in the objects of vision which he can see, and which he will conceive to be in reality clearer than the things which are now being shown to him?

18   True, he said.

19   And suppose once more, that he is reluctantly dragged up a steep and rugged ascent, and held fast until he is forced into the presence of the sun himself, he is not likely to be pained and irritated? When he approaches the light his eyes will be dazzled, and he will not be able to see anything at all of what are now called realities.

20   Not all in a moment, he said.

21   He will require to grow accustomed to the sight of the upper world. And first he will see the shadows best, next the reflections of men and other objects in the water, and then the objects themselves; then he will gaze upon the light of the moon and the stars and the spangled heaven; and he will see the sky and the stars by night better than the sun or the light of the sun by day?

22   Certainly.

23   Last of all he will be able to see the sun, and not mere reflections of him in the water, but he will see him in his own proper place, and not in another; and he will contemplate him as he is.

24 Certainly.

25 He will then proceed to argue that this is he who gives the season and the years, and is the guardian of all that is in the visible world, and in a certain way the cause of all things which he and his fellows have been accustomed to behold?

26 Clearly, he said, he would first see the sun and then reason about him.

27 And then he remembered his old habitation, and the wisdom of the den and his fellow-prisoners, do you not suppose that he would felicitate himself on the change, and pity them?

28 Certainly, he would.

29 And if they were in the habit of conferring honours among themselves on those who were quickest to observe the passing shadows and to remark which of them went before, and which followed after, and which were together; and who were therefore best able to draw conclusions as to the future, do you think that he would care for such honours and glories, or envy the possessors of them? Would he not say with Homer,

'Better to be the poor servant of a poor master,'

and to endure anything, rather than think as they do and live after their manner?

30 Yes, he said, I think that he would rather suffer anything than entertain these false notions and live in this miserable manner.

31 Imagine once more, I said, such an one coming suddenly out of the sun to be replaced in his old situation; would he not be certain to have his eyes full of darkness?

32 To be sure, he said.

33 And if there were a contest, and he had to compete in measuring the shadows with the prisoners who had never moved out of the den, while his sight was still weak, and before his eyes had become steady (and the time which would be needed to acquire this new habit of sight might be very considerable), would he not be ridiculous? Men would say of him that up he went and down he came without his eyes; and that it was better not even to think of ascending; and if any one tried to loose another and lead him up to the light, let them only catch the offender, and they would put him to death.

34 No question, he said.

35 This entire allegory, I said, you may now append, dear Glaucon, to the previous argument; the prisonhouse is the world of sight, the light of the fire is the sun, and you will not misapprehend me if you interpret the journey upwards to be the ascent of the soul into the intellectual world according to my poor belief, which, at your desire, I have expressed — whether rightly or wrongly God knows. But,

whether true or false, my opinion is that in the world of knowledge the idea of good appears last of all, and is seen only with an effort; and, when seen, is also inferred to be the universal author of all things beautiful and right, parent of light and of the lord of light in this visible world, and the immediate source of reason and truth in the intellectual; and that this is the power upon which he who would act rationally either in public or private life must have his eye fixed.

36   I agree, he said, as far as I am able to understand you.

37   Moreover, I said, you must not wonder that those who attain to this beatific vision are unwilling to descend to human affairs; for their souls are ever hastening into the upper world where they desire to dwell; which desire of theirs is very natural, if our allegory may be trusted.

38   Yes, very natural.

39   And is there anything surprising in one who passes from divine contemplations to the evil state of man, misbehaving himself in a ridiculous manner; if, while his eyes are blinking and before he has become accustomed to the surrounding darkness, he is compelled to fight in courts of law, or in other places, about the images or the shadows of images of justice, and is endeavouring to meet the conceptions of those who have never yet seen absolute justice?

40   Anything but surprising, he replied.

41   Any one who has common sense will remember that the bewilderments of the eyes are of two kinds, and arise from two causes, either from coming out of the light or from going into the light, which is true of the mind's eye, quite as much as of the bodily eye; and he who remembers this when he sees any one whose vision is perplexed and weak, will not be too ready to laugh; he will first ask whether that soul of man has come out of the brighter life, and is unable to see because unaccustomed to the dark, or having turned from darkness to the day is dazzled by excess of light. And he will count the one happy in his condition and state of being, and he will pity the other; or, if he have a mind to laugh at the soul which comes from below into the light, there will be more reason in this than in the laugh which greets him who returns from above out of the light into the den.

42   That, he said, is a very just distinction.

43   But then, if I am right, certain professors of education must be wrong when they say that they can put a knowledge into the soul which was not there before, like sight into blind eyes.

44   They undoubtedly say this, he replied.

45   Whereas, our argument shows that the power and capacity of learning exists in the soul already; and that just as the eye was unable to turn from darkness to light without the whole body, so too the instrument of knowledge can only by the movement of the whole soul be

turned from the world of becoming into that of being, and learn by degrees to endure the sight of being, and of the brightest and best of being, or in other words, of the good.

46 Very true.

47 And must there not be some art which will effect conversion in the easiest and quickest manner; not implanting the faculty of sight, for that exists already, but has been turned in the wrong direction, and is looking away from the truth?

48 Yes, he said, such an art may be presumed.

49 And whereas the other so-called virtues of the soul seem to be akin to bodily qualities, for even when they are not originally innate they can be implanted later by habit and exercise, the virtue of wisdom more than anything else contains a divine element which always remains, and by this conversion is rendered useful and profitable; or, on the other hand, hurtful and useless. Did you never observe the narrow intelligence flashing from the keen eye of a clever rogue — how eager he is, how clearly his paltry soul sees the way to his end; he is the reverse of blind, but his keen eye-sight is forced into the service of evil, and he is mischievous in proportion to his cleverness?

50 Very true, he said.

51 But what if there had been a circumcision of such natures in the days of their youth; and they had been severed from those sensual pleasures, such as eating and drinking, which, like leaden weights, were attached to them at their birth, and which drag them down and turn the vision of their souls upon the things that are below — if, I say, they had been released from these impediments and turned in the opposite direction, the very same faculty in them would have seen the truth as keenly as they see what their eyes are turned to now.

52 Very likely.

53 Yes, I said; and there is another thing which is likely, or rather a necessary inference from what has preceded, that neither the uneducated and uninformed of the truth, nor yet those who never make an end of their education, will be able ministers of State; not the former, because they have no single aim of duty which is the rule of all their actions, private as well as public; nor the latter, because they will not act at all except upon compulsion, fancying that they are already dwelling apart in the islands of the blest.

54 Very true, he replied.

55 Then, I said, the business of us who are the founders of the State will be to compel the best minds to attain that knowledge which we have already shown to be the greatest of all — they must continue to ascend until they arrive at the good; but when they have ascended and seen enough we must not allow them to do as they do now.

56 What do you mean?

57 I mean that they remain in the upper world: but this must not be allowed; they must be made to descend again among the prisoners in

the den, and partake of their labours and honours, whether they are worth having or not.

58   But is not this unjust? he said; ought we to give them a worse life, when they might have a better?

59   You have again forgotten, my friend, I said, the intention of the legislator, who did not aim at making any one class in the State happy above the rest; the happiness was to be in the whole State, and he held the citizens together by persuasion and necessity, making them benefactors of the State, and therefore benefactors of one another; to this end he created them, not to please themselves, but to be his instruments in binding up the State.

60   True, he said, I had forgotten.

61   Observe, Glaucon, that there will be no injustice in compelling our philosophers to have a care and providence of others; we shall explain to them that in other States, men of their class are not obliged to share in the toils of politics: and this is reasonable, for they grow up at their own sweet will, and the government would rather not have them. Being self-taught, they cannot be expected to show any gratitude for a culture which they have never received. But we have brought you into the world to be rulers of the hive, kings of yourselves and of the other citizens, and have educated you far better and more perfectly than they have been educated, and you are better able to share in the double duty. Wherefore each of you, when his turn comes, must go down to the general underground abode, and get the habit of seeing in the dark. When you have acquired the habit, you will see ten thousand times better than the inhabitants of the den, and you will know what the several images are, and what they represent, because you have seen the beautiful and just and good in their truth. And thus our State which is also yours will be a reality, and not a dream only, and will be administered in a spirit unlike that of other States, in which men fight with one another about shadows only and are distracted in the struggle for power, which in their eyes is a great good. Whereas the truth is that the State in which the rulers are most reluctant to govern is always the best and most quietly governed, and the State in which they are most eager, the worst.

62   Quite true, he replied.

63   And will our pupils, when they hear this, refuse to take their turn at the toils of State, when they are allowed to spend the greater part of their time with one another in the heavenly light?

64   Impossible, he answered; for they are just men, and the commands which we impose upon them are just; there can be no doubt that every one of them will take office as a stern necessity, and not after the fashion of our present rulers of State.

65   Yes, my friend, I said; and there lies the point. You must contrive for your future rulers another and a better life than that of a ruler, and then you may have a well-ordered State; for only in the State which offers this, will they rule who are truly rich, not in silver and

gold, but in virtue and wisdom, which are the true blessings of life. Whereas if they go to the administration of public affairs, poor and hungering after their own private advantage, thinking that hence they are to snatch the chief good, order there can never be; for they will be fighting about office, and the civil and domestic broils which thus arise will be the ruin of the rulers themselves and of the whole State.

Questions on Content

1   What is the situation of the prisoners in the cave described by Socrates? What can the prisoners perceive in this condition?

2   What happens if one of the prisoners is released? What are the stages in this process of enlightenment?

3   What will be the relations between the released prisoner and the people in the cave?

4   What are the main general ideas represented by Socrates' allegory of the cave?

5   What particular applications does the allegory of the cave have in education? In government?

Questions on Structure and Technique

1   What is the purpose of Socrates' allegory? What does Socrates' use of specific details and images contribute to this purpose?

2   What similarities do you notice between the released prisoner and the people in the cave? What differences do you see?

3   In what paragraph(s) does Socrates' *explain* the comparison between the allegory of the cave and the human condition? In what paragraphs does he *apply* the allegory of the cave to social concerns?

4   What sentence (or sentences) most clearly and concisely expresses Plato's thesis?

5   What key words express Plato's ideals?

Suggestions for Writing

1   Write an essay based on your experiences in which you contrast a situation in which you were a prisoner in "the cave" with a situation where you were released from that "cave." Use specific details and images to show your readers both situations clearly.

2   Write an essay in which you apply Plato's allegory of the cave to a contemporary social situation or problem using either a subject-by-subject or a part-by-part approach for your comparison. Consider in what ways this comparison clarifies the situation or problem, and suggest what conclusions may be drawn from your comparison.

CHAPTER 5

"Very little seems to be known about who actually participates in "community" festivals."

CLASSIFICATION ANALYSIS

*A*n *analysis* is a division of a subject into several parts so that its parts, the relations between those parts, and the relations of the parts to the whole subject may be examined. Three different ways of dividing a whole subject into its parts can be organized and developed by a writer as three basic forms of analysis: a subject divided into categories, or sub-classes, is a *classification analysis*; a subject divided into stages and steps of a whole operation is a *process analysis*; and, a subject divided into its parts as causes and effects is a *causal analysis*. By thinking carefully about a whole subject in terms of its constituent parts in these ways, a writer can use analysis to gain a better understanding of the subject, and then to provide a clear and appropriate form of expression for a purposeful discussion of that subject. You will be studying examples of classification analysis in this chapter, process analysis in chapter six, and causal analysis in chapter seven.

Classification analysis is the division of a general subject into parts which are *categories* or *subclasses* of the whole. A writer's first task in a classifi-cation analysis is to establish such categories. This requires some basic principle of division. A writer must choose a principle of division that is appropriate to an essay's subject and purpose. For example, Richard J. Ossenberg analyses "Social Class and Bar Behaviour During the Calgary Stampede" by classifying bars into lower-class, middle-class, and upper-middle-class establishments according to the social and economic class of the establishments' patrons. Depending on what common characteristic is most relevant to a writer's concerns, any subject may be divided according to any one of a number of principles. Bars, for example, might be al-ternatively classified by their location, size, entertainment, popularity, physical appearance, and so forth. However, a writer should keep in mind the following considerations: approach the subject with a specific purpose in order to determine an appropriate principle of division; use the same principle of division for all categories; and, be sure that these categories do not overlap. After dividing a subject into categories, the categories must be given identifying "labels" (in a word or a phrase), arranged in a logical sequence, and, most importantly, defined.

Definition, in a classification analysis, is an explanation of the main distinguishing characteristics or qualities common to all items, members, or groups contained within a category or subclass of the whole. A good definition of what each category includes under its identifying label in a classification analysis is consistent with the important purpose served by definitions in every form of expression. In general, definition clarifies the meaning of a word or a phrase when we want to be sure as readers and as writers that we have an accurate, precise understanding of the terms being used. When writing about subjects with specialized or technical vocabula-ries, a writer may need to provide a general audience with some words' *denotative* meanings; that is, their dictionary (lexical) definitions. When writing about any subject, a writer must constantly be aware of words' *connotative* meanings; that is, their associated or suggested meanings. In some instances, a writer may want to stipulate the specific denotative or connotative sense in which a word (such as love, beauty, freedom, democracy, truth, faith, time, goodness, etc.) should be understood by readers. Indeed, a writer may even choose to develop an *extended definition* in a paragraph, several paragraphs, or an entire essay in order to elaborate on a word's meaning and significance. As shown in the essays by John Harbron and Margaret Atwood, interesting and effective extended definitions may be developed by writers using classification analysis as well as other rhetorical modes, notably illustration (see William James's "Habit") and comparison and contrast (see Arthur Lower's "The Great God Car").

The organization and development of a classification analysis essay begins with the main categories that a writer has labelled and defined.

I.   Introduction
II. A   Category 1
II. B   Category 2
II. C   Category 3
III.   Conclusion

Using these categories as the basic units of organization, a writer may either continue to subdivide one or more of them further, creating additional but subordinate classifications, or select a different mode to develop them, such as illustration, comparison, or contrast. The essays in this chapter exemplify a variety of the innumerable methods and combinations of techniques a writer may find appropriate to the development of his or her own subject and purpose. Above all else, however, these selections demonstrate that writers should use classification analysis (as well as the other two forms of analysis) as a *means* for organizing and developing the specific details and the particular qualities, features, and characteristics of a whole subject, but not as an end in itself. You will notice how a writer's careful selection of good specific details and examples give substance to an analysis so that it shows the original intricacies and complexities of the subject through the orderly development of its parts. As a result, a writer holds readers' interest and involvement in the subject and avoids classification that appears to be little more than either the stereotyping of people or the oversimplification of ideas and experiences.

Classification analysis offers writers and readers an understanding of a whole subject through an examination of its parts as categories or subclasses. In both our experience and our expression we use classification as a means of ordering the parts of our world, and classification analysis allows us to look more closely and clearly at that world in conventional as well as in unconventional ways.

RICHARD J. OSSENBERG

Richard J. Ossenberg, a professor of sociology at Queen's University, uses classification analysis for his research as well as his writing in this sociological study of three different social groups' participation in a "community festival," the Calgary Stampede. Ossenberg has published a number of research studies on the sociology of Canada, and he has edited two books, Canadian Society : Pluralism, Change, and Conflict *(1971) and* Power and Change in Canada *(1980).*

SOCIAL CLASS AND BAR BEHAVIOUR DURING THE CALGARY STAMPEDE

1   Very little seems to be known about who actually participates in "community" festivals. Social scientists as well as laymen apparently assume that people generally, regardless of status in the community, more or less participate in and benefit from such festivals. In discussing crowds in general, for example, Davis states: "The individuals who constitute any particular crowd are together by accident. Having no organization and being ephemeral, the crowd does not select its participants. Necessarily, the members are drawn from all walks of life and are present in the situation only because, in pursuing their private ends, they have to make use of common conveniences."[1] And in their view of "conventional crowds" (including institutionalized festivals), Killian and Turner state that these "function in facilitating the resolution of cultural conflict,"[2] thereby implying that community solidarity is temporarily restored.

2   It must be obvious from daily observations, however, that such views, while democratic, are anything but accurate. Every community has its distinctive geographical and social boundary lines between rich and poor and between majority and minority ethnic groups. Certainly these lines are not absolute; but there is bound to be disproportionate representation of the various status groups in the crowds that gather for different community activities, whether for nocturnal recreation or Saturday shopping or something else. The "redlight district" thus attracts a rather different clientele than more exclusive entertainment areas, and "hock-shops" and second-hand stores are not frequented by the same persons who patronize exclusive specialty and department stores.

3   Certain social groups also are known to be more likely than others to participate in relatively uncontrolled forms of collective behaviour such as lynchings, race riots, and political separatist movements.[3] On the other hand, it is argued that community festivals (such as the Calgary Stampede discussed here) function specifically to enhance community solidarity through generalized participation in tension-release behaviour.[4] An historical example was the "King-of-Fools" festival of the Middle Ages which was subsidized by the aristocracy who actively participated in the fun and games, but which featured a temporary inversion of the class structure. The annual Japanese village festivals also appear to have the same purpose and consist of extremely unorthodox behaviour as well as inversion of the class structure and other releases from everyday constrictions.[5] Similar ceremonies in urbanized societies have not received, to my knowledge, as much attention from social scientists. As a result, we lack adequate studies of the Oktober-Fest of Germany, the Mardi Gras of New Orleans, the Winter Carnival of Quebec, and the Calgary Stampede of Alberta, not to mention thousands of other community festivals in the United States, Canada, and Western Europe.

4   Both the paucity of analyzed cases and the implicit acceptance by many sociologists and anthropologists of a functionalist view of the integrating effect of community ritual suggested the present study of selective participation. It is based on observations made during a systematic "pub-crawl" on two evenings of the week-long Stampede which is held every July in Calgary, Alberta. The study was prompted by curiosity about the role of social stratification in encouraging or discouraging participation in this type of collective behaviour, which would be designated by Davis as a "planned expressive group" and by Turner and Killian as a "conventional crowd".[6] From a theoretical point of view, it was assumed that variations in the social class structure of communities largely determine differentiated participation in planned community festivals. In *Gemeinschaft* communities where "mechanical solidarity" within a small and homogeneous population prevails, generalized participation in festival occasions is probably usual. In urban *Gesellschaft* communities, however, social class structure seems too complex to expect the same general response.

5   In Canada and the United States we have considerable evidence pertaining to the "life-styles" of the different socio-economic classes. In general, for example, it can be said that middle-class attitudes abound with inhibitions and taboos against progressive and deviant behaviour, while people in lower socio-economic class positions are more concerned with immediate gratifications that sometimes explode into temporary violence. On the other hand, members of the middle class are more sensitive to legal and other restrictive norms and consequently may be more responsive to the relaxation of social

controls represented by the relatively lax enforcement of those norms during community festivals like the Stampede.

6   *It is therefore hypothesized that participation in the Calgary Stampede (as measured by bar behaviour) will be high among middle-class people and low among lower-class people. More specifically, patrons of middle-class drinking establishments during the Calgary Stampede will exhibit more festival-related aggressive/expressive behaviour than patrons of lower-class drinking establishments.*

Background and Methods

7   The annual Calgary Stampede features a rodeo and related "cowboy" themes as central attractions. There is also the usual midway (larger than most), and street dancing is common. In addition, there is a general relaxation of formal social controls, with fewer arrests than usual of ambitious tipplers, "car-cowboys", women of ill repute, and the like.

8   The Stampede is actively promoted in local and national mass media and has become reasonably well known throughout most of North America. As a result, it attracts a generous influx of tourists from the western United States. Since its founding in 1912, it has undergone the usual transition from agricultural fair and exhibition to urban commercial carnival which has accompanied the rapid growth of cities. The population of Calgary has increased from about 20,000 in 1912 to around 350,000 in 1966. Symbolic of this transition was the new "salute to petroleum" theme in 1966, which brought a large and expensive petroleum exhibit to the Stampede grounds. The Western Cowboy and farm themes are still present, but they are somewhat obscured by the many diverse features of the contemporary festival. In 1966, attendance exceeded 600,000 establishing a record.

9   In order to study one important aspect of the festival behaviour, nine beer parlours and cocktail lounges[7] — representing a cross-section of social-class-related drinking establishments in Calgary — were visited on two separate evenings during Stampede Week. I had gained some knowledge previously of the social class characteristics and behavioural patterns of customers usually found in these establishments through periodic visits in the year prior to the Stampede festival. During this year I had casually observed behaviour in all of these bars in the process of searching for a "shorthand" method of discovering social class structure in Calgary. That is, as other researchers have suggested, bars are an effective informal index of the social structure in which they exist.[8] In this connection, each of the drinking establishments was visited on at least three different occasions, including both weekdays and Saturdays.

10   The establishments selected for study are located in the central business district, as well as the surrounding fringe area, or "Zone-in-transition", which contains the cheaper hotels and entertainment areas

found in most medium-to-large cities in North America. This fringe area, which includes Calgary's priority urban renewal project, is populated by economically-deprived people. Unlike many older industrial cities, Calgary's ecological pattern also includes deprived areas in what would normally be "affluent" sectors of other cities. Thus, in areas equidistant from the city centre can be found *nouveau riche* suburbs as well as deprived and ramshackle neighbourhoods. The two types are, of course, separated, and the annexation by the city of Calgary of formerly rural and presently deprived communities largely account for this ecological anomaly.

11   The bars that were visited were chosen both because of my knowledge of their usual social composition and activities and because of their proximity to the Stampede Grounds, thus assuring maximum sample of celebrants. The sample was then divided into "class" groups as follows: two upper-class, three middle-class, and four lower-class. The definition of the social class identity of the bars is admittedly subjective and informal but, I believe, valid.

12   The upper-class establishments are usually patronized by the elite oil and ranching group as well as the *nouveau riche* and the occasional white-collar couple celebrating an anniversary. The middle-class bars are patronized by clerical workers, small businessmen, and generally middle-range employees of the larger local firms, with occasional labourers drifting in. The lower-class bars are the clearest in definition. They are patronized by service personnel, labourers, winos, and deprived Indians as well as by members of newly-arrived immigrant groups. The class distribution of bars in the sample was "biased" toward the lower-status groups. Calgary has a higher proportion of white-collar and professional workers than most cities and if the choice of bars had been based on this consideration, only two or three lower-class bars would have been included. My knowledge of composition and activities of the lower-class bars, however, was greater than that of the middle- and upper-class bars and the choice was made accordingly.

13   Being rather conservative with respect to confirming our hypothesis, we selected two evenings in which cross-class interaction could reasonably be expected to be maximized: namely, the first night of Stampede week, and the night before the final day of festivities. We reasoned that these evenings, unlike the "in-between" nights, would reveal the most frantic collective search for gratifications and, if only accidentally, result in cross-class contacts. The anticipation of festivities is so great in Calgary during the few days prior to the Stampede that the first "green light" day witnesses the greatest crowds, both at the rodeo grounds and in the bars. The last day is perceived as the "last chance"; it was assumed that celebrants would then attempt to "let loose" one last time.

14   We chose drinking establishments rather than other sites of festival activity for the following reasons:

(1) We felt that participant observation would be more easily facilitated in bars than "on the streets" or at the Stampede Rodeo grounds;
(2) It was reasonable to assume that inhibitions concerning cross-class interaction are more easily dissolved with the aid of alcoholic beverages;
(3) We theorized that excessive drinking represents a form of deviant behaviour which becomes "normal" and even goal-directed during many community festivals; and
(4) We enjoy beer.

15   Within the bars, we concentrated on:

(1) The apparent social class composition of patrons;
(2) The wearing of costumes suitable to the "Western cowboy theme" of the Calgary Stampede;
(3) The noise level (including the spontaneity and intent of expressive vocalization); and
(4) Physical and social interaction, including evidences of aggression and general themes of conversation.

Findings

16   *Lower-Class Establishments.* In three of the four beer parlours visited, activities could be described as "business as usual". Beer parlours in general are lower class, and the patrons appeared to be the same as those who frequent these establishments throughout the year. Most of the customers were dressed in their normal work clothes or service-trade uniforms. If anything, there were fewer patrons than usual.

17   Beer parlours normally abound in service personnel, labourers, marginal drifters, and members of economically-depressed minority groups, most of whom live within walking distance. Conversations generally consist of work problems, family problems, sex exploits, cars, dialogue with self (the drifters), and general backslapping and spontaneous camaraderie. Sex distinctions are maintained by segregating the men's parlour from "ladies and escorts", and fights between patrons erupt about once an hour. Police patrols outside of these bars are conspicuous at most times of the year.

18   During the evenings of observation only about one out of ten of the tipplers wore Western cowboy costume, and most of those who did were completely ignored by other patrons. The noise level was lower than usual. There were virtually no "yippees" or "yahoos" or other shouts of the sort commonly associated with rodeos. Social interaction was quite normal, and there were fewer than the usual number of fights between patrons. None of the conversation overheard

dealt even remotely with the Calgary Stampede. Two patrons whom we questioned specifically about the Stampede indicated that they "couldn't care less", and that the Stampede was "a big fraud". One of these, a loner wearing the service-personnel uniform of a local firm, suggested that if he had his way, he would abolish the Stampede because it interfered with his usual drinking activities by "draining" the number of friends he usually found at the bar. When questioned specifically about this, he responded that during Stampede, "they just stay home". The other patron, a travelling resident of a neighbouring province, exclaimed that all he wanted was peace and quiet and he just wished he "had all the money that is spent on the phony Stampede".

19   The most interesting pattern was the maintenance of sex segregation. In Calgary, as in some other Canadian cities, beer parlours are divided by license into rooms for "men" and for "ladies and escorts". During the Stampede the legal ban against an "open" drinking establishment was lifted. However, patrons of three of the four lower-class establishments sampled continued their usual segregated drinking. In fact, several of us were specifically barred from entering the "ladies and escorts' " sections of these bars; and we observed that at least eight of every ten males were in the "men's" section, leaving a more than usual surplus of females in the "ladies and escorts' " section.

20   The only evidence of unusual behaviour was the greater than usual number of "streetwalker" prostitutes in all four of the beer parlours. During a usual evening about one in ten females in these pubs is a prostitute, whereas one in five appeared to be a prostitute during the evenings under study. We concluded that these girls were present for two reasons: (1) some may have anticipated that there would be more "tricks" in the lower-class pubs on the assumption that "slumming" parties would gravitate toward lower-class areas; and (2) some may have been excluded from middle-class establishments by bouncers hired for the occasion, or may have been discouraged by the general confusion of such places at Stampede time.

21   In the fourth beer parlour, patterns of behaviour deviated more from the usual daily routine. About half of the customers were in the Stampede "spirit". This included appropriate costumes, spontaneous "yippees" and "yahoos", physical interstimulation (e.g., back-slapping), cross-sex interaction in the form of indiscriminate necking, and conversations characterized by expressive pleasure-seeking themes such as "sex in the office", "I'll get that bastard (boss)", "let's really rip tonight", "how's about a gang-bang", and the like. The other half of the customers behaved like the patrons of the other three lower-class establishments, but there was very little evidence of any cross-class interaction between them and patrons of different status back-

grounds. Apparently the fourth beer parlour differed from the others because of its proximity to the central "high-class" entertainment core of Calgary and to the Rodeo Grounds. Accidental "drifting" seemed to account for the disruption of normal business. Certainly, this conclusion is reasonable in the light of the following observations of middle-class drinking places.

22 *Middle-Class Establishments.* Two of the three middle-class drinking establishments were cocktail lounges and the other was a beer parlour in a relatively plush hotel. Since the legal requirements for a lounge generally distinguish the "haves" from the "have nots" in Canada, it is not surprising that the majority of customers at Stampede time were apparently middle class. Nevertheless, the middle class constituted a higher percentage than usual at these places. Many of the patrons were frequent and accepted visitors. But some were out-of-towners whose class identification depended on affluent costuming and the spontaneity with which they related to and were accepted by the "regulars". Absent was the usual smattering of blue-collar workers who tend to drift into these bars and are tolerated so long as they "behave themselves".

23 At least 90 per cent of the patrons in these establishments wore cowboy and Western costumes. It is interesting to note that we were consistently ridiculed for not being dressed in similar costumes (hopefully, this will increase our research sophistication in the future although we still may not be able to afford cowboy outfits). The noise level in these middle-class establishments was almost intolerable. There were dozens of spontaneous "yippees" and "yahoos" competing with each other; and verbal and physical stimulation such as males clapping each other on shoulders and couples necking indiscriminately was virtually universal. From the conversation we overheard, we gathered that the collective search for sensate gratifications was extensive. Most of the customers were obviously well along the continuum from sobriety to inebriation. The majority of the table groupings seemed to consist of people who worked in the same office, with executive types freely interacting with secretaries and sundry female assistants. In spite of this clustering, however, there was considerable table-hopping; and tourists were quickly assimilated by locals who seemed ebullient about showing them a good time. For example, a rather lost looking "out-of-towner" who wandered into one of the bars wearing expensive cowboy garb was invited by one of the local celebrants to "come join us, pardner". He was immediately introduced to a newly-acquired "harem" of girls sitting at the table. In another case, a jubilant couple from a neighbouring province invited themselves to a table and were immediately accepted as friends. In this latter case, all of the celebrants, including the visitors, whipped off to a party together. Even in the one middle-class beer parlour

there was absolutely no sex segregation and customers took full advantage of the temporary freedom of cross-sex interaction in contrast to the more highly segregated patterns observed in the lower-class establishments.

24   The prostitutes at the middle-class bars were the more sophisticated call-girl type. Streetwalkers and lower-class revellers generally were barred from entering these establishments by guards and bouncers stationed at all entrances. The few streetwalkers who wandered in seemed confused by the chaos and shortly departed without seriously attempting to solicit "tricks". We concluded that even during community festivals middle-class people tend to be endogamous in their deviate behaviour.

25   *Upper-Middle-Class Establishments.* The two cocktail lounges visited are located in Calgary's most plush and reputable hotels. We had not formulated hypotheses about expected behaviour patterns of patrons in these lounges but did expect that emotional expressive release encouraged during Stampede week would not so directly affect relatively elite members of the community. Actually, the two cocktail lounges throughout the year cater to both upper-middle-class and upper-class customers who for various reasons are not drinking in their private clubs. Our expectation was based on the premise that upper-class people, similar in some ways to members of the lower class in terms of assured status and spontaneity, manage to minimize inhibitions against deviant behaviour in everyday life, and consequently generally engage more in tension-release behaviour.

26   Our speculation was largely confirmed. Although there was a higher proportion of costumed patrons than in the lower-class beer parlours (about 25 per cent), there was very little noise or celebration. Again, it was generally a picture of "business as usual". The costumed customers who were attempting to stimulate behaviour more in keeping with the festival soon became discouraged by the lack of spontaneous emotional contagion and wandered out to seek more gratifying places. We overheard one member of such a group exclaim (with disappointment and disgust), "Let's blow this joint—it's like a graveyard." He was a member of a group of three, all of whom were elaborately costumed and obviously disappointed by the lack of conviviality. He specifically pointed to me as I was jotting down notes and exclaimed, "Jesus, he's working at a time like this!"

Conclusion

27   Observations of behaviour in drinking establishments during the Calgary Stampede confirmed our initial hypothesis. Middle-class customers were obviously engaging in more spontaneous expressive behaviour than either lower- or upper-class patrons. The Stampede week therefore seems more "functional" for people who tend to be in-

hibited in their daily lives and look forward to the "green light" of tolerated deviance during a community festival.

28   We cannot, of course, conclude that our findings suggest similar selective factors relating to participation in all community festivals. As we suggested earlier, the appeal of a festival probably depends on variations in the nature of social class structure of various communities. More specifically, festival participation may depend on the rigidity of the class structure and the extent to which ventilation of frustrations is inhibited and punished through formal social control. For example, we would expect that members of a lower social class group or a minority group who are systematically exploited and punished for deviant behaviour, would participate in "legitimate" community festivals to a much greater extent than found in the present study. We suggest that such situations might include the separate Negro parade and festivities during the Mardi Gras of New Orleans and the widespread "peasant" participation in Rio de Janeiro's "Carnival".

29   The findings suggest that community festivals held in cities such as Calgary reflect social class structure but do not "function" to reinforce social solidarity of members of different social class status groups. The Calgary Stampede, according to our observations, is a middle-class "binge", suggesting that even socially-approved deviant behaviour is endogamous. In a sense, the Calgary Stampede does serve to partially invert social class structure by allowing middle-class celebrants to indulge in the spontaneous and aggressive behaviour permitted to members of the lower class throughout the year. Members of the lower class, if our sample is any indication, view the contrived Stampede as frivolous and phony and apparently attempt to avoid being contaminated by the festivities.

Notes

1. Kingsley Davis, *Human Society* (New York: The Macmillan Co., 1949), 350.

2. Ralph H. Turner and Lewis Killian, *Collective Behavior* (Englewood Cliffs, N.J.: Prentice-Hall, 1957), 155.

3. See, for example, Durward Pruden, "A Sociological Study of a Texas Lynching", *Studies in Sociology*, Vol. 1, No. 1 (1963) 3–9; Howard Odum, *Folk, Region and Society: Selected Papers of Howard W. Odum*, Catherine Jocher, *et al.*, editors and arrangers (Chapel Hill: The University of North Carolina Press, 1964), 37–38; E.V. Essien-Udom, *Black Nationalism*, (Chicago: University of Chicago Press, 1962); and R.J. Ossenberg, "The Conquest Revisited: Another Look at Canadian Dualism", *The Canadian Review of Sociology and Anthropology*, Vol. 4, No. 4, (November, 1967), 201–218.

4. Turner and Killian, *op. cit.*, 153–154.

5. William Caudill, "Observations on the Cultural Context of Japanese Psychiatry", in Marvin K. Opler, ed., *Culture and Mental Health* (New York: The Macmillan Company, 1959), 218–219.

6. David, *op. cit.*, 355; Turner and Killian, *op. cit.*, 153.

7. Distinctions are made in Calgary between "beer parlours", which may only serve beer, and "licensed lounges", which may serve an alcoholic beverage, including beer.

8. See, for example, John Dollard, "Drinking Mores of the Social Classes", in *Alcoholic Studies and Society* (Yale University, Center of Alcoholic Studies, 1954), esp. 96, and Marshall B. Clinard, *Sociology of Deviant Behavior* (New York: Holt, Rinehart and Winston, 1963), 331–332.

Questions on Content

1   What traditional assumptions about different social groups' participation in community festivals does Ossenberg question? What view does Ossenberg propose?

2   Why does Ossenberg study bar behaviour?

3   How does Ossenberg make his study of bar behaviour?

4   What are the major characteristics of bar behaviour in "lower-class" establishments? In "middle-class" establishments? In "upper-middle-class" establishments?

5   What conclusions does Ossenberg draw about social groups' participation in the Calgary Stampede? What general conclusions about people's participation in community festivals does he suggest? Do you agree with Ossenberg's analysis? Why or why not?

Questions on Structure and Technique

1   Why does Ossenberg use "socio-economic class" as his principle of division? Are there any other principles of division Ossenberg could have chosen to investigate his hypothesis? What principles of division might be used to analyse the general subject of bar behaviour?

2   What is Ossenberg's definition of an "upper-class establishment"? A "middle-class establishment"? A "lower-class establishment"? What other examples of formal definitions can you find? What purposes do these definitions serve in the context of the whole study?

3   What subcategories of people are identified under "lower-class establishments"? Under "middle-class establishments"? Under "upper-middle-class establishments"?

4   What specific features of organization and development indicate that Ossenberg's study is an example of writing in the social sciences? What words and phrases that belong to the specialized vocabulary of social scientists does Ossenberg use? What words and phrases belong to the vocabulary of bar patrons?

5   What specific details and examples does Ossenberg include in his analysis that make this writing entertaining as well as informative for readers?

Suggestions for Writing

1   In the light of your own experiences, write a classification analysis of bar behaviour. You may choose to adapt Ossenberg's main classifications to your own thesis, or you may use some other principle of division which is appropriate to your observations.

2   Write a classification analysis of people attending an event that Ossenberg would define as a "community festival," based on your close observation of their participation in the event.

JOHN D. HARBRON

John D. Harbron (b. 1924), a foreign affairs analyst for the Thomson Newspaper Group, draws on his authoritative knowledge and personal interest in ships for this technical classification analysis essay on "Modern Icebreakers" first published in the popular journal Scientific American. *After graduating from the University of Toronto with B.A. and M.A. degrees and studying at the University of Havana, Harbron served as an officer in the Royal Canadian Navy. He taught naval history at the Royal Roads Canadian Services College in Victoria, B.C., from 1948 to 1951. In 1953, he retired from the Navy with the rank of Lieutenant-Commander following service in the Korean War. Harbron then began a distinguished career in journalism, working for* Business Week, Executive *magazine, and the* Toronto Telegram *before joining the Thomson organization. He is also the author of* Communist Ships and Shipping *(1963) and* Canada Without Quebec *(1977) and recipient of several significant awards including the Maria Moors Cabot Medal of the Columbia University Graduate School of Journalism.*

MODERN ICEBREAKERS

1   A substantial fraction of the world's seaborne commerce, particularly in the waters of North America and northern Europe, moves in the high latitudes where ice is an impediment for several months of the year. The nations engaged in such commerce deal with this impediment with a fleet of about 100 icebreakers, which require for their difficult task not only highly specialized construction but also unusual techniques of seamanship. It seems likely that the exploitation of resources such as oil in several regions in the high latitudes will intensify the demands on the icebreakers and their crews in the coming decades.

2   The distinctive features of an icebreaker are its shape, its strong bow, its machinery and its propellers. In shape the icebreaker is characteristically short in length and wide in beam, displaying therefore a stubby profile. The shape is accentuated in modern icebreakers built in Finland, whose shipyards have turned out some 60 percent of the world's fleets, by the piling up of the bridge and the crew's quarters above the deck. This design creates space in the hull for the sturdy main engines, the auxiliary engines and other machinery and the propeller shafts.

3   A look at an icebreaker in profile when the ship is out of the water would reveal another feature of the shape, namely that the draft is

quite shallow at the bow, sloping to a greater depth amidships. This shape is made necessary by the fact that an icebreaker does much of its work not by driving head on into the ice but by riding up on it, so that the increasing weight soon causes the ice under the bow to break. The ship's unusual width contributes to the success of the stratagem by making the weight compact. The design also reduces the strains put on the hull by the fact that the ship is in effect repeatedly running aground.

4   Understandably a vessel doing this kind of work needs a bow that is thick, made typically of steel plate that is about five centimeters (two inches) thick and strongly braced with steel structural members. The hull is also reinforced with thick plate all along the waterline because that area will be often in contact with ice or struck by floes that have been broken loose by the action of the bow. At one time many icebreakers had a weakness in that the welds between the steel plates tended to corrode and fail. Workers at the foundry in the Rautaruukki primary steel mill in Finland developed a microalloyed steel in which the content of manganese, sulfer and silicon was limited compared with conventional steels. The welds in this plate have proved to be resistant to the low-temperature seawater in which icebreakers usually operate.

5   The propulsion machinery of an icebreaker faces severe demands arising from the extreme variations of load on the engines between the times when the ship is breaking ice and the times when it is backing off for another run or is operating at a forward speed in open water. To meet the heavier demands the engines are designed to reach full speed rapidly. In contrast, the engines of a conventional vessel work up slowly to full speed and could be damaged by having to develop maximum power rapidly. The icebreaker's engines must be robust, reliable and able to deliver full power over a range of revolutions. They also must be economical in fuel consumption, since the ship is often operating for extended periods in areas that are remote from fuel supplies.

6   In the days of steam the icebreaker had reciprocating steam engines. Now the diesel-electric system predominates. In these vessels diesel engines power electric generators, and the electricity runs the motors that turn the propellers. A few icebreakers with nuclear power have been built by the U.S.S.R, beginning in 1957 with the *Lenin*. The nuclear reactor in such a vessel is a source of heat for generating steam that runs turbines. Nuclear power is advantageous when an icebreaker is likely to do much of its work in areas remote from fueling stations, such as the high Arctic regions of the U.S., Canada and the U.S.S.R., but otherwise it cannot compete economically with diesel-electric systems.

7   An icebreaker may have as many as four propellers. If there are four, it is likely they will be "wing propellers," meaning that they are

mounted on the sides of the ship, two near the stern and two near the bow. Bow propellers work well in first-year ice, that is, ice that has built up in a single winter and is not more than about 30 centimeters (12 inches) thick. (In some places, such as the Canadian Arctic, first-year ice is much more formidable, attaining a thickness of as much as two meters.) The bow propellers draw water from under the ice, weakening the support of the ice sheet and causing pieces of it to break off. Then the propellers wash water and ice away from the bow of the ship, facilitating forward progress. Reversed, they help the ship to move astern, thereby increasing its maneuverability. Bow propellers have proved to be useless in Arctic and Antarctic waters. The Arctic ice is too hard and the Antarctic ice is too thick to be affected by their action.

There is no single answer to the number of stern propellers an icebreaker should have. The amount of propulsion they must deliver depends on the severity of the ice conditions where the ship is likely to operate. Several types of icebreaker with twin shafts, including the U.S.S.R.'s *Moskva* class in the 1960's and the Canadian Coast Guard's *R* class in the 1970's, have had a good deal of trouble with bent and broken propeller blades and fractured propeller shafts.

One answer to this problem has been to build icebreakers with three propellers, one in the conventional position at the middle of the stern and two on the wings. This configuration too has had trouble in the two icebreakers of the U.S. Coast Guard's *Polar* class. One reason apparently is that because of the dual role of these ships (to break ice in the Arctic and to serve as supply and research vessels in the Antarctic) they have too much shaft horsepower for the size of their hull. The result is a chronic vibration of the hull. Each vessel has 60,000 shaft horsepower (more than any non-nuclear icebreaker), 42,000 from the gas-turbine engine driving the main shaft for breaking ice and 18,000 from diesel-electric engines driving the two wing propellers for running in open water, as on the long trip to the Antarctic.

Since an icebreaker is highly specialized in construction and faces demanding sea and ice conditions, operating one calls for special types of seamanship. Examples are the two modes of operation in ice, known formally as the continuous mode and the ramming mode. In the continuous mode the ship moves steadily ahead at a speed of from three to five knots through ice that is as much as 1.5 meters (five feet) thick. The technique works if the ice is fairly level and offers only average resistance to the ship. Such conditions are normally encountered in several areas where icebreakers operate regularly, including the Gulf of Bothnia, the Gulf of Finland, parts of the Russian Arctic and the Canadian Arctic, the Great Lakes and the St. Lawrence Seaway.

11   In the ramming mode the ship rides up on the ice. When the ice breaks and the vessel is again level in the water, it is backed off several times its length and then driven forward to ride up on the ice sheet again. The technique has to be applied when the ice is notably thick, hard or irregular in surface form.

12   Yet another challenge to seamanship comes when the ship gets stuck in the ice, a not unusual occurrence even though the vessel is designed to break ice. (The *Polar Sea* of the U.S. Coast Guard was embarrassingly beset in the Chukchi Sea north of Alaska from February 18 to May 13, 1981. During much of that time the Coast Guard made the best of the situation by redesignating the ship as a floating research station under the label "Polar Sea Drift Project '81.") Having propellers at both ends of the ship can be helpful by increasing the vessel's maneuverability so that it is less likely to become icebound or has a better chance of breaking free. Another technique still in use on some older icebreakers is heeling, that is, causing the ship to rock from side to side by pumping water or fuel oil back and forth between heeling tanks on opposite sides of the craft. With trimming tanks fore and aft the ship can similarly be made to rock from bow to stern.

13   On more modern vessels the heeling technique is being replaced by an air-bubbling system developed and patented by Wärtsilä, a Finnish shipbuilding firm that is the world's largest builder of icebreakers. The aim of the system is to reduce friction between the hull and the ice or snow. Compressed air is forced through a series of nozzles at intervals near the bottom of the ship. When the air rises along the hull in the form of bubbles, it creates a strong current of water and air that forms a lubricating layer between the hull and the ice. At low speeds (less than two knots) the system reduces friction to about half of what it would be otherwise. As the speed of the ship increases, the effectiveness of the air-bubbling system diminishes, but even at five knots the friction is reduced by about 15 percent.

14   Most people think of the ice covering the sea as being a fairly homogeneous sheet varying mainly in its thickness. Actually it is found in formations ranging from the impenetrable shelf ice of the Antarctic (some of it 100 years old) to the rough polar packs of the high Arctic and the winter-only ice of the Baltic Sea passages, the Great Lakes and the St. Lawrence Seaway. The people concerned with operating icebreakers have to take these many varieties of ice into account.

15   Until about 1966 the U.S., Canadian and Russian government agencies involved with shipping in the Arctic and the Antarctic employed only four rather broad classifications of ice formations: new, young, winter and polar. As the number of the icebreakers increased and the means of determining ice conditions expanded to include surveys by aircraft and photographs from satellites, such generalizations proved to be inadequate for the crews that had to function successfully in

icebreaking work. Now all the nations concerned with major shipping in areas where ice may be a factor maintain detailed and constantly changing definitions of ice formations. The definitions that follow are from Canadian sources, although the other nations recognize parallel categories.

16   The definitions begin with "open water," which is described in the *Sea Atlas of Canada* as "water in which the concentration of ice does not exceed one tenth of the total area." Another major formation is first-year ice, meaning ice that has persisted for less than a year. Second-year ice has survived one summer's melting and is building up again in the following winter. Multiyear ice has remained in place through two summers or more.

17   In addition to these kinds of ice there are other formations that can make an icebreaker's passage either difficult or impossible, depending on the extent of the ice structure. One is rafted ice, in which one sheet of ice has been overriden by another sheet or more than one. Another is hummocked ice, in which ice that has broken is forced upward by pressure and forms hillocks. A ridge is a wall of broken ice that has been formed by the collision of ice masses; its base can be as much as 15 meters below the surface. Finally, snow that has settled on an ice formation can considerably decrease an icebreaker's efficiency.

18   In general such regions as the Gulf of Bothnia, the Gulf of Finland, the Gulf of St. Lawrence, the Great Lakes and the northwest and northeast coasts of the U.S. have from 30 to 90 centimeters (about one foot to three feet) of ice between the middle of December and the middle of May. Severer conditions are faced by icebreakers in the Canadian Arctic and in the high-latitude waters of the U.S.S.R. and the Scandinavian countries, where efforts are made to maintain shipping for at least part of the ice season. Finland keeps the Gulf of Bothnia open throughout the year because of the need to move goods out of the country's many ports there.

19   A point that can be made about the Canadian Arctic also applies to other major ice areas. The Canadian Arctic extends some 3,000 miles from Baffin Island to the North Slope of Alaska and about 2,000 miles northward from Canada's Arctic coastline to the North Pole, with major passages and islands in between. The region has an archipelago of diverse ice-covered areas. Each area has its own historic record of ice, wind, sea-condition and other climatologic factors, and any one of them can change unpredictably in a particular season of icebreaker operations. T.C. Pullen, a retired captain in the Canadian Navy and a specialist on icebreakers, has summarized the situation as follows: "We encounter heavy ice where intelligence has reported ice-free conditions, providing yet another lesson in what

Arctic marine operations are like, namely that they are not necessarily what we should assume to be the case."

20   The variations in the ice give rise to variations in the design of icebreaking vessels. Again the Canadian standards provide a guide. A few years ago the Canadian government published its Canadian Arctic Shipping Pollution Prevention Regulations, which combine a concern for the environmental safety of the Arctic as increasingly larger ships are active in it and an effort to specify the capability of Arctic ships. The regulations define icebreakers and their cousins, ships strengthened for ice, in a range from Arctic Class 1 to Arctic Class 10.

21   A few examples will indicate the gradient embodied in the regulations. A vessel of Arctic Class 3 can maintain a speed of three knots through ice 0.9 meters (three feet) thick. A vessel of Class 7 can maintain a speed of three knots in the continuous mode through ice 2.1 meters (seven feet) thick.

22   The icebreakers of the Baltic type built mainly in Finland and the U.S.S.R. to work in regions with one-year ice can be identified under the regulations as vessels of Class 3 or Class 4. They would not meet the more demanding requirements for a large icebreaker operating throughout the year in the Canadian Arctic. Vessels of this kind are in Arctic Class 8. Canada plans to build its first icebreaker of this class but has not yet begun construction.

23   The most powerful icebreakers today are the nuclear-powered Russian sister ships *Artika* (recently renamed *Leonid Brezhnev*) and *Sibir*, which can be estimated as in the range from Class 5 to Class 7 under the Canadian regulations. Each is a vessel of 35,000 tons' displacement (equivalent to the weight of the ship and everything that it is carrying) with 75,000 shaft horsepower. Another nuclear icebreaker, the *Rossiya* (40,000 tons and an estimated 100,000 shaft horsepower), is now under construction for the U.S.S.R. at the Wärtsilä shipyard in Helsinki.

24   The *Rossiya* will emerge from the shipyard without engines. It will then be towed to Leningrad for the installation of the nuclear power plant. The Russians have not revealed the particulars of these marine nuclear power plants and do not allow foreigners to visit their nuclear icebreakers.

25   The Antarctic icebreakers of the U.S., Argentina, Japan and West Germany are multipurpose vessels compared with the ones that operate in the Northern Hemisphere. The reason is that they must not only deal with ice but also travel long distances in open water to get to the Antarctic, where they function additionally as observation, research and supply ships. Accordingly they are fitted out with extra cabin space for the scientific workers, landing pads for short-range

helicopters that make reconnaissance flights over the ice, heavy deck cranes, cargo elevators and special holds for the supplies they carry to their nation's bases in the Antarctic.

26   An example of the type is the Argentine *Almirante Irizar*, built by Wärtsilä and commissioned in 1979. One of its special features is a helicopter "touch down" system made in Canada. It is designed to cope with the fact that a shallow-draft, stubby icebreaker can roll as much as 40 degrees in open water when the seas are heavy. A cable is lowered from the helicopter to a locking mechanism on the deck, which slowly draws the aircraft down to the level of the deck. By means of a track set in the deck the helicopter is then towed to its hangar. The vessel also has two 16-ton hydraulic cranes for transferring cargo to the shore, an electric towing winch fitted with tension controls (keeping the cable taut at all times when it is loaded) and capable of exerting a maximum pull of 60 tons, and an air-bubbling system.

27   The U.S.S.R. is the major operator of icebreakers and the only nation with nuclear-powered icebreakers in regular service. It is also the only country operating significant numbers of merchant ships with a limited capability for icebreaking. (Many countries operate merchant vessels with hulls strengthened for ice.) Among the Russian vessels are a number of multipurpose container ships with icebreaking capability (at about the level of Arctic Class 2) that can proceed on their own in moderate ice conditions if an icebreaker is not available. Typically they are ships of 18,000 dead-weight tons (the total carried load), shallow draft and an air-bubbling system. They can penetrate the large Siberian rivers flowing into the Arctic seas.

28   Russian icebreakers operate across the immense length of the northern sea route and also, during the ice season, in such peripheral bodies of water as the Gulf of Finland, the Baltic Sea, the Black Sea, the Caspian Sea and the Yenisei, Ob and Lena rivers. The most impressive icebreaker-convoy operations are in the Russian western Arctic, where fleets of commercial vessels are moving in increasing numbers from Murmansk through the Barents Sea and the Kara Sea to the Yenisei River estuary, where they continue upstream to the interior port of Dudinka that serves the timber and nickel-exporting Siberian city of Norilsk.

29   These integrated fleets function in the following way. Nuclear and diesel-electric icebreakers of the *Brezhnev, Kapitan Sorokin* and *Ermak* classes escort the container ships from Murmansk to the Yenisei estuary. The convoy may also include some European cargo ships, mainly British and Scandinavian vessels cleared under Russian ship classifications for navigation behind an icebreaker. At the Yenisei the nuclear icebreakers and the bigger conventional ones stand off the mouth of

the river as the shallow-draft icebreakers of the *Kapitan Sorokin* class continue on into the estuary to the point inland where the convoy is taken over by river icebreakers of the *Kapitan Chechkin* class. They are vessels of 4,490 shaft horsepower and extremely shallow draft (3.2 meters, or 10.5 feet). If the ice conditions are too severe for the river icebreakers and the convoy to proceed to Dudinka, the cargoes are unloaded onto "polar utility vehicles," that is, hovercraft that skim over the ice on a cushion of air. The return passage down the Yenisei and the escort back to Murmansk by the heavier icebreakers complete the journey.

30   It may be that the characteristics of the icebreaker of the future are being developed by a Canadian vessel recently put in service, the *Canmar Kigoriak* of Dome Petroleum Limited. (The first part of its name is an abbreviation for Canadian Marine Drilling Limited, Dome's shipping subsidiary; the second part is the Inuit name for the northern lights.) This Canadian-built vessel serves mainly in the Beaufort Sea to protect Dome's offshore drilling rigs against damage by ice and to assist the firm's high-Arctic fleet, which includes ice-strengthened drilling ships, tugs and self-propelled barges.

31   Among the distinctive features the *Canmar Kigoriak* has for coping with the severe ice conditions of Canada's western Arctic is a single propeller, which contrasts with the twin or triple screws of all other Canadian icebreakers. Its designers see this arrangement as a means of avoiding what they call "one of the main perils of twin- and triple-screw icebreakers, the constant milling of ice with the two outboard screws, which reduces propeller efficiency." The propeller is surrounded by a large protective structure that deflects large pieces of ice moving aft and harmlessly mills small ones. The ship also has bow and stern thrusters and an outsize rudder, which increases its maneuverability.

32   Another feature of the ship is a hull form that distinguishes it from all other icebreakers. Its spoon-shaped bow is meant to break thin ice with a minimum loss of energy. A special reamer is fitted where the bow meets the midsection; it is designed to dig a short distance into the ice, thereby providing a fulcrum that improves the ship's ability to turn. The vessel's capabilities are indicated by the owner's statement that so far it has penetrated first-year ice as thick as 1.73 meters, multiyear ice as thick as 10 meters and first-year ridges grounded in 13 meters of water.

33   The *Canmar Kigoriak* is also a prototype for a giant ship that Dome may build in the 1990's, an icebreaker-tanker of 200,000 deadweight tons. The plan is based on Dome's estimate that enough offshore oil will be found in the Beaufort Sea to justify marine transporters of this size to move it out. Only ships of such size and enormous power

will be equal to the task of operating year-round in the Northwest Passage.

34   If Canada's Arctic Class 8 icebreaker is built, it will be the largest non-nuclear icebreaker in the world. The *Polar 8*, which is its drawing-board name, would be 194 meters long, 32.2 meters wide and 13 meters deep. At 37,000 displacement tons and 100,000 shaft horse-power, the vessel would represent a substantial change in the standard formula for icebreaker design that relates displacement tonnage to shaft horsepower. In non-nuclear icebreakers a characteristic ratio is 15,000 displacement tons to 20,000 shaft horsepower, as in Wärtsilä's widely employed *Kapitan Sorokin* class now in service in Finland, the U.S.S.R. and Argentina. The *Polar 8* would be the first all-weather icebreaker capable of working in Arctic ice conditions that are too severe for the U.S. and Canadian icebreakers in service today.

Questions on Content

1   What is the purpose of icebreakers? Why are icebreakers increasing in importance?

2   What are the four distinctive features of icebreakers?

3   What unusual techniques of seamanship are required in the operation of an icebreaker?

4   Why is the knowledge of ice formations important in the design of icebreaking vessels? How are icebreakers classified?

5   What characteristics and capabilities will the icebreaker of the future have?

Questions on Structure and Technique

1   What sentence clearly established Harbron's subject in paragraph one? In what sentence is Harbron's thesis stated?

2   Harbron's analysis of the subject of modern icebreakers is divided into three major categories: distinctive features (paragraphs two through nine), techniques of seamanship (paragraphs ten through nineteen), and icebreaker designs (paragraphs twenty through thirty-four). What sub-categories are icebreakers' distinctive features divided into? What illustrations of icebreaker seamanship techniques does Harbron provide? How does Harbron classify icebreaker designs? What major illustrations of ice-breaker designs does he present?

3   In what paragraph does Harbron begin to bring his essay to a conclusion? Why is this conclusion effective?

4   The general purpose of Harbron's essay is to inform readers about modern icebreakers by means of an extended definition. Find examples of Harbron's use of description, illustration, comparison, contrast, and classification in individual paragraphs to achieve this purpose.

5   What specialized terms does Harbron define for his readers? What other examples of detailed definitions can you find?

Suggestions for Writing

1   Using the major categories of "distinctive features," "techniques of operation," and "variations in design," write an extended definition of one of the following: video cassette recorders, personal computers, vending machines, calculators, or microwave ovens.

2   Write a classification analysis of a common manufactured product that is useful for some specific purpose. Divide your subject into several categories or subclasses according to an appropriate principle of division (such as features, design, effectiveness, operation, size, etc.). Be sure to label, define, and illustrate each category or subclass so that your analysis supports your thesis in an effective and interesting manner.

MARGARET ATWOOD

Margaret Atwood (b. 1939) is a novelist and poet who has published ten books of poetry, six novels, two collections of short stories, and a half dozen other books including literary criticism. "Survival" is the introductory chapter to Survival: A Thematic Guide to Canadian Literature, *a critical analysis of Canadian fiction and poetry in which Atwood offers four basic categories, or "positions," as "a helpful method of approaching our literature." Atwood, who was born in Ottawa and grew up in Toronto, graduated from the University of Toronto in 1961 and received an M.A. degree from Radcliffe College, Harvard, in 1962. Atwood has taught and lectured at universities across Canada, and she has received many awards and prizes for her work, the most popular being her novels:* The Edible Woman *(1969),* Surfacing *(1972),* Lady Oracle *(1976),* Life Before Man *(1979),* Bodily Harm *(1981), and* The Handmaid's Tale *(1986), for which Atwood received her second Governor General's Award.*

SURVIVAL

When your love is a sour taste
in the mouth, become a matter
for apologies, survive.
. . .
When your face goes flat in
the silvered mirror, endure;
endure, if you can, and survive

— John Newlove, "If You Can"

It is the time of death
and the fear of never
having lived at all
crazes the young
when pigs that escaped slaughter
eat dozens of fermented
apples and charge drunken thru
empty woods
and huntsmen somewhere else
are learning the trade

— Al Purdy, "Autumn"

. . . Lionel was lonely. The months passed. Lionel was lonely. The months passed. They were too close to one another. Secretly Lionel wanted to climb a tree and watch his own funeral. He did not know this . . .

— Russel Marois, *The Telephone Pole*

I'm starting to feel sentimental
only when at home

in my sixty-dollar-a-month slum,
or to feel like a Canadian

only when kissing someone else's bum.

> — John Newlove, "Like a Canadian"

To find words for what we suffer,
To enjoy what we must suffer—
Not to be dumb beasts. . . .

. . . .

. . . We shall survive
And we shall walk

Somehow into summer. . . .

> — D.G. Jones, "Beating the Bushes:
> Christmas 1963"

1   I started reading Canadian literature when I was young, though I
didn't know it was that; in fact I wasn't aware that I lived in a country with any distinct existence of its own. At school we were being
taught to sing "Rule, Britannia" and to draw the Union Jack; after
hours we read stacks of Captain Marvel, Plastic Man and Batman
comic books, an activity delightfully enhanced by the disapproval of
our elders. However, someone had given us Charles G. D. Roberts'
Kings in Exile for Christmas, and I snivelled on my way quickly
through these heart-wrenching stories of animals caged, trapped and
tormented. That was followed by Ernest Thompson Seton's *Wild
Animals I Have Known*, if anything more upsetting because the
animals were more actual—they lived in forests, not circuses—and
their deaths more mundane: the deaths, not of tigers, but of rabbits.

2   No one called these stories Canadian literature, and I wouldn't
have paid any attention if they had; as far as I was concerned they
were just something else to read, along with Walter Scott, Edgar Allan
Poe and Donald Duck. I wasn't discriminating in my reading, and
I'm still not. I read them primarily to be entertained, as I do now.
And I'm not saying that apologetically: I feel that if you remove the
initial gut response from reading—the delight or excitement or simply the enjoyment of being told a story—and try to concentrate on
the meaning or the shape or the "message" first, you might as well
give up, it's too much like all work and no play.

3   But then as now there were different levels of entertainment. I read
the backs of Shredded Wheat boxes as an idle pastime, Captain Marvel
and Walter Scott as fantasy escape—I knew, even then, that wherever I lived it wasn't *there*, since I'd never seen a castle and the Popsicle
Pete prizes advertised on the comic book covers either weren't available in Canada, or cost more—and Seton and Roberts as, believe it

or not, something closer to real life. I *had* seen animals, quite a few of them; a dying porcupine was more real to me than a knight in armour or Clark Kent's Metropolis. Old mossy dungeons and Kryptonite were hard to come by where I lived, though I was quite willing to believe they existed somewhere else; but the materials for Seton's stick-and-stone artefacts and live-off-the land recipes in *Wildwood Wisdom* were readily available, and we could make them quite easily, which we did. Most of the recipes were somewhat inedible, as you'll see if you try Cat-tail Root Stew or Pollen Pancakes, but the raw ingredients can be collected around any Canadian summer cottage.

4   However, it wasn't just the content of these books that felt more real to me; it was their shapes, their patterns. The animal stories were about the struggle to survive, and Seton's practical handbook was in fact a survival manual: it laid much stress on the dangers of getting lost, eating the wrong root or berry, or angering a moose in season. Though it was full of helpful hints, the world it depicted was one riddled with pitfalls, just as the animal stories were thickly strewn with traps and snares. In this world, no Superman would come swooping out of the sky at the last minute to rescue you from the catastrophe; no rider would arrive post-haste with a pardon from the King. The main thing was to avoid dying, and only by a mixture of cunning, experience and narrow escapes could the animal — or the human relying on his own resources — manage that. And, in the animal stories at any rate, there were no final happy endings or ultimate solutions; if the animal happened to escape from the particular crisis on the story, you knew there would be another one later on from which it wouldn't escape.

5   I wasn't making these analytical judgments at the time, of course. I was just learning what to expect: in comic books and things like *Alice in Wonderland* or Conan Doyle's *The Lost World*, you got rescued or you returned from the world of dangers to a cozy safe domestic one; in Seton and Roberts, because the world of dangers was *the same* as the real world, you didn't. But when in high school I encountered — again as a Christmas present — something labelled more explicitly as Canadian Literature, the Robert Weaver and Helen James anthology, *Canadian Short Stories*, I wasn't surprised. There they were again, those animals on the run, most of them in human clothing this time, and those humans up against it; here was the slight mistake that led to disaster, here was the fatal accident; this was a world of frozen corpses, dead gophers, snow, dead children, and the ever-present feeling of menace, not from an enemy set over against you but from everything surrounding you. The familiar peril lurked behind every bush, and *I knew the names of the bushes*. Again, I wasn't reading this as Canlit, I was just reading it; I remember being

elated by some stories (notably James Reaney's "The Bully") and not very interested in others. But these stories felt real to me in a way that Charles Dickens, much as I enjoyed him, did not.

6   I've talked about these early experiences not because I think that they were typical but because I think that — significantly — they weren't: I doubt that many people my age had even this much contact, minimal and accidental though it was, with their own literature. (Talking about how this now makes me feel about 102, because quite a lot has changed since then. But though new curricula are being invented here and there across the country, I'm not convinced that the *average* Canadian child or high school student is likely to run across much more Canadian literature than I did. *Why* this is true is of course one of our problems.)

7   Still, although I didn't read much Canadian writing, what I did read had a shape of its own that felt different from the shapes of the other things I was reading. What that shape turned out to be, and what I felt it meant in terms of this country, became clearer to me the more I read . . . .

8   I'd like to begin with a sweeping generalization and argue that every country or culture has a single unifying and informing symbol at its core. (Please don't take any of my oversimplifications as articles of dogma which allow of no exceptions; they are proposed simply to create vantage points from which the literature may be viewed.) The symbol, then — be it word, phrase, idea, image, or all of these — functions like a system of beliefs (it *is* a system of beliefs, though not always a formal one) which holds the country together and helps the people in it to co-operate for common ends. Possibly the symbol for America is The Frontier, a flexible idea that contains many elements dear to the American heart: it suggests a place that is *new*, where the old order can be discarded (as it was when America was instituted by a crop of disaffected Protestants, and later at the time of the Revolution); a line that is always expanding, taking in or "conquering" ever-fresh virgin territory (be it The West, the rest of the world, outer space, Poverty or The Regions of the Mind); it holds out a hope, never fulfilled but always promised, of Utopia, the perfect human society. Most twentieth century American literature is about the gap between the promise and the actuality, between the imagined ideal Golden West or City Upon a Hill, the model for all the world postulated by the Puritans, and the actual squalid materialism, dotty small town, nasty city, or redneck-filled outback. Some Americans have even confused the actuality with the promise: in that case Heaven is a Hilton hotel with a coke machine in it.

9   The corresponding symbol for England is perhaps The Island, convenient for obvious reasons. In the seventeenth century a poet called Phineas Fletcher wrote a long poem called *The Purple Island*, which

is based on an extended body-as-island metaphor, and, dreadful though the poem is, that's the kind of island I mean: island-as-body, self-contained, a Body Politic, evolving organically, with a hierarchical structure in which the King is the head, the statesmen the hands, the peasants or farmers or workers the feet, and so on. The Englishman's home as his castle is the popular form of this symbol, the feudal castle being not only an insular structure but a self-contained microcosm of the entire Body Politic.

10   The central symbol for Canada — and this is based on numerous instances of its occurrence in both English and French Canadian literature — is undoubtedly Survival, *la Survivance*. Like the Frontier and The Island, it is a multi-faceted and adaptable idea. For early explorers and settlers, it meant bare survival in the face of "hostile" elements and/or natives: carving out a place and a way of keeping alive. But the word can also suggest survival of a crisis or disaster, like a hurricane or a wreck, and many Canadian poems have this kind of survival as a theme; what you might call 'grim' survival as opposed to 'bare' survival. For French Canada after the English took over it became cultural survival, hanging on as a people, retaining a religion and a language under an alien government. And in English Canada now while the Americans are taking over it is acquiring a similar meaning. There is another use of the word as well: a survival can be a vestige of a vanished order which has managed to persist after its time is past, like a primitive reptile. This version crops up in Canadian thinking too, usually among those who believe that Canada is obsolete.

11   But the main idea is the first one: hanging on, staying alive. Canadians are forever taking the national pulse like doctors at a sickbed: the aim is not to see whether the patient will live well but simply whether he will live at all. Our central idea is one which generates, not the excitement and sense of adventure or danger which The Frontier holds out, not the smugness and/or sense of security, of everything in its place, which The Island can offer, but an almost intolerable anxiety. Our stories are likely to be tales not of those who made it but of those who made it back, from the awful experience — the North, the snowstorm, the sinking ship — that killed everyone else. The survivor has no triumph or victory but the fact of his survival; he has little after his ordeal that he did not have before, except gratitude for having escaped with his life.

12   A preoccupation with one's survival is necessarily also a preoccupation with the obstacles to that survival. In earlier writers these obstacles are external—the land, the climate, and so forth. In later writers the obstacles tend to become both harder to identify and more internal; they are no longer obstacles to physical survival but obstacles to what we may call spiritual survival, to life as anything more than a

minimally human being. Sometimes fear of these obstacles becomes itself the obstacle, and a character is paralyzed by terror (either of what he thinks is threatening him from the outside, or of elements in his own nature that threaten him from within). It may even be life itself that he fears; and when life becomes a threat to life, you have a moderately vicious circle. If a man feels he can survive only by amputating himself, turning himself into a cripple or a eunuch, what price survival?

13   Just to give you a quick sample of what I'm talking about, here are a few capsule Canadian plots. Some contain attempts to survive which fail. Some contain bare survivals. Some contain crippled successes (the character does more than survive, but is mutilated in the process).

Pratt: *The Titanic*: Ship crashes into iceberg. Most passengers drown.

Pratt: *Brébeuf and His Brethren*: After crushing ordeals, priests survive briefly and are massacred by Indians.

Laurence: *The Stone Angel*: Old woman hangs on grimly to life and dies at the end.

Carrier: *Is It The Sun, Philibert?* Hero escapes incredible rural poverty and horrid urban conditions, almost makes it financially, dies when he wrecks his car.

Marlyn: *Under The Ribs of Death*: Hero amputates himself spiritually in order to make it financially, fails anyway.

Ross: *As For Me and My House*: Prairie minister who hates his job and has crippled himself artistically by sticking with it is offered a dubious change of escape at the end.

Buckler: *The Mountain and the Valley*: Writer who has been unable to write has vision of possibility at the end but dies before he can implement it.

Gibson: *Communion*: Man who can no longer make human contact tries to save sick dog, fails, and is burned up at the end.

14   And just to round things out, we might add that the two English Canadian feature films (apart from Allan King's documentaries) to have had much success so far, *Goin' Down the Road* and *The Rowdyman*, are both dramatizations of failure. The heroes survive, but just barely; they are born losers, and their failure to do anything but keep alive has nothing to do with the Maritime Provinces or 'regionalism.' It's pure Canadian, from sea to sea.

15   My sample plots are taken from both prose and poetry, and from regions all across Canada; they span four decades, from the thirties to the early seventies. And they hint at another facet of Survivalism: at some point the failure to survive, or the failure to achieve anything beyond survival, becomes not a necessity imposed by a hostile outside world but a choice made from within. Pushed far enough, the obsession with surviving can become the will *not* to survive.

16   Certainly Canadian authors spend a disproportionate amount of time making sure that their heroes die or fail. Much Canadian writing suggests that failure is required because it is felt—consciously or unconsciously — to be the only 'right' ending, the only thing that will support the characters' (or their authors') view of the universe. When such endings are well-handled and consistent with the whole book, one can't quarrel with them on aesthetic grounds. But when Canadian writers are writing clumsy or manipulated endings, they are much less likely to manipulate in a positive than they are in a negative direction: that is, the author is less likely to produce a sudden inheritance from a rich old uncle or the surprising news that his hero is really the son of a Count than he is to conjure up an unexpected natural disaster or an out-of-control car, tree or minor character so that the protagonist may achieve a satisfactory *failure*. Why should this be so? Could it be that Canadians have a will to lose which is as strong and pervasive as the Americans' will to win?

17   It might be argued that, since most Canlit has been written in the twentieth century and since the twentieth century has produced a generally pessimistic or "ironic" literature, Canada has simply been reflecting a trend. Also, though it's possible to write a short lyric poem about joy and glee, no novel of any length can exclude all but these elements. A novel about unalloyed happiness would have to be either very short or very boring: "Once upon a time John and Mary lived happily ever after, The End." Both of these arguments have some validity, but surely the Canadian gloom is more unrelieved than most and the death and failure toll out of proportion. Given a choice of the negative or positive aspects of any symbol — sea as life-giving Mother, sea as what your ship goes down in; tree as symbol of growth, tree as what falls on your head — Canadians show a marked preference for the negative.

18   You might decide at this point that most Canadian authors with any pretensions to seriousness are neurotic or morbid, and settle down instead for a good read with *Anne of Green Gables* (though it's about an orphan . . .). But if the coincidence intrigues you — so many writers in such a small country, and *all with the same neurosis* — then I will offer you a theory. Like any theory it won't explain everything, but it may give you some points of departure.

19   Let us suppose, for the sake of argument, that Canada as a whole is a victim, or an "oppressed minority," or "exploited." Let us suppose in short that Canada is a colony. A partial definition of a colony is that it is a place from which a profit is made, but *not by the people who live there:* the major profit from a colony is made in the centre of the empire. That's what colonies are for, to make money for the "mother country," and that's what — since the days of Rome and, more recently, of the Thirteen Colonies—they have always been for.

Of course there are cultural side-effects which are often identified as "the colonial mentality," and it is these which are examined here; but the root cause for them is economic.

20   If Canada is a collective victim, it should pay some attention to the Basic Victim Positions. These are like the basic positions in ballet or the scales on the piano: they are primary, though all kinds of song-and-dance variations on them are possible.

21   The positions are the same whether you are a victimized country, a victimized minority group or a victimized individual.

22   *Position One: To deny the fact that you are a victim.*

> This uses up a lot of energy, as you must spend much time explaining away the obvious, suppressing anger, and pretending that certain visible facts do not exist. The position is usually taken by those in a Victim group who are a little better off than the others in that group. They are afraid to recognize they are victims for fear of losing the privileges they possess, and they are forced to account somehow for the disadvantages suffered by the rest of the people in the group by disparaging them. As in: "*I* made it, therefore it's obvious we aren't victims. The rest are just lazy (or neurotic, or stupid); anyway it's their own fault if they aren't happy, look at all the opportunities available for them!"
>
> If anger is felt by Victims in Position One, it is likely to be directed against one's fellow-victims, particularly who try to talk about their victimization.
>
> *The basic game* in Position One is "Deny your Victim-experience."

23   *Position Two:*

> To acknowlege the fact that you are a victim, but to explain this as an act of Fate, the Will of God, the dictates of Biology (in the case of women, for instance), the necessity decreed by History, or Economics, or the Unconscious, or any other large general powerful idea.
>
> In any case, since it is the fault of this large *thing* and not your own fault, you can neither be blamed for your position nor be expected to do anything about it. You can be resigned and long-suffering, or you can kick against the pricks and make a fuss; in the latter case your rebellion will be deemed foolish or evil even by you, and you will expect to lose and be punished, for who can fight Fate (or the Will of God, or Biology)?

Notice that:

1   The explanation *displaces* the cause from the real source of oppression to something else.

2   Because the fate cause is so vast, nebulous and unchangeable, you are permanently excused from changing it, *and also* from deciding how much of your situation (e.g. the climate) is unchangeable, how much can be changed, and how much is caused by habit or tradition or your own need to be a victim.

3   Anger, when present — or scorn, since everyone in the category is defined as inferior — is directed against both fellow-victims and oneself.

The basic game in Position Two is Victor/Victim.

24   *Position Three:*

To acknowledge the fact that you are a victim but to refuse to accept the assumption that the role is inevitable.

As in: "Look what's being done to me, and it isn't Fate, it isn't the Will of God. Therefore I can stop seeing myself as a *fated* Victim."

To put it differently: you can distinguish between the *role* of Victim (which probably leads you to seek victimization even when there's no call for it), and the *objective experience* that is making you a victim. And you can probably go further and decide how much of the objective experience could be changed if you made the effort.

This is a dynamic position, rather than a static one; from it you can move on to Position Four, but if you become locked into your anger and fail to change your situation, you might well find yourself back in Position Two.

Notice that:

1   In this position the real cause of oppression is for the first time identified.

2   Anger can be directed against the real source of oppression, and energy channelled into constructive action.

3   You can make real decisions about how much of your position can be changed and how much can't (you can't make it stop snowing; you can stop blaming the snow for everything that's wrong).

The basic game of Position Three is repudiating the Victim role.

25   *Position Four: To be a creative non-victim.*

Strictly speaking, Position Four is a position not for victims but for those who have never been victims at all, for ex-victims: those who have been able to move into it from Position Three because the external and/or the internal causes of victimization have been removed. (In an oppressed society, of course, you can't become an ex-victim — insofar as you are connected with your society — until the entire society's position has been changed.)

In Position Four, creative activity of all kinds becomes possible. Energy is no longer being suppressed (as in Position One) or used up for displacement of the cause, or for passing your victimization along to others (Man kicks Child, Child kicks Dog) as in Position Two; nor is it being used for the dynamic anger of Position Three. And you are able to accept your own experience for what it is, rather than having to distort it to make it correspond with others' versions of it (particularly those of your oppressors).

In Position Four, Victor/Victim games are obsolete. You don't even have to concentrate on rejecting the role of Victim, because the role is no longer a temptation for you.

26   (There may be a Position Five, for mystics; I postulate it but will not explore it here, since mystics do not as a rule write books.)

27   I devised this model not as the Secret of Life or the answer to everything (though you can apply it to world politics or your friends if you like), but as a helpful method of approaching our literature. It's a model about Victims for the simple reason that I found a superabundance of victims in Canadian literature. If I'd been looking at the nineteenth century English novel I'd have devised a table called Characteristics of Gentlemen; or if I'd been investigating American literature I would have found myself thinking about picaresque antiheroes; or if I'd been examining German Roman literature the result would probably have been a diagram of Doppelgängers. But stick a pin in Canadian literature at random, and nine times out of ten you'll hit a victim. My model, then, is a product of my Canadian literary experiences, not a Procrustean bed dreamed up in advance on which Canlit is about to be stretched. Now that I've traced its main outlines, I'll indicate briefly how I intend to use — and not to use — the model.

28   First, three general points about the model:

29   As I said, this is a verbal diagram: it is intended to be suggestive rather than totally accurate. But experience is never this linear: you're

rarely in any Position in its pure form for very long — and you may have a foot, as it were, in more than one Position at once.

30   What happens to an individual who has reached Position Three in a society which is still in Positions One or Two? (Not very nice things, usually.) Or, what happens to an individual who is a victim — like a Black in America — in a society which as a whole is *not* being oppressed by another society? (Again, not very nice things.) If, for instance, your society is in Position Two, perhaps you can't move through Position Three into Position Four except by repudiating your society, or at least its assumptions about the nature of life and proper behaviour. This may eventually make Position Four unreal for you: can you fiddle happily while Rome groans?

31   I've presented the model as though it were based on individual rather than social experience. Perhaps the terms would shift slightly if you were to substitute "we" or "our class" or "our country" for "I", and you'd then get a more complicated analysis of Canadian colonialism. My approach is more modest: it sketches a perspective from which Canadian *Literature* makes a surprising amount of sense.

32   Now, the model as it applies to writing:

33   I assume that *by definition* (mine, and you don't have to believe me) an author is in Position Four at the moment of writing, that is, the moment of creation — though the subject of his book may be Position Two, and the energy for it may come from Position Three. In the rest of his life he shifts around, like everyone else. (The analogous Position Four moment for the reader is not the time it takes to read a book, but the moment of insight — the time when the book makes sense or comes clear). And apart from that comment, I don't want to speculate about the state of authors' souls. Instead, just as in the Preface I proposed the fiction that the literature was being written by Canada, I here propose to regard novels and poems as though they were expressions of Positions, not of authors.

34   This method will, I hope, articulate the skeleton of Canadian literature. It will let you see how the bones fit together, but it won't put flesh on them. That is, the method provides a static dissection, rather than a dynamic examination of a process-in-motion. (A 'static' model facilitates classification. Trying out a dynamic model would also be interesting.)

35   Because I'm not handing out gold stars, I'll try not to do much evaluating — praising or censuring — of books according to this model. Although in real life Position Four may be preferable to Position Two, I do find a consistent and tough-minded Position Two poem preferable to a sloppy and unearned Position Four one. But I'll let you do that kind of evaluation for yourself.

36   You might try to decide whether, in any given work, the actual conditions of the characters' lives are sufficient to account for the doom and gloom meted out to them. Bare Survival isn't a central theme by accident, and neither is the victim motif; the land *was* hard, and we have been (and are) an exploited colony; our literature is rooted in those facts. But you might wonder, in a snowstorm-kills-man story, whether the snowstorm is an adequate explanation for the misery of the characters, or whether the author has displaced the source of the misery in their world and is blaming the snowstorm when he ought to be blaming something else. If so, it is a Position Two story: quite apart from the subject matter, it expresses a premature resignation and a misplaced willingness to see one's victimization as unchangeable.

37   And I'll point out too that a book can be a symptom or reflection of a Position (though not necessarily a bad book); or it can be a *conscious examination* of it (though not necessarily a good one.) The latter seems less fatalistic; a conscious examination of victim experience — including the *need* to be a victim — suggests a more realistic desire to transcend the experience, even if that is not made explicit in the book.

38   I've laid out the skeleton of Canadian literature in a way that was easy for me to manage and I hope will be easy for you to follow.

39   But before you plunge in here are some cheering thoughts:

40   Although negative stances towards theme and image predominate, there are also examples of escapes, positive changes, and revelations.

41   Much of our literature is a diagram of what is *not* desired. Knowing what you don't want isn't the same as knowing what you do want, but it helps.

42   Naming your own condition, your own disease, is not necessarily the same as acquiescing in it. Diagnosis is the first step.

43   Armed with these maxims, you should be proof against some of the murkier depths that lie ahead.

Questions on Content

1   What main theme did Atwood notice in her early reading of Canadian books? How did these books contrast with others she read?

2   What is the function of a "symbol," according to Atwood? What three symbols illustrate this function? What ideas does each one of these symbols represent?

3   What is the result of "a preoccupation with one's survival," according to Atwood? What is the "root cause" of this result?

4   What four "Basic Victim Positions" does Atwood divide "the colonial mentality" into? What are the main characteristics of each position?

5   What is the purpose of Atwood's "model"? Discuss its advantages and its disadvantages.

Questions on Structure and Technique

1   What is the basis for Atwood's analysis of Canadian literature? What are Atwood's definitions of "survival"? Which definition is the main one? Where does Atwood illustrate this definition? Why is this technique of definition effective?

2   What are Atwood's definitions of the "obstacles" to survival? How does Atwood illustrate these definitions? What one word does Atwood repeat as a "label" for "a preoccupation with the obstacles to . . . survival"?

3   What is Atwood's "partial definition" of the term "colony"? Is this a lexical (dictionary) definition? A stipulative one? How is Atwood's definition of colony related to the overall development of her essay's content? Its structure? Are Atwood's "Basic Victim Positions" causes or effects of "the colonial mentality"?

4   Atwood labels her classifications of "Basic Victim Positions" as "Position One," "Position Two," "Position Three," and "Position Four." What are Atwood's main definitions for each one of these classifications?

5   What is the primary purpose of Atwood's analysis? What words, phrases, and sentences indicate her purpose?

Suggestions for Writing

1   Atwood states: "I devised this model not as the Secret of Life or the answer to everything (though you can apply it to world politics or your friends if you like), but as a helpful method of approaching our literature." Take Atwood's suggestion (somewhat) seriously and write a classification analysis of your friends based on the definitions and characteristics of the four "Basic Victim Positions," illustrating each classification with specific details and examples. Keep in mind Atwood's indications of how "to use — and not to use — the model."

2   Analyse your own personal experiences in the light of Atwood's model of the four "Basic Victim Positions." Write a classification analysis of your experiences based on that model's definitions and characteristics.

3   In the light of Atwood's model of "Basic Victim Positions," write a classification analysis of the characters in a Canadian novel that you have read, illustrating your analysis with specific details and examples from the text.

WILDER PENFIELD

Wilder Penfield (1891-1976) was a professor of neurology and neurosurgery at McGill University from 1928 until 1960 when he retired. As founder and director of the Montreal Neurological Institute, Dr. Penfield pioneered its research in the mapping of the human brain. His writings on subjects related to his specialty have appeared in scientific books and journals. He has also expressed his broader concerns with education, language, philosophy, history, and politics, as well as science and medicine, in several books written for a general audience: No Other Gods *(1954), an historical novel about Moses;* The Torch *(1960), an historical novel about Hippocrates, the founder of medical science; and two books of essays,* The Second Career *(1963) and* Second Thoughts *(1970). In "Science, the Arts, and the Spirit," an essay from* Second Thoughts, *Dr. Penfield presents an analysis of the nature of human knowledge in which a basic classification is developed into a complex synthesis of ideas through the use of a variety of rhetorical modes and techniques.*

SCIENCE, THE ARTS, AND THE SPIRIT

1   Each of us, no doubt, is devoted to the common cause—the pursuit of truth — but each makes his own approach. There is in the world today a crying need of distant perspective. It is my purpose, therefore, to view science and the arts from a distance, discussing the frontier boundary that separates them. There is another frontier I propose to examine as well. It comes between the mind and the brain of man. And these two frontiers are related.

2   *Science* may be defined as knowledge of physical phenomena. *The arts* embrace all other forms of human knowledge. Thus, for the purpose of this discussion, the social sciences are not considered a part of science at all. They belong with the humanities, another name for the arts. By *the spirit*, I mean the mind of man. I am not referring to ghosts or superstitions or so-called extra-sensory perceptions. To define man's mind is not so easy. Indeed, this is the great unsolved problem to which I shall return presently.

3   Medicine, of course, deals with the whole man. It is partly concerned with the physical phenomena of the body, partly with mental phenomena. And so the doctor in the medical profession must forever straddle, as best he can, the great dichotomies — that between the arts and the sciences and that between the body and the mind.

4   Language and the arts are old, while science as we know it today is relatively young. It is true that in the fourth century before Christ, Hippocrates founded medical science, defying the unprovable hypotheses of the philosophers, and that Aristotle, shortly afterward, formulated natural science. But, in both cases, this was observational science, not experimental.

5   The whole course of history might have been changed, as Sir William Osler once remarked, had the Greeks discovered the experimental method. It is amusing to reflect on this remark. From the time of Galileo until now (only a little over three centuries), our scientists have transformed man's whole way of life, using the experimental method. In an equal length of time, the Greeks might well have mechanized society before the coming of the Roman Empire. Motor traffic would then have rumbled out over Roman roads and radio might have brought the news that Julius Caesar was crossing the Rubicon!

6   Would experimental science have saved civilization from decadence? That is a question to ask and to answer today. I think not. But there was at hand a new philosophy that might have done it. It was being taught in its purest form at the beginning of the Roman Empire by bands of hardy Christians: "Love . . . thy God . . . and . . . thy neighbour as thyself."[1] But, unfortunately, this basic Christian precept did not reach the Roman populace. It did, however, go out over the Roman roads to our barbarian ancestors. It did live on in the minds of men. It echoed down to us, with changing ecclesiastical overtones, through the dark centuries that followed the fall of Rome.

7   Other things came down to us and were picked up during the renaissance of Greek and Roman learning. This began in Europe during the fourteenth century after Christ. The arts revived then—law, philosophy, medicine, mathematics, painting, sculpture, architecture, literature, poetry, and athletics. But it was not until the seventeenth century that man seemed to stumble on something that the Greeks had missed, *the experimental method.*

8   In 1616 William Shakespeare died. At last, after a lapse of two thousand years, the arts in Europe had come abreast of the arts of ancient Greece! In that same year, the church challenged the new science. The Copernican system, it was announced in the Papal Court, was "dangerous to the faith." Galileo was summoned and forbidden henceforth to teach such heresy.

9   But this accomplished nothing, except to show that men in the church had overstepped the boundary of the spiritual. Truth was on the side of science. Man had already been "dethroned." He was no longer at the centre of a fancied universe created for his benefit. The earth was only a satellite. Men are used to the idea now, but it came as a shock to the people of Christendom.

10   Two hundred years later, they suffered another shock — Darwinian evolution. Man, "the wonder and the glory of the Universe," had descended from nothing more lordly than a monkey! Only gradually during the next hundred years did people come to accept the fact. And then, the final shock to society came in the twentieth century. Scientists dared to create the atom bomb. Men saw with horror that it was possible to destroy mankind and that his civilization would go with him. During the four centuries since the experimental method was introduced, philosophers and priests who ventured across the frontier into this field of physical science have been subjected to a new criticism and, sometimes, to correction.

11   As a result of all this, people of today, the old just as much as the young, are aware of a vast sense of confusion, apprehension, insecurity, and doubt. There is a tacit expectation that, since science has done so much, science will tell us what to think — about God and social morality and the beliefs that have brought men through their trials in the past. Men who are otherwise preoccupied with the business of living are wondering vaguely, "What is it that science has done to society?"

12   To gain the distant perspective we need, let us start at the beginning of time on this cooling planet. Earth, water, and gas came gradually to occupy the relative positions they hold today. Something like two and a half billion years ago, life is said to have appeared — first in simple cells and then in plants, and eventually in animals of ever-greater complexity. This was the biological evolution of Darwin. Forms of life that could survive continued as they were. Many became extinct. New forms kept appearing because of some accidental genetic variation. The fittest forms of new life survived and branching lines of independent evolution developed.

13   Finally — ten or twenty millions of years ago — the line of ancestors that was to end in *homo sapiens* appeared. His origin, according to the fossil evidence, was probably due to variations in the line of the larger apes. These "homonid" newcomers on the earth, as LeGros Clark calls them, lost the pointed teeth of the ape. They stood erect on two feet and had hands more suited to the manipulation of tools than to the climbing of trees. Most important of all, the skulls of these ancestors of ours evidently housed a growing brain.

14   Brain enlargement, it is suggested, made possible their survival in the highly competitive hunting conditions of Europe. Two types appeared. One of them, called Neanderthal Man because of a skeleton found in a cave in Neanderthal Valley in West Germany, had the largest brain of all. But for some reason, now unknown, Neanderthal man seems to have become extinct following the last Ice Age. That is to say, only about fifty thousand years ago. The other branch of the family, with a slightly smaller brain, was man, modern man. To

sum up in the words of LeGros Clark: "Skeletal remains of thirty thousand years ago [in France] are indistinguishable from modern Europeans." This end-result was produced, he concluded, by man's "adaptation to erect bipedalism, rapidly followed by an accelerated expansion of the brain."[2]

15   Now, if man has been what he is today for thirty thousand years, what on earth was he busy about all this time? One major achievement of tribal man was the development of spoken languages. This was of necessity a communal undertaking and it must have been slow. But man did it. He produced a different "tongue" in each of the different parts of the world.

16   The anatomical change responsible for this amazing step forward was this: Additional areas of cerebral cortex, not committed to sensory or motor function, had appeared in the human brain. In this uncommitted cortex and in the new neuronal structures of the brain, lay, hidden, man's potential talents. In the newly added areas of the brain, the keys had come to hand with which he could open his future kingdom and make possible social and intellectual evolution.

17   Thus, mothers began to teach the slowly developing mother tongue to man's children. They matured at a characteristically slow pace in caves and in the huts and the tents that man devised and fabricated with his clever fingers and strong arms. Teaching took the place of the instinctive race-memories that served other species on the earth. The morality and the discipline that parents had to demand in order to preserve those in the family circle developed quite naturally into the morality and the codes of law and the religious teaching of tribe and the nation.

18   Writing is a relatively recent advance. It appeared only five to six thousand years ago, about the time that the culture of wheat made city life possible in the river valleys of Egypt and Mesopotamia. The first writing on clay tablets had to do with trade. It developed rapidly from pictograph to alphabet. The discovery of how to navigate by oar and sail brought trade and communication to the Mediterranean and also farther away along the shores of India and China. This made sea ports possible and provided a means for the spread of culture. Ancient Greece was composed of a hundred competing city-states that lined the Mediterranean shores.

19   Thus, to summarize, language had to be developed first and with it, tribal intercourse. Then writing came in the wake of urbanization. Culture was spread by commerce and conquest. Only then, three and a half to four thousand years ago, did man begin to make a usable written record in which his story can be read. History replaced the buried sequences of fossil remains. From this time onward, the religious thinking of the Jews and the philosophy and art of Greece were saved for us. Although nine-tenths of the Greek papyrus manuscripts

may well have been lost, what remained of these written records formed the basis of the re-establishment of the arts in Europe.

20   But look back again, for a moment, to the beginning of the long, long story of biological evolution. Form altered, developing along a rising scale from cell to plant to animal to man. But, somewhere on the way up, *mind* appeared. It is an accompaniment of life and form, something not easy to describe. Call it a self-awareness, consciousness, mind, spirit.

21   Man has survived through thirty thousand years or so of existence, not because he was stronger than a lion or swifter than an antelope, but because of his mind. During the past four centuries since he discovered the experimental method, he has done more than survive. He has made himself the master of his fate. He has won back the right to be considered the centre of the universe, a universe that can be comprehended, not just imagined.

22   This is the achievement of the mind in the field of science. Science, to repeat the definition, is knowledge of physical phenomena. Whatever the mind is, it is not like the physical phenomena with which science deals. To understand the mind itself and the world of thought and reason is a problem to be studied beyond the field of Science, beyond the frontier, on the other side of the great dichotomy. Scientists will learn in time to understand the brain. But they have not begun to understand the mind. They have thrown no light on man's instinctive urge to worship a God.

23   It is interesting that young Charles Darwin referred, in his journal aboard H.M.S. *Beagle*, to "the primeval forests undefaced by the hand of man. No one," he mused "can stand in these solitudes . . . and not feel that there is more in man than the mere breath of his body."

24   I have studied the brain in conscious men and women, using all the scientific approaches that a modern neurological institute can provide. I have talked with them in the operating room, using local anaesthesia. With the brain exposed, I have measured its electrical activity and stimulated functional mechanisms when it could serve the patient's purpose. And all the while, these patients have used their own minds to help me understand. What have we learned about the nature of the mind and its relation to the body of man? Let me answer that question, as well as I can in a few words, avoiding technical terms.

25   Consider a little girl—I shall call her Mary. Each of you has watched a child in her sleep, no doubt — a wonder far more revealing than Darwin's "primeval forests." Call to her. You see her stir, open her eyes, look about. Then she looks at you and smiles. You have wakened the brain, switching on her "wide-awake mechanism." It is an electrical mechanism made up of living interconnecting neurone cells

located deep beneath the cerebral hemispheres, most of it in the old brain. Fatigue switched it off when she went to sleep. The mechanism was completely inactive during deep sleep and partly active during her dreams.

26   Now, Mary has returned to consciousness. Her mind has *come back*. But the mind did not go anywhere. It was not, I suppose, floating in the room, nor was it perched on the roof. As far as anyone can tell, it has no shape, no weight. It occupies no space. But now Mary's mind is active again. It is making contact with the environment of Mary's body and doing it through Mary's brain. The mind has continuity, now, with Mary's past through the various memory mechanisms in Mary's brain. The mind has established contact with you through Mary's smile. The impact of the smile is real but not to be expressed in the language of a physicist.

27   Here, we have before us the mystery: Mary's mind is Mary-the-person. When Mary's brain is awake and active, her mind takes charge, and she directs the electrical action of certain mechanisms within the brain.

28   When the little girl awoke, she focused her attention on the environment. On recognizing that, she focused on you. When she focuses attention, she is using a remarkable brain mechanism — deciding what is to enter consciousness, what will be remembered by the brain, what will be ignored and leave no trace. Thus she begins at once to learn. To learn is to program, to program the other computer systems of the brain. I call them computer systems because they will act automatically later on. Ivan Pavlov called this process "conditioning," when he studied the learning of dogs. Mary selects what she will learn by focusing her attention.

29   And here are some curious and unexpected facts: although the brain keeps no record of the things the mind ignores, it does form a record of the stream of consciousness and makes other permanent recordings of those things to which Mary pays attention. Mary recognized you, and so she smiled. When she leaves her bed and goes about the house, she will turn her attention to a hundred things, from words and concepts to skills. Many different mechanisms will preserve what she is learning. Some of these mechanisms can be controlled by her afterward and be reactivated by the mind at will. Others cannot be so summoned. But they work automatically at appropriate times. Think of a simple example that is as familiar to you as it is to me:

30   A stream of consciousness flows steadily through your waking hours. (The philosopher, William James, compared this stream to a river.) Like a river, its content is never twice the same. But the comparison is misleading. Man can and does control the stream to a considerable extent. He alters the content by paying attention to this or to that. But he cannot hold it still. The stream of consciousness must

flow. A melody must advance to be a melody. Consciousness is like that. Corresponding with this flow, there is neuronal action in a special mechanism of the brain. I called it Mary's "wide-awake mechanism." It operates continually until sleep returns, or an anaesthetic is given, or a blow "knocks out" the mechanism by concussion at the base of the brain.

31   Before I go on, let me add here a word of explanation. It would be out of place in this discussion to attempt to describe in technical detail the brain mechanisms that form the physical basis of consciousness and thought. In 1966, Dr. J. G. Howells invited me to do just that for his book, *Modern Perspectives in World Psychiatry*. I accepted his challenge for two reasons: first, because, when I retired as a surgeon and scientist in 1960, the records of my experience had not been studied adequately from that point of view and I longed to make a fresh critical analysis. That material, carefully preserved and amplified by my associates in the Montreal Neurological Institute, is, in some ways, unique. Second, it was my growing desire to help the common man, including myself, to understand what science can, and cannot, explain about the mind, which men have so long referred to as the human spirit. The review, which my chapter in Howell's book made necessary, was followed by a succession of scientific addresses and writings to which the interested reader may refer.[3]

32   Scientific study makes steady advance in our understanding of how neuronal conduction makes sensory information available within the brain, and how motor mechanisms send out patterned impulses that cause muscles to execute voluntary as well as reflex movement. We are beginning to understand something about the acquired mechanisms of speech and perception and physical skills and memory and other acquired talents.

33   But the mind is not explained. It seems to be a phenomenon of another order. Somehow it is capable of reason, discretion, initiative, creative thought, considered judgement. Somehow, too, the mind can exert control over attention. Those things that are ignored leave no trace in the brain. The things that come within the searchlight of attention and thus enter the stream of consciousness, leave engrams behind.

34   A dictionary definition of "engram" is, "the lasting trace left in an organism by psychic experience." There are in the human brain different sorts of engrams: for example, the conditioned reflexes that account for the learned skills and also for the acquisition of speech and automatic perception. And there is another sort of engram. It forms a continuous record of the stream of consciousness. A surgeon's electrode applied to the interpretive cortex of the temporal lobe of a conscious patient, and delivering a gentle electrical current, may activate this record. But the record is not in the cortex. The

nerve cells in the cortex, under the electrode, are caused to send neuronal impulses to an area of grey matter at a distance, probably in the higher brainstem. This secondary area of grey matter, then, activates the record as though it were a tape recorder. The stream of consciousness flows again as in some previous period of time, perhaps a period years earlier. Music is heard; people move and speak; and yet the patient is aware of his contemporary experience in the operating room. This awareness comes to him through his senses.

35   The situation in which he finds himself is not unlike that of one who sits at the theatre watching a play and whose attention alternates between the drama of past action and the whispered conversation of his neighbour. He is aware of both. He is free to attend to either one or, indeed, he may attend to neither and thus be able to consider the abstract problem of how these things can be.

36   When a young South African patient cried out to me, as I stimulated his temporal cortex, that he was laughing with his cousins, he marvelled that he could hear them although he knew they were far away on a farm in South Africa. He was turning his attention to the wonder of his strange circumstance, then back to the evoked past experience or back to the present strange experience in the operating room. The ability of the mind of that patient to direct the brain's machinery of attention alternatively to the mechanism of sensory input, or the mechanism of the engram's re-enactment, or to abstract wonder, without losing an awareness of all three, argues that the mind is something distinct, an accompaniment of a different order.

37   In all of our studies of the brain, no mechanism has been discovered that can force the mind to think, or the individual to believe, anything. The mind continues free. This is a statement I have long considered. I have made every effort to disprove it, without success. The mind, I must conclude, is something more than a mechanism. It is, in a certain sense, above and beyond the brain, although it seems to depend upon brain action for its very existence. Yet it is free.

38   The correspondence between mind and brain and the exchange that goes on between the two are problem-projects that will long be studied. Interchange is immediate. Information is delivered to the mind, although how the final delivery is made is still a mystery. The mind controls the brain, at least at times and in part, although how a command is translated into neurone potentials remains a mystery.

39   Clinical medicine throws some light on these matters. During certain types of epileptic fit, there is sudden selective interference with the mechanism that corresponds with mind (the wide-awake mechanism) although the nearby central-motor-control mechanism continues to function automatically. The result is that during these attacks (*petit mal* attacks or attacks of automatism) the patient behaves as an automaton. He may carry out some act in accordance with the

program previously presented by his mind to that mechanism. Thus he continues walking through traffic or playing the piano or even driving a car for a short time. But it is all automatic. The mind can give no further direction. Consciousness is lost, and the brain makes no memory record. The same is true during sleep, of course. But in sleep a man lies quiet, because his central-motor-control mechanism has been switched off together with the mind's mechanism. In sleep-walking, one may suppose that the central-motor-control mechanism wakes up but not the mind-correspondence mechanism.

40   What is one to say to the assertion that brain machinery has accounted for the mind, the spirit of man, and the idea of God? As far as I am aware, this statement has been made by laymen, not by scientists who have studied the brain. It is a philosophical hypothesis. One may call it a declaration of faith. As such, it was incorporated into the doctrine of Karl Marx. It is a basic tenet in the creed of materialism. I find no evidence to support it in studies of the human brain.

41   The early Greek philosophers based their explanations of the universe on just such unprovable hypotheses. The princes of the medieval church based their astronomy on the unprovable hypothesis that man was the centre of the universe. Today we have passed into the modern era in which the experimental method has given man knowledge and power in the field of physical phenomena. For anyone to venture across the frontier that separates physical science from the humanities, supported by nothing more than hypothesis, is to commit the ancient indiscretion of the philosopher and the ecclesiastic in reverse!

42   The nature of brain action is understandable. The mind is an accompaniment of the action in certain brain mechanisms. Some day men, who see more clearly than we, may conclude that the mental and the physical are differing manifestations of one basic element. Who knows? But, now, no scientist can explain the spirit nor can he fashion it directly through any physical mechanism. Scientist, social philosopher, and religious teacher must work on, each in his proper field with a broad perspective.

43   Man's being may well be composed of two fundamental elements. This offers, as Sir Charles Sherrington expressed it, "no greater inherent improbability than that it should rest on one only." Whichever way it is, philosopher and prophet must deal with the spirit. The honest scientist should not pretend to speak with authority beyond the frontier of brain physiology.

44   When we consider the arts and sciences in distant perspective, we must recognize the great dichotomy, the frontier that separates for us physical phenomena from mental phenomena. It separates the human body from the mind. It demarcates the field of science and the field of arts.

45   The common man — and that includes us all — can only adopt what he considers a reasonable faith by which to live and die. Biological evolution has come to an end for man. He can control it. The spirit of men has established a vast body of thought. Men must now learn to control social and intellectual and moral evolution.

46   To understand the ultimate nature of the spirit is a problem man must ponder. To conclude this discussion, I can only repeat: The physical basis of the mind is the brain action in each individual. It accompanies the activity of his spirit. But the spirit is free. It is capable of some degree of initiative. No brain mechanism has yet been demonstrated that directs the action of the mind.

47   I view the situation this way in long perspective: the spirit of each individual grows, evolves, develops from babyhood on through life. It looks out through a man's eyes and listens through his ears and speaks with his mouth. The spirit *is* the man one knows. He must have continuity through periods of sleep and coma. I assume, then, that his spirit must live on somehow after death. I cannot doubt that many make contact with God and have guidance from a greater spirit. But these are the personal beliefs that every man must adopt for himself. If he had only a brain and not a mind, this difficult decision would not be his.

Notes

1. Mark 12: 29–34.
2. W. E. LeGros Clark, *Antecedents of Man: An Introduction to the Evolution of the Primates* (Edinburgh: Edinburgh University Press, 1959).
3. "The Neurophysiological Basis of Thought." A chapter from *Modern Perspectives in World Psychiatry*, ed. J. G. Howells (Edinburgh: Oliver and Boyd, 1968);
   "Consciousness, Memory and Man's Conditioned Reflexes." The William H. Burton Lecture at the Harvard Graduate School of Education, March 8, 1967. A chapter from *On the Biology of Learning* (New York: Harcourt, Brace and World, Inc. 1969);
   "Engrams in the Human Brain: Mechanisms of Memory," *Proceedings of the Royal Society of Medicine*, Vol. LXI (1968), 831–40;
   "Epilepsy, Neurophysiology and Some Brain Mechanisms Related to Consciousness." A chapter from *Basic Mechanisms of the Epilepsies*, ed. H. H. Jasper *et al* (Boston: Little, Brown and Company, 1969);
   "Memory and Perception." Forty-eighth Annual Meeting of the Association for Research in Nervous and Mental Disease, New York, December 6, 1968.

Questions on Content

1   What is the subject of Penfield's essay? What definitions support Penfield's exposition of this subject? What is the significance of the field of medicine?

2   What is the result of the historical process summarized by Penfield in paragraphs four through eleven? What is the relevance of this process to Penfield's subject?

3   Why has "man" survived for over thirty thousand years? Why has "man" "done more than survive"? What is the limitation of experimental science?

4   What distinction does the illustration of Mary introduce? What is the definition of an "engram"? What are the "different sorts of engrams"? What is the relation between the human "brain" and the human "mind"?

5   What is "the ancient indiscretion of the philosopher and the ecclesiastic? What "reverse" indiscretion should we avoid in our own times, according to Penfield? What is "the great dichotomy" that we should recognize? What is its significance?

Questions on Structure and Technique

1   What is Penfield's principle of division? What two categories does Penfield define? What is the relation of "the spirit" to these two categories? What does Penfield suggest is the purpose of his essay?

2   Why are Penfield's introductory definitions important to his method of development in this essay? Does Penfield follow one basic pattern of organization and development? What patterns of organization and development do you find in this essay?

3   What illustrations from Penfield's own personal experience are used to support his analysis? What other kinds of information does Penfield present in his analysis?

4   What questions does Penfield leave unanswered in his essay? Is his essay less effective or more effective as a result? Why?

Suggestions for Writing

1   Write a classification analysis based on Penfield's general statement that "Each of us, no doubt, is devoted to the common cause — the pursuit of truth — but each makes his own approach."

AARON COPLAND

American composer Aaron Copland (b. 1900) was born in Brooklyn, New York City, where he studied music theory, composition, and piano. He went to the American Conservatory in France in 1921 to pursue advanced studies in composition. After he returned to the United States in 1924, Copland composed the Symphony for Organ and Orchestra *(1925), which showed the influences of modern European composers (such as Stravinsky, Bartok, and Schoenberg), and* Music for the Theatre *(1925) and a* Piano Concerto *(1926), in which Copland incorporated jazz music into symphonic music. Both of these influences remained important as Copland developed his own individual style and techniques of composition exemplified in works such as his ballets* Billy the Kid *(1938),* Rodeo *(1942), and* Appalachian Spring *(1944), his film scores for* Of Mice and Men *(1939),* Our Town *(1940),* The Red Pony *(1948), and* The Heiress *(1949), an opera* The Tender Land *(1954), and concert pieces including* Piano Variations *(1930),* Violin Sonata *(1943),* Clarinet Sonata *(1948), and* Piano Fantasy *(1957). Aaron Copland's music has earned him many awards and honours including the Pulitzer Prize (1945). Copland has actively encouraged people's understanding and appreciation of music as well, and he has written several books on the subject, notably* What to Listen for in Music *(1939),* Our New Music *(1941), and* Music and Imagination *(1952). Copland's analysis of "Listening to Music" is a chapter selected from the first of these books, and it offers a classic model of the fundamental principles, organization, and development of an effective and interesting classification analysis essay.*

LISTENING TO MUSIC

1   We all listen to music according to our separate capacities. But, for the sake of analysis, the whole listening process may become clearer if we break it up into its component parts, so to speak. In a certain sense we all listen to music on three separate planes. For lack of a better terminology, one might name these: (1) the sensuous plane, (2) the expressive plane, (3) the sheerly musical plane. The only advantage to be gained from mechanically splitting up the listening process into these hypothetical planes is the clearer view to be had of the way in which we listen.

2   The simplest way of listening to music is to listen for the sheer pleasure of the musical sound itself. That is the sensuous plane. It is the plane on which we hear music without thinking, without considering it in any way. One turns on the radio while doing something

else and absent-mindedly bathes in the sound. A kind of brainless but attractive state of mind is engendered by the mere sound appeal of the music.

3   You may be sitting in a room reading this book. Imagine one note struck on the piano. Immediately that one note is enough to change the atmosphere of the room — proving that the sound element in music is a powerful and mysterious agent, which it would be foolish to deride or belittle.

4   The surprising thing is that many people who consider themselves qualified music lovers abuse that plane in listening. They go to concerts in order to lose themselves. They use music as a consolation or an escape. They enter an ideal world where one doesn't have to think of the realities of everyday life. Of course they aren't thinking about the music either. Music allows them to leave it, and they go off to a place to dream, dreaming because of and apropos of the music yet never quite listening to it.

5   Yes, the sound appeal of music is a potent and primitive force, but you must not allow it to usurp a disproportionate share of your interest. The sensuous plane is an important one in music, a very important one, but it does not constitute the whole story.

6   There is no need to digress further on the sensuous plane. Its appeal to every normal human being is self-evident. There is, however, such a thing as becoming more sensitive to the different kinds of sound stuff as used by various composers. For all composers do not use that sound stuff in the same way. Don't get the idea that the value of music is commensurate with its sensuous appeal or that the loveliest sounding music is made by the greatest composer. If that were so, Ravel would be a greater creator than Beethoven. The point is that the sound element varies with each composer, that his usage of sound forms an integral part of his style and must be taken into account when listening. The reader can see, therefore, that a more conscious approach is valuable even on this primary plane of music listening.

7   The second plane on which music exists is what I have called the expressive one. Here, immediately, we tread on controversial ground. Composers have a way of shying away from any discussion of music's expressive side. Did not Stravinsky himself proclaim that his music was an "object," a "thing," with a life of its own, and with no other meaning than its own purely musical existence? This intransigent attitude of Stravinsky's may be due to the fact that so many people have tried to read different meanings into so many pieces. Heaven knows it is difficult enough to say precisely what it is that a piece of music means, to say it definitely, to say it finally so that everyone is satisfied with your explanation. But that should not lead one to the other extreme of denying to music the right to be "expressive."

8   My own belief is that all music has an expressive power, some more and some less, but that all music has a certain meaning behind the notes and that that meaning behind the notes constitutes, after all, what the piece is saying, what the piece is about. This whole problem can be stated quite simply by asking, "Is there a meaning to music?" My answer to that would be, "Yes." And "Can you state in so many words what the meaning is?" My answer to that would be, "No." Therein lies the difficulty.

9   Simple-minded souls will never be satisfied with the answer to the second of these questions. They always want music to have a meaning, and the more concrete it is the better they like it. The more the music reminds them of a train, a storm, a funeral, or any other familiar conception the more expressive it appears to be to them. This popular idea of music's meaning — stimulated and abetted by the usual run of musical commentator — should be discouraged wherever and whenever it is met. One timid lady once confessed to me that she suspected something seriously lacking in her appreciation of music because of her inability to connect it with anything definite. That is getting the whole thing backward, of course.

10   Still, the question remains, How close should the intelligent music lover wish to come to pinning a definite meaning to any particular work? No closer than a general concept, I should say. Music expresses, at different moments, serenity or exuberance, regret or triumph, fury or delight. It expresses each of these moods, and many others, in a numberless variety of subtle shadings and differences. It may even express a state of meaning for which there exists no adequate word in any language. In that case, musicians often like to say that it has only a purely musical meaning. They sometimes go farther and say that *all* music has only a purely musical meaning. What they really mean is that no appropriate word can be found to express the music's meaning and that, even if it could, they do not feel the need of finding it.

11   But whatever the professional musician many hold, most musical novices still search for specific words with which to pin down their musical reactions. That is why they always find Tchaikovsky easier to "understand" than Beethoven. In the first place, it is easier to pin a meaning-word on a Tchaikovsky piece than on a Beethoven one. Much easier. Moreover, with the Russian composer, every time you come back to a piece of his it almost always says the same thing to you, whereas with Beethoven it is often quite difficult to put your finger right on what he is saying. And any musician will tell you that that is why Beethoven is the greater composer. Because music which always says the same thing to you will necessarily become dull music, but music whose meaning is slightly different with each hearing has a greater chance of remaining alive.

12   Listen, if you can, to the forty-eight fugue themes of Bach's *Well Tempered Clavichord*. Listen to each theme, one after another. You will soon realize that each theme mirrors a different world of feeling. You will also soon realize that the more beautiful a theme seems to you the harder it is to find any word that will describe it to your complete satisfaction. Yes, you will certainly know whether it is a gay theme or a sad one. You will be able, in other words, in your own mind, to draw a frame of emotional feeling around your theme. Now study the sad one a little closer. Try to pin down the exact quality of its sadness. Is it pessimistically sad or resignedly sad; is it fatefully sad or smilingly sad?

13   Let us suppose that you are fortunate and can describe to your own satisfaction in so many words the exact meaning of your chosen theme. There is still no guarantee that anyone else will be satisfied. Nor need they be. The important thing is that each one feel for himself the specific expressive quality of a theme or, similarly, an entire piece of music. And if it is a great work of art, don't expect it to mean exactly the same thing to you each time you return to it.

14   Themes or pieces need not express only one emotion, of course. Take such a theme as the first main one of the *Ninth Symphony*, for example. It is clearly made up of different elements. It does not say only one thing. Yet anyone hearing it immediately gets a feeling of strength, a feeling of power. It isn't a power that comes simply because the theme is played loudly. It is a power inherent in the theme itself. The extraordinary strength and vigor of the theme results in the listener's receiving an impression that a forceful statement has been made. But one should never try to boil it down to "the fateful hammer of life," etc. That is where the trouble begins. The musician, in his exasperation says it means nothing but the notes themselves, whereas the nonprofessional is only too anxious to hang on to any explanation that gives him the illusion of getting closer to the music's meaning.

15   Now, perhaps, the reader will know better what I mean when I say that music does have an expressive meaning but that we cannot say in so many words what the meaning is.

16   The third plane on which music exists is the sheerly musical plane. Besides the pleasurable sound of music and the expressive feeling that it gives off, music does exist in terms of the notes themselves and of their manipulation. Most listeners are not sufficiently conscious of this third plane.

17   Professional musicians, on the other hand, are, if anything, too conscious of the mere notes themselves. They often fall into the error of becoming so engrossed with their arpeggios and staccatos that they forget the deeper aspects of the music they are performing. But from the layman's standpoint, it is not so much a matter of getting over bad

habits on the sheerly musical plane as of increasing one's awareness of what is going on in so far as the notes are concerned.

18 When the man in the street listens to the "notes themselves" with any degree of concentration, he is most likely to make some mention of the melody. Either he hears a pretty melody or he does not, and he generally lets it go at that. Rhythm is likely to gain his attention next, particularly if it seems exciting. But harmony and tone color are generally taken for granted, if they are thought of consciously at all. As for music's having a definite form of some kind, that idea seems never to have occurred to him.

19 It is very important for all of us to become more alive to music on its sheerly musical plane. After all, an actual musical material is being used. The intelligent listener must be prepared to increase his awareness of the musical material and what happens to it. He must hear the melodies, the rhythms, the harmonies, the tone colors in a more conscious fashion. But above all he must, in order to follow the line of the composer's thought, know something of the principles of musical form. Listening to all of these elements is listening on the sheerly musical plane.

20 Let me repeat that I have split up mechanically the three separate planes on which we listen merely for the sake of greater clarity. Actually, we never listen on one or the other of these planes. What we do is to correlate them — listening in all three ways at the same time. It takes no mental effort, for we do it instinctively.

21 Perhaps an analogy with what happens to us when we visit the theater will make this instinctive correlation clearer. In the theater, you are aware of the actors and actresses, costumes and sets, sounds and movements. All these give one the sense that the theater is a pleasant place to be in. They constitute the sensuous plane in our theatrical reactions.

22 The expressive plane in the theater would be derived from the feeling that you get from what is happening on the stage. You are moved to pity, excitement, or gaiety. It is this general feeling, generated aside from the particular words being spoken, a certain emotional something which exists on the stage, that is analogous to the expressive quality in music.

23 The plot and plot development is equivalent to our sheerly musical plane. The playwright creates and develops a character in just the same way that a composer creates and develops a theme. According to the degree of your awareness of the way in which the artist in either field handles his material will you become a more intelligent listener.

24 It is easy enough to see that the theatergoer never is conscious of any of these elements separately. He is aware of them all at the same

time. The same is true of music listening. We simultaneously and without thinking listen on all three planes.

25   In a sense, the ideal listener is both inside and outside the music at the same moment, judging it and enjoying it, wishing it would go one way and watching it go another — almost like the composer at the moment he composes it; because in order to write his music, the composer must also be inside and outside his music, carried away by it and yet coldly critical of it. A subjective and objective attitude is implied in both creating and listening to music.

26   What the reader should strive for, then, is a more *active* kind of listening. Whether you listen to Mozart or Duke Ellington, you can deepen your understanding of music only by being a more conscious and aware listener — not someone who is just listening, but someone who is listening *for* something.

Questions on Content

1   What is "the simplest way of listening to music"? In what situations do we listen to music on this "plane"?

2   What is Copland's view of the "expressive plane"? What other views does he discuss?

3   What is the difference between "professional musicians" and "the man on the street" when they listen to music on the third plane? What will "the intelligent listener" listen for?

4   What experiences at the theatre are analogous to each of these three planes, according to Copland?

5   How can we "deepen our understanding of music"? What do you think Copland means by the phrase "listening *for* something"?

Questions on Structure and Technique

1   What are Copland's labels for the "component parts" of "the whole listening process"? What is the purpose of this division?

2   What is Copland's definition of the "sensuous plane"? What is his definition of the "expressive plane"? What is his definition of the "sheerly musical plane"?

3   What specific details and examples most effectively illustrate the definitions of each one of these planes?

4   What are the purposes of Copland's analogy between listening to music and attending the theatre?

5   What other techniques does Copland use to involve and interest his readers in his analysis of listening to music? For instance, why does he use the pronoun "we"?

Suggestions for Writing

1   Apply Copland's analysis of listening to music to the particular kind of music that you most enjoy, using Copland's labels and definitions to provide your readers with a better understanding and appreciation of its appeal.

2   Write a classification analysis of one of the following common activities: watching television, going out on a date, attending a sports event, or reading a book. Divide this activity into three or four "planes" or "levels," based on Copland's analysis.

CHAPTER 6

"So the small and great cycles of life meet and merge and contribute to the grand design..."

PROCESS ANALYSIS

A process is a whole operation whose sequence of actions or events produces some particular result. Almost any subject, from preparing food to reading or writing to the development of some natural, historical, social, or scientific phenomenon, may be best understood as a process. An analysis divides a whole into constituent parts in order to examine those parts, their interrelations, and their relations to the whole. When a scientist performs a dissection or a mechanic rebuilds a carburetor, they are working with a whole on the basis of its parts: the stages in a process. Analysis can be used by a writer to divide any whole operation into parts for the purpose of explaining to readers either *how* to do something or *how* something was or is done. A process analysis presents a process for either an instructional or an informative purpose and breaks down that process into a well-defined sequence of main *stages*, and often specific *steps* in each stage, so it can then be explained in clear and effective detail.

In a process analysis essay, the writer's introduction of his or her subject should reflect the nature of the process itself. It should also express the writer's attitude toward that subject in terms of the essay's primary purpose; that is, whether it is an instructional discussion of how to do something or an informative presentation of how something was or is done. For instance, in the first sentence of "Reading Plays," Robertson Davies clearly states this subject as a process being analysed for an instructional purpose: "You can train yourself to read plays so that they will give you keen enjoyment." Although the authoritative analysis of stress by Hans Selye in "The Mastery of Stress" is certainly informative, his primary purpose, to give practical directions for handling this problem successfully in our daily lives, is similarly established as follows: "The more we learn about conditioning and about the ways to deal with the stress of life, the more we can enjoy eustress, which is the spice of our existence." In a process analysis where a writer is only concerned with presenting information, not instructions, its purpose of providing the reader with an understanding of how something was done (or is done) should be indicated, as in Wilfred G. Bigelow's account of "The Invention of the Pacemaker" when he states in his introduction that his medical research team "all felt that they were setting the stage for an explosion of knowledge and technology that would profoundly affect the whole practice of medicine."

In both the instructional and the informative approaches to a process analysis, the organization and development is based on the writer's division of the sequence of actions or events in the whole process into several main stages.

I.	Introduction
II. A	Stage 1 — Step 1, Step 2, Step 3
II. B	Stage 2
II. C	Stage 3
III.	Conclusion

instructional (handwritten)

For example, in his analysis of how to "train yourself to read plays," Robertson Davies identifies three basic tasks: "First, you must give the play a fair chance;" "Second, always read it in a theatrical framework;" and, "Above all, read a great many plays." These stages are outlined in general chronological order, but notice that the author explains *how* the process happens, as opposed to a writer's emphasis, in a narrative, on *what* happens. Indeed, in Davies' discussion, as in many process analyses including Selye's "The Mastery of Stress" and Hemingway's "When You Camp Out, Do It Right," the author's interest in explaining *how* to do something is more important than a rigid adherence to chronological order. On the other hand, many process analyses, such as Harold Horwood's "A Wilderness Lake," Farley Mowat's "People of the Sea," and Wilfred G. Bigelow's "The Invention of the Pacemaker," follow a carefully-organized chronological sequence of main stages, and sometimes specific steps in each stage. In all process analyses, however, writers must identify, define, and then illustrate each stage in the process, each part of the whole operation. The writer's development of individual stages must present clear and interesting details that allow the reader both to understand and to become involved in the process; therefore, the writer must keep the reader's needs in mind when selecting and arranging specific details. Neither obvious nor obscure details will necessarily serve a writer's practical purpose of instructing or informing readers about a process.

The reading selections in this chapter demonstrate a number of useful techniques for organizing and developing an effective process analysis essay. Moreover, these selections show how writers' detailed instructions and information on a variety of subjects make their readers more aware of the relations between things as processes — those operations, developments, and changes that contribute so much to our experiences.

ROBERTSON DAVIES

Robertson Davies (b. 1913) grew up in Thamesville, Renfrew, and Kingston, Ontario. He attended Upper Canada College in Toronto, Queen's University in Kingston, and received his B.Litt. degree from Balliol College, Oxford, in 1938. Davies' studies in drama led to the publication of his thesis Shakespeare's Boy Actors *(1939) and two years of theatre work in England with the Old Vic Company. After returning to Canada, Davies continued directing and writing plays while making a career as a writer and editor for* Saturday Night *magazine, the* Peterborough Examiner, *and the* Toronto Star. *Many of Davies' plays as well as several collections of his prose journalism have been published, including the review articles in* A Voice from the Attic *(1960) from which the following selection on the process of "Reading Plays" has been excerpted. From 1963 until 1981, Davies taught literature and drama at the University of Toronto, and he has published several books of literary criticism and scholarship. Robertson Davies' work as a director, playwright, critic, and patron has contributed greatly over the years to the development of Canadian theatre and drama, but his national and international reputation as a writer has rested more in recent years on his achievements in fiction. These works include:* Tempest-tost *(1951),* Leaven of Malice *(1954),* A Mixture of Frailties *(1958),* Fifth Business, *(1970),* The Manticore *(1972),* World of Wonders *(1975), and* The Rebel Angels *(1981). Davies' most recent novel is* What's Bred in the Bone *(1985).*

READING PLAYS

1   You can train yourself to read plays so that they will give you keen enjoyment. The directions are few. First, you must give the play a fair chance; it is not a novel, and it should not be read in scraps; try to complete it in an evening. Second, always read it in a theatrical framework; it was written for the stage, and you must, to the best of your ability, visualize it as a stage production. This takes some doing, for you may not have a strong theatrical imagination. When a play is well performed in the theater, a crowd of experts have all worked to give you pleasure; you will not at first trial provide in your mind a director, a designer, and a cast of talented actors. Do not be disappointed if your early attempts seem a little heavy. If you persist, the art will come, in a sufficient measure, for it is a law of the imagination that the more you want, the more it will provide. Persist, and the reading of plays can become a splendid private indulgence.

2   Let me warn you, as a rule, against play-reading groups. The sheer physical technique required to make reading aloud a pleasure is not to be found among people who try it only occasionally, and who have not made a study of the text. Play readings are, as a general thing, prolonged butcheries. Read plays to yourself, bringing all the

imagination, feeling, and wit that you possess to bear upon the feat. Be a Gielgud in your own bosom, and do not encourage your friend, the lawyer, to read the role of Hamlet aloud in his courtroom voice.

3   Above all, read a great many plays, both for the pleasure it will give you and for the mastery that can be gained only in that way. The imaginative skill which you pick up in the reading of a dozen trivial comedies will bear fruit when you attempt a great one; much of the disappointment which undergraduates feel when they first read great plays arises simply from the fact that they do not know how to go about it; such texts demand the most expert work of the most gifted actors and directors to give them life on the stage; why expect them to leap into brilliance at the behest of an unexercised imagination?

4   Read much, and do not expect every play to be a perfect experience when you read it, any more than you do when you go to the theater. In this department of reading more than in any other, catholicity and bulk are the secrets of pleasure.

Questions on Content

1   What does Davies indicate is the main purpose for training yourself to read plays? In which sentences does Davies state this purpose?

2   In what ways is "imagination" important in the process of training yourself to read plays, according to Davies?

3   What are Davies' basic directions for this process? What errors should the reader avoid at each stage in this process?

4   Why is the last stage most important?

Questions on Structure and Technique

1   Why does Davies arrange his directions in this particular order?

2   What words and phrases does Davies use to introduce each main stage? What other words and phrases might he have chosen?

3   What techniques does Davies use that emphasize his instructional purpose?

4   How is this instructional purpose also apparent in Davies' choices of specific details?

Suggestions for Writing

1   Choose an activity that you enjoy. Complete the thesis statement, "You can train yourself to____," so that it is appropriate to your subject. Then, write an instructional process analysis in which you give three or four basic directions necessary for your readers to enjoy the activity too.

2   Write a process analysis in which you instruct your readers how to read one kind of writing other than plays, such as novels, poems, biographies, histories, romances, newspaper or magazine articles, letters, reports, and so forth.

HANS SELYE

Hans Selye (1907–1982) was a medical research scientist whose pioneering studies, lectures, and writing on the concept of stress earned him recognition as an authority on the subject. Born in Vienna and educated at several universities in Europe, Selye taught biochemistry at McGill University from 1932 on and also worked at the Institute of Experimental Medicine and Surgery at the Université de Montréal. Hans Selye's books on stress include: The Stress of Life *(1956),* From Dream to Discovery *(1964), and* Stress Without Distress *(1974). "The Mastery of Stress" is from a chapter in Selye's account of his life and work,* The Stress of My Life *(1977), and it is a presentation of a well-defined sequence of stress which affords readers a better understanding of stress as well as practical advice on dealing with stress situations.*

THE MASTERY OF STRESS

1   The term "stress" has been used so loosely and applied to so many areas that it is probably easier to understand what stress is *not*. Contrary to widespread public opinion, stress is not synonymous with nervous depression, tension, fatigue or discouragement. The only way to characterize stress is to call it a nonspecific response of the body to any demand. Under given circumstances, stress may cause exhaustion, a nervous breakdown, a cardiac accident, asthma or muscular fatigue. Still, these disturbances are not stress, but rather its diverse effects upon certain individuals.

2   You *should not and cannot avoid stress*, because to eliminate it completely would mean to destroy life itself. If you make no more demands upon your body, you are dead. Whatever we do — run up a flight of stairs, play tennis, worry or fight starvation — demands are made upon us. A lash of the whip and a passionate kiss can be equally stressful! Although one causes distress and the other eustress, both make certain common demands, necessitating adaption to a change in our normal resting equilibrium. Even while we sleep, the heart must continue to beat, we must move the muscles that help the lungs to breathe, we continue to digest last night's meal, and even the brain does not cease to function as we dream. Consequently, it would be quite unthinkable that anyone could, or would even want to, avoid stress. However, the more we learn about conditioning and about the ways to deal with the stress of life, the more we can enjoy eustress, which is the spice of our existence. It gives us the only outlet we have to express our talents and energies, to pursue happiness.

3   Every one of us must learn to recognize what for him is "overstress" (hyperstress), when he has exceeded the limits of his adaptability; or "understress" (hypostress), when he suffers from lack of self-realization (physical immobility, boredom, sensory deprivation). Being over-wrought is just as bad as being frustrated by the inability to express ourselves and find free outlets for our innate muscular or mental energy.

4   The way I see it, the stress of life has four basic variations, although in their most characteristic nonspecific manifestations they all depend upon the same central phenomenon. This might be illustrated as follows:

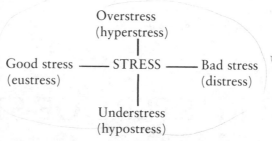

Overstress
(hyperstress)
|
Good stress ——— STRESS ——— Bad stress
(eustress)   (distress)
|
Understress
(hypostress)

5   Our goal, then, is to strike a balance between the equally destructive forces of hypo- and hyperstress, to find as much eustress as possible and minimize distress. . . .

6   Once we really understand stress, each of us will be his own best physician, for no one can appreciate your mental needs better than you yourself. Everyone must learn to measure the stress level at which he personally functions best and then not go either above or below that. By careful self-observation we can gradually develop an instinctive feeling telling us that we are running above or below the stress level that corresponds to our own nature. In practice, no refined chemical tests can do more for you. I know when I have just "had enough of it," and then I stop. I don't need any complex scientific machinery for this.

7   Judging what is best for us personally is a matter of training through experience, which everybody has to acquire for himself. But in this task we can be greatly aided by a thorough knowledge of the basic natural laws that have been clarified through research on stress. You must learn to balance the pleasures and stimulation of social engagements, trips and successful work against your requirements for peace, solitude and serenity. Everybody will arrive at this aim in a somewhat different manner, always characteristic of his own individuality. Some understand their inner needs through mediation and silence; others may only find their own stress level through danger signs such as insomnia, irritability, indigestion, headaches or depression. First of all, we must learn to analyze and be honest with ourselves. Then,

step by step, an intelligent person will usually succeed in developing his own techniques, limiting his unnecessary telephone calls, his participation in social life, committee meetings, civic activities, etc., which he has blindly undertaken because "they were expected of him." This will leave much more time to do other things at which he is really good and which may be more useful both to himself and to society. Don't accept social obligations that people try to impose upon you if you dislike them. "Worthy causes" are not natural obligations and will only bore you, so disregard them. Do what you like and respect, without worrying about criticism, scandal or even all the money that you lose by deviating from generally accepted standards.

8   If you read the daily papers or watch news programs on television that do not interest you, just give that up and turn your attention to other things that you find more edifying. Don't allow the verbal terrorism of others to give you guilt feelings. Instead, save your energy for activities that are really meaningful.

9   "Even if you have the misfortune of having badly chosen your wife, at least choose your occupation wisely, because you will spend much more time with it than with her." I do not remember the author of this advice but, in any event, I fully agree with him — and by "occupation" I don't mean only your job, but whatever you decide to do throughout each day.

10   You must satisfy yourself first of all. Pleasure will come only from what you have done to earn it. As much as possible, try to awaken the creativity that may lie buried in your subconscious mind. Whatever steps you must take to exteriorize your talents, the accomplishment of this is the basic prerequisite for your development and satisfaction. It really doesn't matter whether you are a scientist, gardener, poet, musician, athlete or even a beachcomber; the essential thing is that you unfold your personality as far as you can, and thereby achieve happiness.

11   You should try very honestly to establish what you consider a noble aim in life, a goal worthy of your efforts, a pursuit which gives you maximal satisfaction. This is not always easy. You must be extremely sincere with yourself; you have to remember to choose only what *you* really want to do, not what your parents, friends, neighbors, teachers or preachers have virtually brainwashed you to do. To establish this is of the utmost importance because it helps you avoid some of the major frustrations in life, which are the principal sources of distress.

12   After that you must fight hard to attain your goal, but always stay within the limits of your capacity to withstand stress. We must learn how to face life gracefully from what we have established about the actions of syntoxic and catatoxic hormones. We need to know how to accept defeat when it is not worthwhile to win, or when the goal

we have set for ourselves turns out to be unattainable; but we must also fight stubbornly until death if under given conditions, without defense, death would be inevitable anyway.

13   Each time you are the victim of some family disagreement or a disappointing experience at work, examine carefully whether it is really worth your while to defend your point of view. If not, just ignore the friction or, if necessary, cut your ties with the offender; if the goal is important, fight with all your strength. After the combat is over, whether you win or lose, return to solitude, breathe calmly, relax your muscles and empty your mind and body of all the aftermaths of the struggle, gradually returning to your normal pace of life. I once summarized these thoughts in a jingle that I am fond of quoting:

> "Fight for your highest
> Attainable aim
> But do not put up
> Resistance in vain."

14   Fifty years of research in laboratories and clinics have convinced me that the physiological mechanisms of adaptation to the stress of life are essentially the same on the cellular and molecular level as they are with regard to interpersonal and international relationships.

15   To my mind, the general syndrome of adaptation to the demands of life, which I have already outlined, is at the root of the great tensions characteristic of our time that manifest themselves in the relations between individuals and nations. Perhaps humanity's greatest problem today is determining how to face interpersonal and international stress situations as well as those created by changes in our inanimate environment.

Questions on Content

1   What is Selye's definition of "stress"? What is his thesis concerning stress?

2   What is the first main stage in the process of dealing with stress? Why is it important to understand the four variations of stress?

3   What is the second stage in this process? What does it mean to be one's "own best physician," according to Selye? What detailed steps and suggestions does Selye discuss in this stage?

4   What is the third stage that follows from this second stage? What difficulties are involved in choosing an aim, a goal, or a pursuit in life?

5   What is the fourth and final stage in the process of dealing with stress? Why is this stage most important?

Questions on Structure and Technique

1   Why does Selye need to define the term "stress"? How does Selye support and develop this definition in paragraphs one and two? How does Selye develop this definition even further at the first stage of his analysis in paragraphs three through five?

2   What purpose does Selye's diagram serve in paragraph four? Is this diagram useful or necessary? Why?

3   Why is the following topic sentence in paragraph six effective: "Once we really understand stress, each of us will be his own best physician"?

4   In which paragraph does Selye begin discussing the third stage in the process of handling stress? What is his topic sentence for this stage? What is his topic sentence for stage four?

5   What readers is Selye writing for? What specific details are directed toward this audience? What techniques other than his choice of illustrations does Selye use effectively to present this instructional process analysis to his audience?

Suggestions for Writing

1   Consider an aim, a goal, or a pursuit that you established for yourself, and then write an *informational* process analysis in which you explain the stages involved for you in trying to attain it.

2   Choose another significant problem that many people must learn how to handle in their daily lives, and write an instructional process analysis in which you present an effective approach or method for dealing with that problem.

FARLEY MOWAT

In this informative analysis of the historical process whereby Newfound-landers "evolved into a unique people," Farley Mowat (b. 1921) combines a firm grasp of historical facts with his personal understanding of the people of Newfoundland. Mowat lived for several years in a Newfoundland outport, Burgeo, and he has written several books about Newfoundland, including This Rock Within the Sea: A Heritage Lost *(1968),* A Whale for the Killing *(1972), and* The Wake of the Great Sealers *(1973). Born in Belleville, Ontario, raised in Saskatchewan, and educated at the University of Toronto, Mowat has frequently drawn on his own experiences for what he terms his "subjective non-fiction" writing, which includes over two dozen books. In addition to his books on Newfoundland, Mowat is best-known for books about the Arctic, its people, and its history:* People of the Deer *(1952),* Coppermine Journey *(1958),* The Desperate People *(1959),* Ordeal by Ice *(1960),* The Polar Passion *(1967),* Canada North *(1967),* Siber: My Discovery of Siberia *(1970),* Tundra *(1973),* Snow Walker *(1975), and* Canada North Now: The Great Betrayal *(1976). Mowat's sincere, often controversial, concern for the sanctity of nature and its processes is a dominant one in much of this writing as well as in* Never Cry Wolf *(1963). Mowat has also written several books specifically for young people, among them* Lost in the Barrens *(1965) which won a Governor General's Award, and* The Boat Who Wouldn't Float *(1968) for which he received the Leacock Medal for Humour. Mowat's most recent writing includes* And No Birds Sang *(1979), a book about his experiences serving in the Hastings and Prince Edward Regiment during the Second World War.*

PEOPLE OF THE SEA

1 Discovered in 986 by Greenland Norse who made an abortive settlement in the north part, Newfoundland began to take shape as a European entity in the west as early as 1450, by which time Basque and Portuguese whalers and fishers were regularly sailing to the Grand Banks, into Belle Isle Strait, and probably to most of the good harbors that ring the island. The early history is dim, principally because until the 1700's it was illegal to settle in Newfoundland. The wealthy west coast fish merchants of England had engineered such laws in an attempt to prevent the establishment of a native fishery in the "New Land". But laws are mostly made to be broken. By 1510 runaways from fishing ships—the Masterless Men, as they are known in tradition — had spread like a slow, silent tide into remote Newfoundland

bays. They lived hard lives in a hard land — but they lived. There were six thousand miles of rock-ribbed, sea-roaring coasts to hide them, and here they built their little "tilts" of sod or logs, concealing themselves from strangers and passing ships, getting a little "country meat" from the land, but subsisting mainly on the fish they caught from open boats. Historians have ignored these early planters, remembering only the grandiose attempts of men like Lord Baltimore, which mostly failed. Nevertheless by 1550 a large part of the Newfoundland coast was occupied and these early "liveyers" (people who "live here" — a name still in use on the Labrador coast) slowly increased in numbers.

2   The odds against them were terrible. Starvation was the common lot through the first three centuries of Newfoundland's recent history, and chronic hunger filled most of the fourth. But a steady flow of new blood came in from Ireland, the Southern Counties of England and the Channel Islands, in the form of indentured labor brought over by great English and Jersey merchant companies to man their fishing victories. These indentured people, men and women both, were practically slaves and a good many of them slipped quietly off to seek freedom in the secret little coves. The English outporters met French fishermen-settlers and Micmac Indians and, since all men were equal before the sea, marriages took place freely across the lines of race and blood.

3   So the Newfoundlanders early evolved into a unique people — a true "People of The Sea" who eventually ringed the island with more than thirteen hundred outports, ranging in size from two or three families to as high as fifty. Most of these settlements had no contact with one another or with the world outside except by water.

4   They struggled for survival as few human beings in our time have had to struggle. In small open boats the men fished the year round, with time off for grueling voyages in small schooners carrying salt cod to Europe and the West Indies; while the women "made" (dried and treated) the salt cod which was the great product of the northern seas. Every September at "settling up time" the salt fish was carried to the merchant who bought it, at his price — not for cash, but as payment against the debts, the endless debts, of the fisherman and his family.

5   The merchant class of Newfoundland held the people in a deadly vice; as inescapable and as ruthless a trap as any that was ever devised by a trader to ensnare a simple Indian. From its beginnings until as late as the 1950's in some remote outports, a man was born, grew up and died in debt to the merchant.

6   The long centuries slipped by and a score of times Newfoundland became a battlefield, usually between French and English, during

which the outporters often lost all they possessed and had to start again with nothing but their hands. During all those years nothing really changed. The system remained the same. The poor stayed desperately poor, and the rich grew fabulously rich. St. John's was the only real town the island boasted, and it was the home of the great merchants — the "Water Street men". Even as late as 1950 St. John's had more millionaires per capita than any other city in North America, including the capital of Texas! And in 1949 the majority of the people of Newfoundland still knew grinding poverty.

7   Here is the way it was [according to Newfoundlander Harvey Pink]: "In the thirties — the 'Hard Times', we called it — there was nothing to be had. The merchants would give out no more credit and the people had no money, of course. Fish was a glut. Nobody would buy our fish. People all up and down the coasts were starving. Nobody will ever know how many children died, but a good many grown men starved to death. If there happened to be a doctor handy, he'd write it down as heart failure, which was true enough. The government gave out the dole — six cents a day for a family and you took it 'in kind', and the kind, often enough, was rotten or weevily flour. My people were a little better off than most, and many's the time neighbors would come to our kitchen for a feed. I mind how they smelled. My mother told me: 'Son,' she says, 'That is the smell of poverty. Don't you forget it.' I knew one man, poor fellow, set out to ask for help from the relieving officer one day in winter time. But he froze to death on the way. When we found him, all he was wearing was a pair of trousers and a jacket made of wore-out flour sacks. He had no socks — only a torn pair of rubber boots on his feet . . . ."

8   Hard times! Yes. But a Newfoundlander was used to hard times, having known little else for centuries. He begat immense families, often fifteen to eighteen children, but it was rare for more than a handful of them to reach maturity, and when they were grown-up the sea would take its toll of the men — "Bridegrooms of the Sea", they called the drowned — while tuberculosis took a toll of the women — a heavy toll.

9   It was like that right up until Confederation in 1949. And yet when union with Canada was mooted, the "Water Street men" fought a bitter battle to prevent it. They preferred things to stay as they were. But they lost. One day in April of 1949 Newfoundland ceased to be the oldest European settlement in North America and became the youngest of the ten Canadian provinces. And an ancient mold was shattered, almost overnight — not by a bomb or by a similar catastrophe, but . . . by the baby bonus!

10   The baby bonus accomplished in a few years what the merchants had been able to prevent through three or four centuries. It brought

cash, and therefore a measure of freedom to the people. The change was unbelievable. My neighbors in the outport of Burgeo, where I live now, never tire of recalling what happened.

11   "Before my wife got her first bonus money," one of them told me, "nobody in our family had ever seen a five-dollar bill. If we saw five dollars in silver a year — that was a lot. Everything we sold went to one merchant, and everything we bought had to come from him. He owned us, do you see?"

12   Here is how things now stand in this old Island after 18 years of being part of Canada. Nobody starves to death anymore, not even children. Nobody, or at least not many people, die because of a lack of medical services. For the first time, every child can learn to read and write, even if the educational standard is much lower than on the mainland. Men who never had anything to lean on except their own strong muscles, can now draw unemployment insurance, sick benefits, or relief assistance, while their wives gather in the baby bonus cheques. Old people, who used to survive (or try to), on a government pension of $120.00 a year, are now so relatively affluent that they hardly know what to do with their money. The population is exploding; not because more children are being born, but because a lot more of them are surviving.

13   It all looks very good indeed. And yet there is a shadow over the paradise created by Confederation. Having tasted the fruits of the Canadian way of life, more and more and more Newfoundlanders are turning their backs on the pitiless grey sea which made them what they were. The Newfoundland merchant fleet, mostly under sail, was so impressive that as late as 1939 about five hundred sailing vessels were operating out of Newfoundland ports, many of them engaged in the trans-Atlantic salt fish trade, while others carried cargo to and from Canadian and Caribbean ports. Employment in the fisheries has fallen sharply as, indeed, it must. Where once fifty men, working for starvation wages, could land a certain weight of fish, now four or five men, better paid and operating a modern dragger, do the same job.

14   Standards of living go up, and the number of acceptable jobs at these new standards go down. The birth rate goes up, and there are not enough jobs available even for those presently employable. And so Newfoundland, once noted as the greatest exporter in the world of salt fish, is now exporting men and women as its major produce. They go because they must, and because the new generation will not accept the kind of life their fathers knew.

15   But more than the physical presence of the new generation is being lost. The tough, impervious core of courage, resourcefulness, ability, endurance, and personal pride that was a product of the evolution of

the outport man and woman — the byproduct of adversity — is disappearing in the interval between one generation and the next.

16   Newfoundland demonstrates with pitiless clarity the terrible paradox of our times: as we make life easier, more tolerable, less demanding, so do we weaken the sustaining fabric of pride and strength which made us men in the first place.

17   In Burgeo, as in most of Newfoundland, the older men still go fishing in their little boats, although there is no longer any need for men of sixty or seventy to endure the cold seas and the cutting gales. They go because they love the life, not for the money that is in it. But they know they are the last of their kind — that the young fellows who are their sons and grandsons will soon be gone from the little outports; from Heart's Ease, Pushthrough, Fransway, and all the others. They know that in the past ten years more than three hundred outports have died, or been abandoned. They know that the young people will go to the Mainland, where they will become real Canadians — whatever that may be; but they have a feeling that these men of a new age will somehow be less than the men their fathers were.

Questions on Content

1   Who were the first people to settle in Newfoundland? When?

2   During the next four centuries, who settled in Newfoundland? Why did they evolve into a "unique people"? How did they struggle for survival?

3   What startling contrast had gradually developed by 1950, at the end of those four centuries?

4   After Newfoundland joined Confederation in 1949, what made an "unbelievable" change there, and why?

5   What is "the terrible paradox of our times" that Mowat sees in the people of Newfoundland following "18 years of being part of Canada"?

Questions on Structure and Technique

1   In recounting a chronological history of the people of Newfoundland, into what four stages does Mowat divide his process analysis? Can you assign dates to these stages?

2   What is the real subject of Mowat's analysis of this historical process? What sentences state this subject in the first four paragraphs? What is the effect of these repeated statements?

3   Why are Mowat's quotations of two Newfoundlanders' own views of their experiences effective? What other detailed illustrations do you find most effective in this essay?

4   What is Mowat's thesis statement? What is the effect of presenting this statement toward the conclusion of the essay rather than at the beginning? What is a "paradox"?

5   From whose point of view are we told that "these men of a new age will somehow be less than the men their fathers were"? Does Mowat's own analysis support this view? How?

Suggestions for Writing

1   Write a process analysis of your family's history, dividing it into stages and developing specific details in order to support your thesis about that history.

2   Write a process analysis of another contemporary situation that demonstrates what Mowat defines as "the terrible paradox of our times: as we make life easier, more tolerable, less demanding, so do we weaken the sustaining fabric of pride and strength which made us men [and women] in the first place."

3   Based on historical research as well as your own experience, write a concise process analysis of the history of your home province and its people. Be sure that you not only establish a clear thesis statement about that history, but also that the stages you define and the detailed illustrations you choose provide relevant support for your thesis.

HAROLD HORWOOD

Harold Horwood (b. 1923) is the author of two novels, Tomorrow
Will be Sunday *(1966) and* White Eskimo: A Novel of Labrador *(1973),
a collection of essays,* Newfoundland *(1969), and several other books.
"A Wilderness Lake" is a chapter from* The Foxes of Beachy Cove *(1967), a
non-fiction prose study of nature that has been favourably compared to
Thoreau's* Walden. *In "A Wilderness Lake," Horwood explains the natural cycle of life as a process whose stages correspond with the seasons of
the year. Horwood's detailed and knowledgeable description of this particular process concludes with an insightful discussion of the profound
processive quality of all creation. Born in St. John's and living in Newfoundland for most of his life, Horwood's major concerns as a writer reflect a
radical dissatisfaction with "civilized" society and an exploration of alternative ideas and lifestyles.*

A WILDERNESS LAKE

1   Half a mile from my front gate lies a body of water with the official
name of Beachy Cove Pond. But no one calls it that. Ever since a
family of beavers moved into it from some remote region five years
ago, and completely altered its size and shape and character, it has
been known to the people of Witch Hazel Ridge as the Beaver Pond.
Formerly it was very small and shallow; now it covers almost one-
third of a square mile, averaging four feet in depth. Except for a
lily-free swimming hole near the inlet, you can reach any part of the
bottom with a canoe paddle. Well hidden from roads and human
habitations, it is a true wilderness lake.

2   I have seen it in all its seasons — when the moon caught the long
needles of frost creeping on its surface in autumn, and the lonely
night cries of thrushes in migration dropped from the darkness overhead; in the stillness of winter when a single ax rang over its snow,
and the long straight tracks of a horse sled were the only sign of life
in a world rapt in the deep trance of hibernation; in spring when the
ice cracked in a great flood and went roaring to sea with a prolonged
clap of thunder over the numerous rocky falls of Beachy Cove River;
and in the summer, amid the ceaseless hum and twitter of burgeoning life, when the very bottom of the pond erupted with birth, when
the deeps and the shallows, the marshy margins and the surrounding
banks hopped and crawled and whispered and sang with the miracle
of procreation. Disregarding the microscopic world, and counting

only what can be seen with the naked eye, there are more living animals in the Beaver Pond than there are human beings upon this entire planet.

3   Under the lock and key of winter, when scarcely a ray of sunshine penetrates its surface, life in the pond is near its lowest ebb, with only a few hundred fish and a few million insects, down among the very roots of life, swimming or crawling in slow motion. Under the ice the beavers come and go. A muskrat emerges briefly from his burrow in the bank to feed on the root of a pond lily. Even these hardy animals are seen but rarely. Everything else is buried in the mud, or stuck to the stems of the plants and benumbed into deep sleep by the cold. Some have died utterly, down to the last individual of the species, leaving only the tiny blueprint of their lives, coiled and recoiled like a multi-stranded cord within the nucleus of a microscopic egg, awaiting the warmth of another year to replenish the earth with their kind. Others have left larvae, rolled into balls in a death-like stupor, also awaiting the touch of the sun to revive them. Even the few creatures that move, such as the fish and the larger beetles, do so at a snail's pace, barely flexing their muscles in the near-freezing water. The little food needed for this slow-motion life comes from the bottom—dormant larvae and eggs of summer's turbulent children.

4   Around the end of March the ice melts, or, more rarely, cracks and "goes out" in a cascading breakup under pressure from a spring flood. At the same time the first migratory birds arrive — horned larks and fox sparrows, closely followed by robins. By mid-April every suitable spruce and fir on the dry banks of the Beaver Pond has its pair of songbirds. The yellow-shafted flickers have set up house in dead trees a few yards back from the water. Then snipe and swamp sparrows begin building nests around the edges of the peat bog at the end of the pond, where the brook comes snaking in from the upper gully. Savannah sparrows lay claim to the shrubs and herbs on the bank above. Rusty blackbirds inhabit the stunted spruces along the drowned shore where the beavers have backed the water into the forest, and a little later, flocks of warblers take over the leafy woods at the lower end. Soon every scrap of territory is annexed by one bird or another, and the air is loud with their songs. The various scraps of earth which they claim fit together like the pieces of a jigsaw puzzle, each to his own peculiar tastes. The warblers do not nest on the marsh, nor the snipe in the spruces. Nor are there any blank spaces. There are always more birds than nest sites, and whenever an empty bit of real estate occurs on the banks of the pond, some creature whose needs are exactly suited by this particular vacant lot comes along and stakes a claim.

5   At almost the same time as the birds, fish arrive in large numbers, tumbling downstream from the chain of lakes that runs across the country a mile or so away. Some of them come to rest in the deep

holes of the bottom, and along the shady, food-laden banks. Others flop over the beaver dam and continue downstream, making spectacular dives over the high falls of Beachy Cove River (dives that no warm-blooded creature could hope to survive) until they reach the beach and the sea, where they are occasionally caught in nets, or taken by children with shop-line fishing gear, looking for nothing more spectacular than a sculpin or a flat-fish, but pleased beyond measure by the unexpected appearance of a rainbow trout.

6   For the trout it is always a one-way trip. They obey the age-old instinct to go down to the sea, as their ancestors did in quieter waters than these for countless generations, but no fish ever hatched could get upstream past even the first waterfall in this wild river.

7   Meanwhile, as if on purpose to provide food for the hordes of hungry birds and fish, there has been a great stirring and awakening in the pond itself. Green frogs and their tadpoles that were buried in the mud all winter, looking as dead as last year's leaves, wake up and wriggle to the surface. The tadpoles dine on algae, which are now burgeoning into an underwater meadow under the shock of the sunlight. Soon they begin to sprout legs and to absorb their tails. The frogs hop out among the reeds, searching for the first swarms of flies that are hatching even now in the sun-warmed corners of marsh and pond, and will soon be followed by explosive swarms of caddis flies and May flies, rising by the million out of the sun-warmed water.

8   Each has its own place in the pattern. As with insects, so with larger animals. Besides beavers and muskrats, the pond has mink, a pair of loons, and a rough-legged hawk. This magnificent bird, exceeded in majesty only by the eagle, lives at the very peak of the food chain, and rides the air securely, with no enemies that it need fear, traveling on slow wingbeats around the bend of the lake, or soaring through summer mornings as the pond air rises above the night-chilled land.

9   Each follows the pattern that has existed since its beginnings: the muskrats gather leaves and burrow for roots, the loons dive for fish, as each is taught to do by the immortal mysteries buried deep within the mortal frame. Each stays inside the narrow limits prescribed by its nature. Muskrat food could nourish the loon, perhaps even fatten it, yet it does not trespass upon the muskrat's domain. If the fishing is poor it will go hungry rather than eat leaves and roots. The mink, on the other hand, ignores the vegetable food that grows so lushly along its native bank, and competes with the loon for fish. It will wait patiently in the shadow of an alder shrub for a fish to rise near shore. Then it will dive into the water like an arrow, rising a moment later with the fat trout clamped in its sleek black jaws. It vanishes into the woods, to be seen no more until hunger or curiosity sends it back to the bank.

10   The mink and the muskrat live not without danger. Should it show itself too often on the surface of the pond, the mink might be struck by the rough-legged hawk. The muskrat might as easily be killed by the mink, which is perfectly at home in the water and well able to pursue him through all the passages of his burrow. And both have to keep a wary eye on the young foxes, which have moved down from the brood den on the mountain, and are growing stronger and more cunning every day.

11   The cubs, still linked by an invisible tie to their mother, who is never more than a few hundred yards away from them, already know the taste of muskrat meat. They have come to the pond to be near water and good hunting, for here is the very well of life in Beachy Cove Valley. The pond and its banks, open to the sun as the forest is not, provide a rapid growth of food. Here the sun's energy is not stored in great pillars of wood but is turned quickly into succulent leaf and stem, and living juice and flesh, and so mounts through its chemical transformations up the ladder of the living world from alga and insect all the way to the foxes and the hawk.

12   The cubs slink through the kalmia bushes and thickets of Labrador tea, poking sharp black snouts and whiskers out above the water only when they feel sure there is no larger animal about, for they might be seized by a roaming dog, by the solitary lynx that patrols this patch of woods, or perhaps the hawk that cruises the length of the Beaver Pond watching intently through its telescopic eyes for any movement of prey worthy of its attack.

13   Throughout the summer the shallows are filled with frogs, multiplying at a fantastic rate, consuming vast numbers of flies, and in turn falling easy victims to everything from hawks to feral cats, which constantly prowl these woods on velvet feet. The young foxes usually disdain to hunt frogs, but the smaller and weaker cats must take whatever they can get.

14   The frogs that came out of the mud in spring have been mostly eaten by mid-summer, but have been replaced by a new generation of frogs in much larger numbers than before. It is then that they peak tirelessly, all night long, from the thickets of cattails, in a language that has no words and only two syllables. This chanting out of the age of amphibians contrasts and competes with another sound that crackles down through the clouds from the icy regions ten miles above the earth — jet bombers on a night mission toward the North Pole. But the sound out of the remote past, full of melancholy and ageless sadness, goes on, undisturbed even by the sound of the end of the world.

15   Autumn comes slowly to the Beaver Pond, creeping through the blue and yellow haze of Indian summer. Already by early July the first of the butterflies have crept under the bark of trees or among

leaves on the banks to hibernate until spring. Many species of insects have vanished altogether, leaving only eggs or larvae behind. Soon the first of the birds are gathering into flocks, stirred by a restlessness to travel, while the beavers are busy cutting great stacks of tender twigs to store in the pond beside the door of their lodge against the months when they will be unable to climb the banks and feed in the forest. The single, mournful notes of migrating thrushes again are heard at night, and soon, from the north, will come the wild bugle calls of Canada geese.

16 So the wheel of the year circles above the pond, carrying life up to its triumphant climax in August, and down to its still, small diminuendo in December. It is a cycle with much struggle and ferocity, but also with much beauty and symmetry, not only in its individual forms, but in its total pattern, as well.

17 Beyond this annual cycle, the pond has a life cycle of its own. Like a living creature, it is born, it grows, and it dies. It began far back in time, more than seven thousand years ago, when a part of Beachy Cove Valley was blocked with rocks and clay left by a melting glacier. Here the stream that followed the glacier down the valley widened into a stretch of still water. The pond reached its climacteric when the beavers backed it up into the forest, creating a vast new territory for the nurturing of countless lives. But the very life which fills the pond slowly brings it to an end. The thick growth of underwater plants, the husks of insects, the inedible parts of animals that fall to the bottom in a steady rain throughout the summer—all combine to raise it year by year toward the surface. At last the water will become too shallow for the beavers, no matter how many outlets they plug with dams, and then they will desert the pond, or lingering, will be frozen into their lodge to die of starvation. Their dam will be broken, and they will not be there to repair it. Then the water level will suddenly fall, and the pond will become a marsh, with a stream flowing through it. As the lip where the dam once stood is worn down, the bed of the stream will slowly deepen, the marsh will dry out and become a rich meadow with a thick deposit of organic soil created so many years before by the swarming of life of the pond. When that happens a new sort of life history will begin along new routes and patterns, and the meadow will be home to millions of new creatures, all vastly different from the hordes of living things that inhabit the Beaver Pond today.

18 So the small and the great cycles of life meet and merge and contribute to the grand design, forever changing and growing into something new. Most of the swamp sparrows lost their nests the year the vixen brought her growing cubs to the pond. The vixen herself disappeared soon after, and perhaps no more than two of the cubs lived long enough to mate. But the Platonic idea of the swamp sparrow

lives on like that of the fox, forever pure and bright, as though always freshly coined from the mint of creation, weaving the life and death of the individual — and even the life and death of his world — into the great, glowing tapestry of eternity.

Questions on Content

1   Horwood's general subject is "a true wilderness lake" known as the Beaver Pond, as established in paragraph one. What is Horwood's real subject, as expressed in paragraph two?

2   What are the four stages in the process Horwood describes in "A Wilderness Lake," as summarized in paragraph two? What stage seems most significant to Horwood in his detailed description of this process? How is this significance emphasized? Why is this emphasis appropriate to Horwood's real subject?

3   What is Horwood's thesis statement about the cyclical process he describes?

4   After summarizing (in paragraph sixteen) the life cycle of the animals in the pond and then stating that "It is a cycle with much struggle and ferocity, but also with much beauty and symmetry, not only in its individual forms, but in its total pattern, as well," Horwood discusses that cycle's relation to the life cycle of the pond itself in the two other concluding paragraphs, seventeen and eighteen. What are the main ideas developed in these two paragraphs?

5   What is the purpose of Horwood's process analysis in "A Wilderness Lake"?

Questions on Structure and Technique

1   What senses do the descriptive images in paragraph one and two appeal to? What images did you feel were most effective in subsequent paragraphs? Why?

2   How are the descriptive images in paragraph two arranged? Why is this pattern appropriate to Horwood's organization and development of the essay as a whole? Outline how this basic pattern is organized into paragraphs.

3   What distinct steps is the second stage, spring, divided into (paragraphs four through twelve)? What words and phrases help to define this sequence of steps?

4   Why is the contrast of the jet bombers in paragraph fourteen so effective? What purpose does this contrast serve in the essay as a whole, with specific reference to Horwood's conclusion?

5   Why do you think Horwood withholds his thesis statement until paragraph seventeen? Particularly in the light of Horwood's thesis and conclusion in paragraphs seventeen through nineteen, why is process analysis an effective mode of organization and development for this essay?

Suggestions for Writing

1   Choose a specific place that you have observed closely and thoroughly. Analyse the process whereby this place changes during the year in accordance with the four seasons. Write an informational process analysis based on your analysis, using specific detailed descriptions to develop your essay.

2   Analyse the life cycle of a particular person, animal, place, or thing, dividing the cycle into appropriate stages and steps within each stage. Write an informational process analysis of this life cycle, describing the specific details of what occurs at each stage and how they are related to the whole process.

ERNEST HEMINGWAY

*Ernest Hemingway (1899–1961) wrote this instructional essay on camp-
ing for the* Toronto Star *where he worked as a journalist. He later became
the author of short stories and novels such as* The Sun Also Rises *(1926),*
A Farewell to Arms *(1929), and* For Whom the Bell Tolls *(1940). Hemingway was born and raised in Oak Park, Illinois, near Chicago, and his early
experiences camping, fishing, and hunting during summers spent with his
family in northern Michigan began a lifelong interest in the outdoors and
sporting activities reflected in this selection as well as in many of his major
fictional works. Hemingway's passion for experience and for doing the
"right" thing with grace and dignity were always expressed in his writing
with simplicity, clarity, and insight from his apprentice years as a journalist to his masterpiece,* The Old Man and the Sea *(1953), for which he was
awarded both Pulitzer and Nobel Prizes. Hemingway took his own life in
1961 following a long period of despair and illness.*

WHEN YOU CAMP OUT, DO IT RIGHT

1   Thousands of people will go into the bush this summer to cut the
high cost of living. A man who gets his two weeks' salary while he is
on vacation should be able to put those two weeks in fishing and
camping and be able to save one week's salary clear. He ought to be
able to sleep comfortably every night, to eat well every day and to
return to the city rested and in good condition.

2   But if he goes into the woods with a frying pan, an ignorance of
black flies and mosquitoes, and a great and abiding lack of knowledge about cookery the chances are that his return will be very different. He will come back with enough mosquito bites to make the
back of his neck look like a relief map of the Caucasus. His digestion
will be wrecked after a valiant battle to assimilate half-cooked or
charred grub. And he won't have had a decent night's sleep while he
has been gone.

3   He will solemnly raise his right hand and inform you that he has
joined the grand army of never-agains. The call of the wild may be
all right, but it's a dog's life. He's heard the call of the tame with both
ears. Waiter, bring him an order of milk toast.

4   In the first place he overlooked the insects. Black flies, no-see-ums,
deer flies, gnats and mosquitoes were instituted by the devil to force

people to live in cities where he could get at them better. If it weren't for them everybody would live in the bush and he would be out of work. It was a rather successful invention.

5   But there are lots of dopes that will counteract the pests. The simplest perhaps is oil of citronella. Two bits' worth of this purchased at any pharmacist's will be enough to last for two weeks in the worst fly and mosquito-ridden country.

6   Rub a little on the back of your neck, your forehead and your wrists before you start fishing, and the blacks and skeeters will shun you. The odor of citronella is not offensive to people. It smells like gun oil. But the bugs do hate it.

7   Oil of pennyroyal and eucalyptol are also much hated by mosquitoes, and with citronella they form the basis for many proprietary preparations. But it is cheaper and better to buy the straight citronella. Put a little on the mosquito netting that covers the front of your pup tent or canoe tent at night, and you won't be bothered.

8   To be really rested and get any benefit out of a vacation a man must get a good night's sleep every night. The first requisite for this is to have plenty of cover. It is twice as cold as you expect it will be in the bush four nights out of five, and a good plan is to take just double the bedding that you think you will need. An old quilt that you can wrap up in is as warm as two blankets.

9   Nearly all outdoor writers rhapsodize over the browse bed. It is all right for the man who knows how to make one and has plenty of time. But in a succession of one-night camps on a canoe trip all you need is level ground for your tent floor and you will sleep all right if you have plenty of covers under you. Take twice as much cover as you think that you will need, and then put two-thirds of it under you. You will sleep warm and get your rest.

10   When it is clear weather you don't need to pitch your tent if you are only stopping for the night. Drive four stakes at the head of your make-up bed and drape your mosquito bar over that, then you can sleep like a log and laugh at the mosquitoes.

11   Outside of insects and bum sleeping the rock that wrecks most camping trips is cooking. The average tyro's idea of cooking is to fry everything and fry it good and plenty. Now, a frying pan is a most necessary thing to any trip, but you also need the old stew kettle and the folding reflector baker.

12   A pan of fried trout can't be bettered and they don't cost any more than ever. But there is a good and bad way of frying them.

13   The beginner puts his trout and his bacon in and over a brightly burning fire the bacon curls up and dries into a dry tasteless cinder and the trout is burned outside while it is still raw inside. He eats them and it is all right if he is only out for the day and going home to a good meal at night. But if he is going to face more trout and bacon

the next morning and other equally well-cooked dishes for the remainder of two weeks he is on the pathway to nervous dyspepsia.

14   The proper way is to cook over coals. Have several cans of Crisco or Cotosuet or one of the vegetable shortenings along that are as good as lard and excellent for all kinds of shortening. Put the bacon in and when it is about half cooked lay the trout in the hot grease, dipping them in corn meal first. Then put the bacon on top of the trout and it will baste them as it slowly cooks.

15   The coffee can be boiling at the same time and in a smaller skillet pancakes being made that are satisfying the other campers while they are waiting for the trout.

16   With the prepared pancake flours you take a cupful of pancake flour and add a cup of water. Mix the water and flour and as soon as the lumps are out it is ready for cooking. Have the skillet hot and keep it well greased. Drop the batter in and as soon as it is done on one side loosen it in the skillet and flip it over. Apple butter, syrup or cinnamon and sugar go well with the cakes.

17   While the crowd have taken the edge from their appetites with flapjacks the trout have been cooked and they and the bacon are ready to serve. The trout are crisp outside and firm and pink inside and the bacon is well done — but not too done. If there is anything better than that combination the writer has yet to taste it in a lifetime devoted largely and studiously to eating.   *hyperbole*

18   The stew kettle will cook your dried apricots when they have resumed their predried plumpness after a night of soaking, it will serve to concoct a mulligen in, and it will cook macaroni. When you are not using it, it should be boiling water for the dishes.

19   In the baker, mere man comes into his own, for he can make a pie that to his bush appetite will have it all over the product that mother used to make, like a tent. Men have always believed that there was something mysterious and difficult about making a pie. Here is a great secret. There is nothing to it. We've been kidded for years. Any man of average office intelligence can make at least as good a pie as his wife.

20   All there is to a pie is a cup and a half of flour, one-half teaspoonful of salt, one-half cup of lard and cold water. That will make pie crust that will bring tears of joy into your camping partner's eyes.

21   Mix the salt with the flour, work the lard into the flour, make it up into a good workmanlike dough with cold water. Spread some flour on the back of a box or something flat, and pat the dough around a while. Then roll it out with whatever kind of round bottle you prefer. Put a little more lard on the surface of the sheet of dough and then slosh a little flour on and roll it up and then roll it out again with the bottle.

22   Cut out a piece of the rolled out dough big enough to line a pie tin. I like the kind with holes in the bottom. Then put in your dried apples that have soaked all night and between sweetened, or your apricots, or your blueberries, and then take another sheet of the dough and drape it gracefully over the top, soldering it down at the edges with your fingers. Cut a couple of slits in the top dough sheet and prick it a few times with a fork in an artistic manner.

23   Put it in the baker with a good slow fire for forty-five minutes and then take it out and if your pals are Frenchmen they will kiss you. The penalty for knowing how to cook is that the others will make you do all the cooking.

24   It is all right to talk about roughing it in the woods. But the real woodsman is the man who can be really comfortable in the bush.

Questions on Content

1   According to Hemingway, what "ought" a person be able to do when going camping? What dangers does an uninstructed camper face?

2   What is the first main problem that a camper should not overlook? What steps should be taken to overcome this problem?

3   What is the second major concern that a camper must address? What important details must be attended to?

4   What is the third main thing that must be done correctly by a camper? What steps and specific details illustrate this task?

5   What is Hemingway's definition of "the real woodsman"? How is this definition supported by the preceding discussion of camping?

Questions on Structure and Technique

1   In paragraph one, what sentence clearly establishes Hemingway's subject? In what sentence does he most clearly state his attitude toward that subject? Why are paragraphs two and three important?

2   What are the three main aspects of camping that Hemingway develops in this essay? How are these aspects introduced in paragraphs one and two? To what extent can these aspects be considered as chronologically-ordered stages in a whole process? Outline Hemingway's organization of this essay.

3   Where does Hemingway develop detailed steps within a major stage? What details makes these steps interesting to the reader? What specific details indicate Hemingway's authoritative knowledge of his subject?

4   Examine Hemingway's use of both third-person and second-person nouns and pronouns in this essay. When does he use third person? When does he use second person? Why? When does he shift from third-person to second-person, and vice versa? Why?

5   What examples of words, phrases, and sentences can you find that seem intended to encourage as well as to instruct the reader in the necessary skills for a successful camping experience?

Suggestions for Writing

1   After studying Hemingway's essay, with particular attention to paragraphs eleven through twenty-three, write an instructional process analysis on how to prepare a favourite dish or perhaps a whole meal. Be sure to establish a clear thesis and to develop your instructions effectively dividing them into several main stages as well as specific steps within those stages (where appropriate). Use specific details that will appeal to your readers' senses and general interest in the process you discuss.

2   Write an instructional process analysis of an activity that you do well, one that requires careful attention to the correct procedures in order to be performed successfully. Your use of specific details and examples should reflect both your authority on the subject and the dangers or problems posed to a novice.

CHAPTER 7

"O my tiger city!"

CAUSAL ANALYSIS

A causal analysis is a division of a whole subject into several parts so that the relations between causes and effects may be examined. This division is made in response to an explicit or an implicit expression of a question or problem. If we ask *why* something happens, then we are considering its *causes*. If we ask what *results* when something happens, then we are considering its *effects*. In other words, an inquiry into a subject's cause and effect relations may proceed either from effect to cause or from cause to effect, beginning with what is known and investigating what is unknown.

Causal analysis provides writers with another practical means of both understanding and expressing ideas and experiences, but any causal explanation presents writers as well as readers with several important questions about what is unknown: Are all possible causes or effects being considered? Are the causes, effects, and cause-effect relations "real" ones? Are the cause-effect relations oversimplified? Consequently, a writer must cautiously and carefully organize and develop a causal explanation with sufficient evidence to support his or her analysis.

First, a writer should outline all possible causes or effects of something happening. Then, a writer can select the most significant ones and examine their relations so that they can be arranged in a logical manner. For example, if you consider *why* you are living in a particular town or city, as Morley Callaghan does in "Why Toronto?", you may decide that there is really only one single reason, or cause, such as attending your college or university. In this basic illustrative pattern of cause and effect as well as in more complex ones, you must provide specific details to substantiate that your explanations are real ones and not oversimplifications. Callaghan, for instance, begins his analysis by suggesting several plausible reasons why he lives in Toronto, and then shows us why he does not believe them to be the real causes before offering us his explanation. More often, you will identify several related causes that can be arranged as either a causal classification or a causal process (or a combination of these two patterns). You will need to apply the principles of classification or process analysis in doing so.

I. Introduction [Effect]
II. A Cause 1
II. B Cause 2
II. C Cause 3
III. Conclusion

For example, you may decide that there are several categories, or kinds, of causes that explain why you live in a place, such as education, family, and friends, in which case you should organize and develop your essay as a causal classification. On the other hand, the causes may be related as a sequence of causes and effects whereby one cause results in an effect which, in turn, is the cause of a second effect, and so on, in which case you should organize and develop your essay as a causal process. For instance, family problems may have brought you closer to your friends who, in turn, encouraged you to attend university with them; therefore, you decided to move to the town where that university is located. Conversely, either a causal classification or a causal process may also be used to arrange the related effects that *result* when something happens, such as the kinds or the sequence of effects that result from your decision to live in a new place.

I.   Introduction [Cause]
II. A   Effect 1
II. B   Effect 2
II. C   Effect 3
III.   Conclusion

In the following selections, you will study how writers organize and develop causal analysis essays that proceed from effect to cause(s) or from cause to effect(s) using causal classification or causal process. In practice, a writer's subject and purpose, point of view, and specific knowledge of the subject usually indicate which basic patterns would be most effective. You will also discover how these patterns can be developed into complex analyses of complicated subjects when writers are taking many possibilities into account, substantiating the real possibilities with details and examples, and avoiding simplified explanations in favour of a thoughtful and knowledgeable discussion of the relations between causes and effects.

MORLEY CALLAGHAN

Morley Callaghan (b. 1903) has lived in Toronto for almost all of his life, and he offers us an insightful analysis of the reasons why in this essay. After graduating from the University of Toronto in 1925 and completing a law degree at Osgoode Hall in 1928, Callaghan pursued a career as a writer with the encouragement of Ernest Hemingway and F. Scott Fitzgerald. Following the publication of his first novel, Strange Fugitive *(1928), and a collection of short stories,* A Native Argosy *(1929), Callaghan spent time in Paris with these two young American writers and others including James Joyce, an experience described in his autobiographical book,* That Summer in Paris *(1963). Among Callaghan's most popular other works are the novels* Such is My Beloved *(1934),* They Shall Inherit the Earth *(1935),* More Joy in Heaven *(1937),* The Loved and the Lost *(1951),* The Many Colored Coat *(1960), and* Close to the Sun Again *(1951), and the collection of short stories entitled* Morley Callaghan's Stories *(1959).*

WHY TORONTO?

1 People sometimes ask me a strange question. They say, 'Why do you live in Toronto?' This question comes not only from those I have met casually for the first time, but often from people who have lived most of their lives in Toronto, and it always leaves me with an apologetic air and an evasive answer never quite expressed. I know what they mean. They mean that I don't own a bank, an industrial plant, or an advertising agency that links me to this one spot on the earth; being a writer I could just as easily live in Montreal, Mexico City, or among the palms and temples of the south. To make it worse, even my wife the other day asked me in a puzzled tone why we had gone on living in Toronto.

2 To the professor from St. Louis who asked me why I lived in Toronto, I tried saying casually, 'Why, I was born in Toronto.' For a moment he was silent and I thought I might have found the right easy answer. 'How odd,' he said finally. 'You're the only writer I know who lives in the place where he was born.'

3 Others have suggested that possibly I like being surrounded by a group of friends, 'makers of Canadian literature', in this new Athens of the north, but then I have to explain shyly that I don't seem to have many literary friends and that the great new cultural wave seemed to have missed my street, as the tornado that struck Windsor last summer missed many of the streets of that town. Is my publisher in

Toronto? No. When I write fiction stories do they appear in the Toronto magazines? No, the American magazines. Is my business, such as it is, conducted in Toronto? No, my agent is in New York. Is there anything on earth that I do in Toronto, as a writer, that I couldn't do just as well, if not better, somewhere else? And the answer is 'No.'

4   Even the fact that my children go to school in Toronto never seems to be sufficient justification for living here to those who would lead me beyond the horizon. So I have stretched myself out on a couch, pretending that a psycho-analyst is just behind me, leading me on, and I have torn into my dreams and broken thoughts, trying to reveal to myself the cause of my Toronto bondage. And I find myself defending Toronto, laughing at it and being cynical about those other cities recommended to me.

5   New York is always there in my mind as the right city, but I have lived in New York and I don't know many writers who go on living there year after year without getting a little sour or brittle or tired. Of course, that's true of New York, but isn't it also true that I have been sour and tired in Toronto? Oh, it is indeed. And there are places to pass the time in New York, comfortable places with pretty faces, and in that city you want more and more of the life around you — you want to possess it and it gets that it eats you up, and when enough of you has been eaten away, you get tired and alcoholic.

6   A friend of mine in Montreal, Frank Scott, the professor-poet, is always saying that Montreal is the right place, for that lovely city seethes with ideas and has an intellectual life that is foreign to Toronto. But I think he has it all wrong. The English-speaking people of Montreal are pretty much like the people of Toronto; in fact, walking along the Montreal streets I'm always meeting somebody who used to live in Toronto, and they all swear they are much happier than they were in the Ontario Athens; but they look just the same to me and they talk just the same and they have the same ideas and the intellectual structure of their lives was clearly shaped in Toronto and they can't get away from it. This I perceive with a certain feeling of glee. These Ontarians have run four hundred miles trying to catch falling stars, and they have dug themselves into Montreal and have quaffed wine and heard moon songs and made themselves comfortable in ways in which the time passes easily. But they don't fool me — Toronto is in the mind. The notion that Montreal has a dazzling intellectual life like that of Paris, which makes the intellectual life of Toronto seem pathetically provincial, is a myth. Montreal has charm and fine restaurants and happy bistros, and there one can forget easily that Toronto is deep in the mind; one can laugh and struggle to maintain the illusion, but the truth is that the English-speaking people of Montreal and Toronto think the same thoughts. This they refuse to believe. It may be, of course, that I have gone a bit crazy and think

of myself as a leader in the underground resistance movement, and whisper to myself the story of those glorious days in France during the German occupation when French writers of the resistance went right on creating and publishing their writing under the noses of the watchful conquerors. Their resistance gave them a creative strength and their attic rooms and their cellars were their temples of art, and they felt a certain contempt for those writers who had run from the conquerors and were living in comfort abroad.

7   The people of Toronto are a quiet, pleasant people who like to lead an orderly life. They are reasonably polite. They don't like the social life of the cafés, and the crowded boulevards have no charm for them, but they like an indoor life, and their living rooms and drawing rooms take the place of the cafés and the bistros. I should say rather that this was the Toronto of twenty-five years ago when the polite cultural life represented a vast imitation British Dullness. This dullness is still all-pervading among the nicer people, but in the meantime, under their noses, the life around them has changed. Toronto in the last ten years has become a big, hard, rough, sprawling North American city with a Bay Street that is one of the biggest gambling markets in North America. The town crawls with taverns, the streets are filled with strange accents. It is the centre for whatever there is of the publishing, painting, writing, music, and theatre life of English-speaking Canada. It has become a hard-driving city, a great place for a hard guy after a fast buck. And it has the biggest university in Canada and probably more intellectual apathy than any other city of its size.

8   I come now to my acceptance of the reality of my life in Toronto. I walk around the streets, I go from house to house, nursing my necessary illusion that the orderly life of the place and the simple friendliness of the people is a discipline for me. I deceive myself into thinking that I live a monastic life, but that like a monk in his cell in the long night, my imagination may be stretched and strained and fired and make for me the stuff of exalted dreams. The hard routine of a strict monastic rule may be very good for the soul. The orderly, unexciting, strict Toronto life, I go on telling myself year after year, cannot distract me, cannot give the illusion of gay living, and if the flesh groans the spirit may grow stronger.

9   There is one other aspect of the matter. I have tried wandering into other cities, and pressing on to distant shores, and have found after a few weeks in a strange place, the urge to move on grows strong, the old weariness gripping me, makes me believe that each new place will be charming because it is new. Well, a writer can stand only so much of this restless boredom; he will go on and on, once he starts wandering, seeking the unexpected scene, the new lovely face, with the charm of novelty always pulling him on and finally wearying

him to death. If you stay in Toronto, the longing remains deep in the soul, and since it can't be satisfied you can't be wearied, and your mind and your imagination, should become like a caged tiger. O Toronto! O my tiger city!

Questions on Content

1   Why do people ask Morley Callaghan "Why do you live in Toronto?" What plausible answers to this question does Callaghan consider? What general attitude toward Toronto does Callaghan express?

2   What two cities are "recommended" to Callaghan as good places for a writer to live in? Why doesn't Callaghan want to live in New York? Why doesn't he want to live in Montreal? What is the main similarity between New York and Toronto, according to Callaghan? Between Montreal and Toronto?

3   What aspects of Toronto does Callaghan "defend"? What does he "laugh at"?

4   What is Callaghan's "necessary illusion" about his life in Toronto? What does he "deceive" himself into thinking? Why does Callaghan accept the "reality" of his life in Toronto? What is the relation between "illusion" and "reality" that Callaghan shows us?

5   Why does Callaghan call Toronto "my tiger city"?

Questions on Structure and Technique

1   Does Callaghan's analysis proceed from effect to cause or from cause to effect? What sentence first establishes the general purpose of Callaghan's analysis? What is his purpose? In what subsequent sentence does he express this purpose as a statement of the problem to be solved?

2   In what sentence does Callaghan express his general attitude toward Toronto? How is this sentence related to Callaghan's subsequent organization and development of his analysis?

3   Is Callaghan's "cynicism" about New York and Montreal a real "cause" for living in Toronto? Why does Callaghan point out the similarities between these cities and Toronto?

4   In what paragraphs does Callaghan present the real reason why he lives in Toronto? What sentences contain general statements of this reason? What similes provide specific images that clarify these general statements for a reader?

5   Why does Callaghan choose the verb form "should become" in his concluding paragraph?

Suggestions for Writing

1   Ask yourself the question "Why do I live in this city (or town)?" Organize and develop your answer to this question in a causal analysis essay. Support your general statements with specific details and images that clearly *show* your readers why you live where you do.

2   Write a causal analysis essay in which you discuss why you need to engage in a particular activity that other people sometimes question, using specific details and examples to support your analysis.

3   Ask a variety of people the following question: "Why do you live in this city (or town)?" Classify their responses into three or four logical categories. Use these categories as the basis for your organization and development of a causal analysis essay in which you report and explain the results of your survey. Provide your readers with selected details and illustrations that clarify your analysis.

WILFRED G. BIGELOW

In this selection from a chapter in his book entitled Cold Hearts *(1984), heart surgeon, researcher, and educator, Dr. Wilfred G. Bigelow (b. 1913) explains to his readers the causal process whereby he and other medical researchers at Toronto's Banting Institute developed an electric pacemaker for the heart in 1949. Dr. Bigelow effectively guides the lay reader through a complex series of stages and steps in the scientific research process by using clear definitions, avoiding technical jargon, and introducing interesting narrative details into his writing. Educated at Brandon College and the University of Toronto and the recipient of many awards and honors for his contributions to the field of medicine, Dr. Bigelow has been Senior Surgeon and Head of Cardiovascular Surgery at Toronto General Hospital and he is Professor Emeritus in the Department of Surgery at the University of Toronto Medical School.*

THE INVENTION OF THE PACEMAKER

1   It is 1949. Visualize, if you will, Room 64 in the basement of the Banting Institute in Toronto — home of the cardiovascular surgical experimental laboratory. The room is 23 × 14 feet. A small, high window is below ground level. As it houses two major research projects, the room is very congested. The adjoining Room 65 has recently been acquired. . . .

2   Opening the door of Room 64 released the hum of activity of four to seven or eight busy people: my team of two research fellows (John Callaghan and Ross Fleming), two technicians, a chemist, and assorted representatives from departments that were collaborating in the hypothermia and microcirculation research. To say that they were occupied is an understatement. They all felt that they were setting the stage for an explosion of knowledge and technology that would profoundly affect the whole practice of medicine.

3   Capillary circulation (microcirculation) was being observed through a microscope in a living animal. This was a new and exacting technique, hitherto viewed by only a few anatomists. It gets at the business end of the circulation, where all the action is. The hypothermia studies, we hoped, would allow direct-vision correction of heart defects, until now virtually unassailable. It was an awesomely fertile field.

4   Microcirculation and hypothermia were initiated as two different research projects. Astoundingly, as work progressed it became apparent that they were closely interrelated. Cooling an animal below a certain body temperature produced some serious obstruction to flow in the capillary circulation.

5   The excitement of work in hypothermia was overshadowed by a great cloud of frustration. As noted earlier, the heart would cease to function (cardiac arrest) at some point when the laboratory animal was cooled below a body temperature of 24°C. And yet infant animals could be safely cooled and resuscitated from body temperatures near the freezing level (5°C). We were in a hurry to solve the problem so that we could study deep hypothermia. Why did the cold heart suddenly stop? We pondered, discussed, and read about the subject.

6   The heart stoppage or cardiac arrest was in two forms: cardiac standstill — a motionless heart; and ventricular fibrillation, where the auricles may still be beating, but the strong ventricles are ineffectively squirming. There had been three years' research with no answer.

7   One morning a standard experiment was planned. As I entered the laboratory, an anaesthetized dog was already being cooled in refrigeration blankets with ice bags. At a body temperature of 22°C with regular heart action and adequate blood pressure, the cooling was discontinued and the top blanket removed. After surgical preparation of the shaven skin, the chest was opened by a surgical incision. Cardiac arrest was not expected at 21°C in this particular animal. The pericardium was opened, exposing the normal pink heart beating slowly, forcibly, and gracefully. We were now ready to make certain physiological observations regarding hypothermia, after which the pericardium and chest would be closed and the animal rewarmed.

8   Just as we were about to begin the tests the heart unexpectedly stopped. It lay quietly in standstill. Cardiac massage did not restart it. This meant that our experiment would have to be postponed for another day while we attempted to revive the animal.

9   I looked at the heart. It was quiet, cool, pink, and the muscle was firm. It was of normal appearance in all respects. What was wrong with the little rascal? Out of interest and in desperation, I gave the left ventricle a good poke with a probe I was holding. There was an immediate and sudden strong contraction that involved all chambers — then it returned to standstill. I did it again, with the same result. What an unexpected observation!

10   I poked it regularly every second. Lo and behold, it resembled a normal beating heart. Were these phony beats or real contractions expelling blood into the circulation? A technician acting as anaesthetist said, "Hey, I'm getting a blood pressure here." This meant that these were real contractions, that the heart was not only beating but forcibly expelling blood in a normal manner.

11   The heart had stopped while it appeared to be perfectly capable of continued function. An electrical impulse had the same effect as a poke. Perhaps all the cold heart needed was a pacemaker. What a fascinating idea! Perhaps we could keep the heart beating while we cooled the animal to deep hypothermia levels. We had read reports of research indicating that in laboratory animals, and presumably humans, nerve impulses were not conducted along the nerve below a body temperature of 9 or 10°C, while in hibernators conduction was not affected down to body temperatures of 2 or 3°C. . . . Our experimental animal was successfully resuscitated. He recovered to full activity little knowing that he had created the germ of an idea that would eventually bring health and happiness to thousands of people.

12   Hopps and Callaghan, with the assistance of senior technicians Don Hughes and Ken Burly, commenced a careful and painstaking series of experiments: to assess the electrical activity on a normal heart; to determine comparable pulse characteristics that were most effective and safest; to decide on the best method of delivering a stimulus to the heart.

13   It became apparent to the electric stimulus applied to the heart must be of short duration. The electrical activity of what was called a "sine wave" or "square wave" form might persist into the late stage of heart contraction where the ventricle was in a sensitive state. This might precipitate a cardiac arrest. It was finally decided that a pulse wave with sharp rise and a two-millisecond duration stimulated the normal p-wave on the electrocardiogram. The current should be low. With the heart exposed, the sinoauricular node (the area of the heart containing the natural pacemaker) could be stimulated using an electrode at the tip of an insulated rod. It was a single electrode with the other "dispersive" electrode on the chest wall.

14   To stimulate the heart without opening the chest, Hopps took a standard cardiac catheter and adapted it by passing a wire down the inside of the tube with a ring electrode mounted at the tip. This catheter electrode could be passed down a vein in the neck of a dog to be inside the heart and near the sinoauricular node. The second electrode was attached to the edge of the wound. It proved effective.

15   With great perception, he decided that having both electrodes in the one catheter would channel the electrical stimulation to the desired area and avoid muscle twitching caused by the second electrode. Would it work? He passed both wires down the catheter that attached to two small ring electrodes insulated from each other at the tip. It did work, and more effectively. This was the first so-called "bipolar" catheter electrode to stimulate the lining of the heart. It is still used in pacemakers today.

16   Once the desired pulse features were determined, Hopps retired with the experimental data to his sophisticated electronics laboratory in the National Research Council in Ottawa. Assisted by the skilled technicians and equipment, he designed and built an efficient portable pacemaker unit incorporating the desired electrical features with a specialized circuit.[2] It delivered what had been established as the ideal current and electrical pulse wave (monophasic or biphasic). It allowed dial control of heart rate and voltage. The unit was about twelve inches long and seven inches high — the size of a mantel radio of that era. It was portable, but something that you didn't carry around with you.

17   It was a great day when Jack arrived back in the Banting laboratory with a big smile and carrying our first pacemaker unit carefully packaged. It was viewed with awe and pride. Here was a machine that could duplicate the electrical impulse that stimulated the heart to beat 40 million times a year. We all had a peek at the complicated circuitry and nodded gravely as Jack explained its function.

18   Setting ourselves the goal of duplicating the electrical impulse of a normal heart had meant many animal experiments and long hours of work. As one contemplated the future use of pacemakers for long periods of time, the goal appeared to have justified the effort. But what did we expect from a pacemaker?

19   Our greatest hope was that by providing an artificial pacemaker for the heart, an experimental animal (and later a human) could be safely cooled to low body temperatures (deep hypothermia) and be rewarmed with no ill effect. This was based on our new theory that the heart stopped functioning below 20°C because the cardiac nerves were paralysed by the cold.

20   If we did not succeed in achieving safe deep hypothermia, at least a heart that arrested in standstill during an operation with moderate hypothermia could be "paced" until the body was rewarmed sufficiently to allow return of normal heart action.

21   Pacing the heart might improve its effectiveness and reduce the congestion that usually occurred at 20–24°C body temperature, thereby lessening the incidence of ventricular fibrillation.

22   Its use in hearts at normal body temperature would have to be studied. This was a huge, unexplored continent.

23   In anticipation of the arrival of the pacemaker, the team had prepared an experiment with all hands on deck in our basement laboratory. A routine cooling procedure was carried out. A dog was anaesthetized and a tube was inserted into its trachea to control breathing. The electrocardiogram and blood pressure were recorded. The pacemaker electrode had been sterilized. Through a one-inch incision in

the animal's neck, the catheter was passed down a vein into the heart. When the stimulating tip was in the region of the sinoauricular node, there was evidence on the electrocardiogram to confirm its position. The blood pressure and heart rate were recorded by a fine pointer that produced a tracing on some smoked paper mounted on a rotating drum — a Kymograph. This was 1950, before medical researchers had acquired some of the existing modern electronic techniques used by engineers.

24   The dog was cooled and all things proceeded without a hitch. At 21 °C body temperature, the electrocardiogram showed changes we recognized as indicating that the heart was beginning to falter. It stopped at 20°C body temperature. The pacemaker was quickly switched on at a rate that was optimum for that body temperature. It immediately took control of the heart. The blood pressure and electrocardiogram improved.

25   There was a murmur and some cheerful expletives from the group huddled around watching the electrocardiogram and blood pressure. Cooling progressed without event: 19°C . . . 18°C . . . with a good, stable-appearing electrocardiogram. There were wary smiles exchanged among the watchers. Were we about to have the privilege of being the first to see safe deep hypothermia in an animal with the use of a pacemaker? A body temperature of 17°C had just registered on the thermometer when suddenly the heart stopped. Changing the voltage current or position of the electrode had no effect. The pacemaker had failed us. It had reduced the lower limits of cooling by perhaps 2°C, but that was not enough to make it worthwhile. It did not solve our major problem.

26   This did not appear to be the answer to deep hypothermia. However, pacemaker research in hypothermia continued, and further experiments showed that the pacemaker could be used to improve the safety at moderate levels of hypothermia.[3]

27   The next obvious step was to study the use of the pacemaker at normal body temperatures.[4] Would the pacemaker produce expulsive beats if the heart stopped? We wanted dependable proof from well-controlled experiments using a physiological stimulus.

28   An unexpected problem was immediately encountered. How does one stop a heart? The situation had not been anticipated. An animal can be asphyxiated or chemically poisoned, producing cardiac arrest and death. This was not a reasonable solution. The heart would be damaged and attempts to restore such post-mortem hearts in animals and humans were seldom successful. Experimental surgical techniques to stop the heart or paralyse the sinoauricular node were not dependable in those days.[5] How to stop a heart without damaging it? How to simulate the human condition where, in an otherwise

healthy state, the heart slows or suddenly stops due to faulty impulse formation?

29   The literature indicated that turtle, rabbit, and dog hearts could be stopped temporarily by applying a continuous electric current (tetanizing) to the right vagus nerve in the neck. Callaghan tested all three animals and elected to use dogs and rabbits. It was fair to say that our past experience had not been extensive with turtles. The heart could be stopped for only about half a minute, but that was long enough to test the effectiveness of our pacemaker.

30   In the experiments the animals were anaesthetized. When the vagus nerve was exposed by a small incision in the neck and stimulated electrically, the heart stopped and the blood pressure fell precipitously. In each experiment the pacemaker would restore the heart beats and blood pressure during the arrest period.

31   During the course of these experiments the pacemaker was applied to the normal beating heart. A dog's normal heart rate is about 120 per minute. It was amazing to discover that the heart rate was effectively controlled by the pacemaker. It dominated the natural pacing mechanism. This finding was consistent. With a normal rate of 120, the pacemaker could regulate the heart action and increase the rate to 200 or lower it to 60 per minute. The blood pressure, interestingly enough, remained unchanged regardless of the heart rate, due to built-in reflexes.

32   Experiments during hypothermia and at normal body temperature were duplicated using a bipolar stimulating electrode applied to the sinoauricular node; to the external surface of the exposed left ventricle; and, without opening the chest, by way of the intravenous electrode inside the heart at the level of the sinoauricular node.

33   All of these experiments were repeated many times with control studies and careful collection and analysis of data. The experiments had no effect upon the animals. The majority required only a nick in the neck. Once again the heart rate and blood pressure were recorded on a smoked drum. To make doubly sure that we convinced the medical men and scientists who would hear this report, John Callaghan recorded key experiments by a motion picture, which still survives. In making an announcement to the medical world that a safe physiological pacemaker had been designed for human use, that could actually control the heart rate, the team had to be very sure of its ground.

34   Where should this be recorded? With the advice of Professor Robert Janes it was decided to send an abstract requesting a place on the program at the next meeting of the Annual Surgical Congress of the American College of Surgeons. This was and still is the largest meeting of surgeons in the world. What a relief it was when we were notified that our paper had been one of those selected for what is

called the Surgical Forum. John was to make the presentation, and his name would appear first in our published report because he and Jack Hopps had done the lion's share of the work, particularly the normal body temperature studies. . . .[6]

35   This was the beginning of an explosion of knowledge that has produced the incredible era of heart pacemakers that we know today.

Notes

1. W.G. Bigelow, J.C. Callaghan, and J.A. Hopps, "General Hypothermia for Intracardiac Surgery," *Annals of Surgery*, 132 (1950), 531.

2. Hopps received support from his section head, C.F. Pattenson, at the National Research Council. J.R. Charbonneau was the technician who actually constructed the unit and assisted at the Banting Institute laboratory. Electronic recording devices were used by engineers in the 1950's, but electronics had not yet been married to medicine and the medical researchers here were unaware of existing electronic devices.

3. J.C. Callaghan and W.G. Bigelow, "An Electrical Artificial Pacemaker for Standstill of the Heart," *Annals of Surgery*, 134 (1951), 8.

4. *Ibid.*

5. A dependable technique for producing heart block in experimental animals was not available until 1955. See T.E. Starzyl and R.A. Gaertner, in *Circulation*, 12 (1955), 259.

6. J.C. Callaghan and W.G. Bigelow, "An Electrical Artificial Pacemaker for Standstill of the Heart," *Surgical Forum*, American College of Surgeons, 1950.

Questions on Content

1   What problem was Dr. Bigelow and his research team trying to solve initially?

2   What did they learn one morning after three years of research?

3   Why was a series of experiments necessary before Jack Hopps could design and build an efficient portable pacemaker unit?

4   What were the researchers' expectations for the new machine that Hopps constructed? To what extent were these expectations fulfilled during subsequent experiments?

5   What were the results of this research at the Banting Institute?

Questions on Structure and Technique

1   Dr. Bigelow's introduction concludes with the question: "Why did the cold heart suddenly stop?" Why is this statement of a problem effective in introducing the research process presented in this essay? Is this question answered?

2   The research process itself presented in this essay can be divided into five main stages: the preliminary experiment, the investigative experiments, the pacemaker experiments, and, the presentation of results. Each of these main stages is composed of specific steps. Make a detailed paragraph outline of the main stages and specific steps involved in this process.

3   What examples of interesting and effective specific details that appeal to a general audience can you find? What kinds of material do you think would be eliminated from this writing if it were written only for an audience of cardiovascular specialists? What kind of information would be added for the benefit of this audience?

4   What examples of colloquial words and phrases can you find in this essay? What distinctly technical terminology is employed by Dr. Bigelow?

5   What is the purpose of Dr. Bigelow's conclusion? In what way does this conclusion contribute to the effectiveness of the essay as a whole?

Suggestions for Writing

1   Write a causal process analysis in which show either how you solved a significant problem in your own experience or how you made a discovery of importance to you.

2   Write a causal process analysis of a medical procedure performed on you by a doctor. Although you should present the sequence of causes and effects involved in this process from a patient's point of view, you may choose to supplement your own memory and knowledge with some research into this procedure.

HEATHER MENZIES

Although computer technology has profoundly revolutionized many aspects of our daily experiences during the past several years, its development has been an integral part of the whole history of civilization. In this chapter from her book entitled Computers on the Job: Surviving Canada's Microcomputer Revolution *(1982), Heather Menzies (b. 1949) traces this historical process of innovations in the handling of information in order to give her readers a better understanding of how computer technology developed. She then analyses its present and future effects in our society. Menzies, who was born and educated in Quebec, is a journalist and the author of several books on computer technology including* The Railroad's Not Enough: Canada Now *(1978).*

COMPUTERS, CHIPS AND AUTOMATION

1   About half the work done in North America can be labelled "information work." However it's pigeonholed, as financial analysis, management, secretarial, sales and other services or even manufacturing, the work involves handling information — information that computers can handle for you, and possibly instead of you. But the use of machines to manipulate information isn't a product of the contemporary business world. Throughout history, people who needed to make tabulations, keep records or run manufacturing processes dealt with information, too — and looked for tools to make the work easier.

2   The humble abacus, pioneered by the Chinese six centuries before Christ, is the first well-known example of a tool that can store information as the altered state of a physical thing, which in turn can be manipulated. In this case, the altered state is achieved by moving the beads along the rods of the abacus. Today the same principle is applied in the computer, through electric switches. While this early calculator seems crude today, the abacus nevertheless gave considerable power to its early users: the power of information.

3   Information at its simplest is difference. Black exists, for instance, because it is different from white. Similarly, a percentage communicates information because it expresses a difference between the part and the whole. Numbers and letters are the building blocks of information. They are coded concepts for representing the reality we have observed. The code can be processed according to commonly accepted

logical routines to yield insight, the power of being informed. Sometimes reducing our world to these codes is frustrating, like completing a multiple-choice questionnaire when the answer you want lies somewhere between boxes 1 and 2, or between 3 and 4. Information that won't fit into these boxes, such as nuances and subjective or qualitative information, is lost. Still, once information has been codified or, in computer jargon, digitized, it can then be processed automatically by the computer. This is what makes computers so important to jobs today: they can take over handling any information once it has been coded into digital symbols and entered into the computer as input data. Essentially the computer manipulates the data by following a fixed pattern of instructions (akin to a recipe or knitting pattern) spelled out in computer programs. This manipulation is called data processing, and a data bank is an electronic file where data is stored.

4   Between the heyday of the abacus and the advent of the modern computer came many innovators who sought to increase their information power. In 1642, the philosopher and mathematician Blaise Pascal, the son of a French tax collector, substituted toothed wheels for abacus beads in the world's first known mechanical adding machine. He also incorporated some of the manipulation routine, or program, into the machine itself. As numbers were dialled in on one of the interlocking wheels of the machine, the levers inside were set to trip a movement in the wheel representing the next order of magnitude (the hundreds were next after the tens, for instance). A speedometer runs on the same principle.

5   Charles Babbage, a British mathematician, made two significant additions to the computer's development. In 1822 he invented the difference machine, a calculator that set Pascal's principles to work on a scale never before dreamed of, by solving equations. It was really a special-purpose computer, limited to that one function. But Babbage still wanted a general-purpose machine. Instead of building a series of pattern-of-action choices into one machine, he went for the truly inventive. He designed a set of identical moving parts that could be manipulated to perform innumerable functions according to different patterns of action, equivalent to modern programs. Although it was never completely built, the analytical engine achieved the theoretical leap from calculating machine to programmable computer.

6   The analytical engine incorporated the five component parts, or functions, that are found in all modern computer systems. There were the input and output functions, which fed numbers and instructions into the mechanism and yielded the results as printed numbers. Inside, the arithmetic or processing function, which Babbage called the "mill," actually did the calculations. The store or memory function held numbers waiting to be processed. Finally, the control function or unit

ensured that the machine completed all the calculations in the right sequence before going on to another task.

7   In planning the analytical engine, Babbage recycled from his difference machine the cogs and wheels to handle the calculation functions, the mechanical rods and levers to perform the memory functions and the numbered wheels for recording the information output. For the all-important input and control functions, he borrowed from the French weaver Joseph Jacquard, who in 1804 had automated the control function of a weaving loom.

8   Jacquard had designed a series of stiff cards with holes punched in them that corresponded to the intricate floral patterns being woven. At each throw of the shuttle, one of these cards was placed in the path of the rods, which were pulled forward to complete the weave. Where there were holes in the card, the rods slipped through; where there were none, the rods were held back. Card by card, each with its program of punched holes, the weaving pattern was created. In Babbage's analytical engine the punched cards replaced the hand-controlled levers for setting the calculation function in motion and controlled the sequence of calculations that the mill performed.

9   One contemporary observer — Lord Byron's daughter, Ada, the Countess of Lovelace, who was an intimate friend of Babbage's (his mistress, some say) — made some prophetic observations about the computer's role as an intellectual tool: "The Analytical Engine has no pretensions whatever to originate anything. It can do [only] whatever we know how to order it to perform. It can follow analysis; but it has no power of anticipating . . . any truths. Its province is to assist us in making available what we are already acquainted with."

10   The invention of electricity moved computers from the realm of the possible into that of the practical. In 1890, the American Herman Hollerith employed electricity in his tabulating machine, which was used for calculating the American census of that year. He used the punched cards Jacquard had pioneered and the idea of rods going through the holes. But instead of moving wool and silk threads into position to complete a weaving pattern, Hollerith's rods dipped into a bowl of mercury to complete an electric current that, in turn, caused a clock dial to advance by one turn. The success of this machine, able to "read" punched cards from the census returns, led to the formation of the Computing Tabulating and Recording Company, later renamed International Business Machines, or IBM.

11   The next developments were technical improvements, such as the use of vacuum tubes or electronic valves instead of electromagnetic relays for processing data. Electronic valves can perform hundreds or even thousands of data processing steps, called cycles, per second, while electromagnetic relays could only handle five or ten cycles

per second. The first tube computer was the Colossus, developed by the British under a blanket of secrecy during the Second World War. By helping to crack the German intelligence codes, it is credited with helping to win the war for the Allies. This was but a preview of the vital importance information technology would assume in modern society.

12   Ironically, the Germans believed that their codes were impregnable because they were generated by an information-scrambling computer of their own invention, called the Enigma machine; but it had electromagnetic components. The British, with their faster vacuum tubes, devised a series of the codes and processed the German information signals against them until, finally, intelligible data sequences appeared on the printout. The information was fed in on punched paper tape and "read" by a photoelectric reader that could absorb 5,000 characters per second, an impressive rate at that time. Then it was processed through 2,000 vacuum tubes.

13   An American computer, the ENIAC, boasted 19,000 vacuum tubes. Although it could only be reprogrammed by extensive rewiring, it nonetheless was a stored-program computer, which was a significant development. Still, both machines were restricted to the role of glorified adding machines.

14   Another turning point was the development of the transistor, in 1947. The new invention replaced the vacuum tubes as the switching mechanism (logic gates) in the computer that actually processes data into information. It represented a dramatic new application of electricity: instead of moving an electric current, transistors registered difference by displacing a few electrons in a tiny globule of semiconductor material, which normally doesn't conduct electricity. The transistor consisted of layers of silicon, a semiconductor, that had been treated with impurities to make it conduct electricity across the areas that had been treated. This breakthrough greatly increased the reliability of computers and overcame the physical encumbrances of the vacuum tube computers. The process of getting computer equipment into progressively smaller spaces had begun.

15   Years later, when the planar oxidization process was developed for etching on these impurities to create the logic gates, which correspond to the possible choices in processing, the microelectronic revolution was launched. It became possible to etch several logic gates (or transistors) onto the surface of one piece, or chip, of silicon no bigger than a baby's fingernail.

16   The planar etching process started a war of miniaturization and economies of scale that popularized computer technology and left the ad writers scrambling for new and better descriptive labels. At first it seemed a miracle that one logic gate was etched on a chip. By

the mid-1960s, though, these were replaced with small-scale integrated circuits, chips with ten or more logic gates. Then came medium-scale integrated circuits with hundreds of components. The early 1970s would see the manufacture of large-scale integrated circuits with thousands of components or logic gates per chip. The greater the miniaturization, the lower the price. The lower the price, the more information work computers could take on, and the more work functions could be automated.

17   Despite miniaturization, the computer in the 1950s and 1960s was still rather like the steam engine of the industrial revolution. It was big, clumsy and expensive. Just as the steam engine made it impractical to mechanize anything but large mass-production activities, so computers made it uneconomical to automate anything but large-scale production processes. The majority of installations in industry were in continuous-flow production processes, consisting of a series of interlocking standard steps or procedures, with the product literally flowing automatically from one place to another. Applications included smelting, oil refining, pulpwood processing, grain cleaning and brewing. Product handling, which included assembly work and inventory, could not be automated. Nor could most information handling.

18   What information-related work could be automated was originally confined to major statistical projects with massive data processing requirements, mainly in the tertiary or service sector of the economy. Governments installed computers for processing income tax returns and, later, payroll deductions and other data on their own employees. Airlines used them for tabulating airline reservations and cargo statistics. Banks installed them for processing cheques and calculating interest. Insurance companies used them to calculate and process insurance premiums. Companies in retail trade bought them to process sales-return data. Companies in the rail, truck and shipping business used them to process ticket sales and waybill data.

19   The first wave of computer automation slowly but surely had some major effects on both organizational hierarchies and the larger employment scene. When computers were first installed in the service-sector businesses, they were seen as something alien, and their operators were regarded with awe, if not suspicion. Initially, the work was distinctly alien as well; data processing was called "number crunching" and left at that. A sideline of the primary tasks in the office, it didn't really affect the regular office staff, who carried on their paper-base information work with only a touch of paranoia showing in the general disdain with which they regarded the "computer types."

20   The computer types, meanwhile, were steadily enlarging the scope of their information work. In manufacturing, they expanded from

simple financial recordkeeping to inventory management and production scheduling. In service industries, they automated marketing functions such as sales and advertising feedback analysis. And in corporate head offices everywhere, they expanded into costing, cashflow analysis and long-range forecasting and planning.

21   In their expansion, the computer types also created a whole hierarchy of new information occupations. The new positions ranged from systems analysts and designers, who drew up the general requirements of a data processing job or automation project, to computer programmers who translated these into orders the computer could follow, computer operators who ran the computer and data-entry clerks (originally keypunch operators) who fed the data into the computer.

22   Later, tape librarians and data network personnel were added to the hierarchy. Their jobs were to maintain and store the magnetic tapes full of data and to begin creating data banks, the electronic files of the office of the future.

23   Few people noticed the similarities between these occupations and those associated with a traditional office hierarchy of information workers. Yet the systems analysts and designers were obviously the equivalent of corporate planners, the computer programmers were akin to office managers and administrators, and computer operators, data clerks and tape librarians resembled secretaries, administrative assistants and other office support staff. One group worked with computerized or automated information systems; the other worked with print-based information systems. Neither group realized it was in competition with the other, and for the time being this redundancy was allowed.

24   The organizational shakeup that computers were to cause was not yet evident in the first wave era of the 1950s and 1960s, but there were predictions that computer automation would lead to mass unemployment. The catastrophe never materialized, because of the state of the technology, the state of the workplace organization and the state of the economy.

25   The first computers were just too big and, more to the point, too expensive, to push into all the nooks and crannies where people worked. This was particularly true of the emerging service industries— banks, insurance companies, telephones and other utilities. Although head-office statistical functions could be automated, a lot of the work, particularly in the branches, was widely distributed and rather unsystematic, not like work in processing industries, which was tightly organized, standardized and centralized. Also, since much of the work in service industries involved creating and handling information, which defied available productivity measures except when reduced

to data for processing, it escaped productivity pressures. There was little pressure for productivity, in any case. The world economy was booming, and there was an abundance of people willing to work for relatively low wages.

26   Some of these were people being displaced by automation in the processing industries. But mostly they were women entering the paid labour force. The increasing participation of women in the paid labour force has been one of the most dramatic developments in the post-war era. Women doubled their participation rate between 1950 and 1980.

27   While the state of the economy kept predictions of widespread unemployment from coming true, the accompanying bullish state of mind also made people pay little attention to doomsayers. The 1960s were a time of confidence in technology and in society's ability not only to shape its collective destiny but also to generate more health and wealth for all. Meanwhile in scholarly circles there was a successful battle to redefine the industrial revolution as an unblemished triumph of technology, and an American presidential commission on automation concluded that technological change shouldn't lead to unemployment in any self-respecting economy. Quite the reverse was true: increased productivity produced by technological change will lead to increased economic activity, which will lead, in turn, to increased employment, it said.

28   The formula did not deal with the question of skill loss, which has accompanied technological change since Joseph Jacquard invented his punch-card-controlled loom. Yet when automation was introduced to the pulp and paper, grain-cleaning and other processing plants in the 1950s and 1960s, the skill, knowledge and personal discretion associated with turning wood pulp into paper, cleaning grain and operating the other processing plants were absorbed into the computer-controlled machines. Employees who previously had been required to know the production process enough to fine-tune it, run chemical tests and adjust equipment were now reduced to bored machine operators watching dials and meters all day. The higher rates of alcoholism, drug abuse and absenteeism reflected the lower job satisfaction of workers in these plants.

29   The formula also ignored possible jobless economic growth, and the problems associated with occupational mobility—the difference in skills and other qualifications between jobs being automated and new jobs created. The estimated 1.5 million people displaced when the processing industries were automated did not find new work in these same industries. Their unemployment just happened to coincide with the emergence of the new service industries, which could absorb them not because they had the right qualifications, but because few skills were required in most of the new jobs: driving trucks, buses

and taxis, filling out forms, waiting on customers and the like.

30   How will this formula hold up in the second wave of automation, which arrived with the microprocessor in 1971? The first wave did not yield the terrible disruption predicted, because the economy was booming, because the technology had tight perimeters of application and because many large enterprises just weren't ready to automate. But now the economy is sluggish, more companies have standardized their operations and are looking for ways to cut costs, and the technology has few limits.

31   The microprocessor, a "computer on a chip," has allowed computers to go anywhere and automate almost any mechanical process. Packaged as tiny microprocessors, computers have become flexible, accessible and cheap. The microprocessor could be installed in this small corner to automate a minor control function or in that small corner to automate a recording function. It could also be incorporated into a hierarchy of computer control for maximum value per computer-power dollar. In terms of the hierarchies in any organization, the microprocessor and microcomputer are ideal for automating small local tasks such as filing, typing or parts assembly; at the equivalent of department management level, a medium-sized computer (a minicomputer, perhaps) can coordinate supplies, scheduling and other administrative functions automatically. Finally, at a senior management level, the traditional large computer (called a mainframe) can maintain overall control and supervision while monitoring and coordinating the entire operation.

32   In applicability, the difference between the original large computer and the versatile, cheap little chip is as profound as the difference between the steam engine and electricity. It is also as important to the spread of automation as electricity was to the spread of mechanization. When machines required an external power source such as the steam engine, it was feasible to mechanize only large-mass-production activities — such as in manufacturing and processing plants. With electricity, however, mechanical power was incorporated into every conceivable mechanical process, not only in large factories but in small shops, farms and homes as well. Today all that a microprocessor needs is electricity, and it can be incorporated into almost anything that's already been mechanized. The cost of its power, roughly five dollars per chip in 1980, is declining at some 35 percent a year.

33   On farms, microprocessors incorporated into mechanical feeding systems can monitor and control the amount of chop being channelled from the silo into the feedlot. In homes, they can monitor the furnace, the humidifier and even the stove, and guard against break-ins. In office copiers, they can react to commands encoded in the information beamed to them from a word processor down the hall.

In factories, they can monitor temperatures, test chemical solutions and control the arms of assembly-line robots. All told, it has been estimated (in *Business Week*) that nearly half of all jobs could be eliminated, deskilled or otherwise changed by the current second wave of automation.

34   Never before has one invention had such a widespread application. Nor has history recorded such a short time lag — less than ten years — between invention and adoption, or such a blinding rate of implementation. But microprocessor technology is called revolutionary for another, still more important reason: because of the transformation it triggers. It transforms by adding the dimension of "intelligence" — the capacity to inform and be informed. Equally important, and arising from its distributed-power characteristics, the technology of computers can be integrated with compatible technologies — such as telephones, cables and other communications systems. One of the most potent examples of this integration is called computer communications, or informatics. A combination of computer and communications technologies, informatics is creating a revolution in its own right.

35   Just what sort of future this new technology will create is being determined now in the way it's being applied . . . in offices, in service-sector business such as banks, insurance companies and stores, and in industry.

Bibliography

On the history of computers, some sources of particular note are Christopher Evans's book, *The Micro Millennium* (New York: Washington Square Press, 1979); and among Canadian sources, "The Effects of Microelectronics on Employment and Income," a 1980 discussion paper by Katherine McGuire for the Canadian Labour Congress; and *The Microelectronic Revolution*, by Lydia Dotto (Toronto: Housser & Co. Ltd., 1981). Finally, *Computer Consciousness: Surviving the Automated 80s*, by H. Dominic Covvey and Neil Harding McAlister (Don Mills: Addison-Wesley, 1980), is an excellent introduction to computer technology.

Questions on Content

1   Why have "machines to manipulate information" been developed?

2   Who were the major innovators in information processing between the ancient abacus and the "first wave" of computers in the 1950s and 1960s? What were their major contributions to the development of modern computers?

3   What two main aspects of society did the first wave of computer automation affect? What were the most important effects on each aspect of society?

4   What are the most important effects of the second wave of computer automation? What is "revolutionary" about microprocessor technology?

Questions on Structure and Technique

1   What sentence in paragraph one is Menzies' statement of her essay's subject? In what sentences does Menzies state her thesis as a causal analysis of why something happened?

2   Does Menzies develop her analysis of how computers were developed as a causal process or a causal classification? Is this explanation presented as a sequence of events or of cause and effect relations?

3   In what paragraph does Menzies make a transition from an analysis of the causes to an analysis of the effects of computer technology on society? What rhetorical modes does Menzies use to organize and develop her discussion of these effects?

4   What is the main purpose of Menzies' analysis? What audience is she writing for? How does Menzies effectively adapt her purpose to her audience? Why is this task of the writer an important one?

Suggestions for Writing

1   What are the effects of computer technology on you? Organize the most significant effects as either a causal process or a causal classification, and write an essay based on your analysis. Be sure to establish a clear thesis for your discussion and support that thesis with specific details and examples from your own experience.

2   In a well-organized and well-developed causal analysis essay, explain both the causes and the effects of the development of one specific kind of contemporary electronic technology for a general audience. If you use your own specialized knowledge or research materials for your analysis, adapt it to the needs of your audience where necessary.

MARSHALL McLUHAN

Marshall McLuhan (1911-1980) gained an international reputation with his books on the history and theory of communications, culture, and technology, most notably The Mechanical Bride: Folklore of Industrial Man *(1951),* The Gutenberg Galaxy: The Making of Typographic Man *(1962),* Understanding Media: The Extension of Man *(1964), and* The Medium is the Message *(1967). In* "The Medium is the Message," *a chapter from* Understanding Media, *McLuhan discusses the fundamental and profound effect of a variety of media on our lives: "It is the medium that shapes and controls the scale and form of human association and action." McLuhan clarifies and develops this thesis through his presentation of a number of extended modern and historical illustrations. Born in Edmonton, McLuhan grew up in Winnipeg and attended the University of Manitoba. He continued his education at Cambridge University where he received a doctorate in English Literature. He taught English at several universities in the United States and Canada before joining the faculty of St. Michael's College, University of Toronto, in 1946. McLuhan's innovative work there as a teacher, editor, scholar, and writer continued until shortly before his death, and his intellectual accomplishments have significantly contributed to our understanding of the relations of our means of expression to human experience itself.*

THE MEDIUM IS THE MESSAGE

1   In a culture like ours, long accustomed to splitting and dividing all things as a means of control, it is sometimes a bit of a shock to be reminded that, in operational and practical fact, the medium is the message. This is merely to say that the personal and social consequences of any medium — that is, of any extension of ourselves — result from the new scale that is introduced into our affairs by each extension of ourselves, or by any new technology. Thus, with automation, for example, the new patterns of human association tend to eliminate jobs, it is true. That is the negative result. Positively, automation creates roles for people, which is to say depth of involvement in their work and human association that our preceding mechanical technology had destroyed. Many people would be disposed to say that it was not the machine, but what one did with the machine, that was its meaning or message. In terms of the ways in which the machine altered our relations to one another and to ourselves, it mattered not

in the least whether it turned out cornflakes or Cadillacs. The restructuring of human work and association was shaped by the technique of fragmentation that is the essence of machine technology. The essence of automation technology is the opposite. It is integral and decentralist in depth, just as the machine was fragmentary, centralist, and superficial in its patterning of human relationships.

2   The instance of the electric light may prove illuminating in this connection. The electric light is pure information. It is a medium without a message, as it were, unless it is used to spell out some verbal ad or name. This fact, characteristic of all media, means that the "content" of any medium is always another medium. The content of writing is speech, just as the written word is the content of print, and print is the content of the telegraph. If it is asked, "What is the content of speech?," it is necessary to say, "It is an actual process of thought, which is in itself nonverbal." An abstract painting represents direct manifestation of creative thought processes as they might appear in computer designs. What we are considering here, however, are the psychic and social consequences of the designs or patterns as they amplify or accelerate existing processes. For the "message" of any medium or technology is the change of scale or pace or pattern that it introduces into human affairs. The railway did not introduce movement or transportation or wheel or road into human society, but it accelerated and enlarged the scale of previous human functions, creating totally new kinds of cities and new kinds of work and leisure. This happened whether the railway functioned in a tropical or a northern environment, and is quite independent of the freight or content of the railway medium. The airplane, on the other hand, by accelerating the rate of transportation, tends to dissolve the railway form of city, politics, and association, quite independently of what the airplane is used for.

3   Let us return to the electric light. Whether the light is being used for brain surgery or night baseball is a matter of indifference. It could be argued that these activities are in some way the "content" of the electric light, since they could not exist without the electric light. This fact merely underlines the point that "the medium is the message" because it is the medium that shapes and controls the scale and form of human association and action. The content or uses of such media are as diverse as they are ineffectual in shaping the form of human association. Indeed, it is only too typical that the "content" of any medium blinds us to the character of the medium. It is only today that industries have become aware of the various kinds of business in which they are engaged. When IBM discovered that it was not in the business of making office equipment or business machines, but that it was in the business of processing information, then it began to navigate with clear vision. The General Electric Company makes

a considerable portion of its profits from electric light bulbs and lighting systems. It has not yet discovered that, quite as much as A.T.&T., it is in the business of moving information.

4 The electric light escapes attention as a communication medium just because it has no "content." And this makes it an invaluable instance of how people fail to study media at all. For it is not till the electric light is used to spell out some brand name that it is noticed as a medium. Then it is not the light but the "content" (or what is really another medium) that is noticed. The message of the electric light is like the message of electric power in industry, totally radical, pervasive, and decentralized. For electric light and power are separate from their uses, yet they eliminate time and space factors in human association exactly as do radio, telegraph, telephone, and TV, creating involvement in depth.

5 A fairly complete handbook for studying the extensions of man could be made up from selections from Shakespeare. Some might quibble about whether or not he was referring to TV in these familiar lines from *Romeo and Juliet*:

> But soft! what light through yonder window breaks?
> It speaks and yet says nothing.

6 In *Othello*, which, as much as *King Lear*, is concerned with the torment of people transformed by illusions, there are these lines that bespeak Shakespeare's intuition of the transforming powers of new media:

> Is there not charms
> By which the property of youth and maidhood
> May be abus'd? Have you not read Roderigo,
> Of some such thing?

7 In Shakespeare's *Troilus and Cressida*, which is almost completely devoted to both a psychic and social study of communication, Shakespeare states his awareness that true social and political navigation depend upon anticipating the consequences of innovation:

> The providence that's in a watchful state
> Knows almost every grain of Plutus' gold
> Finds bottom in the uncomprehensive deeps,
> Keeps place with thought, and almost like the gods
> Does thoughts unveil in their dumb cradles.

8 The increasing awareness of the action of media, quite independently of their "content" or programming, was indicated in the annoyed and anonymous stanza:

> In modern thought, (if not in fact)
> Nothing is that doesn't act,
> So that is reckoned wisdom which
> Describes the scratch but not the itch.

9   The same kind of total, configurational awareness that reveals why
the medium is socially the message has occurred in the most recent
and radical medical theories. In his *Stress of Life*, Hans Selye tells of
the dismay of a research colleague on hearing of Selye's theory:

> When he saw me thus launched on yet another enraptured descrip-
> tion of what I had observed in animals treated with this or that
> impure, toxic material, he looked at me with desperately sad eyes
> and said in obvious despair: "But Selye, try to realize what you are
> doing before it is too late! You have now decided to spend your
> entire life studying the pharmacology of dirt!"

(Hans Selye, *The Stress of Life*)

10   As Selye deals with the total environmental situation in his "stress"
theory of disease, so the latest approach to media study considers
not only the "content" but the medium and the cultural matrix within
which the particular medium operates. The older unawareness of
the psychic and social effects of media can be illustrated from almost
any of the conventional pronouncements.

11   In accepting an honorary degree from the University of Notre Dame
a few years ago, General David Sarnoff made this statement: "We
are too prone to make technological instruments the scapegoats for
the sins of those who wield them. The products of modern science
are not in themselves good or bad; it is the way they are used that
determines their value." That is the voice of the current somnambu-
lism. Suppose we were to say, "Apple pie is in itself neither good nor
bad; it is the way it is used that determines its value." Or, "The small-
pox virus is in itself neither good nor bad; it is the way it is used that
determines its value." Again, "Firearms are in themselves neither good
nor bad; it is the way they are used that determines their value." That
is, if the slugs reach the right people firearms are good. If the TV
tube fires the right ammunition at the right people it is good. I am
not being perverse. There is simply nothing in the Sarnoff statement
that will bear scrutiny, for it ignores the nature of the medium, of
any and all media, in the true Narcissus style of one hypnotized by
the amputation and extension of his own being in a new technical
form. General Sarnoff went on to explain his attitude to the technology of print, saying that it was true that print caused much trash to
circulate, but it had also disseminated the Bible and the thoughts of
seers and philosophers. It has never occurred to General Sarnoff that
any technology could do anything but *add* itself on to what we already
are.

12   Such economists as Robert Theobald, W. W. Rostow, and John
Kenneth Galbraith have been explaining for years how it is that "classical economics" cannot explain change or growth. And the paradox
of mechanization is that although it is itself the cause of maximal
growth and change, the principle of mechanization excludes the very

possibility of growth or the understanding of change. For mechanization is achieved by fragmentation of any process and by putting the fragmented parts in a series. Yet, as David Hume showed in the eighteenth century, there is no principle of causality in a mere sequence. That one thing follows another accounts for nothing. Nothing follows from following, except change. So the greatest of all reversals occurred with electricity, that ended sequence by making things instant. With instant speed the causes of things began to emerge to awareness again, as they had not done with things in sequence and in concatenation accordingly. Instead of asking which came first, the chicken or the egg, it suddenly seemed that a chicken was an egg's idea for getting more eggs.

13   Just before an airplane breaks the sound barrier, sound waves become visible on the wings of the plane. The sudden visibility of sound just as sound ends is an apt instance of that great pattern of being that reveals new and opposite forms just as the earlier forms reach their peak performance. Mechanization was never so vividly fragmented or sequential as in the birth of the movies, the moment that translated us beyond mechanism into the world of growth and organic interrelation. The movie, by sheer speeding up the mechanical, carried us from the world of sequence and connections into the world of creative configuration and structure. The message of the movie medium is that of transition from lineal connections to configurations. It is the transition that produced the now quite correct observation: "If it works, it's obsolete." When electric speed further takes over from the mechanical movie sequences, then the lines of force in structures and in media become loud and clear. We return to the inclusive form of the icon.

14   To a highly literate and mechanized culture the movie appeared as a world of triumphant illusions and dreams that money could buy. It was at this moment of the movie that cubism occurred, and it has been described by E. H. Gombrich (*Art and Illusion*) as "the most radical attempt to stamp out ambiguity and to enforce one reading of the picture—that of a man-made construction, a colored canvas." For cubism substitutes all facets of an object simultaneously for the "point of view" or facet of perspective illusion. Instead of the specialized illusion of the third dimension on canvas, cubism sets up an interplay of planes and contradiction or dramatic conflict of patterns, lights, textures that "drives home the message" by involvement. This is held by many to be an exercise in painting, not in illusion.

15   In other words, cubism, by giving the inside and outside, the top, bottom, back, and front and the rest, in two dimensions, drops the illusion of perspective in favor of instant sensory awareness of the whole. Cubism, by seizing an instant total awareness, suddenly announced that *the medium is the message*. It is not evident that the

moment that sequence yields to the simultaneous, one is in the world of the structure and of configuration? Is that not what has happened in physics as in painting, poetry, and in communication? Specialized segments of attention have shifted to total field, and we can now say, "The medium is the message" quite naturally. Before the electric speed and total field, it was not obvious that the medium is the message. The message, it seems, was the "content," as people used to ask what a painting was *about*. Yet they never thought to ask what a melody was about, nor what a house or a dress was about. In such matters, people retained some sense of the whole pattern, of form and function as a unity. But in the electric age this integral idea of structure and configuration has become so prevalent that educational theory has taken up the matter. Instead of working with specialized "problems" in arithmetic, the structural approach now follows the lines of force in the field of number and has small children meditating about number theory and "sets."

16 Cardinal Newman said of Napoleon, "He understood the grammar of gunpowder." Napoleon had paid some attention to other media as well, especially the semaphore telegraph that gave him a great advantage over his enemies. He is on record for saying that "Three hostile newspapers are more to be feared than a thousand bayonets."

17 Alexis de Tocqueville was the first to master the grammar of print and typography. He was thus able to read off the message of coming change in France and America as if he were reading aloud from a text that had been handed to him. In fact, the nineteenth century in France and in America was just such an open book to de Tocqueville because he had learned the grammar of print. So he, also, knew when that grammar did not apply. He was asked why he did not write a book on England, since he knew and admired England. He replied:

> One would have to have an unusual degree of philosophical folly to believe oneself able to judge England in six months. A year always seemed to me too short a time in which to appreciate the United States properly, and it is much easier to acquire clear and precise notions about the American Union than about Great Britain. In America all laws derive in a sense from the same line of thought. The whole of society, so to speak, is founded upon a single fact; everything springs from a simple principle. One could compare America to a forest pierced by a multitude of straight roads all converging on the same point. One has only to find the center and everything is revealed at a glance. But in England the paths run criss-cross, and it is only by travelling down each one of them that one can build up a picture of the whole.

18 De Tocqueville, in earlier work on the French Revolution, had explained how it was the printed word that, achieving cultural saturation in the eighteenth century, had homogenized the French nation. Frenchmen were the same kind of people from north to south. The

typographic principles of uniformity, continuity, and lineality had overlaid the complexities of ancient feudal and oral society. The Revolution was carried out by the new literati and lawyers.

19　　In England, however, such was the power of the ancient oral traditions of common law, backed by the medieval institution of Parliament, that no uniformity or continuity of the new visual print culture could take complete hold. The result was that the most important event in English history has never taken place; namely, the English Revolution on the lines of the French Revolution. The American Revolution had no medieval legal instructions to discard or to root out, apart from monarchy. And many have held that the American Presidency has become very much more personal and monarchial than any European monarch ever could be.

20　　De Tocqueville's contrast between England and America is clearly based on the fact of typography and of print culture creating uniformity and continuity. England, he says, has rejected this principle and clung to the dynamic or oral common-law tradition. Hence the discontinuity and unpredictable quality of English culture. The grammar of print cannot help to construe the message of oral and non-written culture and institutions. The English aristocracy was properly classified as barbarian by Matthew Arnold because its power and status had nothing to do with literacy or with the cultural forms of typography. Said the Duke of Gloucester to Edward Gibbon upon the publication of his *Decline and Fall*: "Another damned fat book, eh, Mr. Gibbon? Scribble, scribble, scribble, eh, Mr. Gibbon?" De Tocqueville was a highly literate aristocrat who was quite able to be detached from the values and assumptions of typography. That is why he alone understood the grammar of typography. And it is only on those terms, standing aside from any structure or medium, that its principles and lines of force can be discerned. For any medium has the power of imposing its own assumption on the unwary. Prediction and control consist in avoiding this subliminal state of Narcissus trance. But the greatest aid to this end is simply in knowing that the spell can occur immediately upon contact, as in the first bars of a melody.

21　　*A Passage to India* by E. M. Forster is a dramatic study of the inability of oral and intuitive oriental culture to meet with the rational, visual European patterns of experience. "Rational," of course, has for the West long meant "uniform and continuous and sequential." In other words, we have confused reason with literacy, and rationalism with a single technology. Thus in the electric age man seems to the conventional West to become irrational. In Forster's novel the moment of truth and dislocation from the typographic trance of the West comes in the Marabar Caves. Adela Quested's reasoning powers cannot cope with the total inclusive field of resonance that is India. After the Caves: "Life went on as usual, but had no consequences, that is to say, sounds did not echo nor thought develop. Everything seemed cut off at its root and therefore infected with illusion."

22   *A Passage to India* (the phrase is from Whitman, who saw America headed Eastward) is a parable of Western man in the electric age, and is only incidentally related to Europe or the Orient. The ultimate conflict between sight and sound, between written and oral kinds of perception and organization of existence is upon us. Since understanding stops action, as Nietzsche observed, we can moderate the fierceness of this conflict by understanding the media that extend us and raise these wars within and without us.

23   Detribalization by literacy and its traumatic effects on tribal man is the theme of a book by the psychiatrist J. C. Carothers, *The African Mind in Health and Disease* (World Health Organization, Geneva, 1953). Much of his material appeared in an article in *Psychiatry* magazine, November, 1959: "The Culture, Psychiatry, and the Written Word." Again, it is electric speed that has revealed the lines of force operating from Western technology in the remotest areas of bush, savannah, and desert. One example is the Bedouin with his battery radio on board the camel. Submerging natives with floods of concepts for which nothing has prepared them is the normal action of all of our technology. But with electric media Western man himself experiences exactly the same inundation as the remote native. We are no more prepared to encounter radio and TV in our literate milieu than the native of Ghana is able to cope with the literacy that takes him out of his collective tribal world and beaches him in individual isolation. We are as numb in our new electric world as the native involved in our literate and mechanical culture.

24   Electric speed mingles the cultures of prehistory with the dregs of industrial marketeers, the nonliterate with the semiliterate and the postliterate. Mental breakdown of varying degrees is the very common result of uprooting and inundation with new information and endless new patterns of information. Wyndham Lewis made this a theme of his group of novels called *The Human Age*. The first of these, *The Childermass*, is concerned precisely with accelerated media change as a kind of massacre of the innocents. In our own world as we become more aware of the effects of technology on psychic formation and manifestation, we are losing all confidence in our rights to assign guilt. Ancient prehistoric societies regard violent crime as pathetic. The killer is regarded as we do a cancer victim. "How terrible it must be to feel like that," they say. J. M. Synge took up this idea very effectively in his *Playboy of the Western World*.

25   If the criminal appears as a nonconformist who is unable to meet the demand of technology that we behave in uniform and continuous patterns, literate man is quite inclined to see others who cannot conform as somewhat pathetic. Especially the child, the cripple, the woman, and the colored person appear in a world of visual and typographic technology as victims of injustice. On the other hand, in a culture that assigns roles of jobs to people—the dwarf, the skew, the child create their own spaces. They are not expected to fit into some uniform and repeatable niche that is not their size anyway. Consider the phrase "It's a man's world." As a quantitative observation endlessly repeated from within a homogenized culture, this phrase refers to the men in such a culture who have to be homogenized Dagwoods in order to belong at all. It is our I.Q. testing that we have produced the greatest flood of misbegotten standards. Unaware of our typographical cultural bias, our testers assume that uniform and continuous habits are a sign of intelligence, thus eliminating the ear man and the tactile man.

26   C. P. Snow, reviewing a book of A. L. Rowse (*The New York Times Book Review*, December 24, 1961) on *Appeasement* and the road to Munich, describes the top level of British brains and experience in the 1930s. "Their I.Q.'s were much higher than usual among political bosses. Why were they such a diasaster?" The view of Rowse, Snow approves: "They would not listen to warnings because they did not wish to hear." Being anti-Red made it impossible for them to read the message of Hitler. But their failure was as nothing compared to our present one. The American stake in literacy as a technology or uniformity applied to every level of education, government, industry, and social life is totally threatened by the electric technology. The threat of Stalin or Hitler was external. The electric technology is within the gates, and we are numb, deaf, blind, and mute about its encounter with the Gutenberg technology, on and through which the American way of life was formed. It is, however, no time to suggest strategies when the threat has not even been acknowledged to exist. I am in the position of Louis Pasteur telling doctors that their greatest enemy was quite invisible, and quite unrecognized by them. Our conventional response to all media, namely that it is how they are used that counts, is the numb stance of the technological idiot. For the "content" of a medium is like the juicy piece of meat carried by the burglar to distract the watchdog of the mind. The effect of the medium is made strong and intense just because it is given another medium as "content." The content of a movie is a novel or a play or an opera. The effect of the movie form is not related to its program content. The "content" of writing or print is speech, but the reader is almost entirely unaware either of print or of speech.

27   Arnold Toynbee is innocent of any understanding of media as they have shaped history, but he is full of examples that the student of media can use. At one moment he can seriously suggest that adult education, such as the Workers Educational Association in Britain, is a useful counterforce to the popular press. Toynbee considers that although all of the oriental societies have in our time accepted the industrial technology and its political consequences: "On the cultural plane, however, there is no uniform corresponding tendency." (Somervell, I. 267) This is like the voice of the literate man, floundering in a milieu of ads, who boasts, "Personally, I pay no attention to ads." The spiritual and cultural reservations that the oriental peoples may have toward our technology will avail them not at all. The effects of technology do not occur at the level of opinions or concepts, but alter sense ratios or patterns of perception steadily and without any resistance. The serious artist is the only person able to encounter technology with impunity, just because he is an expert aware of the changes in sense perception.

28   The operation of the money medium in seventeenth-century Japan had effects not unlike the operation of typography in the West. The penetration of the money economy, wrote G. B. Sansom (in *Japan*, Cresset Press, London, 1931) "caused a slow but irresistible revolution, culminating in the breakdown of feudal government and the resumption of intercourse with foreign countries after more than two hundred years of seclusion." Money has reorganized the sense of life of peoples just because it is an *extension* of our sense lives. This change does not depend upon approval or disapproval of those living in the society.

29   Arnold Toynbee made one approach to the transforming power of media in his concept of "etherialization," which he holds to be the principle of progressive simplification and efficiency in any organization or technology. Typically, he is ignoring the *effect* of the challenge of these forms upon the response of our senses. He imagines that it is the response of our opinions that is relevant to the effect of media and technology in society, a "point of view" that is plainly the result of the typographic spell. For the man in a literate and homogenized society ceases to be sensitive to the diverse and discontinuous life of forms. He acquires the illusion of the third dimension and the "private point of view" as part of his Narcissus fixation, and is quite shut off from Blake's awareness or that of the Psalmist, that we become what we behold.

30   Today when we want to get our bearings in our own culture, and have need to stand aside from bias and pressure exerted by any technical form of human expression, we have only to visit a society where that particular form has not been felt, or a historical period in which

it was unknown. Professor Wilber Schramm made such a tactical move in studying *Television in the Lives of Our Children*. He found areas where TV had not penetrated at all and ran some tests. Since he had made no study of the peculiar nature of the TV image, his tests were of "content" preferences, viewing time, and vocabulary counts. In a word, his approach to the problem was a literary one, albeit unconsciously so. Consequently, he had nothing to report. Had his methods been employed in 1500 A.D. to discover the effects of the printed book in the lives of children or adults, he could have found out nothing of the changes in human and social psychology resulting from typography. Print created individualism and nationalism in the sixteenth century. Program and "content" analysis offer no clues to the magic of these media or to their subliminal charge.

31   Leonard Doob, in his report *Communication in Africa*, tells of one African who took great pains to listen each evening to the BBC news, even though he could understand nothing of it. Just to be in the presence of those sounds at 7 p.m. each day was important for him. His attitude to speech was like ours to melody—the resonant intonation was meaning enough. In the seventeenth century our ancestors still shared this native's attitude to the forms of media, as is plain in the following sentiment of the Frenchman Bernard Lam expressed in *The Art of Speaking* (London, 1696):

> 'Tis an effect of the Wisdom of God, who created Man to be happy, that whatever is useful to his conversation (way of life) is agreeable to him . . . because all victual that conduces to nourishment is relishable, whereas other things that cannot be assimulated and be turned into our substance are insipid. A Discourse cannot be pleasant to the Hearer that is not easie to the Speaker; nor can it be easily pronounced unless it be heard with delight.

32   Here is an equilibrium theory of human diet and expression such as even now we are only striving to work out again for media after centuries of fragmentation and specialism.

33   Pope Pius XII was deeply concerned that there be serious study of the media today. On February 17, 1959, he said:

> It is not an exaggeration to say that the future of modern society and the stability of its inner life depend in large part on the maintenance of an equilibrium between the strength of the techniques of communication and the capacity of the individual's own reaction.

34   Failure in this respect has for centuries been typical and total for mankind. Subliminal and docile acceptance of media impact has made them prisons without walls for their human users. As A. J. Liebling remarked in his book *The Press*, a man is not free if he cannot see where he is going, even if he has a gun to help him get there. For each of the media is also a powerful weapon with which to clobber other media and other groups. The result is that the present age has been

one of multiple civil wars that are not limited to the world of art and entertainment. In *War and Human Progress*, Professor J. U. Nef declared: "The total wars of our time have been the result of a series of intellectual mistakes."

35   If the formative power in the media are the media themselves, that raises a host of large matters that can only be mentioned here, although they deserve volumes. Namely, that technological media are staples or natural resources, exactly as are coal and cotton and oil. Anybody will concede that society whose economy is dependent upon one or two major staples like cotton, or grain, or lumber, or fish, or cattle is going to have some obvious social patterns of organization as a result. Stress on a few major staples creates extreme instability in the economy but great endurance in the population. The pathos and humor of the American South are embedded in such an economy of limited staples. For a society configured by reliance on a few commodities accepts them as a social bond quite as much as the metropolis does the press. Cotton and oil, like radio and TV, become "fixed charges" on the entire psychic life of the community. And this pervasive fact creates the unique cultural flavor of any society. It pays through the nose and all its other senses for each staple that shapes its life.

36   That our human senses, of which all media are extensions, are also fixed charges on our personal energies, and that they also configure the awareness and experience of each one of us, may be perceived in another connection mentioned by the psychologist C. G. Jung:

> Every Roman was surrounded by slaves. The slave and his psychology flooded ancient Italy, and every Roman became inwardly, and of course unwittingly, a slave. Because living constantly in the atmosphere of slaves, he became infected through the unconscious with their psychology. No one can shield himself from such an influence [*Contributions to Analytical Psychology*, London, 1928].

Questions on Content

1   What is McLuhan's definition for his phrase "the medium is the message"? Is it the medium or its message that affects our experiences? How do the specific examples (in paragraphs one through four) clarify McLuhan's thesis? What awareness do Shakespeare and Selye have in common?

2   What views are promoted by the "conventional pronouncements" about content and message illustrated by Sarnoff's statements? What subsequent illustrations (in paragraphs eight through twelve) demonstrate that all media, and not simply "the way they are used," unify form and function in their effects on our experiences? Discuss how "the medium is the message" in each illustration.

3   What contrast between England and America did Alexis de Tocqueville understand? What fundamental contrast in "medium" explains this effect, according to McLuhan? What similar contrasts are illustrated in E. M. Forster's *A Passage to India*?

4   Why is it imperative that we understand the specific effects of modern media that McLuhan presents in his subsequent illustrations? What is the significance of the statement by Pope Pius XII in this regard?

5   Why is the statement about slavery by the psychologist C. G. Jung relevant to McLuhan's analysis of the effects of all media?

Questions on Structure and Technique

1   In what sentences in paragraph one does McLuhan state his thesis? What sentences in paragraph three are general restatements of this thesis?

2   McLuhan develops this complex causal analysis essay by using many extended illustrations to demonstrate both why "the medium is the message" in specific instances and what effects such media have on our experiences. Why does McLuhan find it necessary to present so many illustrations? How is this method of development related to the general purpose of his overall analysis?

3   What patterns of development in addition to illustration does McLuhan employ within his analysis? Provide one or two good examples of each pattern.

4   Why is McLuhan's conclusion (in the last five paragraphs) an effective one?

Suggestions for Writing

1   In the second half of his analysis, McLuhan uses summaries of works by other authors for the development of his own ideas. Study these examples of effective summary. Then write an essay in which you summarize McLuhan's essay in the context of your own understanding of media's effects on people's experiences.

2   After studying McLuhan's analysis thoughtfully and carefully, select one example of contemporary electronic media and write an analysis of its effects in which you support McLuhan's statement that " 'the medium is the message' because it is the medium that shapes and controls the scale and form of human association and action." Develop your analysis by presenting details and examples from your own experience of the "medium" you have chosen for your subject.

E. M. FORSTER

English novelist E. M. Forster (1879-1970) wrote "My Wood" after the success of his best-known novel, A Passage to India *(1924), enabled him to buy a small country estate in England. In "My Wood," an essay in* Abinger Harvest *(1936), Forster analyses "the effect of property upon the character" based on his own experience. Born in London, England, and educated at King's College, Cambridge, Forster lived and wrote in Italy, Greece, and India before finally settling in England. During this time, he published four other novels:* Where Angels Fear to Tread *(1905),* The Longest Journey *(1907),* A Room with a View *(1908), and* Howard's End *(1910). His other works include several collections of short stories and essays, a book of literary criticism entitled* Aspects of the Novel *(1927), and a posthumously published novel,* Maurice *(1971).*

MY WOOD

1   A few years ago I wrote a book which dealt in part with the difficulties of the English in India. Feeling that they would have had no difficulties in India themselves, the Americans read the book freely. The more they read it the better it made them feel, and a cheque to the author was the result. I bought a wood with the cheque. It is not a large wood — it contains scarcely any trees, and it is intersected, blast it, by a public footpath. Still, it is the first property that I have owned, so it is right that other people should participate in my shame, and should ask themselves, in accents that will vary in horror, this very important question: What is the effect of property upon the character? Don't let's touch economics; the effect of private ownership upon the community as a whole is another question — a more important question, perhaps, but another one. Let's keep to psychology. If you own things, what's their effect on you? What's the effect on me of my wood?

2   In the first place, it makes me feel heavy. Property does have this effect. Property produces men of weight, and it was a man of weight who failed to get into the Kingdom of Heaven. He was not wicked, that unfortunate millionaire in the parable, he was only stout; he stuck out in front, not to mention behind, and as he wedged himself this way and that in the crystalline entrance and bruised his well-fed flanks, he saw beneath him a comparatively slim camel passing through the eye of a needle and being woven into the robe of God.

The Gospels all through couple stoutness and slowness. They point out what is perfectly obvious, yet seldom realized: that if you have a lot of things you cannot move about a lot, that furniture requires dusting, dusters require servants, servants require insurance stamps, and the whole tangle of them makes you think twice before you accept an invitation to dinner or go for a bathe in the Jordan. Sometimes the Gospels proceed further and say with Tolstoy that property is sinful; they approach the difficult ground of asceticism here, where I cannot follow them. But as to the immediate effects of property on people, they just show straightforward logic. It produces men of weight. Men of weight cannot, by definition, move like the lightning from the East unto the West, and the ascent of a fourteen-stone bishop into a pulpit is thus the exact antithesis of the coming of the Son of Man. My wood makes me feel heavy.

3   In the second place, it makes me feel it ought to be larger.

4   The other day I heard a twig snap in it. I was annoyed at first, for I thought that someone was blackberrying, and depreciating the value of the undergrowth. On coming nearer, I saw it was not a man who had trodden on the twig and snapped it, but a bird, and I felt pleased. My bird. The bird was not equally pleased. Ignoring the relation between us, it took fright as soon as it saw the shape of my face, and flew straight over the boundary hedge into a field, the property of Mrs. Henessy, where it sat down with a loud squawk. It had become Mrs. Henessy's bird. Something seemed grossly amiss here, something that would not have occurred had the wood been larger. I could not afford to buy Mrs. Henessy out, I dared not murder her, and limitations of this sort beset me on every side. . . .

5   In the third place, property makes its owner feel that he ought to do something to it. Yet he isn't sure what. A restlessness comes over him, a vague sense that he has a personality to express — the same sense which, without any vagueness, leads the artist to an act of creation. Sometimes I think I will cut down such trees as remain in the wood, at other times I want to fill up the gaps between them with new trees. Both impulses are pretentious and empty. They are not honest movements towards money-making or beauty. They spring from a foolish desire to express myself and from an inability to enjoy what I have got. Creation, property, enjoyment form a sinister trinity in the human mind. Creation and enjoyment are both very, very, good, yet they are often unattainable without a material basis, and at such moments property pushes itself in as a substitute, saying, "Accept me instead — I'm good enough for all three." It is not enough. It is, as Shakespeare said of lust, "The expense of spirit in a waste of shame": it is "Before, a joy proposed; behind, a dream." Yet we don't know how to shun it. It is forced on us by our economic system as the alternative to starvation. It is also forced on us by an internal

defect in the soul, by the feeling that in property may lie the germs of self-development and of exquisite or heroic deeds. Our life on earth is, and ought to be, material and carnal. But we have not yet learned to manage our materialism and carnality properly; they are still entangled with the desire for ownership, where (in the words of Dante) "Possession is one with loss."

6   And this brings us to our fourth and final point: the blackberries.

7   Blackberries are not plentiful in this meagre grove, but they are easily seen from the public footpath which traverses it, and all too easily gathered. Foxgloves, too — people will pull up the foxgloves, and ladies of an educational tendency even grub for toadstools to show them on the Monday in class. Other ladies, less educated, roll down the bracken in the arms of their gentlemen friends. There is paper, there are tins. Pray, does my wood belong to me or doesn't it? And, if it does, should I not own it best by allowing no one else to walk there? There is a wood near Lyme Regis, also cursed by a public footpath, where the owner has not hesitated on this point. He had built high stone walls each side of the path, and has spanned it by bridges, so that the public circulate like termites while he gorges on the blackberries unseen. He really does own his wood, this able chap. And perhaps I shall come to this in time. I shall wall in and fence out until I really taste the sweets of property. Enormously stout, endlessly avaricious, pseudo-creative, intensely selfish, I shall weave upon my forehead the quadruple crown of possession until those nasty Bolshies come and take it off again and thrust me aside into the outer darkness.

Questions on Content

1   What is the first effect of property ownership that Forster discusses? What practical issue is illustrated by the Biblical parable?

2   What is the second effect that Forster presents? What human emotions does the bird incident illustrate?

3   What is the third effect that Forster examines? Why is this a "pretentious and empty" feeling in Forster's view?

4   What effect of property ownership do the blackberries illustrate?

5   Who are the "nasty Bolshies"?

Questions on Structure and Technique

1   What is the purpose of Forster's questions in paragraph one? Why does he present three questions rather than one?

2   Is Forster's analysis organized as a causal classification or a causal process? What principle of division is established by Forster in paragraph one?

3   How would you describe the tone of Forster's analysis? What examples, sentences, and phrases establish Forster's tone most effectively?

4   What are the sources of Forster's examples and allusions?

5   Why is Forster's final sentence effective? In what way does this sentence reflect the essay's organization and development? What attitude toward his subject does Forster express in this sentence? Is Forster's attitude supported by his analysis?

Suggestions for Writing

1   In "My Wood," E. M. Forster asks his readers this question: "If you own things, what's their effect on you?" Write a causal classification analysis of the effects of ownership in which you answer Forster's question in terms of one thing that you own.

2   Think about decisions and experiences that resulted in changes in the way you felt about yourself. Choose one specific decision or experience and write a causal analysis of its effects on you, using very specific details and examples to illustrate clearly your more abstract ideas and emotions.

CHAPTER 8

"A Planet for the Taking"

ARGUMENT

An argument is a form of writing which attempts to convince readers that a writer's claim or belief is valid. Although a writer's argument may be expressive or informative, it is directed primarily at readers' rational and emotional capacities of understanding to fulfil its main purpose: to convince readers to accept and, sometimes, to act on the writer's views. Your previous reading in this book, and elsewhere, has made you familiar with writing whose purpose, in whole or in part, has been to gain your acceptance or adoption of other people's ideas or beliefs. You were probably conscious of this purpose when you read, for example, Pierre Berton's "The Religion of Work and the Dirtiest Job in the World," Arthur Erickson's "Ideation and Creativity," Margaret Atwood's "Survival," and Marshall McLuhan's "The Medium is the Message." Similarly, your acceptance of claims or beliefs is sought daily by writers of newspaper and magazine editorials, advertisements, political speeches, and ceremonial addresses. As Northrop Frye argues in "The Vocation of Eloquence," this social or public use of language — rhetoric — exerts considerable power over our experiences, and yet its effectiveness depends upon our own power to make choices and judgments. In this chapter, you will study how arguments can serve to influence and even to change people's attitudes, ideas, and convictions. The reading selections not only offer a variety of general, thought-provoking perspectives on our experiences as Canadians, but also deal with a number of more specific subjects such as national unity, native rights, social reform, ecology, euthanasia, economic models, and commercial advertising, among others. Although the authors' viewpoints as well as their subject matter vary a good deal, you will find that their genuine concern with the nature and meaning of our most fundamental assumptions and values provide a general sense of unity to these selections. In your reading, you are encouraged to seek out the similarities and differences among these authors' arguments, and to compare and contrast them with your own views on issues of importance in your experience. For your writing, you should study how these authors apply the rhetorical patterns and techniques that you have used for expressive and informative purposes to the formal features characteristic of an argument.

An effective argument involves three kinds of appeals to its readers: the appeal to *reason and intellect*; the appeal to *emotions and feelings*; and, the appeal of a writer's *ethical character*. A writer's specific subject and audience require an appropriate balance of these appeals that will make an argument most convincing. For instance, the poetic quality of Bruce Hutchison's patriotic essay on Canada as an "Unknown Country" makes a strong emotional appeal to a Canadian audience. In his "Lament for Confederation," Chief Dan George combines emotional and ethical appeals by identifying himself with all of Canada's native people in order to express their experience of oppression and their hopes for the future. The essays by Rick Salutin and David Suzuki appeal to reason as well as to emotion, as does Northrop Frye's "The Vocation of Eloquence," but Frye's argument is a rigorous intellectual analysis that depends upon his careful, logical development of ideas and clear presentation of supporting evidence for its effectiveness. In his classic satire, "A Modest Proposal," Jonathan Swift's speaker invokes both rational and ethical appeals in a "mock argument" in which Swift undercuts these appeals in favour of his readers' emotional as well as reasonable human sensibilities. The kinds of appeals emphasized by these writers exemplify how the practical task of composing an effective argument should be based on a sound knowledge of the fundamental uses (and abuses) of reason, emotion, and ethical appeal in argument.

An argument's appeal to *reason and intellect* requires that a writer support one or more claims with good evidence, and present such evidence in a logical manner. A writer's *claim*, or proposition, is a statement of an arguable point of view on a subject. A claim responds to a perceived question about the meaning, value, causality, or solution of X with an assertion that a reader will not or may not accept as valid. Therefore, a writer provides *evidence* that a reader will accept or is likely to accept as valid, and demonstrates that some significant relation, or *warrant*, exists between the evidence and the claim. In other words, a writer wants to prove to a reader that given the evidence, and in view of the warrant, the claim must therefore be accepted as valid. For example, a basic argument would take the following written form:

Evidence:	Lindsay is an honours graduate of The University of Winnipeg Collegiate.
Warrant:	Since honours graduates of The University of Winnipeg Collegiate always do well at university, and
Support Warrant:	because a recent study shows that no honours graduate of the Collegiate ever had a cumulative GPA of less than 3.0 in his or her first year of university
(Optional) Claim:	work, Lindsay may be expected to do well in his university studies.

Note that an argument may be expressed in five other versions of this form: C, W, E; C, E, W; W, E, C; E, C, W; W, C, E. In some cases it may also be desirable or necessary to justify the warrant for a claim with supporting data or details termed a *support warrant*, as indicated above. A complex argument arranges several of these basic arguments into either a chain or a cluster:

In an argument chain, a writer progresses from the evidence to the claim through a closely-linked sequence of intermediary arguments. In an argument cluster, a writer presents independent basic arguments or argument chains on related issues which all support the same general claim. In both forms of a complex argument, a writer can organize and develop the presentation of detailed evidence in a logical sequence by using the basic expository patterns of illustration, comparison-contrast, classification analysis, process analysis, and causal analysis.

An argument's persuasive appeal to *emotions and feelings*, such as love, compassion, admiration, contentment, fear, frustration, or anger, depends on a writer's careful selection of examples, details, words, and phrases that will best evoke readers' responses to the subject. A writer should choose examples that will enhance readers' interest and involvement in an argument as well as their sense of its relevance and significance; for instance, examples of personal experiences, or allusions to familiar people, places, and situations. Similarly, detailed images may be used to appeal to readers' senses, and figurative language such as similes, metaphors, and analogies can be used to encourage readers to make comparisons and associations. A writer must also choose words and phrases whose connotations will evoke desired emotional responses from readers. A writer's diction will also influence readers by the tone it conveys: authority, confidence, irony, sympathy, and so forth. Description, narration, and illustration are effective modes of developing examples and details that appeal to readers' emotions.

An argument is most convincing to readers when it reveals rather than conceals the truth value of a writer's claim or belief. An argument's *ethical appeal* is based on a writer's character. A writer's use of reason and emotion in argument should establish his or her qualities of honesty, fairness, reliability, and sincerity in the reader's mind. A writer must develop the trust and respect of readers if he or she expects them to accept or to act on the ideas or beliefs presented in an argument. The rational, emotional, and ethical appeals of an argument will be unconvincing if they are flawed by a writer's errors in logic or abuses of persuasive techniques. *Fallacies*, as such flaws are termed, include the following: a "hasty generalization," where there is too little evidence to warrant a claim ("I am bilingual. You are bilingual. Therefore, everyone in our class is bilingual"); an "unqualified generalization," where a claim is not qualified to account for contradictory evidence ("Exercise is good. Therefore, everyone should exercise"); a "hypothetical claim," where an assertion contrary to fact is used as evidence to support a claim ("If Brian Mulroney had not been elected as Prime Minister in 1984, our country would be in an economic depression today"); "name-calling," where the issue is avoided by disparaging an individual or a group ("The Premier of our province would lie to his own mother"); "stereotyping," where the issue is avoided by classifying all individuals under one label ("All ballet dancers are homosexuals"); and, "bandwagon," where a claim is supported by the evidence that everyone else is said to accept that claim ("Everyone knows that abortion is murder").

In writing an argument, a writer has the opportunity to formulate and clarify his or her ideas and beliefs. By assembling and evaluating the evidence for one's convictions in an open-minded and objective inquiry, a writer can further strengthen or modify his or her position. The organization and development of an argument is then a matter of adapting basic rhetorical modes to a logical and clear arrangement of the evidence so that it supports, or warrants, a writer's claim or belief. A writer's emotional and ethical appeals in the presentation of an argument enhance readers' willingness to accept that viewpoint. The following selections demonstrate how writers' arguments involve readers in the enduring relation between experience and expression.

BRUCE HUTCHISON

Journalist Bruce Hutchison (b. 1901) was a reporter, columnist, and editor who worked for the Victoria Times, *the Vancouver* Sun, *and the Winnipeg* Free Press. *The winner of three National Newspaper Awards and three Governor General's Awards, Hutchison also wrote over a dozen books including* The Unknown Country *(1942) and* Canada: Tomorrow's Giant *(1957). The following selection is the lyrical introduction to* The Unknown Country. *Hutchison's vivid images, figurative language, and connotative words and phrases present a very descriptive impression of Canada which is designed to support his patriotic belief in the country's future. As you read this selection, remember that he was writing during World War II when most readers were strongly inclined to share and be moved by the sentiments he expresses. In this historical context, consider what would have been Hutchison's specific persuasive purposes. What persuasive power does his writing have on your emotions? What contemporary forms of expression, if any, employ language similar to Hutchison's for persuasive purposes?*

THE UNKNOWN COUNTRY

1   No one knows my country, neither the stranger nor its own sons. My country is hidden in the dark and teeming brain of youth upon the eve of its manhood. My country has not found itself nor felt its power nor learned its true place. It is all visions and doubts and hopes and dreams. It is strength and weakness, despair and joy, and the wild confusions and restless strivings of a boy who has passed his boyhood but is not yet a man.

2   A problem for America they call us. As well call a young thoroughbred a problem because he is not yet trained and fully grown. A backward nation they call us beside our great neighbor — this though our eleven millions have produced more, earned more, subdued more, built more than any other eleven millions in the world. A colony they have thought us though we have rebelled and fought and bled for the right to our own government and finally produced the British Commonwealth of equal nations. A timid race they have called us because we have been slow to change, because we have not mastered all the achievements nor all the vices of our neighbors.

3   They have not known Canada. Who but us can feel our fears and hopes and passions? How can aliens or even blood brothers know our inner doubts, our secret strengths and weaknesses and loves and lusts and shames?

4   Who can know our loneliness, on the immensity of prairie, in the dark forest and on the windy sea rock? A few lights, a faint glow is our largest city on the vast breast of the night, and all around blackness and emptiness and silence, where no man walks. We flee to little towns for a moment of fellowship and light and speech, we flee into cities or log cabins, out of the darkness and the loneliness and the creeping silence. All about us lies Canada, forever untouched, unknown, beyond our grasp, breathing deep in the darkness and we hear its breath and are afraid.

5   No, they could not know us, the strangers, for we have not known ourselves.

6   Long we have been a-growing, but with strong bone and sure muscle — of two bloods, French and British, slow to be reconciled in one body. We have been like a younger boy in the shadow of two older brothers, and, admiring their powers, watching the pageant of England and the raging energy of America, we have not learned our own proud story nor tested our own strength. But no longer are we children. Now our time is come and if not grasped will be forever lost.

7   Now must we make our choice. Now must the heaving, fluid stuff in Canada take shape, crystallize, and harden to a purpose. No people of our numbers has ever occupied such a place before in the flood tide of history, for we are of two worlds, the Old and the New, one foot in each, knowing England, knowing America, joined to each by blood and battle, speech and song. We alone are the hinge between them, and upon us hangs more than we know.

8   Wondrous and very sweet is our name. Canada! The very word is like a boy's shout in the springtime, is like the clamor of geese going north and the roar of melting rivers and the murmur of early winds.

9   Can we not hear the sound of Canada? Can we not hear it in the rustle of yellow poplar leaves in October, and in the sudden troutsplash of a silent lake, the whisper of saws in the deep woods, the church bells along the river, the whistle of trains in the narrow passes of the mountains, the gurgle of irrigation ditches in the hot nights, the rustle of ripe grain under the wind, and the bite of steel runners in the snow?

10   Have we not felt the texture and living stuff of Canada? Have we not felt it in the damp, springy forest floor, in the caress of the new grass upon our face, in the salt spray off Fundy or Juan de Fuca, in the hot sun of the prairies, in the beat of blizzards and the fierce surge of summer growth?

11   And the colors of Canada, those also have we seen. We have seen them in the harsh sweep of prairie snow, in sunlight and shadow vibrant across the heavy-headed wheat, in foaming apple orchards and in maple woods, crimson as blood, and in bleeding sumac by the

roadside, and in white sails of schooners out of Lunenburg and in the wrinkled blue face of mountains. And we have smelled the clean, manly smell of Canada, in pine forest and settlers' clearing fires, and alkali lakes and autumn stubble and new sawdust and old stone.

12   Yes, but we have not grasped it yet, the full substance of it, in our hands, nor glimpsed its size and shape. We have not yet felt the full pulse of its heart, the flex of its muscles, the pattern of its mind. For we are young, my brothers, and full of doubt, and we have listened too long to timid men. But now our time is come and we are ready.

Questions on Content

1   What comparison in paragraph one clarifies Hutchison's statement that "No one knows my country"?

2   What alternate views of Canada does Hutchison present in paragraph two? How does Hutchison account for the inadequacy of such views (paragraphs three through five)?

3   What view of Canada does Hutchison restate in paragraph six? Why is this comparison appropriate? What problem does it establish?

4   What is the dominant impression produced by Hutchison's detailed images in paragraphs eight through eleven? Where does Hutchison clarify this impression? What general belief does this impression support?

Questions on Structure and Technique

1   What sentence in paragraph one is Hutchison's thesis statement? What basic pattern of organization does this sentence establish? Where does Hutchison restate his thesis?

2   What is the unifying metaphor of Hutchison's essay? In what paragraph is this metaphor introduced? In what other paragraphs is this metaphor developed?

3   What images can you find that appeal to our sense of sight, sound, touch, taste, and smell? In what paragraphs are these images most important? Why?

4   Is Hutchison's conclusion effective? Why? Why not?

5   Discuss the questions posed in the introduction to Hutchison's essay. Support your answers with relevant examples of contemporary issues and forms of expression.

Suggestions for Writing

1   Write a descriptive essay about a place by using specific images and figurative language in order to support your belief in the true significance of that place and to convince readers to accept that belief as their own.

DAN GEORGE

Chief Dan George (b. 1899) has been an influential and effective spokes-person for Canada's native people. This address read on July 1, 1967 at a public celebration of Canada's centennial held in Vancouver's Empire Sta-dium is a compelling statement of his most fundamental beliefs. His speech's strong emotional and ethical appeals result, in part, from his effective use of questions, repetition, personification, simile, metaphor, and illustrative imagery. Consider what other examples of persuasive expression involve extensive use of such techniques. Although formal oratory may not be the usual form of your own persuasive expression, a more limited use of these rhetorical techniques in any argument enhances its emotional and ethical effect on an audience. Chief Dan George was born and raised on the Burrard Reserve in North Vancouver, B.C., and he worked as a logger and long-shoreman before becoming a musician and entertainer as well as chief of the Squamish Indians. Best-known for his television, film, and theatrical performances, Chief Dan George was nominated for an Academy Award for his role in Little Big Man *(1970).* My Heart Soars *(1974) is a collection of his meditations on Indian experience.*

LAMENT FOR CONFEDERATION

1   How long have I known you, Oh Canada? A hundred years? Yes, a hundred years. And many many *seclanun* more. And today, when you celebrate your hundred years, oh Canada, I am sad for all the Indian people throughout the land.

2   For I have known you when your forests were mine; when they gave me my meat and my clothing. I have known you in your streams and rivers where your fish flashed and danced in the sun, where the waters said come, come and eat of my abundance. I have known you in the freedom of your winds. And my spirit, like the winds, once roamed your good lands.

3   But in the long hundred years since the white man came, I have seen my freedom disappear like the salmon going mysteriously out to sea. The white man's strange customs which I could not understand, pressed down upon me until I could no longer breathe.

4   When I fought to protect my land and my home, I was called a savage. When I neither understood nor welcomed this way of life, I was called lazy. When I tried to rule my people, I was stripped of my authority.

5   My nation was ignored in your history textbooks — they were little more important in the history of Canada than the buffalo that ranged the plains. I was ridiculed in your plays and motion pictures, and when I drank your fire-water, I got drunk — very, very drunk. And I forgot.

6   Oh Canada, how can I celebrate with you this Centenary, this hundred years? Shall I thank you for the reserves that are left me of my beautiful forests? For the canned fish of my rivers? For the loss of my pride and authority, even among my own people? For the lack of my will to fight back? No! I must forget what's past and gone.

7   Oh, God in Heaven! Give me back the courage of the olden Chiefs, let me wrestle with my surroundings. Let me again, as in the days of old dominate my environment. Let me humbly accept this new culture and through it rise up and go on.

8   Oh God! Like the Thunderbird of old I shall rise again out of the sea: I shall grab the instruments of the white man's success — his education, his skills, and with these new tools I shall build my race into the proudest segment of your society. Before I follow the great Chiefs who have gone before us, oh Canada, I shall see these things come to pass.

9   I shall see our young braves and our chiefs sitting in the houses of law and government, ruling and being ruled by the knowledge and freedoms of *our* great land. So shall we shatter the barriers of our isolation. So shall the *next* hundred years be the greatest in the proud history of our tribes and nations.

Questions on Content

1   What is Chief Dan George's attitude toward Canada's centenary celebration?

2   What are the main reasons he gives for this attitude?

3   What is his general response to the problems of the past?

4   What specific actions does he recommend for the future?

5   What kind of future does he envision for native people in Canada?

Questions on Structure and Technique

1   What is the main pattern of organization in this speech? What other rhetorical modes of development are used?

2   How does Chief Dan George appeal to our sense of reason? How does he appeal to our emotions? How does he provide an ethical appeal?

3   What is the purpose of Chief Dan George's questions? What is the purpose of his repetition of words and phrases?

4   Why is Chief Dan George's use of the pronouns "I", "you," and "our" effective? Why are some nouns capitalized?

5   What examples of personification, simile, and metaphor are most effective? Why?

Suggestions for Writing

1   Write an essay in which you illustrate your reasons for holding a strong conviction or belief on a subject in order to convince readers to accept and possibly act on the validity of your viewpoint.

2   Write an essay in which you argue for a solution to a problem faced by members of a minority group of which you consider yourself a member.

RICK SALUTIN

Rick Salutin (b. 1942) is a writer who has expressed his views on Canadian culture in articles appearing in magazines such as Harper's, Maclean's, Weekend, Today, *and* This Magazine *as well as in numerous plays including* Les Canadiens. *"Marginality" is the introduction to a collection of his work entitled* Marginal Notes: Challenge to the Mainstream *(1984). In this thought-provoking essay, Salutin provides an extended definition of the term "marginality" and then illustrates its cultural significance in an argument designed to challenge his readers' ideas and beliefs as well as to gain their acceptance of his own. Salutin, who was born in Toronto, studied at Brandeis University, Columbia University, and the New School for Social Research in New York, before returning to Canada to pursue his interests in contemporary social, cultural, and political issues.*

MARGINALITY

1   Canada, for most of those who live here, is a lengthy margin, perhaps the longest in the world. For five thousand miles it stretches, a thin strip pinned across the top of the United States. The Canadian landmass spreads north, along with a smattering of Canadians. The vast majority, though, huddle within that strip, and their attention focuses southward more often than northward — or inward. We feel ourselves at the edge of something vast, teeming, variegated and contentedly self-absorbed, something that expects to be the object of attention from the outside. We are to it as the margin to a densely printed page.

2   We experience this marginality most sharply in the area of our culture. It exists elsewhere: the political sphere, where decisions that affect us seem often to be made in foreign capitals; or the economic realm, in which ownership and control frequently reside abroad. But we *feel* it every day culturally. The images that populate our fields of vision are rarely our own, and are mostly American. When Canadians see an American movie set in a small Texas town, they are prone to say, "That's just how it was in Barrie!" If they saw a movie actually set in Barrie, they might well feel it wasn't quite "real" — because all the images of small towns that have conditioned their expectations are American. If you saw someone else's reflection every time you looked in a mirror, you'd soon begin to feel that was how you looked. You'd squint doubtfully at your *own* reflection. The same effect happens with our experience of events: a Canadian election or scandal doesn't seem quite real in the manner of British or U.S. equivalents.

What would make a Canadian event thoroughly believable? Probably TV coverage by the American networks.

3   Marginality, then, is not a matter of location; it is a matter of attitude. It can exist in many spheres: within the economy, within a family, a work-place, a team, the United Nations — almost anywhere there is collective human activity. Canadian marginality as expressed by that five-thousand-mile geographical strip, is just a metaphor.

4   Marginality is largely a matter of attitude, but it concerns reality. There genuinely are centres of power, control and attention — as there are margins. Those who feel marginal consider their feeling to reflect their reality. There is a complex relation between what *is* (central or marginal) and what is felt to be so. My friend Clayton believes his house is at the exact geographical centre of Toronto. There may be topographical arguments in favour of his belief, but I know he thinks it because he lives there. Americans have good reasons for thinking their society is the centre of the universe: economic power, military might, ability to impose their political will. But they also have an unshakable conviction that they are *it* and everywhere else is periphery. And—although they also border us, and indeed our country is larger than theirs—we share their attitude as to who is central and who is marginal.

5   The difference between being and feeling (central and marginal) leads to some oddities. Those who are marginal can feel central — and the reverse. Any beggar in this society may identify with those at the summit of wealth and power. He can mime their posture and sincerely mouth their values. He may be a social outcast yet not feel so in the least, though at some point we may suspect his sense of belonging approaches self-delusion. (This is known in the technical literature as false consciousness and is worth, in my opinion, at least a lifetime of study.) Conrad Black on the other hand should not feel marginal. The attitudes and platitudes in newspaper editorials, the education system and the political arena suit him perfectly. Yet he says he feels persecuted when a national magazine describes just how he adroitly bends the political and judicial structures to his will. We may surmise though that his sense of marginality is fleeting and he will awake next day to a sense of order restored with Himself at its centre.

6   One can also be (and feel) marginal in some ways and not in others. A child can feel central among its peers and marginal with its siblings — or vice versa. A man or woman may feel central at home and marginal in the workforce — or the unemployment line. A Canadian corporate magnate, say the president of the Canadian branch of a multinational, may feel quite insignificant at headquarters in Houston or Detroit. One can even become marginal, in odd ways, to parts of one's own life — though that is a messier case.

7   When I look over things I have dealt with since I began writing in 1971, I am amazed at how much could be tucked under the heading of marginality. A self-hating Canadian in the U.S. A nationalist in the country that has always suspected nationalism. Among nationalists, a Marxist. A middle-class writer in the labour movement, and within labour a dissenter against the mainstream. A Quebec *indépendantiste* in English Canada. A Jew among Gentiles, and among Jews an outsider for criticizing the community and Israel. The first writing money I ever made came from a radio program called *Inside from the Outside*. I wrote about Canadian revolutions that failed and Canadian heroes who were unknown. My first play was set in China, and I went to Mozambique to learn about culture and politics.

8   I don't suppose it's accidental. It's true that the Canadian geographical strip is only a metaphor. Coming from here doesn't mean one is destined or doomed to marginality. But it's a hell of a starting-point.

9   No one wants to feel like a pariah among his own people. You write about your fellow Jews because this is a part of yourself and as a writer you choose to explore it. But parts of this part cause you concern, pain and anger. You describe these with care. You weigh and test each nuance, trying to be honest and fair. You step carefully through this minefield, emerge at the other side and publish. The first phone call is an anguished, accented woman's voice — a survivor. 'How could you write this?' It's like Hitler coming back. Your immediate thought: Am I an anti-Semite? Did I write hatefully? You walk and wonder and re-examine every phrase. A relative's letter: 'If you said this in a Jewish publication we would hail your courage, but in a national magazine — it's like handing the noose to the hangman.' Your mother, in and out of the hospital with one of the illnesses of age: you warn her something else will soon appear, it's about Israeli policy, it's critical, she may get more calls from people blaming her for what that son of hers has done now. She has been your most devoted reader. She has found and kept pieces even you forgot you wrote. This time she says, 'I may not read it, dear.'

10   You don't choose to be marginal. You see things a certain way and express this view. Marginality is a gradual consequence. Others start to view you in ways that startle you. I once criticized the editor and critic Robert Fulford in *This Magazine*. Fulford wrote back in *Saturday Night*, I can imagine the excitement with which his discovery was greeted in the offices of *This Magazine*. 'Someone has said something slightly favourable to The System. Call the cops! Get him!'

11   I wondered, how does Fulford picture us and our 'offices' — as a rabbit warren of radicals with typewriters, like the caves at Yenan where the Red Army licked their wounds after the Long March? Would he be surprised at the one sunny corner, with hanging plants

over Lorraine's desk, on the spacious floor we share with *Canadian Forum*, the Association of Canadian Publishers and the Canadian Book Information Centre—a few blocks from *Saturday Night* itself? At a garden party with media figures: am I wrong, am I just projecting, or do they expect me to slip a Molotov cocktail from my shirt and fling it into the kidney-shaped pool?

12   The fact you are marked as marginal starts to affect your work. You lack some of the writing outlets you might have if your views were more conventional. But you're not cut off completely. In some ways the mainstream even requires you to provide something different from time to time, and to prove they are open to many opinions. Anyway, no one said life was going to be easy.

13   Something more insidious happens. What you write in the mainstream starts to sound quirky, unlikely or bizarre—not just to others, but even to yourself. This has little to do with the plausibility of your ideas. The context makes your words sound strange.

14   As I write, new leaders are being proposed by the Liberals and the Progressive Conservatives (itself an outlandish phrase but one we all nod to from habit). It seems to me the field of candidates is an insult to the Canadian people, yet it would be hard to express this view. It would require mountains of evidence, rigorous reasoning and a mild inoffensive tone. *The Globe and Mail* editorialist can pontificate into his (or her) beard about the heroic virtues of the same lot and no eyebrow is raised. The arguments from my view are not weaker than the *Globe*'s (I am already being inoffensive); it is the context of accepted and repeated opinion which makes my statement sound questionable. Not wrong—unrespectable. The contribution tends to be dismissed before it is entertained, due to its marginality.

15   At times marginality can seem attractive, even romantic: marginal man, the existential hero, standing alone against the currents of the time. This may be fine for characters you create, or admire, but not for the character you are. Perhaps some artists of nihilistic turn enjoy occasional marginality, especially if it is marketable that season. But most writers wish to connect, not withdraw. And the place where marginality inevitably aches is politics. (By politics I don't mean just parties and elections; I mean that entire area in which we are concerned with the shape and thrust of our society, as far as these are within human control.) As a writer with political concerns, you want to affect your fellow citizens, join in the process of government and change, act as a member of your community. Being right and principled is no compensation for being miles from everyone else.

16   You fall into an emotional double peril. You may grow bitter. With all good will you have tried to make a contribution to your society, yet have been consigned to irrelevance. Or you become self-righteous, even smug: you offered, they didn't listen—let them rot. You waver

between despair and arrogance, self-pity and contempt — and help along the process of your own marginalization.

17   You may even embrace the role, enthusiastically identifying with every victim and loser of the past and present. This involves a loss of perspective. I may feel deep sympathy with the peasants of southern Africa, but my main economic concern is paying the mortgage every month, not eking out enough protein to make it to tomorrow. You overplay the marginal card, you take yourself too tragically, you even misplace your sense of humour.

18   Marginalization starts to take an unforeseen toll, penetrating areas of your life unrelated to writing. You live alone. Socially, when in doubt, you are surly; they expect it. You import that stance of outsider into your private life. Perhaps you were inclined this way for earlier reasons; now that bent links up with your experience as a writer. You distance yourself not just from prevailing opinion, but from people who come towards you: you stand aside and let them by. 'How easily substance can become style,' says a friend. You intended to take a principled stand on the pernicious fashions of your time; you have become a walking emotional margin.

19   None of this was sought. You wrote to take a stand, to share your view, to cut a route to the centre of your society. Yet a funny thing happened on the way: you became marginal. We are not marginal because of the quirkiness of our ideas or the inadequacy of our arguments, but because of the power of those who define the centre. Those with the ability to issue the definitions— through the broadcast media, the newspapers and magazines, the schools and universities — control the criteria of centrality. They live there.

20   As for those of us who heartily abominate these criteria, we cannot deny that we are marginal. There is no point, our marginality is real. We can however reject the evaluation which those at the centre make, and which our society largely accepts, about our marginality. We can deny that marginality is negative. We can claim it as a strength.

21   The main trait of those at the centre in our society is surely smugness. They assume there is no better place to be, there could be no finer view. They swallow their canapés and pat their bellies. They find it unthinkable that any location less central could offer a superior vantage-point.

22   Yet what do their versions of reality accomplish? Their nostrums may reassure but do they clarify? Do they make sense of the world? 'I could never understand how the Causes of the War caused the war,' laments a bewildered ex-student. 'I tried to start reading the newspapers again,' says a housewife, 'but I gave up. I couldn't understand any of it. What is power? Why do countries go to war? Why do they care about territory?' Only through habit do the rest of us nod as if the explanations delivered to us daily mean anything. 'I started to

cry on the subway,' says a man during a political crisis; 'I didn't go to work, I just wandered. I don't understand any of it. Why is it happening?' You cannot make sense of this society with explanations from the centre because the centre has too much to hide: all the levers and forces which operate from there, including the motives of the explainers themselves.

23   The centre is grandiose but it is tiny. Its charter members, the truly rich and/or powerful plus their faithful retainers, are few in number. They swell their ranks by conscripting many who agree to subscribe to their values without sharing in the perks. This adherence is often tenuous. The immigrants, the native peoples, the majority of women, the unemployed youth, the peripheralized middle executives (even), the surplus Ph.D.s — of what use are the definitions of centrality to them? They already are — and many already feel — marginalized. Others join them, especially as economic crisis deepens. We move towards a society which is mainly margin.

24   It is an odd society which offers its members only the choice between centre and margin. Why not a different centre or centres? A true opposition? Yet the only alternatives granted legitimacy by the centre itself are no real alternatives at all: Conservatives instead of Liberals, or an NDP providing it is indistinct from either. Any basically critical, fundamentally different stance is instantly consigned to the margin. No wonder people are reluctant to abandon the centre.

25   Yet the margin declares itself anyway. The history of the human race over the past two hundred years has been the progressive assertion of the margin over the centre. In the American Revolution an outpost of the British Empire asserted itself against the centre. In the French Revolution the marginalized mass — *le peuple* asserted itself against the court of Versailles, centre of the political universe. In our own time it is the marginalized peoples of the Third World, from China to Cuba to Vietnam to Mozambique to Nicaragua, who assert themselves against the imperial centres again and again. Within our own society the last hundred years have seen the self-assertion of the working class, the native peoples, women — all the internal margins of the Western world. It is the major movement of our age, these defiant self-assertions by those deemed outsiders. There is far more historical relevance on the periphery today than among any of the smug elites at the centre. A Mozambican peasant raises a fist against the forces of might and tradition and becomes the locus of the human quest in our time. We are fully human, he — or she — says, and we will no longer accept the negative consequences of our marginality. It is a scandal from the point of view of the centre: these scruffy dissenters stepping out of the bush directly onto the stage of history. Or from the factory, or from the office. Those at the centre gawk.

26   In the world today the margin is the only place from which you gain a clear view of what is happening; the view from the centre is hopelessly distorted. Its only recommendation is its respectability: it carries credentials — the *Toronto Star*, *Maclean's*, *The National*, the University of So-and-So.

27   Finally, I want to argue that the margin is where you have more fun. This is a somewhat ponderous statement, but I cannot believe those who carry the burdens of hypocrisy, self-delusion and smugness are having fun too. It's true they often look as though they're enjoying themselves, but I choose to believe it's a façade. Real fun (a word unique to the English language) comes with a clear conscience and a clear view.

Questions on Content

1   In what ways is Canada "marginal," according to Salutin? What does Salutin mean when he writes that "Canadian marginality . . . is just a metaphor"?

2   What illustrations does Salutin use to demonstrate "a complex relation between what *is* (central or marginal) and what is felt to be so"?

3   What main negative effects of marginality does Salutin discuss?

4   What are the main positive strengths of marginality, according to Salutin?

5   What is the historical significance of marginality? What is marginality's contemporary significance?

Questions on Structure and Technique

1   In what sentence in paragraph one does Salutin most concisely define the term "marginality"? What illustrations in paragraphs one and two clarify this definition? Why are these illustrations effective for Salutin's argument?

2   Why does Salutin make a distinction "between what *is* (central or marginal) and what is felt to be so"? How does Salutin attempt to make this distinction convincing?

3   What kind of appeal does Salutin emphasize when he discusses his own experience as a writer? What examples of the two other kinds of appeals can you find in his essay?

4   Why does Salutin discuss both negative and positive aspects of marginality?

5 In what ways is Salutin's treatment of his definition of marginality in the concluding paragraphs different from its presentation in the introductory paragraphs? Is Salutin's development of his essay inductive or deductive? Why?

Suggestions for Writing

1 After studying Salutin's argument in favour of "marginality," write an essay in which you argue for a "marginal" idea or belief that you hold in opposition to the "central" mainstream view taken by most other people in a group in which you consider yourself a member.

2 Write an essay in which you agree or disagree with one of the following statements in Salutin's essay: "The history of the human race over the past two hundred years has been the progressive assertion of the margin over the centre"; or, "the margin is the only place from which you gain a clear view of what is happening; the view from the centre is hopelessly distorted."

DAVID T. SUZUKI

David T. Suzuki (b. 1936) is a scientist, educator, and broadcaster whose numerous science programs on radio and television such as Science Magazine *and* The Nature of Things *have made a major contribution to the popularization of science in Canada. In his essay "A Planet for the Taking" Suzuki analyses the causes and effects of "our faith in the power of science and technology," arguing his claim that we need "a profound perceptual shift" in our view of nature. He examined this issue in detail in an eight-part television series of the same name. Born and raised in Vancouver, Suzuki received his B.A. from Amherst College and his Ph.D. in Genetics from the University of Chicago. He was a professor of zoology at the University of British Columbia from 1963 to 1975, and he has been a lecturer and speaker at many universities and scientific conferences throughout the world.*

A PLANET FOR THE TAKING

1   Canadians live under the remarkable illusion that we are a technologically advanced people. Everything around us denies that assumption. We are, in many ways, a Third World country, selling our natural resources in exchange for the high technology of the industrialized world. Try going through your home and looking at the country of origin of your clothes, electrical appliances, books, car. The rare technological product that does have Canada stamped on it is usually from a branch plant of a multinational company centred in another country. But we differ from traditional Third World countries. We have a majority population of Caucasians and a very high level of literacy and affluence. And we have been able to maintain our seemingly advanced social state by virtue of an incredible bounty of natural resources.

2   Within the Canadian mystique there is also a sense of the vastness of this land. The prairies, the Arctic, the oceans, the mountains are ever present in our art and literature. This nation is built on our sense of the seeming endlessness of the expanse of wilderness and the output of nature and we have behaved as if this endlessness were real. Today we speak of renewable resources but our "harvest" procedures are more like a mining operation. We extract raw resources in the crudest of ways, gouging the land to get at its inner core, spewing

our raw wastes into the air, water and soil in massive amounts while taking fish, birds, animals and trees in vast quantities without regard to the future. So we operate under a strange duality of mind: we have both a sense of the importance of the wilderness and space in our culture and an attitude that it is limitless and therefore we needn't worry.

3   Native cultures of the past may have been no more conservation-minded than we are but they lacked the technology to make the kind of impact that we do today. Canadians and Americans share one of the great natural wonders, the Great Lakes, which contain 20 per cent of world's fresh water, yet today even this massive body of water is terribly polluted and the populations of fish completely mixed-up by human activity. We speak of "managing" our resources but do it in a way that resembles the sledgehammer-on-the-head cure for a head-ache. On the west coast of Canada, Natives lived for millennia on the incredible abundance of five species of salmon. Today, the massive runs are gone and many biologists fear that the fish may be in mortal jeopardy because of both our fishing and management policies. Having improved fishing techniques this century to the point of endangering runs yet still knowing very little of the biology of the fish, we have assumed that we could build up the yield by simply dumping more back. But it wasn't known that sockeye salmon fry, for example, spend a year in a freshwater lake before going to sea. Millions of sockeye fry were dumped directly into the Fraser River where they died soon after. In Oregon, over-fishing and hydroelectric dams had decimated coho populations in the Columbia River. In one year, over 8 million fry were released of which only seven were ever caught. No one knows what's happening to the rest.

4   We act as if a fish were a fish, a duck a duck or a tree a tree. If we "harvest" one, we renew it by simply adding one or two back. But what we have learned is that all animals and plants are not equivalent. Each organism reflects the evolutionary history of its progenitors; in the case of salmon, each race and subrace of fish has been exquisitely honed by nature to return to a very specific part of the Pacific water-shed. Similarly, in the enormous area of prairie pothole country in the centre of the continent, migratory birds do not just space them-selves out according to the potholes that are empty. Scientists have discovered that the birds have been selected to return to a very restricted part of that area. And of course, our entire forestry policy is predicated on the ridiculous idea that a virgin stand of fir or cedar which has taken millennia to form and clings to a thin layer of topsoil can be replaced after clear-cut logging simply by sticking seedlings into the ground. How can anyone with even the most rudimentary understanding of biology and evolution ignore the realities of the

complex interaction between organisms and the environment and attempt to manipulate wild populations as if they were tomato plants or chickens?

5   I believe that in large part our problems rest on our faith in the power of science and technology. At the beginning of this century, science, when applied by industry and medicine, promised a life immeasurably better and there is no doubt that society, indeed the planet, has been transformed by the impact of new ideas and inventions of science. Within my lifetime, I've seen the beginning of television, oral contraception, organ transplants, space travel, computers, jets, nuclear weapons, satellite communication, and polio vaccine. Each has changed society forever and made the world of my youth recede into the pages of history. But we have not achieved a technological utopia. The problems facing us today are immense and many are a direct consequence of science and technology. What has gone wrong?

6   I believe that the core of our 20th century dilemma lies in a fundamental limitation of science that most scientists, especially those in the life sciences, fail to recognize. Most of my colleagues take it for granted that our studies will ultimately be applicable to the "big picture," that our research will have beneficial payoffs to society eventually. That is because the thrust of modern science has been predicated on the Newtonian idea that the universe is like an enormous machine whose entire system will be reconstructed on the basis of our understanding of the parts. This is the fundamental reductionist faith in science: the whole is equal to the sum of its parts. It does make a lot of sense—what distinguishes science from other activities that purport to provide a comprehensive "world view" is its requirement that we focus on a part of nature isolated to as great an extent as possible from the rest of the system of which it is a part. This has provided enormous insights into that fragment of nature, often accompanied by power to manipulate it. But when we attempt to tinker with what lies in the field of our view, the effects ripple far beyond the barrel of the microscope. And so we are constantly surprised at the unexpected consequences of our interference. Scientists only know nature in "bits and pieces" and assume that higher levels of organization are simply the expression of the component parts. This is what impels neurobiologists to study the chemical and electrical behaviour of single neurons in the faith that it will ultimately lead to an understanding of what creativity and imagination are, a faith that I don't for a moment think will ever be fulfilled (although a lot of useful information will accrue).

7   Physicists, who originally set this view in motion, have this century, with the arrival of relativity and quantum theory, put to rest the notion

that we will ever be able to reconstruct the entire universe from fundamental principles. Chemists know that a complete physical description of atoms of oxygen and hydrogen is of little value in predicting the behaviour of a water molecule. But biologists scream that any sense that there are properties of organization that don't exist at lower levels is "vitalism," a belief that there is some mystical life force in living organisms. And so biochemists and molecular biologists are intent on understanding the workings of organisms by learning all they can about sub-cellular organization.

8   Ironically, ecology, long scorned by molecular biologists as an inexact science, is now corroborating physics. In studying ecosystems, we are learning that a simple breakdown into components and their behaviour does not provide insight into how an entire collection of organisms in a natural setting will work. While many ecologists do continue to "model" ecosystems in computers in the hope that they will eventually derive a predictive tool, their science warns of the hazards of treating it too simply in management programs.

9   At present, our very terminology suggests that we think we can manage wild plants and animals as though they were domesticated organisms. We speak of "herds" of seals, of "culling," "harvesting," "stocks." The ultimate expression of our narrow view (and self-interested rationalizations) is seen in how we overlook the enormous environmental impact of our pollution, habitat destruction and extraction and blame seals and whales for the decline in fish populations or wolves for the decrease in moose — and then propose bounties as a solution!

10   But Canadians do value the spiritual importance of nature and want to see it survive for future generations. We also believe in the power of science to sustain a high quality of life. And while the current understanding of science's power is, I believe, misplaced, in fact the leading edges of physics and ecology may provide the insights that can get us off the current track. We need a very profound perceptual shift and soon.

Questions on Content

1   What "strange duality of mind" do Canadians' views of nature reveal, according to Suzuki?

2   What illustrations show the effects of this attitude toward nature?

3   What is the main cause of this attitude toward nature, according to Suzuki?

4   What is the "fundamental limitation of science that most scientists . . . fail to recognize"?

5   What do studies in physics and ecology demonstrate about our faith in science and technology? What does Suzuki conclude?

Questions on Structure and Technique

1   What claim does Suzuki attempt to disprove in paragraphs one and two? What evidence does he offer to refute this claim? What alternative claim does Suzuki make? What specific evidence in paragraphs three and four support Suzuki's claim?

2   What other claims does Suzuki make in paragraphs five and six? How are these claims causally related to his claim in paragraph two? How does Suzuki support his claims in paragraphs seven, eight, and nine? What conclusion does he draw from his analysis? Does Suzuki develop this argument inductively or deductively?

3   What is the relation between Suzuki's concluding paragraph and paragraphs one and two? Why is this conclusion effective?

4   What audience is this argument written for? What aspects of this argument appeal to reason? What aspects of this argument appeal to emotion? What appeal does Suzuki emphasize? Why?

5   What effects does Suzuki achieve by using the pronouns "we" and "I" throughout this essay?

Suggestions for Writing

1   Select a problem that has resulted from "a sense of the importance of the wilderness and space in our culture and an attitude that it is limitless and therefore we needn't worry." Write an argumentative essay in which you attempt to convince readers of the seriousness of the problem and then discuss what direction efforts to solve the problem should take.

2   Write an essay in which you agree or disagree with Suzuki's claim that "in large part our problems rest on our faith in the power of science and technology." Choose one significant issue with which to illustrate your view, and organize and develop your argument by supporting your claims with good, specific evidence.

3   Write an argument about an important problem that you believe can only be solved by "a very profound perceptual shift" in our view of that problem.

VIVIAN RAKOFF

The many complex and difficult moral, ethical, social, and economic questions arising from the development of modern medical technology have no easy answers. A Professor of Psychiatric Education at the University of Toronto and Head of the Department of Psychiatry at Toronto's Sunnybrook Medical Centre, Vivian Rakoff (b. 1928) offers a carefully reasoned and balanced analysis of our responses to these problems in order to indicate a clearer direction to our arguments in the future. Consider both why this approach to argument is effective, and when it is a most appropriate one to adopt.

THE FATAL QUESTION

1   Human beings sustained in a state of technical "life" through complex machinery present to society and medicine a terrible and increasingly familiar dilemma. All the meaning and pleasure of ordinary life are absent and there's no hope of return to dignified existence. Who has the authority to decide that the time has come to stop the machines? The patient (if conscious), the family, the physician, or the law? Who has the power to commit euthanasia? Or, putting it closer to the emotional core of the problem, to commit murder? Who had the authority to start the machines in the first place?

2   There are no immediate answers, but there's already a repertoire of responses, many of them secret or unspoken. A hospital may give its permission for the patient to go home after discussion with physicians, family, and, where possible, the patient — indeed sometimes at the request of the patient — with the clear knowledge that he or she will die shortly after the machines have been detached. A deliberately careless nurse or doctor may disconnect the power lines, or someone may appeal to the courts to make the decision. Or people may make "living wills" in which they decide, while they are well, that they should be allowed to die "naturally."

3   Once the problem is made explicit it becomes a horrifying moral issue. The decision to withhold life-sustaining measures flies in the face of ordinarily accepted law and morality. Mercy killing is tainted by moral revulsion and the memory — very close to us — of eugenic killing and so-called medical experiments by the Nazis. There is also the hovering doubt that medical opinion may be wrong, that someone who appears permanently comatose, may, in fact, recover. A life-taking decision goes against the fundamental aim of medicine, the preservation of life.

4   The dilemma is not new. Poor societies have often been forced to make similar choices: the Inuit, in times of great stress, put the enfeebled old onto ice floes, and in many societies weak babies were exposed to the elements. In wartime or on dangerous expeditions wounded comrades have had to be abandoned. What is new is the enormous scale of the problem, and its pervasiveness. The proportion of medically needy old people is rapidly increasing. Technology has changed everything by expanding our choices. Our range of control has broadened and we now find ourselves caught by a magic that, when it was new, seemed marvellous and only good.

5   Something has gone wrong, and suspicion naturally falls on medicine and its apparently mindless embrace — without regard for the human implications — of science, technique, and expensive machines.

6   In one of his madder essays, the German-American political philosopher Herbert Marcuse suggested that mankind should not willingly accept the inevitability of death. In his view to accept a limit, any limit, was to accept the authoritarian structure of a tyrannical society and thereby to adopt a world view of diminished possibilities. That radical thought makes all other revolutionary slogans in history seem frivolous. It's a call to the barricades to plunder and redistribute the greatest of all the limited-access treasures — time.

7   Marcuse was merely expressing hyperbolically the notions of limitless growth and the perfectibility of man which are almost orthodox in modern Western society. He articulated in extreme form a current of belief common to our world: that old age, the decay of the body, and physical suffering are not inevitable, are in fact a kind of cosmic mistake — and a hurdle for Western man to overcome. In these terms, the attack on death itself is only an expansion of our very common assumption that anything can be fixed, that there is no obstacle that cannot be overcome with the right technology.

8   And in a sense it now seems that this crazy rejection of mortality is based on solid ground. Life expectancy has increased from about forty years two centuries ago to seventy-two years for men and seventy-nine years for women (in Canada at the moment). Because of immunization and antibiotics, the infectious diseases that wiped out generations of children are no longer the threat they once were. Surgery benignly invades the body to carve out tumours, excise damaged pieces, and, most dramatically, replace nonfunctioning or malfunctioning parts. The middle-aged can now defend themselves against the reality of being old with spectacles, good dentistry, face-lifts, herniorrhaphies, cataract operations, varicose vein strippings, haemorrhoidectomies, and any number of similarly undramatic manoeuvres.

9   But, of course, Herbert Marcuse's dream has not been fulfilled. People die, and they tend to die more and more of circulatory diseases

or cancer. In a curious way it is a privilege — a specifically modern privilege — to die of circulatory disease or cancer. It implies that one has weathered the infections of childhood and middle age, and that social policy is so advanced that lethal accidents and industrial poisoning (despite our beliefs to the contrary) are much reduced. Heart attacks and cancers signify that one has survived.

10   Relatively good health and medical care are among the most manifest benefits available in our society. Health has been democratized, and is now within the domain of expectation rather than charity. People in the developed countries no longer wait for religious organizations to provide bandages, hospital beds, and nursing, as they no longer expect charity to provide education and pensions. And this fact has changed expectations about existence in general. The young mothers dying in childbirth, the sick and dying children, the constant presence of illness that provided so many plot devices for nineteenth-century fiction — these are no longer the casually accepted facts of our lives. Only three or so generations ago, death was everyone's life companion. It was impossible to grow up without watching a number of childhood contemporaries die along the way; furthermore, it was not impossible but highly unlikely for parents to see all of their children grow to adulthood.

11   The other day I glanced at a nineteenth-century story by Israel Zangwill in which the very regularity of death is part of the plot's background. Zangwill is describing the situation of a certain Mrs. Drabdump, a widow: "The late Mr. Drabdump had scratched the base of his thumb with a rusty nail, and Mrs. Drabdump's foreboding that he would die of lockjaw had not prevented her wrestling day and night with the shadow of Death, as she had wrestled with it vainly twice before, when Katie died of diphtheria and little Johnny of scarlet fever. Perhaps it is from overwork among the poor that Death has been reduced to a shadow." Today a child who is born will, with moderate good luck, become an adult. Our expectations have so changed that it is as if nature itself has been changed. The field of forces in which we make our plans has been dramatically altered. The frail old and the terminally resuscitated patients are the result of a continuum of technology that starts at birth and stretches like a safety net under the entire population.

12   This safety net is now perceived as a necessity, and in the United States union leaders — who reflect the general level of social aspiration — increasingly demand extensive health care as part of labour settlements. In Canada, care is provided generally, as a public entitlement. The result in financial terms is an extraordinary increase in the cost of health care to society as a whole, whether the money is paid through governments or through corporations. Most industrialized countries,

whatever their health plans, now spend about $800 a year per person on health; there are more than 150 physicians per 100,000 people. Quite apart from the controversy as to whether the costs can be trimmed, or whether doctors, nurses, and other health-care workers are overpaid, these costs reflect an extraordinary and historically unprecedented mobilization of energies. The rise in medical costs is usually presented as a social problem, and it is. It may also represent, from another perspective, a marvellous change in social thinking. It can be interpreted as a concrete expression of the value we place on the preservation and extension of life.

13   Now that health care is assumed to be a necessary benefit, it has also become suspect. There is a probably inevitable seesaw of attitudes toward all social forces — what was good becomes bad, what was progressive becomes reactionary. So a number of questioning, negative responses have coalesced into a serious and widespread criticism of modern medicine. Each of the critical positions has its own historical antecedents, its serious proponents, its zealous, hyperbolic loonies. And each of them articulates, in a different way, our profound historical disappointment with the promises of technological Utopianism — as it applies not just to medicine but to society as a whole. This is not new; suspicion of the machine has run like a shadow alongside the triumphs of the machine.

14   The rational surface of the industrial world in the nineteenth century quickly generated a yearning for simplicity and innocence, a feeling of loneliness and directionlessness, a fear that Western man was courting disaster by rejecting ancient truths. Philosophers expressed these terrors more than a hundred years ago, when the greatest triumphs of expanding technology, particularly the almost miraculous achievements of technological medicine, were yet to come. And now that undreamed-of miracles have become ordinary, fears and disappointments are even more universal and are expressed in ways that range from the theological and abstract to the folkloric.

15   Even if all of these objections to technological medicine are for the moment pushed to the side as too soft-minded and sentimental, the economic reservations remain. They seem to stand like a huge barrier against further development of more machines with even more specialized functions — and against the ever-growing spread of supportive services to an expanding pool of old people.

16   One part of the argument against medical technology is based on simple cost effectiveness. "Do you really think that it's worth it to develop a primitive artificial heart which has, so far, been used only a few times — and renders the patient unable to lead anything like a normal life, without carrying around a suitcase full of equipment? Is that life? And at such cost, who is going to be able to support it?

Everybody threatened with imminent death from a barely functioning heart will want one — and we can't afford it."

17   For the artificial heart one might substitute elaborate neonatal units: "We spend millions to maintain the lives of some very frail, perhaps even genetically damaged, infants, and down the street they're building abortion clinics and selling contraceptives." Or, "How many specialized neurosurgery units do we really require? They operate principally on people whose doom is sealed. Certainly they alleviate some suffering, and every now and again they get rid of a benign tumour, or their post-traumatic work is occasionally spectacular and useful — but the contribution to overall health statistics is minimal."

18   The reservations are even more forceful when applied to techniques still in their infancy, such as the hugely expensive imaging devices that show bodily structures and functions without having to invade the body's interior with surgery. The PET and NMR scanners require special facilities, cyclotrons, physicists, and millions of dollars in capital investment — all to show soft structures, for example, or the ongoing metabolism of the brain. As yet, they are little more than experimental and the cost is mind-boggling. The promise for research and diagnosis is just as mind-boggling, but in the whole of Canada there are no more than a half-dozen of these machines. "They cost too much."

19   The second part of this argument against medical technology refers to simple medical services — nursing, meals for the housebound elderly, and the more-or-less routine surgical repair jobs we now regard as part of growing older. Applied to a population of the aged, these measures represent a colossal financial liability to society. A warning about the future usually accompanies this line of thought. We have a drop in the birth rate and in forty years the old will sit like a heavy burden on the shoulders of a smaller work force. Many of the old, kept alive by antibiotics, will be as dependent on technology as someone plugged into electrical respirators and infusion pumps. They may not be wired into visible machines, but they will be just as dependent on a panoply of services. In their case, there will be no particular plug to pull but instead a structure devoted to the maintenance of semi-existence, much more difficult to dismantle than a machine. Presented carefully with the appropriate graphs and figures, this nightmare is persuasive and economically terrifying.

20   The larger philosophical questions come into public focus, with more emotional impact than the economic issue, in cases such as that of Karen Ann Quinlan — someone who apparently had no realistic hope of independent survival but was kept technically alive. In this scenario, physicians, technologically expert and morally bankrupt, are presented as villains. They are seen as behaving with arrogant triumphalism, interested only in doing things to human beings as a

display of their virtuosity — or, worse, to satisfy their greed. People who should be allowed to die "in dignity" are artificially kept alive, apparently without regard for their real needs. The criticism becomes more general when it reflects attitudes beyond medicine. At this point it questions the lack of imagination inherent in this medical expression of society's denial of psychological and spiritual man. In this scenario, man has been reduced to a piece of machinery to be shaped according to a technological imperative.

21   Jacques Ellul, the French theologian, has devoted his most earnest efforts to questioning the faith modern man has placed in the idea that there are technological ways to solve or escape from ancient moral dilemmas. In Canada, the philosopher George Grant has raised the same sort of suspicion of what he considers our mindless rush toward technological toys: "Nearly all our current moral discourse about technological society falls back to rest upon such unthought concepts as 'values' and 'ideals.' By so doing, it revolves within the hard-rimmed circle of technological society and cannot issue in thought. The moral exhortations of our politicians, our scholars, our psychiatrists, our social scientists are caught in this circle, so that their words become a tired celebration of technological society."

22   The problem of technology is particularly important as it relates to the newest systems — computers, recombinant DNA, long-distance communication satellites. These things make the old technology of levers, cogs, and electrical wires seem domestic and familiar. The new technology has gone a long way beyond the old idea of the machine as an extension of some ordinary human function such as speaking, walking, or digging. The distinction between the person and the machine is clear in the older technologies, but some of the newer instruments become part of the human being, a new element of anatomy — most dramatically, an artificial heart. If the technological artefact can be integrated into a human, then is a human simply a very complex machine? When technology reaches this level, a new channel of perception has been opened. It is not hard to understand why this transforming metaphor should worry theologians.

23   Miraculous extensions of life expectation offer a new kind of immortality, but the ambiguity of survival has not been sufficiently questioned. Immortality for what? A person or a supermachine? If for a human being, then the quality of life, relationships, and continued creativity are in question. If for a machine, then physical function is enough. The machine metaphor, which is fairly understandable in the workings of advanced medicine, may be dangerous if it is thoughtlessly extended. Is the comatose patient sustaining the use of the machine, or vice versa?

24   Moral speculations such as these echo an old argument. Classically, it takes the form of a debate between the humble acceptance of an

assigned place in God's universe and the so-called Faustian urge to open up our place in the universe and stake out territory without thought of any boundaries. The argument has no real resolution. The expansive, forward-moving vision generates a weary "Whoa" and we are reminded by Jacques Ellul or George Grant to look at what we may be losing or destroying in our rush toward what they consider the illusory possibilities of the future.

25   In a pluralist intellectual climate, the battle is constant. We do not exist in a small city-state like Renaissance Florence; we will not have a period of elaborate inventiveness, followed by drastic penance and tyranny in the form of someone like Savonarola. Our Savonarolas are with us all the time, playing a stern obbligato behind our technological triumphs. The problem involves much more than getting hospitals to accept "do not resuscitate" orders for the dying. We are all involved in the larger issue. When we refuse to limit our ambitions we all take part in the act of resuscitation.

26   Another objection to medical technology also represents the re-emergence of a perennial current: the belief that wisdom is not acquired, that knowledge is a human endowment like eyes and ears, and that proper social and educational opportunities will bring it out. This belief found its expression in Jean-Jacques Rousseau's notion of a natural man who possesses true wisdom. It comes in many variations, the most appealing being the Walden Pond school of social criticism. It is manifestly attractive because it lacks the pursed lips and theological rigours of the Ellul position or the smell of gloomy stuff such as "spiritual pride."

27   The *Walden* version depicts a tamed, comfortable world on the margins of technology. Henry David Thoreau did not go into the wilderness as many American contemporaries did. He essentially stayed home in New England, close to his mother's kitchen, visited by literary luminaries. He simplified his life in the middle of a relatively secure reality; he criticized the excess and complexity of the technologically burdened life without entirely leaving it.

28   And, like Thoreau, the Walden Pond critic of medical technology does not want to give up the triumphs of medicine. No-one calls for the abandonment of penicillin or the polio vaccine. The widespread demand is for a return to the natural — as in natural childbirth or natural foods — as opposed to the dreadful and frightening machine. The aesthetic discomfort with the machine is a central component of this stance. It rejects the frontiers of medicine and the dangerous options of the new technological wilderness. The concern is not only with the tragic example of a dying person with a thousand tubes but also with the more ordinarily cold manoeuvres of medicine: the alien and apparently dehumanized world of glass, metal, and wire. While purporting to be kindly, the working surface of modern medicine is

perceived by many patients as icily repellent, and has associations of puncturing, cutting, hurting. It does not come across as caring and charitable. It comes across as heartless.

29   In the background are the machines, obscenely doing what should not be done. Apart from representing a new version of spiritual pride, high-tech medicine arouses all the profound suspicions of science that regularly reemerge in Western consciousness—suspicions expressed in the story of Frankenstein and other mad scientists of fiction, the lineal descendants in popular mythology of the medieval wizard, alchemist, and necromancer, both wise and malign. The machine, for those who do not know how to use it, is never "user-friendly." It may turn on us, like the computer HAL in *2001: A Space Odyssey*, particularly when it is the instrument of esoteric power.

30   Esoteric knowledge is antidemocratic. The suspicion of high technology borrows from a general rejection of professionalism, and medicine provokes some of the most furious antiprofessionalism. Populist critics refer to institutionalized medicine in terms of its self-important pretensions to omniscience, esoteric language, undemocratic decisions, self-serving greed, and the profession's institutional need to maintain its own power while pretending altruistic concern with suffering. Anti-professionalism, with its push to demystify medical authority, is close to the naturalist ambitions of the Walden Pond position, but it may carry with it a wish not only for simplicity but for magic, the folklorically simple.

31   The rejection of the authoritarian claims of medicine carries, paradoxically, a yearning for unsubstantiated magical alternatives. Along with a rejection of medical authority goes an eagerness to confer authority on less rationally supported authorities. During a difficult television exchange between Dick Cavett and the heart surgeon Christiaan Barnard, Cavett proposed that physicians had no more understanding than laymen of how to make life-and-death decisions in difficult circumstances. If anything, he suggested, physicians were more heartless and thoughtless than many laymen. Barnard rejected this position and wagered his years of engagement with the crises of medical practice against the assumptions of equal authority, or charity, by those who had not been in the trenches. Barnard's stance is not common even among physicians, and the authority of medicine can no longer depend on the good will of a grateful or awed public or the simple assertion of authority based on experience.

32   Yet no matter how unsubstantiated a claim for a new miracle cure may be—a decoction of peach pips for cancer, diagnostic wonders from hair analysis, infinite therapeutic possibilities in the soles of the feet, or acupuncture for everything—someone will come forward to support it. The populist rejection of scientifically based medicine may seem rational, but its association with a rush to embrace quackery

may reveal an underlying wish for simplicity. Who does not want to be released from the limitations on hope embodied in cool, unsentimental science?

33 Costs inhibit choice. The vision of the enfeebled old, sucking the resources of the world through the feeding bottle of health services, is terrifying when presented in terms of fiscal reality. One cannot have what one cannot afford. The survival of the old in numbers constituting a burden on the able-bodied represents one of the major forms of ecological pollution generated by the industrial society's love of comfort and ease without regard for ecological or monetary cost. By implication we are asked to choose the rationing of services and, perhaps through education, the introduction of different expectations, a more stoical vision of what one is entitled to. Perhaps we must consciously decide that we will not have all available machines simply because they are available. It is often proposed that education in preventive medicine — exercise, diet, no smoking, little alcohol — would do infinitely more for the cardiac health of the population than millions of dollars spent on an artificial heart.

34 Are these, in fact, real choices? Can we really choose not to develop the expensive machines for investigation, such as the PET scanners, or for intervention, such as kidney-stone-smashing devices, or artificial substitutes for hearts, kidneys, pancreases? Can we refuse these things because they cost too much?

35 The choices are not clear, or mutually exclusive. Health education does not exclude the development of specific health instruments. And technology does not become more expensive, it becomes cheaper: great lumbering machines are steadily miniaturized. Yesterday's outlandish luxury becomes today's affordable necessity. (As for absolute cost, none of these things costs anything like modern society's weapons programme.) The currently suspect devices for life-maintenance or resuscitation are part of the same historic impulse that generated penicillin and the polio vaccine. There is a technological imperative that cannot be easily denied. Do we regret the saved lives and the relative medical safety we now expect? Most of us recognize that, on balance, we have benefited, and we want to generate further benefit. Apart from the dangers of needless resuscitation and thoughtless life maintenance, who would not want a safer childhood or old age? The techniques to provide these manifestly good things are essentially the same techniques now presented as the horrifying instruments of thoughtless resuscitation and life maintenance.

36 The prophecy that generates most economic terror is the picture of a society oppressed by a thick layer of parasitic old people. The number of old who will drain our resources in the near future has to be seriously considered, but this vision contains questionable assumptions. While the old certainly use more facilities than the young, they

are not uniformly or normatively decrepit. Sixty-five need not represent the end of productive life.

37   The vision of the old as nothing but a drain on society extends far beyond the overuse — as economists like to term it — of medical goods and services to the entire range of social services. To some degree this fear is only a fresh manifestation of North American gerontophobia. The old in North American life have never had much of a place and have been perceived as more decrepit than they are. Old people are not only an economic burden, they can also be generators of wealth, a resource as well as a drain. Along with extended survival, there can also be extended productivity accompanied by the right to continued work.

38   The notion of a finite pocket of social wealth which the old will steadily devour is probably short-sighted. The creation and maintenance of prosperity is a constantly changing social enterprise and many dire economic prophecies are disastrously mistaken extrapolations of the contemporary into the future. (The increase in urban horses in the late nineteenth century held a promise of twentieth-century covered in dung.) The future should be planned for and anticipated, but apparently rational and economically determined numbers may conceal an ungenerous and phobic vision that requires correction. We can take comfort from the old statistics relating the numbers of farmers to agricultural production. There are now far fewer working farmers in North America than there were fifty years ago, but food productivity has enormously increased.

39   The moral and ethical problems arising from technology are also, in some ways, a restatement of notions of original sin. We shelter a fantasy in which the machine is unnatural and artificial — a work of man, as opposed to nature, the work of God. In this sense, the machine is alien to the universe of the ordained moral order, and dangerously amoral. But the level of debate around this topic as it pertains to medicine demonstrates that as a society we do not thoughtlessly worship mere instruments for their own sake.

40   The machine as an instrument of will makes constant demands on our judgment and integrity. It also demonstrates our lack of objectively defined ethical standards. Because we cannot appeal to church or state for hard guidelines, we have to arrive at our standards of behaviour through continuing discussion. In this process medicine has one advantage over many other human occupations: in its ideal form it is explicitly committed not only to maintaining life but to enhancing it. The use of the machine by medicine is mediated by an ancient but persistent belief that, above everything else, we should do no harm.

41   We are involved in an unending process of questioning and adaptation — an adaptation that, with luck, will not fall into a simple-minded

rejection of the machine as the work of the devil. It is at least equally valid to see the manufacture of machines and goods as the continuous unfolding of human endowment in a cumulative history. Man the tool-maker is man expressing an ancient and important component of his true nature.

Questions on Content

1   What is the "dilemma" presented to us by modern medical technology?

2   What was Herbert Marcuse's response to this dilemma? In what ways does Marcuse's radical view now seem "almost orthodox"?

3   What arguments against medical technology does Rakoff summarize?

4   In what sense are the problems arising from technology "a restatement of original sin," according to Rakoff?

5   What is Rackoff's own response to these problems? What future direction should our arguments concerning the use of medical technology take, according to Rakoff? What moral principle is his argument based on? Do you agree or disagree with Rakoff's view of the problem? Why?

Questions on Structure and Technique

1   In what sentence does Rakoff most succinctly state the dilemma presented to us by modern medical technology? In paragraphs one through five, what techniques does Rakoff use to establish the nature and significance of this dilemma for his readers?

2   What is the purpose of paragraphs six through twelve? What is the purpose of paragraphs thirteen through thirty-two? What is the purpose of paragraphs thirty-three through forty-one? What dominant mode of organization does Rakoff use to structure his argument? What other modes does he employ?

3   Is the overall pattern of development in Rakoff's argument inductive or deductive? Why is this pattern effective?

4   Does Rakoff's argument appeal primarily to our reason or our emotions? What role does the writer's ethical appeal play in the argument?

5   Why is Rakoff's conclusion effective? Is his conclusion warranted by his preceding evidence?

Suggestions for Writing

1   In the light of Vivian Rakoff's essay, "The Fatal Question," write an argument in which you set forth your own views on the subject of euthanasia.

2   Write an essay in which you summarize both positive and negative aspects of one type of modern medical technology, and then argue for your own view regarding its use based on that analysis.

DIAN COHEN AND
KRISTIN SHANNON

Dian Cohen is president of an economic communications consulting firm in Montreal, a columnist for Canadian Living *and* Maclean's *magazines, a business and economics commentator for the CBC, an advisor to several corporations, and a director of Hydro Quebec and Immedia Telematics. Cohen has won two National Business Writing Awards and has received honours for her work in economic and business education from several institutions. Kristin Shannon is founder, chairperson, and publisher of* Canadian Trend Report, *an economic and political forecasting publication serving private and Crown corporations as well as federal and provincial departments and agencies. Educated in Japan in economics and industrial relations, Shannon is also a strategic-planning consultant for an international clientele and a director of Pacific Rim Research, the Niagara Institute, the Couchiching Institute on Public Affairs, and A.T. International. For their book,* The Next Canadian Economy (1984), *Cohen and Shannon interviewed a wide variety of business people, labour leaders, and politicians about the future of our economy. They discovered that one of three conventional solutions were usually proposed to solve problems of economic development: "war, reflection, or mate-like-rabbits." However, Cohen and Shannon also found other more innovative and long-range approaches to our economy were offered by some people, ideas that form the basis for this analysis of the next Canadian economy which they argue for in the concluding section of their book.*

THE NEXT CANADIAN ECONOMY

1   Institutions are more than just the buildings we live and work in; they are also the unwritten rules we live by. While we may not see the cracks or hear an audible rumble, the ground beneath them is shaking. Our proud pillars of permanence are caging us in, holding us back from a smooth transition to the next economy.

2   Forged by the iron of an industrial age, Canada's institutions both evolved from and reinforced the values of a materialistic age. It is not too surprising, therefore, that we are accustomed to visualizing institutions as "hardware" structures, as fixed three-dimensional "things" rooted firmly to the ground.

3   It is more difficult to see the "software" systems, customs and rules that make up our cultural institutions. Yet, these intangible, software institutions shape our present lives and our future choices. The tax system, the parliamentary system, the collective bargaining system, education, social welfare, the health care system, all grew up as part of the "rules of the game" for the industrial age. How we handle changes in these intangible institutions will be crucial in determining Canada's place internationally in the next economy.

4   The old rules of the game served us relatively well, evolving slowly and usually peacefully over more than a century. In an era of rapid growth, there was every confidence that virtually any problem could (would) eventually be solved. We could afford to be patient and trusting . . . after all, we all understood the rules of the game.

5   But the game is now rapidly changing—and the old rules we played by may be a poor guide for the new one. Tom Axworthy: "Our large institutions aren't very adaptive, and that's why I say that we'll likely try to muddle along. I don't think we have to, but we haven't gone through enough yet to face up to it. Our institutions, be they parliament, the party system or others, are pretty slow to adapt."

6   While some institutions are crumbling quietly in the rapid onslaught of the next economy, others resist any threat to their power or prominence, hard-won in the last economy. This stubbornness is often reinforced by fear that institutions will vanish leaving nothing to replace them; after all, they were created for that purpose.

> *If large collective-bargaining units dissolve, what will replace them to ensure fairness in the workplace?*
>
> *If our religions diversify, do we risk having Christian values "watered down"?*
>
> *What if the Third World loans are not repaid; will Canada's banking system absorb the shock?*
>
> *What if we cannot meet the pension plan premiums required to keep the system intact for the huge baby boom generation?*
>
> *What if tax rules become so out of step that entire communities stop supporting the system?*

7   The industrial age ushered in an era of highly-structured institutions. Virtually everything became associated with a formal institution, performed within the secure confines of the appropriate hallowed halls under the official auspices of the right specialist. Even birth and dying take place in sanctuaries: hospitals and funeral parlors, respectively presided over by medical experts and make-up artists.

8   Institutions of the industrial age are *place-, time- and manner-bound*, each one guarded by an established guild or priesthood.

Everything has an exclusive place, a set time and a firm, sequenced series of rules and procedures. It is only recently, for example, that we even started planning homes with multi-purpose areas, family rooms, instead of parlors and bedrooms.

9   Education happens at school, healing at the hospital, lawyering at the courthouse, working at the office, negotiating at the bargaining table, legislating at the parliament buildings . . . .

10   Education is spooned out to children aged 5 to 18, between the rings of a bell at nine o'clock and at three o'clock, from September to June; medical care is rendered by appointment—only in an emergency at any time; justice is administered when court is in session; work is done between nine and five by people from 18 to 65 years of age, Monday to Friday, except for bank holidays and a two-week shut-down in late July; negotiations take place according to the terms of the last contract; legislation is passed when the house is sitting—and the bells are *not* ringing . . . .

11   Each institution maintains its own select guild or priesthood that holds rank in the social order through exclusive access to a proprietary set of information. Teachers are listened to in classrooms since they provide the curriculum needed to pass final exams; doctors' orders are followed because they hold a monopoly on medical information; lawyers are raised above contempt for their ability to comprehend legal documents; managers' directives are heeded because they read the latest sales report; campaign strategists are courted if they have the results of the latest public opinion poll . . . .

12   We play by the rules of the game established by the information holder, or we are simply "left out." But what happens if individuals gain direct access to the information that is now the exclusive custody of revered guilds and priesthoods? What happens to teachers and classrooms if video-taped lessons can be borrowed from the local library? Can we envision a generation reflecting nostalgically on an old computer-tutor instead of cherishing memories of ivy-covered walls? What happens to doctors and hospitals if computerized home diagnosis and treatment is made available? What happens to lawyers and courtrooms if computers are programmed to search legal precedents and predict case outcomes? What happens to business executives and boardrooms if pieces of a corporation are bought and sold five times in five minutes? What happens to parliamentarians and legislative assemblies if "instant referenda" are held?

13   These place-, time- and manner-bound restrictions that have so neatly shaped the contours of institutions in the industrial-age economy are being dissolved. Rather than patching up the cracks in the old institutions, let's look at some of the troubling questions about this transition period that are now beginning to emerge. The soft revolution in our institutions is not simply about what we *can* do,

but about what we *choose* to do. For *families*, this soft revolution that has occurred in our homes over the last dozen years, for example, is very difficult to pin down. But we do know that women seeking a paycheque, jobless children in their 20s moving back in with their parents, marriages breaking down or being redefined, families mending, blending and extending, are all part of the transition.

14   In *business*, although Frank Tyaack outlines some exciting options, we don't know how to picture or respond to a sudden and silent transformation in the dominant means of production. We vacillate between fear of robots stealing our jobs and excitement about "putting the brains back in the shop." Some say we can do this for all jobs, others say that 80 percent of jobs will be de-skilled. One thing is sure: the questions from the tide of micro-electronic technologies are not just "technical," but generate a sometimes frightening undertow of political, economic and social choices. No single invention since the steam engine will sweep over our lives as much as the integrated circuit and the thinking machines will.

15   Some telling clues to the secrets of the next economy are whispered in the new passwords that people who already dwell in the information age use in conversation: "to be interdependent," "to keyboard," "to network" — a vocabulary that would offend the sensitive ear of any English-grammar teacher, but a good indication of the values of the next economy.

16   This language signals the demise of a way of life that is harnessed to the formal, tightly structured, hierarchical, fixed requirements of industrial tasks: people with specialized duties, both at work and at home; employees concentrated around a central workplace; families oriented to a rigid division of time between the work world and their home life; an education system geared to producing able workers.

17   This language foreshadows a way of life that links up through informal, loosely-structured networks. There are new horizontal flows of information, new ways of structuring time. There will be people with a variety of income-earning skills; worker/owners running cottage industries at home; families operating like small businesses; educational systems doing more than just slotting people into career niches.

18   The pyramid, the vertical hierarchy, is no longer the shape for our institutions. In the next economy, authority, power and communication channels might look more like interlocking circles than tight boxes or straight lines. Authority, respect and loyalty will be collegial and earned rather than paternal or maternal and dutifully rendered. According to Jacques Vallée, author of *The Network Revolution*, "Computer conferencing is a first step toward the creation of such a medium: a revolutionary network where each node is equal in power to all the others."

19   **The Structure of Work** The tightly-knotted concept of a "job," for example, the most basic bond of Canadians to the economy, is unravelling. It is very difficult now — especially after the last three years — for us as parents to justify telling our teenagers to "work hard and follow all the rules" when we (and particularly our children) know so many people who always did just that, but are currently without jobs.

20   "My biggest fear is what the people of the Big Generation, those born in the fifties and early sixties, are going to do with their lives," says John Kettle, editor of the *Futureletter*. Most of this generation will be forced to explore a wider range of options throughout their lives than did their parents and grandparents. Many will have to invent their work or create their own business, not just find a job.

21   Alternating between work and parenting and frequent career shifts are becoming commonplace, partly by choice, partly by necessity. The average family recognizes that this means a great deal more fluctuation in income as his and her paycheques vary over the years. But Canada has been slow to realize and respond to the chaos that these new patterns are creating in its institutions — for example, in the design of pension plans and the health care system.

22   In the words of Dr. Russell Robinson, assistant deputy minister, Consumer and Corporate Affairs: "Our social institutions, especially government, are slow to catch on . . . . Our basic security programs — pensions, social insurance — can't be a leading edge for these changes, because even if we knew how to construct them, they couldn't be the areas of first change; they represent our security blanket. But we must start soon to look at them because the processing time in changing them takes so long. You have to start now in order to look at the question, for example, of what a model for the social security system might be 15 years from now."

23   Canada, however, has yet to address openly, much less confront, the question of a permanent income support system that can be sustained for as long as it takes to "unbundle" jobs and redefine "work." Our present systems of unemployment insurance, welfare, and job retraining evolved as a *temporary* response to a *temporary* problem. They were designed to meet the basic income needs of a few people at the margins of an economy for only a short period of time. That was an acceptable model for the last economy, but it is ill-suited to a lengthy transition period of high, structural unemployment among the mainstream of the Canadian middle class.

24   The biggest obstacles we face now are invisible, leftover assumptions, expectations, institutional systems and social rules rather than visible landmarks of physical geography. The mountains to be conquered rise in the minds of national and provincial capitals and Toronto boardrooms, rather than in the Rockies. The elements to

be battled have less to do with the laws of nature than with the laws of Canadian society. It is the restrictive institutional systems and social rules — man-made limits — that have to be loosened.

25   Take the institution of law, for example. Legal experts are discovering that trying to make property law from the industrial age fit the incorporeal information-age products — ideas, software, brilliant but easy to copy systems — is a formidable task. Not unlike economists who are trying to sort out the value of information-age products, lawyers are trying to figure out who owns these invaluable "brain" products. Similar problems occur in biotechnology.

26   DATELINE LOS ANGELES A leukemia patient whose blood may have unique disease-fighting properties filed suit Tuesday for a stake in a potentially lucrative patent his doctors took out on a product developed from his cells. John Moore's lawyers say their client has a right to share in the billions of dollars that the substance, called the Mo-cell line, could generate in licensing fees.

    Although Moore knew and consented to the use of his blood for research, he was never told it might have commercial applications, says his lawyer.

27   Our laws evolved in the days when the respective value of land, labor and capital had a fairly stable relationship. Wealth was derived largely from tangibles, with value tied to physical things we could count, measure or hold in our hand. *Natural resources were the common source of wealth; money was the common currency.*

28   **Wealth** Put simply, this notion of wealth means having stuff, having usually the exclusive possession of some "thing" of value. The value of the thing depends on its scarcity, not on its holder. Each thing has a fixed value in relation to other things of the same kind. For example, the value of one gold bar is the same as the value of another, no matter who owns them. If gold bars are hoarded, their value increases; but owning a second one doesn't alter the value of the first.

29   In the information age, these relationships are changing dramatically. Increasingly, much of our wealth will be in intangibles, in what Roy Cottier calls "brain industries." And much of the value and wealth created will be through sharing, not hoarding. *In the next economy, people are the source of wealth, and information is the currency.*

30   Wealth in the next economy is aligned in some mysterious way with sharing, not exclusive possession. The value of a data bit is less dependent on availability, but much more dependent on its holder. Each bit has a value that varies in relation to other bits. For example, the value of information on the stock market changes according to how many other bits of information you have.

31   Many companies who appear to be selling stocks and bonds are in fact selling information. As Brian Fabbri, asked about hoarding information in the competitive Wall Street atmosphere explains: "Educating our clients means more business for us. So, information about how we see markets develop is something that we disseminate rather than hold as proprietary."

32   Hoarding a bit of information, therefore, adds little to its value. In the next economy, information, with some exceptions, may be more valuable when it is shared. Data bits become information when there is a context to give them meaning. Information becomes knowledge when there is a receptive environment.

33   Knowledge — information plus context — then, is both a product and a capital good. This quantum jump in the importance of knowledge poses tough questions for the transition. For example, how do you transpose an industrial-age tax system to these patterns of wealth creation?

34   For the next economy, *relationships are becoming as valuable as possessions*. In a volatile world, there may be more stability, for example, in friendships than in where you work or what you do. Relationships become key elements of wealth creation in the information age. Who you know, what they know, and how to pursue it together are crucial skills.

35   **Education** The people we talked with are worried about Canada's education system. Their concerns stem from an understanding of some elements critical to a successful knowledge-based economy: excellent data banks, open access to information, rich individual diversity of perspectives, and cumulative learning processes.

36   "How will we be able to change education?" asks Saskatchewan's finance minister, Bob Andrew. "How do we shake it loose? The education institutions, which we were taught were the leading edge of new ideas, are static today, are perhaps the most conservative. The university system is awful. It's an area that used to be the leading edge of change. Now, it is the leading edge of holding things back."

37   Roy Cottier, senior vice-president of Northern Telecom, says bluntly: "When we recognize that brains are the passport to a post-industrial future, and not just resource activity, then we'll start to solve our problems. How will we bring that about? That is a hell of a good question. Most people are still unaware of the transition that is taking place in the total economy . . . . What we have to get understood is that we have to make drastic changes in the education structure. Another problem with education is that it is a provincial responsibility. That was fine in 1867, but this is 1984."

38   "If our comparative advantage is intellectual capital," warns Westinghouse CEO Frank Tyaack, "then the thing that we should be

investing in like fury is education. And my perception of the education system is that it is shrinking in terms of its support and its facilities. If I had to pick *the* priority area for government policy to enter, I'd pick that one first. I'll forego the tax incentives, the grants, the export aid and so on; if they would shovel the billions into education, I'd be happier."

39   Frank Tyaack's advice for becoming an educated, adaptable, high "intellectual-capital" person: "Learn to be generalists." Trevor Eyton, Brascan's CEO, worries about the narrow perspectives that executives bring to strategic planning: "A lot of our senior management comes out of the same kind of environment; they've gone to Upper Canada College and they've learned to think in pretty straight paths. Well, the world has changed a lot and we can adapt to it, and we can perform, but we've got to have different ways of teaching and learning. I don't think I'm all that much smarter, but I found it an advantage not to go to Upper Canada — where I went it was down and dirty and you really learned to think in a lot of different directions."

40   Banker Scott McCreath takes his children to factories and farms "so they will know something about how we make things, grow things; I want them to be curious about how it all works." Money manager Milton Wong feels that a "spirit of curiosity is the most important attitude" for the next economy, and stresses that it should be coupled with a determination "to go find out."

41   The cost of restructuring education will be high. Northern Tel's Roy Cottier points out: "We can still afford it, if we decide we want it. But if we decide we don't, we sure as heck will not be able to afford it later because we won't be in business. . . . One of the things that has to be done is we, as a society, have to take a look at our gross national cash flow and say, 'OK, are we going to continue to spend X amount on social services, X amount on defence, X amount on education?' And we're going to find that we're going to have to make changes, because the needs of the last decade are not the needs of the next decade."

42   Bob Andrew summed up well the delicate issue of capital use in this sensitive transition period: "Every country has a finite amount of capital, some more than others, but each with a finite amount. The success of a country to a large degree depends upon how that country employs its capital: human capital, investment capital, renewable and non-renewable resource capital . . . and how they are able to adapt the application of that capital to the changing world in which they live and function.

43   "Our country tends to be slower to adapt to change because of our poor use of capital. Too much of our capital is employed in protected, uncompetitive industries that clearly will not survive internationally. They are propped up to survive almost one day at a time. We resist

either facing up to the fact that we should wind them down, and redirect both the investment and human capital into something that can grow, whether it is an entirely new industry or a refit of the present one.

44 "We must approach that problem both from the economic side and from the human side. And it will not be without some pain, but nevertheless we must address the problem.

45 "Our tax system hardly encourages adaption; rather it tends to preserve the status quo, to lock in the old industrial-age values, or what is even worse, tries to redirect it to fashionable ideas of the politicians . . . perhaps we should go back to using revenue gathering for that purpose alone, rather than trying to 'manage' the economy with it. Our tax system is important because we have become a country where taxes (or avoiding taxes) too often is the main rationale for making decisions on how capital will be employed. Even governments seem to be getting into the game . . . if that isn't taking it to absurd lengths."

46 The security of an established "known" is always tempting to cling to—until it no longer comforts with a firm, steady hand, or it chafes too much like a tiresome parent, or it simply blows away. But, too many of our institutions that serve as homes (and provide livelihoods) are resisting the process of change, and hamstringing the transition to the next economy. "Muddling through," as Tom Axworthy warned, is in the long run likely to be more painful than trying to form a picture, together, of what comes next, and how our institutions should help. We run the risk, however, of violating the first law of wing walking. . . .

Dressed in a brown leather bomber jacket, a long white scarf billowing out behind him in the full force of the wind rushing past, he grins at us, waiting far below on the ground. We all wave. He moves one arm in a curving gesture. Bravado.

One foot begins to slide forward, just as the pilot starts a wide lazy circle. His knee moves up and out a bit, jarred by the blast of air currents, then down and forward, edging over towards the next strut. Both hands stiffen while the lower body shifts weight, leaning into the wind, arching to the right.

He stands on the wing of the bi-plane, arms in a pair of fixed right angles locked onto the struts. Blinded by the wind, one arm extended, groping ahead, pressing in the direction of where the second strut should be. He thrusts his arm forward once more against the powerful current and catches it. Arms wide, buffeted, he slides more of his body weight over; tension grows in his left arm. Arms outstretched, he is pulled by his own weight off centre again and again, until he lets go and draws himself—smiling once more, remembering to look towards us—to the second strut. On the ground there is an audible wave, a sigh rippling through us as the plane completes another lazy circle.

47   "Never let go of what you've got, until you've got hold of something else" cautions the first law of wing walking. Preparing for the future is like wing walking. No one can be blamed for refusing to yield the relative security of a good firm grip on what they knew.

48   We cling to the old-but-familiar structural elements even when we feel them dissolving in our hands, or holding us back. Among the people we interviewed, there was a remarkable degree of consensus that the institutions that served us well in the past, now don't; that the experts who served us well, now don't; and that the politics of the industrial age may not fit the needs of the next Canadian economy.

49   New ones have to be invented at the same time that we find a way to let the old ones go, lest they impede us. Attitudes and values appropriate to the last economy affect the strategies and tactics required for managing our personal, corporate and national security. They have to be revised to fit the demands of the next economy. Those courageous and probing people we met stressed a number of recommendations about some key things that are holding us back, moving us forward.

50   The first view they share: *We are not likely to get anywhere if we don't ask the right questions.* That means having the courage to put the necessary questions — no matter how uncomfortable — on the table. It means having the courage to face a "gloomy" economic forecast, or a tough set of anxious feelings about technology choices. These forecasts or trends in the culture are nothing more than starting points; a place to begin to confront what effect they might have on our personal and mutual choices.

51   Unfortunately, one of the hold-over groups from the last economy, the "mood managers," are accustomed to framing issues in such a way that it makes it virtually impossible to ask the right questions. Those who do, risk being called critical, impolite, or gloomy about the future — at the furthest extreme, a "danger to the unfolding economy," if you want to believe, as we are repeatedly told, that "our worst economic enemy is pessimism."

52   Let's take the brutal and painful question of who gets a job and who gets a welfare cheque during the transition to the next Canadian economy. The tacit assumption in our culture is that the guys who have jobs are "good citizens," and those who do not are "lazy bums." This social and economic roulette carves deep scars on those who land on the wrong number. Yet, part of the pain is tied to our being too polite (or too frightened) to ask the more fundamental question about how we are going to distribute income in this country.

53   There are many of these kinds of questions — that have to be asked openly and discussed openly, rather than closeted or tucked away on the hidden agendas of closed-to-the-public meetings of finance ministers or secret sessions in the Privy Council Office.

54   Other questions of high national priority that are also very politically sensitive, but need to be openly addressed, include, for example, the problem of developing excellent research on the new technologies. Achieving this at a level that will enable Canada to keep pace in the game of world-class competition implies a concentration of resources at a particular university, or within a few companies. This need to focus resources conflicts sharply with our habit of trying to distribute all the new factories, government labs, or grants as evenly as possible. If we try to use the same formula, and spread knowledge capital too thinly, we may fail to concentrate and develop our key to wealth in the next economy, our human resources.

55   Many more questions are directed at the security issues; trying to agree on a list of the things we want to cling to from the last economy is one of the biggest challenges facing the present government. What was "waste" or a "frill" in the last economy may well be an essential in the next. For example, educational funds that have been quietly cut back in the last several years by provincial governments will not only have to be restored, but augmented. Knowledge capital is certainly one ticket to our security in the next economy.

56   The next shared conclusion, although there is no agreement on how to go about it, is that *our institutions need to become more flexible.*

57   In addition to questioning attitudes that hinder a wide-ranging search for the future, we must now focus on the economic, political and cultural institutions which have become so rigid that they limit our range of choices in managing a transition to the next Canadian economy.

58   Some of these institutions are easy to spot — schools that do not teach computer literacy, for example. Others are virtually invisible; they are simply established practice — automatically depositing money in a bank, for instance. We rarely ask: "What happens to this money?" Is it invested in new, job-creating small businesses, or does it go offshore, to finance a Brazilian loan?

59   These multi-level trade-off questions about our institutions are barely being acknowledged, much less spelled out. In the last chapter some of the symptoms of this soft revolution are described. The transition to the next economy is pressuring individuals to constantly re-examine their choices. So much of what we used to take for granted is now up in the air: not just when, but whether to have children, or, which second-career training to pursue, just in case the first set of job plans breaks down.

60   The challenge implicit in the second conclusion is that we have to identify the rigid and inappropriate institutions that are blocking us, and then transform or abandon them. For example, a tax system that is tied to the last economy will hamper a transition. The carrots

and sticks tucked into our process of collecting revenue, designed to shape behavior towards certain industrial-age objectives, are not going to work as well in the next economy. We'll have a different set of needs and goals. Recognition of this set of blocks is one of the things that is fostering the grass roots resistance to the "overly complex" (or put less delicately, "manipulative") nature of the present tax structure.

61   A third perspective that emerged clearly from our coast-to-coast discussions is that *while we are negotiating the rapids of the transition, we should not constantly change the rules of the game*. Points out Don Johnston: "If entrepreneurs are the catalysts of economic growth in our future, nothing stimulates capital investment as much as a supportive fiscal regime that features a tax system which is stable, predictable and fairly administered." The basic terms of reference need to be clarified, not constantly or capriciously altered to suit a short-term situation.

62   Much of the push for deregulation is born in the natural reluctance to hear the latest change in an already cumbersome, rigid and often outdated set of rules. Both the pressure to simplify the tax system and the urge to reduce the paperwork reflect a collective sense that it is time to simplify the rules of the game. With fewer and simpler rules, there may be, so the argument goes, more room for people to experiment and adapt to the transition to the next economy. It's tough enough living with a tangled set of guidelines when things are stable. When the basic premises of the economy are being shaken, the web of our regulatory structure can strangle us.

63   These pressures are not just a simple-minded "step to the right" or a "swing to conservatism" in the traditional sense. These cumulative pressures for deregulation and tax simplification also represent a feeling that people are less inclined to merrily follow the piper, or accept being told what they can or can't do, when they sense that the system as a whole is increasingly out of sync with the emerging economy. "Get off my back" is a loud and legitimate cry during an era when people are trying to gain a little more manoeuvering room for their own personal security.

64   The heavy emphasis on personal security accounts for the wide concern about the strength of the safety net. A corollary to the third conclusion becomes: *Don't mess around much with the safety net*. Shaking the moorings of the safety net implies changing the rules of the game at a time when people cannot tolerate more uncertainty. The healthcare system and pensions, for example, become even stronger symbols of long-term stability than in a more predictable era. They become those struts we don't want to let go of. A strong safety net helps a transition, reduces fear, and allows us to experiment and become more adaptable.

65   The fourth conclusion is that *we need ways to decide, that fit the size, scope and duration of the problems we face; these being strategic decisions, we need to include a wide range of perspectives*. This is a particularly acute need when the traditional balance points within the system — the old left and right perspectives — are so clearly outdated by the emerging realities of the next economy. There is little room for ideology, blame, or nostalgia for the good old days in the transition to the next economy.

66   Ritual political contests between "socialists," "conservatives" and "liberals" not only lose meaning in this context, but get in the way. This is underscored by the size of the Conservative "win" in the last federal election, which swept candidates of every political orientation into office at the same time and created a participant pool that is so huge it is virtually unwieldy. A clear-cut win which could have been argued as an endorsement of a particular set of conservative principles would have been, for example, a thirty-seat gain. But a victory of 211 seats means the government has to speak for all of the people, not just count on an opposition voice to represent a dissenting, or coherent point of view. One result of the last federal election is that the task of government has grown larger, and at the same time, of necessity more respectful of the diverse participants in the winning coalition.

67   The Mulroney government's early choice to emphasize process and consultation was a fitting one for the times. "Canadians expect our new government to be open and honest, and to introduce new concepts of consultation and cooperation" the prime minister emphasized repeatedly in the period just before and just following the election. His advisors in cabinet and on the policy side, such as Michael Wilson and Charles MacMillan, carried the day in the early stages of the Mulroney government. They emphasized the need to get broad participation rather than handing things off to the backroom boys. The former PC government of Joe Clark also drew its highest marks for pursuing a course of openness.

68   A major change in institutional direction that is in harmony with the pull of the next economy implies a need for strategic, not just operational planning. Shorter-term *operational planning*, with well-defined goals, can be carried out by a group of managers with relatively uniform values and even a narrow perspective. But *strategic planning* demands a wider array of values, more voices at the table, more room for dissent, and greater diversity of opinion. As Milton Wong points out, in making strategic decisions about a billion dollars of investment funds, there is a strong need for "open, constructive conflict of perspectives in order to get to a creative strategic recommendation."

69   The final conclusion, and the one that is hardest to see through the spectacles of our old institutions, and the one that we explore in this chapter is: *Canadians need to develop for themselves effective strategies for facing the transition to the next economy.* We have begun the painful process of backing away from our old reliance on government to "solve" everything for us. There is always anger associated with breaking free of a dependency, and the last federal election result reflected some of those feelings. But the research evidence has been steadily mounting — Canadians are begining to do it themselves.

70   **Effective Strategies** In this context, let's look at some winning strategies for the next economy. Those we interviewed certainly presented some good ideas, but let's start by stepping back and looking at how we got our ideas about what would be a winning strategy for the last economy.

71   Political and personal strategies are built on sets of assumptions about the nature of conflict, as well as the nature of success. These ideas come almost from the primordial ooze, as we base many of our pictures of the future on what we believe to be the truth about our past. Similarly, our values about decision and conflict are often based on our beliefs about the evolution of human nature or who *won* a place on the great chain of being. Our ideas about winning strategies and the nature of conflict are intimately intertwined with our sense of the history of the species and the descent of man.

72   Was it *always* a fight to win an ecological niche, or does cooperation play a part in our view of evolution? Does the notion of "survival of the fittest" underly our view of how the strongest and best won the right to reproduce? Does the idea of "survival of the fittest" form the basis for our belief as to why capitalism works? Are we sometimes using "competition" as a quick shorthand for saying "After all, Darwin was right — survival strategies are always a question of the fittest, the fastest, and the most fiercely competitive"?

73   Does a vague belief in social Darwinism inform our perspective on why some families always seem to wind up on welfare, while others prosper? Have we learned, either consciously or subconsciously, that competition and struggle are implied in any winning strategy? Do we believe that "toughest," most "aggressive," of necessity mean the "best" or minimally "the winner"? How does that make us feel about our potential for success in, for example, highly-competitive international markets if we are simultaneously so proud as Canadians of our traditions of being "nice," "polite," and "cooperative"?

74   A brief look at some of the contemporary research and thinking on the subject of conflict resolution and winning suggests these issues are intimately tied together. Yet, the last thirty years has given us a surprising volume of new information on the evolution of the spe-

cies, and on conflict versus cooperation. Perhaps we can make use of that new information.

75   In the field of anthropology, for example, views have run the gamut from Ardrey's turf and power-oriented "mighty hunter" theories to Elaine Morgan's perspective that "what saved the species was a group [of women] who cooperated in fighting against the savage drought by running into the ocean . . . for a few thousand years." You can look up the rest of the theory in her provocative and humorous answer to Darwin, called *Descent of Woman.*

76   Both of these authors have presented their arguments in popular forms. Both have wide followings who look to the story of evolution to prove their views about the nature of man (or woman), and more importantly, to reinforce their beliefs that their values are the "right" ones.

77   Both are using shards of evidence based on a mixture of fossil findings, judgments about how those fossils correlate with other things going on at the same time, and, of course, their respective personal value systems. But one of the advantages of pursuing research questions at this point in the twentieth century is that we are now allowed to probe past the statement that the authors used an "objective scientific method." The part played by an investigator's value system in his conclusions is now a matter for more open examination.

78   Another advantage in living at this time of the twentieth century is that we have developed some additional research techniques to supplement the intellectual digs of the anthropologists. We aren't just dependent on watching them battle it out in print. And we aren't just forced to resign ourselves to saying, "Well, one informed opinion against another — who is to know?" No, in addition to supplementing what they tell us with our own personal experience and observation, we now have some additional options. One of the most effective learning and research tools is the use of *simulations.*

79   Simulations create situations in miniature for testing or exploring the whole bunch of "what if" questions with as much fun and as little risk as possible. Simulations are also extremely effective in teaching environments, when it is important for the participants to understand and integrate a number of complex factors all at once. A short word for "simulations" is "games."

80   A game takes some basic rules, agreed upon goals, and then, if it is a good game, provides an opportunity for the full force of personality to work itself out, within a rational framework. The games and simulations played in the last thirty years which have the most to offer in an examination of conflict and decision making fall into three clusters: *management games, war games, and peace games.*

81   Management games and simulations have been principally developed and financed by business as the quickest and most efficient way to get complex ideas integrated into the system. Because executive time is expensive, businessmen must learn quickly. Business schools, too, consider simulations to be one of their most effective teaching tools. They use a lot of these teaching games, ranging from case studies to computer-simulated portfolio management programs.

82   War games have largely been financed through the various defence establishments around the world and were, at first, usually played in secret at think tanks, or on military bases. Vast sums of money have been dedicated to this branch of game theory. Much of the early work on war games was classified and secret, but quite a bit has found its way into the open literature of political science.

83   The two we are going to concentrate on are *war games* and *peace games*.

84   Let's start with *peace games* because they are the least familiar. The idea and the name *Peace Game* originated with the Quakers when they were trying to resolve a post-war problem with their neighbors. In particular, they needed to reconcile their beliefs of conscience with the strong social disapproval they received when they refused to go to war. This "act of conscience" and their religious beliefs, especially their value of "non-violence" were in conflict with the values of many of their neighbors. So the Quakers started holding Peace Games to simulate some of the situations that had been faced in earlier wars and in the aftermath of those wars, as neighbors tried to reconcile their wartime views, actions, and values with one another, so they could be friends again.

85   The Peace Game is an event designed for a fairly large community, involving from fifty to a few hundred people. The community is divided up into "attackers" and "defenders" who are assigned logical roles. The Peace Game script is written setting the stage, and then all the participants who are assigned roles have to stay in character until the game is over, even while eating or performing other ordinary chores. If they break character, they are asked to leave the game. Usually those assigned to be attackers or invaders "believe" in force and violence, and in competition as the only way to resolve conflict. The defenders, by contrast, "believe" in non-violence.

86   Quite a lot of "what if" questions can be explored when a community of that size acts out the issues over an extended period of time. Some peace games have been played for up to two weeks. People become deeply involved in their roles, exploring not only their intellectual beliefs about winning strategies, but they also test their feelings in a very intense environment. The object of the Peace Game is to develop a wider array of ways to "win" in a life-like situation.

87   Perhaps the most fundamental question in its simplest terms that these real life simulations try to address is: "What is the best strategy, cooperation or conflict?"

88   By contrast, the study of War Games began with a narrower question than Peace Games. The War Games question was: "How do you win?" Interestingly enough, War Games have evolved to ask the broader strategic question of "How do you avoid conflict?" or, at the diplomatic level, "How do you win the maximum number of negotiations in the theatre of world opinion?"

89   The recent popular movie "War Games," ended with the war-room computer being instructed to play an almost endless progression of tic-tac-toe games in a process designed to teach it about the futility of world conflict.[1] The computer concludes: "Global Thermonuclear war. A curious game: the only winning move is not to play."

90   Early war games were much simpler, starting off with maps and models of planes and tanks, assessing the arithmetic of two opposing forces. The choice of ground, timing, and the volume of the forces arrayed against one another were the central elements. The classic battle scenes were transformed by the high-speed computer simulations into more abstract mathematical modelling exercises. What would be our gains, what would be our potential losses, under the following conditions — were the standard questions.

91   In the earliest stages, they were viewed as straight power conflicts, mostly a matter of sheer weight of armaments determining the outcome. But as hundreds of millions of dollars were poured into these military "what if" exercises, they became far more sophisticated and complex. A much wider range of factors were explored than just the physical weight of weapons. Theories of personality were applied, perspectives on leadership, the political will of the combatants was assessed, and questions of the strategic worth of different cultural values were incorporated into the game.

92   Sophisticated war games, not unlike their cousins, econometric models, became much more difficult to quantify. The softer-sided issues of personality, politics and cultural values, and especially political will, became more critical concerns as the models matured. New fields of inquiry were developed to fuel the models, such as content-analysis techniques which can assess the evolving political will in a country, even if those being studied don't wish to cooperate.

93   Information about the War Games procedures and research findings began to be available outside the military think tanks as academics from many different disciplines were called upon to consult on the games. A wider variety of players took a look at the technologies and theories of the games and began to apply them to civilian life and to decision-making in the political arena. The games came out from behind closed doors and some of the software has even turned

up at the local video arcade. Open, widely-publicized tournaments are now held.

94   **New Games** Recently, a political scientist and games theorist, Robert Axelrod, held two rounds of an international tournament posing this question: "In the absence of a higher authority, when should a person (business, province, country) cooperate, and when should a person try to gain maximum personal advantage?"

95   Axelrod used a fairly simple game to try to identify a *strategy that would win over the long haul*. The game that he employed makes a number of important assumptions. First, it assumes that, like "real life," the players are likely to see each other again, and no one knows when one might move to another city, change jobs, or die. So, when one round is over, it doesn't mean the game is over. The next assumption is that you will always know what the other person did last, but not what he is likely to do next. Again, quite like real life. We know a lot about history, but very little about the future. Even if someone tells you what they are going to do, you don't really believe it until you see it.

96   Axelrod picked a well-tested game called "The Prisoner's Dilemma" to try to discover the best, most "robust" strategy, the one that would be most likely to win consistently. The game itself is quite straightforward. Two "prisoners" have been arrested and are being questioned separately. Their guards try to get each one to "defect," to agree to testify against the other one in hopes of a lighter sentence for himself. Each "prisoner" has to choose to either continue to hope that his accomplice "cooperates," and also keeps quiet, or he must decide if there is going to be a "defection." If so, it is to his advantage to defect first.

97   In the computer model, points are assigned for each choice, and the points are known in advance by both players. You get a good solid score if you both cooperate. You get a lousy score if you cooperate and the other guy chooses to defect (this is called the "sucker's payoff"). You get a higher score (at least for the one move) if you choose to defect while the other guy chooses to cooperate. But the worst score is if both choose to defect at the same time.

98   The reason it is called the prisoner's "dilemma" is that if both defect, both do far worse over the course of the game than if they both cooperated. Just reading a description of the game and the points system doesn't seem all that hopeful for a strategy of cooperation. Axelrod invited competitors from all over the world, both experts and kids who are hackers (computer wizards). Some of the entries were very complex; some were sneaky; some used subterfuge and psychology. (You can read about the interesting ones in Axelrod's book.)[2]

99   Yet, despite the tough competition and more than three decades of game theory, and the arrival of bigger, better and cheaper computers and more complex software for simulations, a relatively simple strategy called *tit for tat* won the international tournament.

100   *Tit for tat* has only four rules:

1   Start off *nice*. Never be the first to "defect."

2   *Retaliate*. If the other player starts by defecting, return his move, "tit for tat."

3   Always be *forgiving*. If the other player cooperates, makes a nice move, then forget the past; return to making nice moves.

4   Be very *clear* and *open* about your strategy. Let the other players around you know that these are your rules; communicate clearly. Above all, keep it simple.

101   After the tournament, Axelrod published the results and explained why *tit for tat* was such a robust strategy. Then he held a second, larger, round. Most people tried to improve on *tit for tat*, making it trickier, slightly less forgiving, for example. Most of those people ignored the fourth rule, "Keep it clear and simple."

102   But the person who had submitted *tit for tat* in the first round, Anatol Rappaport, a professor at the University of Toronto, remembered the rule and simply resubmitted the same entry. He won again. Decisively.

103   It seems ironic that even the cold mathematical rules of computer-simulation game theory drawn from the chest of war games, rather than peace games, suggest some kind of cooperative strategy works best over the long haul. The findings show that a "nice" and "cooperative" strategy, but one that is ready to retaliate if the other guy is playing by different rules, works best when the future is uncertain.

104   Those who think and write about theories of conflict resolution have argued a long time whether a positive, cooperative value system would have the stamina to endure, without a higher authority provided by a creed, a belief in God, a formal value system or just a solid authority figure. Even those who teach the tactics of non-violence, drawing on the teachings of Gandhi and the experience of Martin Luther King, sometimes wind up expressing doubts about human "nature." They wonder whether the precepts of non-violence and cooperative resolution of conflict will hold up without the presence of a great spiritual leader.

105   What is particularly interesting and useful about some of the game theory results (such as the Prisoner's Dilemma tournament) that are tested to see how they work without higher authority, is that cooperative strategies often work whether or not people even know or like each other. What does seem to matter is that they have to notice

that they inhabit the same small planet, and may see each other again, for another "round," on another day.

106   This is where we stand in our dilemma; no matter whether one politician wins or loses, or whether one side wins or loses a round, a sufficient framework must remain so that we can continue to play another round.

107   For, to take an issue of growing proportions, it doesn't matter whether Ottawa wins or loses against the provinces on a question such as who should pay the bill for the *UIC-welfare shuttlebus*. We do all live in the same country and are likely to see that unemployed person again. No matter whose budget he is lodged in right now, unless there is some fundamental adjustment in his situation, we will be all paying the cost of structural unemployment for a long time. Games theory tells us there is no free lunch; and it is becoming harder and harder to declare some factor, or some person to be unimportant in the equation. Evolving research in this area, whether it is for war games, peace games, or predicting the shape of the next economy, tells us we have to be more inclusive in our respect for the things that count.

108   These sophisticated simulations also tell us that each decision counts, and that each of us can affect the outcome. Simple-minded win-lose strategies based on mutual distrust appear to win only if it is game-over in one move. As soon as there is any likelihood that we are going to keep playing together, then the cooperative strategies begin to look like the long-term winners.

109   The challenges that we face in the transition to the next economy are not likely to be resolved in a few years, or by a limited number of players. Ironically, the more you add complexity to the trade-offs, the more likely it is that cooperative strategies are the most effective approach.

110   That is the situation we face in the transition to the next Canadian economy.

111   One hint on how to face it comes from the Dutch cultural historian, Johan Huizinga, who argued that the most civilizing pastime man has is play; that games and explorations over the long history of the race have given rise to new ideas and vision . . . and progress.[3] Why call us "homo-sapiens," man-the- knower, he asked, when our character of "homo-ludens," man-the- player, has been so very important to the evolution of the race? Why not indeed?

112   It is in this spirit that we invite you not only to explore the existing options for the transition to the next economy, but to "play" with developing a much wider array of new political and personal choices. Your suggested solutions to our present quandary may well go beyond *war*, *reflection*, or *mate-like-rabbits*.

113   Let us know what you come up with.

Notes

1. Jacques Vallée, *The Network Revolution* (Berkeley, Ca.: And/Or Press, 1982).
"In November, 1979, in an 'incident' that passed generally unnoticed in American newspapers, the entire North American continent was in a state of nuclear war for seven minutes because of what seems to have been an operator error. Whether the computer detected the wrong set of patterns, or was fed an emergency training tape, the result was the same: It appeared that a massive enemy attack was being directed at the United States. Going through regular procedures, officers at NORAD—The North American Radar system located under Cheyenne Mountain in Colorado—gave takeoff orders to fighter-bombers from Montana to Canada to meet the unexpected onslaught, while the entire military system of the United States and Canada was placed on alert status. The Strategic Air Command did not take off because a Presidential order is required for that, and after seven minutes nobody had been able to reach the President, the Vice-President, or the Secretary of Defense. Finally, an officer who thought it was strange that the Russians would attack during 'a period of relative detente,' ordered his staff to run a check of the computer, and the mistake was found."

2. Robert Axelrod, *The Evolution of Cooperation*, Basic Books, New York, NY, 1984.

3. Johan Huizinga, *Homo Ludens*, Routledge & Kegan, Boston, MA, 1980.

Questions on Content

1   How do Cohen and Shannon define Canadian institutions? What examples do they present to clarify and develop their definition? What general changes are occurring in the structure of our institutions?

2   What three types of institutional change do the authors then analyse? What changes do the authors foresee in the structure of work? Wealth? Education?

3   What is the "first law of wing walking," and why is it significant in the context of the authors' analysis?

4   What five recommendations do the people interviewed by the authors offer in order to reshape institutions more appropriate to the demands of the next Canadian economy? Do you agree or disagree with each one of these recommendations? Why?

5   Why are "game" strategies important? What different kinds of "games" do the authors discuss? What game strategy do the authors recommend? Why? What general context do they provide for their argument in the conclusion?

Questions on Structure and Technique

1   Why is the word "game" important in the authors' introductory definition of institutions? What further significance does the term "game" take on in the final section of their argument? In what ways is the "game" metaphor effective in their argument?

2   What classifications do the authors use to organize and develop their argument? Are those classifications clearly labelled, defined, and illustrated? What examples support your answer?

3   What examples of effective transitional sentences and paragraphs can you find in this selection?

4   What audience is this argument directed toward? What examples of words, phrases, sentences, and illustrations can you find that appeal most effectively to this audience?

5   Is the appeal of this writing directed toward readers' reason or emotions? Support your answer with some good examples of this appeal.

Suggestions for Writing

1   Write an essay in which you argue for or against significant changes taking place in one "institution" with which you are familiar.

2   Write an argument on any subject supporting the following statement in which Cohen and Shannon summarize the work of the Dutch cultural historian, Johan Huizinga: "The most civilizing pastime man has is play; . . . games and explorations over the long history of the race have given rise to new ideas and vision . . . and progress. Why call us 'homo-sapiens', man-the-knower, . . . when our character of 'homo-ludens', man-the-player, has been so very important to the evolution of the race?"

JONATHAN SWIFT

Jonathan Swift (1667–1745) is an eighteenth-century essayist and satirist whose finest works include A Tale of a Tub *(1704),* The Battle of the Books *(1704),* The Drapier's Letters *(1724),* Gulliver's Travels *(1726), and the following essay entitled "A Modest Proposal" (1729). Swift's argument in "A Modest Proposal" is a parody of British solutions to Ireland's problems of starvation and overpopulation. Swift creates a speaker, a persona, whose practical and economical recommendations are undercut by Swift's own emphasis on how such limited criteria result in this outrageous and inhumane view of human life. You will note Swift's use of eighteenth-century conventions such as spelling and capitalization. As you study Swift's classic "mock argument" on an important issue of his time, you should consider how you might update and adapt more fundamental features of his content and technique in a similar argument that deals with an important contemporary problem. Swift was born in Dublin, Ireland, and educated at Trinity College, Dublin, and Oxford University in England. He was then ordained in the Anglican Church and eventually was appointed Dean of St. Patrick's Cathedral in Dublin, a position he held until his death.*

A MODEST PROPOSAL

1   It is a melancholly Object to those, who walk through this great Town or travel in the Country; when they see the Streets, the Roads and Cabbin-doors crowded with Beggars of the Female Sex, followed by three, four, or six Children, all in Rags, and importuning every Passenger for an Alms. These Mothers, instead of being able to work for their honest Livelyhood, are forced to employ all their Time in stroling to beg Sustenance for their helpless Infants; who, as they grow up, either turn Thieves for want of Work; or leave their dear Native Country, to fight for the Pretender in Spain, or sell themselves to the Barbadoes.

2   I think it is agreed by all Parties, that this prodigious number of Children in the Arms, or on the Backs, or at the Heels of their Mothers, and frequently of their Fathers, is in the present deplorable state of the Kingdom, a very great additional Grievance; and therefore, whoever could find out a fair, cheap, and easy Method of making these Children sound and useful Members of the Commonwealth, would deserve so well of the Publick, as to have his Statue set up for a Preserver of the Nation.

3   But my Intention is very far from being confined to provide only for the Children of professed Beggars: It is of a much greater Extent, and shall take in the whole Number of Infants at a certain Age, who are born of Parents in effect as little able to support them, as those who demand our Charity in the Streets.

4   As to my own Part, having turned my Thoughts, for many Years, upon this important Subject, and maturely weighed the several Schemes of other Projectors, I have always found them grossly mistaken in their Computation. It is true, a Child, just dropt from its Dam, may be supported by her Milk, for a Solar Year with little other Nourishment; at most not above the Value of two Shillings; which the Mother may certainly get, or the Value in Scraps, by her lawful Occupation of Begging: and it is exactly at one Year old that I propose to provide for them in such a manner, as, instead of being a Charge upon their Parents or the Parish, or wanting Food and Raiment for the rest of their Lives; they shall, on the contrary, contribute to the Feeding and partly to the Cloathing, of many Thousands.

5   There is likewise another great Advantage in my Scheme, that it will prevent those voluntary Abortions, and that horrid practice of Women murdering their Bastard Children, alas! too frequent among us; Sacrificing the poor innocent Babes, I doubt, more to avoid the Expence than the Shame; which would move Tears and Pity in the most Savage and inhuman breast.

6   The number of Souls in Ireland being usually reckoned one Million and a half; of these I calculate there may be about Two hundred Thousand Couples whose Wives are Breeders; from which number I subtract thirty Thousand Couples, who are able to maintain their own Children, although I apprehend there cannot be so many under the present Distresses of the Kingdom; but this being granted, there will remain an Hundred and Seventy Thousand Breeders. I again Subtract Fifty Thousand, for those Women who miscarry, or whose Children die by Accident, or Disease, within the Year. There only remain an Hundred and Twenty Thousand Children of poor Parents, annually born: The Question therefore is, How this Number shall be reared, and provided for? Which, as I have already said, under the present Situation of Affairs, is utterly impossible, by all the Methods hitherto proposed: For we can neither employ them in Handicraft or Agriculture; we neither build Houses, (I mean in the Country) nor cultivate Land: They can very seldom pick up a Livelyhood by Stealing until they arrive at six Years old; except where they are of towardly Parts; although, I confess, they learn the Rudiments much earlier; during which Time, they can, however be properly looked upon only as Probationers; as I have been informed by a principal Gentleman in the County of Cavan, who protested to me, that he never knew above one or two Instances under the Age of six, even in

a part of the Kingdom so renowned for the quickest Proficiency in that Art.

7   I am assured by our Merchants, that a Boy or a Girl before twelve Years old, is no saleable Commodity; and even when they come to this Age, they will not yield above Three Pounds, or Three Pounds and half a Crown at most, on the Exchange; which cannot turn to Account either to the Parents or the Kingdom; the Charge of Nutriment and Rags, having been at least four Times that Value.

8   I shall now therefore humbly propose my own Thoughts; which I hope will not be liable to the least Objection.

9   I have been assured by a very knowing American of my Acquaintance in London, that a young healthy Child, well nursed is, at a Year old, a most delicious, nourishing and wholesome Food, whether Stewed, Roasted, Baked, or Boiled; and I make no doubt that it will equally serve in a Fricasie, or Ragoust.

10   I do therefore humbly offer it to publick Consideration, that of the Hundred and Twenty Thousand Children, already computed, Twenty thousand may be reserved for Breed; whereof only one Fourth Part to be Males; which is more than we allow to Sheep, black Cattle, or Swine; and my Reason is, that these Children are seldom the Fruits of Marriage, a Circumstance not much regarded by our Savages; therefore, one Male will be sufficient to serve four Females. That the remaining Hundred thousand, may, at a Year old be offered in Sale to the Persons of Quality and Fortune, through the Kingdom; always advising the Mother to let them suck plentifully in the last Month, so as to render them plump, and fat for a good Table. A Child will make two Dishes at an Entertainment for Friends; and when the Family dines alone, the fore or hind Quarter will make a reasonable Dish; and seasoned with a little Pepper or Salt, will be very good Boiled on the fourth Day, especially in Winter.

11   I have reckoned upon a Medium, that a Child just born will weigh Twelve Pounds; and in a solar Year, if tolerably nursed, increaseth to 28 Pounds.

12   I grant this Food will be somewhat dear, and therefore very proper for Landlords; who, as they have already devoured most of the Parents, seem to have the best Title to the Children.

13   Infant's Flesh will be in Season throughout the Year; but more plentiful in March, and a little before and after; for we are told by a grave Author an eminent French Physician, that Fish being a prolifick Dyet, there are more Children born in Roman Catholic Countries about Nine Months after Lent, than any other Season: Therefore reckoning a Year after Lent, the Markets will be more glutted than usual; because the Number of Popish Infants, is, at least, three to one in this Kingdom; and therefore it will have one other Collateral advantage; by lessening the Number of Papists among us.

14   I have already computed the Charge of nursing a Beggar's Child (in which List I reckon all Cottagers, Labourers, and Four fifths of the Farmers) to be about two Shillings per Annum, Rags included; and I believe no Gentleman would repine to give Ten Shillings for the Carcase of a good fat Child; which, as I have said, will make four Dishes of excellent nutritive meat, when he hath only some particular Friend, or his own Family, to dine with him. Thus the Squire will learn to be a good Landlord, and grow popular among his Tenants; the Mother will have Eight Shillings net Profit, and be fit for Work till she produceth another Child.

15   Those who are more thrifty (as I must confess the Times require) may flay the Carcase; the Skin of which, artificially dressed, will make admirable Gloves for Ladies, and Summer Boots for fine Gentlemen.

16   As to our City of Dublin; Shambles may be appointed for this Purpose, in the most convenient Parts of it, and Butchers we may be assured will not be wanting; although I rather recommend buying the Children alive, and dressing them hot from the Knife, as we do roasting Pigs.

17   A very worthy Person, a true Lover of his Country, and whose Virtues I highly esteem, was lately pleased, in discoursing on this Matter, to offer a Refinement upon my Scheme. He said, that many Gentlemen of this Kingdom, having of late destroyed their Deer; he conceived that the Want of Venison might be well supplied by the Bodies of young Lads and Maidens, not exceeding fourteen Years of Age, nor under twelve; so great a Number of both Sexes in every Country being ready to Starve, for want of Work and Service: And these to be disposed of by their Parents, if alive, or otherwise by their nearest Relations. But with due reference to so excellent a Friend, and so deserving a Patriot, I cannot be altogether in his Sentiments. For as to the Males, my American Acquaintance assured me from frequent Experience, that their Flesh was generally tough and lean, like that of our School-boys, by continual Exercise, and their Taste disagreeable; and to fatten them would not answer the Charge. Then, as to the Females, it would, I think, with humble Submission, be a Loss to the Publick, because they soon would become Breeders themselves: And besides it is not improbable, that some scrupulous People might be apt to censure such a Practice, (although indeed very unjustly) as a little bordering upon Cruelty; which, I confess, hath always been with me the strongest Objection against any Project, how well soever intended.

18   But in order to justify my Friend; he confessed, that this Expedient was put into his Head by the famous Salmanaazor, a Native of the Island Formosa, who came from thence to London, above twenty Years ago, and in Conversation told my Friend, that in his Country,

when any young Person happened to be put to Death, the executioner sold the Carcase to Persons of Quality, as a prime Dainty, and that, in his Time, the Body of a plump Girl of fifteen, who was crucified for an Attempt to poison the Emperor, was sold to his Imperial Majesty's prime Minister of State, and other great Mandarins of the Court, in Joints from the Gibbet, at Four hundred Crowns. Neither indeed can I deny, that if the same Use were made of several plump young girls in this Town, who, without one single Groat to their Fortunes, cannot stir Abroad without a Chair, and appear at the Play-house, and Assemblies in foreign fineries, which they never will pay for; the Kingdom would not be the worse.

19 Some Persons of a desponding Spirit are in great Concern about that vast Number of poor People, who are Aged, Diseased, or Maimed; and I have been desired to imploy my Thoughts what Course may be taken, to ease the Nation of so grievous an Incumbrance. But I am not in the least Pain upon that Matter; because it is very well known, that they are every Day dying, and rotting, by Cold and Famine, and Filth, and Vermin, as fast as can be reasonably expected. And as to the younger Labourers, they are now in almost as hopeful a Condition: They cannot get Work, and consequently pine away for Want of Nourishment, to a Degree, that if at any Time they are accidentally hired to common Labour, they have not Strength to perform it; and thus the Country, and themselves, are in a fair Way of being delivered from the Evils to come.

20 I have too long digressed; and therefore shall return to my Subject. I think the Advantages by the Proposal which I have made are obvious, and many, as well as of the highest Importance.

21 For First, as I have already observed, it would greatly lessen the Number of Papists, with whom we are Yearly overrun; being the principal Breeders of the Nation, as well as our most dangerous Enemies; and who stay at home on Purpose, with a Design to deliver the Kingdom to the Pretender; hoping to take their Advantage by the Absence of so many good Protestants, who have chosen rather to leave their Country, than stay at home, and pay Tithes against their Conscience, to an idolatrous Episcopal Curate.

22 Secondly, The poorer Tenants will have something valuable of their own, which, by Law, may be made liable to Distress, and help to pay their Landlord's Rent; their Corn and Cattle being already seized, and Money a Thing unknown.

23 Thirdly, Whereas the Maintenance of an Hundred Thousand Children, from two Years old, and upwards, cannot be computed at less than ten Shillings a Piece per Annum, the Nation's Stock will be thereby encreased Fifty Thousand Pounds per Annum; besides the Profit of a new Dish, introduced to the Tables of all Gentlemen of

Fortune in the Kingdom, who have any refinement in Taste; and the Money will circulate among ourselves, the Goods being entirely of our own Growth and Manufacture.

24 Fourthly, The constant Breeders, besides the Gain of Eight Shillings Sterling per Annum, by the Sale of their Children, will be rid of the Charge of maintaining them after the first Year.

25 Fifthly, This Food would likewise bring great Custom to Taverns, where the Vintners will certainly be so prudent, as to procure the best Receipts for dressing it to Perfection; and consequently, have their Houses frequented by all the fine Gentlemen, who justly value themselves upon their Knowledge in good Eating; and a skilful Cook, who understands how to oblige his Guests, will contrive to make it as expensive as they please.

26 Sixthly, This would be a great Inducement to Marriage, which all wise Nations have either encouraged by Rewards, or enforced by Laws and Penalties. It would encrease the Care and Tenderness of Mothers towards their Children, when they were sure of a Settlement for Life, to the poor Babes, provided in some Sort by the Publick, to their annual Profit instead of Expence. We should soon see an honest Emulation among the married Women, which of them could bring the fattest Child to the Market. Men would become as fond of their Wives, during the Time of their Pregnancy, as they are now of their Mares in Foal, their Cows in Calf, or Sows when they are ready to farrow; nor offer to beat or kick them, (as is too frequent a Practice) for fear of a Miscarriage.

27 Many other Advantages might be enumerated. For instance, the Addition of some Thousand Carcases in our Exportation of barrel'd Beef: The Propagation of Swine's Flesh, and Improvement in the Art of making good Bacon; so much wanted among us by the great Destruction of Pigs, too frequent at our Tables, and are no way comparable in Taste, or Magnificence, to a well-grown, fat yearling Child; which, roasted whole, will make a considerable Figure at Lord Mayor's Feast, or any other publick Entertainment. But this, and many others, I omit; being studious of Brevity.

28 Supposing that one Thousand Families in this City, would be constant Customers for Infants Flesh, besides others who might have it at merry Meetings, particularly Weddings and Christenings; I compute that Dublin would take off, annually, about Twenty Thousand Carcases; and the rest of the Kingdom (where probably they will be sold somewhat cheaper) the remaining Eighty Thousand.

29 I can think of no one Objection, that will possibly be raised against this Proposal; unless it should be urged, that the Number of People will be thereby much lessened in the Kingdom. This I freely own; and it was indeed one principal Design in offering it to the World. I desire the Reader will observe, that I calculate my Remedy for this

one individual Kingdom of Ireland, and for no other than ever was, is, or, I think, ever can be upon Earth. Therefore, let no man talk to me of other Expedients: Of taxing our Absentees at five Shillings a Pound: Of using neither Cloaths, nor Household Furniture, except what is of our own Growth and Manufacture: Of utterly rejecting the Materials and Instruments that promote foreign Luxury: Of curing the Expensiveness of Pride, Vanity, Idleness, and Gaming in our Women: Of introducing a Vein of Parsimony, Prudence and Temperance: Of learning to love our Country, wherein we differ even from Laplanders, and the Inhabitants of Topinamboo: Of Quitting our Animosities, and Factions; nor act any longer like the Jews, who were murdering one another at the very Moment their City was taken: Of being a little cautious not to sell our Country and Consciences for nothing: Of teaching Landlords to have, at least, one Degree of Mercy towards their Tenants. Lastly, of Putting a Spirit of Honesty, Industry, and Skill into our Shopkeepers; who, if a Resolution could now be taken to buy only our native Goods, would immediately unite to cheat and exact upon us in the Price, the Measure, and the Goodness; nor could ever yet be brought to make one fair Proposal of just Dealing, though often and earnestly invited to it.

30   Therefore, I repeat, let no Man talk to me of these and the like Expedients; till he hath, a least, a Glimpse of Hope, that there will ever be some hearty and sincere Attempt to put them in Practice.

31   But, as to my self; having been wearied out for many Years with offering vain, idle, visionary Thoughts; and at length utterly despairing of Success, I fortunately fell upon this Proposal; which, as it is wholly new, so it hath something solid and real, of no Expence and little Trouble, full in our own Power; and whereby we can incur no Danger in disobliging England: For this Kind of Commodity will not bear Exportation; the Flesh being of too tender a Consistence, to admit a long Continuance in Salt; although, perhaps, I could name a Country, which would be glad to eat up our whole Nation without it.

32   After all, I am not so violently bent upon my own Opinion, as to reject any Offer, proposed by wise Men, which shall be found equally innocent, cheap, easy, and effectual. But before something of that Kind shall be advanced in Contradiction to my Scheme, and offering a better; I desire the Author, or Authors, will be pleased maturely to consider two Points. First, As Things now stand, how they will be able to find Food and Raiment, for a Hundred Thousand useless Mouths and Backs? And Secondly, There being a round Million of Creatures in human Figure, throughout this Kingdom; whose whole Subsistence, put into a common Stock, would leave them in Debt two Millions of Pounds Sterling; adding those, who are Beggars by Profession, to the Bulk of Farmers, Cottagers and Labourers, with the Wives and Children, who are Beggars in Effect; I desire those

Politicians, who dislike my Overture, and may perhaps be so bold to attempt an Answer, that they will first ask the Parents of these Mortals, Whether they would not at this Day think it a great Happiness to have been sold for Food at a Year old, in the Manner I prescribe; and thereby have avoided such a perpetual Scene of Misfortunes, as they have since gone through; by the Oppression of Landlords; the Impossibility of paying Rent, without Money or Trade; the Want of common Sustenance, with neither House nor Cloaths, to cover them from the Inclemencies of the Weather; and the most inevitable Prospect of intailing the like, or greater Miseries upon their Breed for ever.

33   I profess, in the Sincerity of my Heart, that I have not the least personal Interest, in endeavouring to promote this necessary Work, having no other Motive than the publick Good of my Country, by advancing our Trade, providing for Infants, relieving the Poor, and giving some Pleasure to the Rich. I have no Children, by which I can propose to get a single Penny; the youngest being nine Years Old and my Wife past Child-bearing.

Questions on Content

1   What problem does the speaker define in paragraphs one and two? What goal does he seek?

2   What general proposal does the speaker offer in paragraph four? What will this proposal prevent?

3   Why is it "utterly impossible" for the one hundred and twenty thousand children of poor parents to be reared, and provided for, according to the speaker? What is the speaker's specific proposal for solving this problem? What "refinement" on this scheme was suggested to the speaker?

4   What six advantageous effects of his proposal's implementation does the speaker outline? What other advantages does he mention?

5   What "other expedients" does the speaker reject? Why? What two points must be considered by those who would offer other proposals, according to the speaker? What does the speaker claim as his motive for making his proposal? On what basis does the speaker make this claim?

Questions on Structure and Technique

1   What is the speaker's purpose in paragraphs one through seven? In what sentence in this section does the speaker first introduce his proposal? How does this sentence differ from the statement of his proposal in paragraphs nine through eleven?

2   What words and phrases in paragraphs one through seven undercut the speaker's ethical appeal? When do you first become aware that Swift's essay is ironic? What subsequent words, phrases, and sentences not only confirm this awareness but also provoke strong emotional responses against the speaker's proposal?

3   Why does the speaker make extensive use of statistics in the presentation of his proposal? What image of himself does he attempt to project? What other methods does he use to enhance this image?

4   After presenting the problem (paragraphs one through seven) and proposing his solution (paragraphs eight through nineteen), the speaker lists the advantages to be gained by the implementation of his proposal (in paragraphs twenty through twenty-eight). On what criteria does the speaker base this analysis of his scheme's beneficial effects? In what other previous paragraphs does the speaker also evaluate his proposal's effects by using such criteria? What criteria does the speaker's proposal ignore?

5   What is the speaker's purpose in paragraphs twenty-nine through thirty-two? What is Swift's purpose? What is the speaker's intention in paragraph thirty-three? How does Swift undercut the speaker's ethical appeal?

Suggestions for Writing

1   Using Swift's structure and technique in "A Modest Proposal" as a model, write a mock argument in which you create a speaker whose proposal for solving a current problem is opposite to the real issues you want to raise in your essay.

2   Select a newspaper or magazine article, editorial, or letter to the editor in which a writer's solution to a problem is morally or ethically unacceptable to you. Write an essay in which you argue against the writer's position and offer a more reasonable and acceptable alternative approach or solution to the problem.

NORTHROP FRYE

Northrop Frye (b. 1912) is a scholar, critic, and professor of literature whose books include Fearful Symmetry: A Study of William Blake *(1947),* Anatomy of Criticism *(1957), and* The Great Code *(1982). Frye, born in Sherbrooke, Quebec, graduated from the University of Toronto in 1933, and after studying theology at Emmanuel College, Toronto, was ordained as a United Church minister in 1936. He then studied at Oxford University, receiving his M.A. in 1940. Northrop Frye has been a professor and administrator at Victoria College, University of Toronto, since 1939. "The Vocation of Eloquence" is the concluding lecture in a CBC radio series of addresses by Frye entitled* The Educated Imagination *(1963), one of more than fifteen published collections of his lectures and essays on English and Canadian literature and culture.*

THE VOCATION OF ELOQUENCE

1   The title I'm using for this talk, 'The Vocation of Eloquence', comes from a gorgeous French poem called *Anabase*, by a writer whose pen-name is St. John Perse. It's been translated into English by T. S. Eliot. Its theme is the founding of a city and a new civilization, and naturally the author, being a poet, is keenly aware of the importance of the use of words in establishing a society. . . . I don't think of myself as speaking primarily to writers, or to people who want to be writers: I'm speaking to you as consumers, not producers, of literature, as people who read and form the public for literature. It's as consumers that you may want to know more about what literature can do and what its uses are, apart from the pleasure it gives.

2   . . . Nothing can be more obviously useful than learning to read and write and talk, but . . . a lot of people, especially young and inexperienced people, don't see why studying literature should be a necessary part of this . . . I've been trying . . . to distinguish the language of the imagination, which is literature, from two other ways of using words: ordinary speech and the conveying of information. It's probably occurred to you already that these three ways of using words overlap a good deal. Literature speaks the language of the imagination, and the study of literature is supposed to train and improve the imagination. But we use our imagination all the time: it comes into all our conversation and practical life: it even produces

dreams when we're asleep. Consequently we have only the choice between a badly trained imagination and a well trained one, whether we ever read a poem or not.

3   When you stop to think about it, you soon realize that our imagination is what our whole social life is really based on. We have feelings, but they affect only us and those immediately around us; and feelings can't be directly conveyed by words at all. We have intelligence and a capacity for reasoning, but in ordinary life we almost never get a chance to use the intellect by itself. In practically everything we do it's the combination of emotion and intellect we call imagination that goes to work. Take, for example, the subject that in literary criticism is called rhetoric, the social or public use of words. In ordinary life, as in literature, the way you say things can be just as important as what's said. The words you use are like the clothes you wear. Situations, like bodies, are supposed to be decently covered. You may have some social job to do that involves words, such as making a speech or preaching a sermon or teaching a lesson or presenting a case to a judge or writing an obituary on a dead skinflint or reporting a murder trial or greeting visitors in a public building or writing copy for an ad. In none of these cases is it your job to tell the naked truth: we realize that even in the truth there are certain things we can say and certain things we can't say.

4   Society attaches an immense importance to saying the right thing at the right time. In this conception of the 'right thing', there are two factors involved, one moral and one aesthetic. They are inseparable, and equally important. Some of the right things said may be only partly true, or they may be so little of the truth as to be actually hypocritical or false, at least in the eyes of the Recording Angel. It doesn't matter: in society's eyes the virtue of saying the right thing at the right time is more important than the virtue of telling the whole truth, or sometimes even of telling the truth at all. We even have a law of libel to prevent us from telling some truths about some people unless it's in the public interest. So when Bernard Shaw remarks that a temptation to tell the truth should be just as carefully considered as a temptation to tell a lie, he's pointing to a social standard beyond the merely intellectual standards of truth and falsehood, which has the power of final veto, and which only the imagination can grasp. We find rhetorical situations everywhere in life, and only our imaginations can get us out of them. Suppose we're talking to somebody, let's say a woman, who's in a difficult mood. We're faced at once with the problem: does what she is saying represent her actual meaning, or is it just a disguised way of representing her emotional state of mind? Usually we assume the latter but pretend to be assuming the former. This is a problem in rhetoric, and our decision is an act of literary criticism. The importance of rhetoric proves, once again,

that the imagination uses words to express a certain kind of social vision. The social vision of rhetoric is that of society dressed up in its Sunday clothes, people parading in front of each other, and keeping up the polite, necessary and not always true assumption that they are what they appear to be.

5   In our use of words in ordinary life, . . . we are all bad poets. We read stories in our newspapers about Britain and Russia and France and India, all doing that and thinking that, as though each of these nations was an individual person. We know, of course, that such a use of language is a figure of speech, and probably a necessary figure, but sometimes we get misled by such figures. Or we get into the opposite habit of referring to the government of Canada as 'they', forgetting that they're our own employees and assuming that 'they' are carrying out plans and pursuing interests of their own. Both of these habits are forms of misapplied mythology or personification.

6   The central place of the imagination in social life is something that the advertisers suddenly woke up to a few years ago. Ever since, they've been doing what they call projecting the image, and hiring psychologists to tell them what makes the most direct appeal to the imagination . . . . Advertising is one example, though a very obvious one, of the deliberate creation of an illusion in the middle of real life. Our reaction to advertising is really a form of literary criticism. We don't take it literally, and we aren't supposed to: anyone who believed literally what every advertiser said would hardly be capable of managing his own affairs. I recently went past two teen-age girls looking at the display in front of a movie which told them that inside was the thrill of a lifetime, on no account to be missed, and I heard one of them say: 'Do you suppose it's any good?' That was the voice of sanity trying to get its bearings in a world of illusion. We may think of it as the voice of reason, but it's really the voice of the imagination doing its proper job . . . . I spoke of irony, which means saying one thing and meaning another, as a device which a writer uses to detach our imaginations from a world of absurdity or frustration by letting us see around it. To protect ourselves in a society like ours, we have to look at such advertising as that movie display ironically: it means something to us which is different from what it says. The end of the process is not to reject all advertising, but to develop our own vision of society to the point at which we can choose what we want out of what's offered to us and let the rest go. What we choose is what fits that vision of society.

7   This principle holds not only for advertising but for most aspects of social life. During an election campaign, politicians project various images on us and make speeches which we know to be at best a carefully selected part of the truth. We tend to look down on the person who responds to such appeals emotionally: we feel he's behav-

ing childishly and like an irresponsible citizen if he allows himself to be stampeded. Of course there's often a great sense of release in a purely emotional response. Hitler represented to Germany a tremendous release from its frustrations and grievances by simply acting like a three-year-old child: when he wanted something he went into a tantrum and screamed and chewed the scenery until he got it. But that example shows how dangerous the emotional response is, and how right we are to distrust it. So we say we ought to use our reason instead. But all the appeals to us are carefully rationalized, except the obviously crackpot ones, and we still have to make a choice. What the responsible citizen really uses is his imagination, not believing anybody literally, but voting for the man or party that corresponds most closely, or least remotely, to his vision of the society he wants to live in. The fundamental job of the imagination in ordinary life, then, is to produce, out of the society we have to live in, a vision of the society we want to live in. Obviously that can't be a separated society, so we have to understand how to relate the two.

8   The society we have to live in, which for us happens to be a twentieth-century Canadian society, presents our imagination with its own substitute for literature. This is a social mythology, with its own folklore and its own literary conventions, or what corresponds to them. The purpose of this mythology is to persuade us to accept our society's standards and values, to 'adjust' to it, as we say. Every society produces such a mythology: it's a necessary part of its coherence, and we have to accept some of it if we're to live in it, even things that we don't believe. The more slowly a society changes, the more solidly based its mythology seems to be. In the Middle Ages the mythology of protection and obedience seemed one of the eternal verities, something that could never change. But change it did, at least all of it that depended on a certain kind of social structure. A hundred years ago a mythology of independence, hard work, thrift and saving for a rainy day looked equally immortal, but, again, everything that was based on weak social services and stable values of money had to go. If a society changes very rapidly, and our society certainly does, we have to recognize the large element of illusion in all social mythology as a simple matter of self-protection. The first thing our imaginations have to do for us, as soon as we can handle words well enough to read and write and talk, is to fight to protect us from falling into the illusions that society threatens us with. The illusion is itself produced by the social imagination, of course, but it's an inverted form of imagination. What it creates is the imaginary, which as I said earlier is different from the imaginative.

9   The main elements of this social mythology will be familiar to you as soon as I mention them. I spoke of advertising, and what's illusory about that is the perverted appeal it so often makes to the imagination:

the appeals to snobbery and to what are called 'status symbols', the exploiting of the fear of being ridiculed or isolated from society, the suggestion of an easy way of getting on the inside track of what's going on, and so on. Then there's the use of cliché, that is, the use of ready-made, prefabricated formulas designed to give those who are too lazy to think the illusion of thinking. The Communists of course have made a heavy industry of clichés, but we have our own too. Hard-headed business man; ivory tower; longhair; regimentation; togetherness; airy-fairy. Anybody who believes literally what these clichés express, as far as any thinking for himself is concerned, might just as well be in Moscow reading about fascist hyenas and the minions of imperialist aggression.

10   Then there's the use of what we call jargon or gobbledegook, or what people who live in Washington or Ottawa call federal prose, the gabble of abstractions and vague words which avoids any simple or direct statement. There's a particular reason for using gobbledegook which makes it a part of social mythology. People write this way when they want to sound as impersonal as possible, and the reason why they want to sound impersonal is that they want to suggest that the social machine they're operating, usually a government agency, is running smoothly, and that no human factors are going to disturb it. Direct and simple language always has some force behind it, and the writers of gobbledegook don't want to be forceful; they want to be soothing and reassuring. I remember a report on the classification of government documents which informed me that some documents were eventually classified for permanent deposition. The writer meant that he threw them away. But he didn't want to say so, and suggest that somebody was actually tearing up paper and aiming it at a wastebasket; he wanted to suggest some kind of invisible perfect processing. We get similar euphemisms in military writing, where we read about 'anti-personnel bombs', meaning bombs that kill men, designed not to give us any uncomfortable images of legs torn off and skulls blown open. We can see here how the ordinary use of rhetoric, which attempts to make society presentable, is becoming hypocritical and disguising the reality it presents beyond the level of social safety.

11   Then there's all the mythology about the 'good old days', when everything was simpler and more leisurely and everybody was much closer to nature and got their milk out of cows instead of out of bottles. Literary critics call these reveries pastoral myths, because they correspond to the same kind of convention in literature that produces stories about happy shepherds and milkmaids. Many people like to assume that the society of their childhood was a solid and coherent structure which is now falling apart, as morals have become looser and social conditions more chaotic and the arts more unintelligible to ordinary people, and so forth. Some time ago an archaeologist in

the Near East dug up an inscription five thousand years old which told him that 'children no longer obey their parents, and the end of the world is rapidly approaching'. It's characteristic of such social myth-making that it can swing from one extreme to the other without any sense of inconsistency, and so we also have progress myths, of the kind that rationalize the spreading of filling stations and suburban bungalows and four-lane highways over the Canadian landscape. Progress myths come into all the phoney history that people use when they say that someone is a 'Puritan', meaning that he's a prude, or that someone else is 'medieval' or 'mid-Victorian', meaning that he's old-fashioned. The effect of such words is to give the impression that all past history was a kind of bad dream, which in these enlightened days we've shaken off.

12   The various . . . diagrams and doodles that people carry around in their minds help them sort things out. Sometimes they sort things the wrong way. For instance, there's the diagram of left-wing and right-wing in politics, where you start with Communism at the extreme left and go around to Fascism at the extreme right. We use this diagram all the time, but suppose I were to say: 'the Conservatives are nearer to being Fascists than the Liberals, and the Liberals are nearer to being Communists than the Conservatives.' You recognize that statement to be nonsense; but if it's nonsense, the diagram it's founded on is more misleading than it is useful. The person it's most useful to is the person who wants to turn abusive, which is my next point.

13   Ordinary speech is largely concerned with registering our reactions to what goes on outside us. In all such reactions there's a large automatic or mechanical element. And if our only aim is to say what gets by in society, our reactions will become almost completely mechanical. That's the direction in which the use of clichés takes us. In a society which changes rapidly, many things happen that frighten us or make us feel threatened. People who can do nothing but accept their social mythology can only try to huddle more closely together when they feel frightened or threatened, and in that situation their clichés turn hysterical. Naturally that doesn't make them any less mechanical. Some years ago, in a town in the States, I heard somebody say 'those yellow bastards', meaning the Japanese. More recently, in another town, I heard somebody else use the same phrase, but meaning the Chinese. There are many reasons, not connected with literary criticism, why nobody should use a phrase like that about anybody. But the literary reason is that the phrase is pure reflex: it's no more a product of a conscious mind than the bark of a dog is.

14   We said that the person who is surrounded with advertisers, or with politicians at election time, neither believes everything literally nor rejects everything, but chooses in accordance with his own vision

of society. The essential thing is the power of choice. In wartime this power of choice is greatly curtailed, and we resign ourselves to living by half-truths for the duration. In a totalitarian state the competition in propaganda largely disappears, and consequently the power of imaginative choice is sealed off. In our hatred and fear of war and of totalitarian government, one central element is a sense of claustrophobia that the imagination develops when it isn't allowed to function properly. This is the aspect of tyranny that's so prominently displayed in George Orwell's *1984*. Orwell even goes so far as to suggest that the only way to make tyranny permanent and unshakable, the only way in other words to create a literal hell on earth, is deliberately to debase our language by turning our speech into an automatic gabble. The fear of being reduced to such a life is a genuine fear, but of course as soon as we express it in hysterical clichés we are in the same state ourselves. As the poet William Blake says in describing something very similar, we become what we behold.

15   Too often the study of literature, or even the study of language, is thought of as a kind of elegant accomplishment, a matter of talking good grammar or keeping up with one's reading. I'm trying to show that the subject is a little more serious than that. I don't see how the study of language and literature can be separated from the question of free speech, which we all know is fundamental to our society. The area of ordinary speech, as I see it, is a battleground between two forms of social speech, the speech of a mob and the speech of a free society. One stands for cliché, ready-made idea and automatic babble, and it leads us inevitably from illusion into hysteria. There can be no free speech in a mob: free speech is one thing a mob can't stand. You notice that the people who allow their fear of Communism to become hysterical eventually get to screaming that every sane man they see is a Communist. Free speech, again, has nothing to do with grousing or saying that the country's in a mess and that all politicians are liars and cheats, and so on and so on. Grousing never gets any further than clichés of this kind, and the sort of vague cynicism they express is the attitude of somebody who's looking for a mob to join.

16   You see, freedom has nothing to do with lack of training; it can only be the product of training. You're not free to move unless you've learned to walk, and not free to play the piano unless you practice. Nobody is capable of free speech unless he knows how to use language, and such knowledge is not a gift: it has to be learned and worked at. The only exceptions, and they are exceptions that prove the rule, are people who, in some crisis, show that they have a social imagination strong and mature enough to stand out against a mob. In the recent row over desegregation in New Orleans, there was one mother who gave her reasons for sending her children to an integrated school with

such dignity and precision that the reporters couldn't understand how a woman who never got past grade six learned to talk like the Declaration of Independence. Such people already have what literature tries to give. For most of us, free speech is cultivated speech, but cultivating speech is not just a skill, like playing chess. You can't cultivate speech beyond a certain point, unless you have something to say, and the basis of what you have to say is your vision of society. So while free speech may be, at least at present, important only to a very small minority, that very small minority is what makes the difference between living in Canada and living in East Berlin or South Africa. The next question is: where do the standards of a free society come from? They don't come from that society itself, as we've just seen.

17   Let us suppose that some intelligent man has been chasing status symbols all his life, until suddenly the bottom falls out of his world and he sees no reason for going on. He can't make his solid gold cadillac represent his success or his reputation or his sexual potency any more: now it seems to him only absurd and a little pathetic. No psychiatrist or clergyman can do him any good, because his state of mind is neither sick nor sinful: he's wrestling with his angel. He discovers immediately that he wants more education, and he wants it in the same way that a starving man wants food. But he wants education of a particular kind. His intelligence and emotions may quite well be in fine shape. It's his imagination that's been starved and fed on shadows, and it's education in that that he specifically wants and needs.

18   What has happened is that he's so far recognized only one society, the society he has to live in, the middle-class twentieth-century Canadian society that he sees around him. That is, the society he does live in is identical with the one he wants to live in. So all he has to do is to adjust to that society, to see how it works and find opportunities for getting ahead in it. Nothing wrong with that: it's what we all do. But it's not all of what we all do. He's beginning to realize that if he recognizes no other society except the one around him, he can never be anything more than a parasite on that society. And no mentally healthy man wants to be a parasite: he wants to feel he has some function, something to contribute to the world, something that would make the world poorer if he weren't in it. But as soon as that notion dawns in the mind, the world we live in and the world we want to live in become different worlds. One is around us, the other is a vision inside our minds, born and fostered by the imagination, yet real enough for us to try to make the world we see conform to its shape. This second world is the world we want to live in, but the word 'want' is now appealing to something impersonal and unselfish in us. Nobody can enter a profession unless he makes at least a

gesture recognizing the ideal existence of a world beyond his own interests: a world of health for the doctor, of justice for the lawyer, of peace for the social worker, a redeemed world for the clergyman, and so on.

19   I'm not wandering away from my subject, or at least I'm trying not to. My subject is the educated imagination, and education is something that affects the whole person, not bits and pieces of him. It doesn't just train the mind: it's a social and moral development too. But now that we've discovered that the imaginative world and the world around us are different worlds, and that the imaginative world is more important, we have to take one more step. The society around us looks like the real world, but we've just seen that there's a great deal of illusion in it, the kind of illusion that propaganda and slanted news and prejudice and a great deal of advertising appeal to. For one thing, as we've been saying, it changes very rapidly, and people who don't know of any other world can never understand what makes it change. If Canada in 1962 is a different society from the Canada of 1942, it can't be real society, but only a temporary appearance of real society. And just as it looks real, so this ideal world that our imaginations develop inside us looks like a dream that came out of nowhere, and has no reality except what we put into it. But it isn't. It's the real world, the real form of human society hidden behind the one we see. It's the world of what humanity has done, and therefore can do, the world revealed to us in the arts and sciences. This is the world that won't go away, the world out of which we built the Canada of 1942, are now building the Canada of 1962, and will be building the quite different Canada of 1982.

20   A hundred years ago the Victorian poet and critic Matthew Arnold pointed out that we live in two environments, an actual social one and an ideal one, and that the ideal one can only come from something suggested in our education. Arnold called this ideal environment culture, and defined culture as the best that has been thought and said. The word culture has different overtones to most of us, but Arnold's conception is a very important one, and I need it at this point. We live, then, in both a social and a cultural environment, and only the cultural environment, the world we study in the arts and sciences, can provide the kind of standards and values we need if we're to do anything better than adjust.

21   I spoke . . . of three levels of the mind, which we have now seen to be also three forms of society and three ways of using words. The first is the level of ordinary experience and of self-expression. On this level we use words to say the right thing at the right time, to keep the social machinery running, faces saved, self-respect preserved, and

social situations intact. It's not the noblest thing that words can do, but it's essential, and it creates and diffuses a social mythology, which is a structure of words developed by the imagination. For we find that to use words properly even in this way we have to use our imaginations, otherwise they become mechanical clichés, and get further and further removed from any kind of reality. There's something in all of us that wants to drift toward a mob, where we can all say the same thing without having to think about it, because everybody is all alike except people that we can hate or persecute. Every time we use words, we're either fighting against this tendency or giving in to it. When we fight against it, we're taking the side of genuine and permanent human civilization.

22   This is the world revealed by philosophy and history and science and religion and law, all of which represent a more highly organized way of using words. We find knowledge and information in these studies, but they're also structures, things made out of words by a power in the human mind that constructs and builds. This power is the imagination, and these studies are its products. When we think of their content, they're bodies of knowledge; when we think of their form, they're myths, that is, imaginative verbal structures. So the whole subject of the use of words revolves around this constructive power itself, as it operates in the art of words, which is literature, the laboratory where myths themselves are studied and experimented with.

23   The particular myth that's been organizing this talk, and in a way the whole series, is the story of the Tower of Babel in the Bible. The civilization we live in at present is a gigantic technological structure, a skyscraper almost high enough to reach the moon. It looks like a single world-wide effort, but it's really a deadlock of rivalries; it looks very impressive, except that it has no genuine human dignity. For all its wonderful machinery, we know it's really a crazy ramshackle building, and at any time may crash around our ears. What the myth tells us is that the Tower of Babel is a work of human imagination, that its main elements are words, and that what will make it collapse is a confusion of tongues. All had originally one language, the myth says. That language is not English or Russian or Chinese or any common ancestor, if there was one. It is the language of human nature, the language that makes both Shakespeare and Pushkin authentic poets, that gives a social vision to both Lincoln and Gandhi. It never speaks unless we take the time to listen in leisure, and it speaks only in a voice too quiet for panic to hear. And then all it has to tell us, when we look over the edge of our leaning tower, is that we are not getting any nearer heaven, and that it is time to return to earth.

Questions on Content

1   Why does Frye entitle his essay "The Vocation of Eloquence"?

2   What are the three ways of using words, according to Frye? How do we use imagination in our ordinary speech? How is the imagination used in conveying information? What is literature, according to Frye?

3   What are the "main elements" of our social mythology, according to Frye? What is "the essential thing" we must remember about our social mythology? What are the two forms of social speech?

4   "Where do the standards of a free society come from," according to Frye? Explain.

5   What is "genuine and permanent civilization"? What created this "world", according to Frye? Why is the story of the Tower of Babel most significant, in Frye's view?

Questions on Structure and Technique

1   What general claim about literature does Frye make in paragraphs one and two?

2   What classifications of our use of words does Frye introduce in paragraph two? How are these classifications important to his organization and development of the whole essay? In what paragraphs does Frye summarize the significance of his classifications and their interrelations?

3   Who is Frye's audience? What is Frye's purpose in addressing this audience? Why are Frye's classifications appropriate for this purpose?

4   What illustrations does Frye use to appeal specifically to his audience? What illustrations appeal to their sense of reason? What illustrations appeal to their emotions?

5   How would you describe the "tone" of Frye's essay? What examples of Frye's use of language can you find that contribute to this tone?

Suggestions for Writing

1   Write an essay in which you argue in favour of the study of literature and language, basing your discussion on your own experiences and ideas as well as on your understanding of Northrop Frye's argument.

2   Write an essay in which you agree or disagree with one of the following statements in Frye's essay: "In society's eyes the virtue of saying the right thing at the right time is more important than telling the whole truth, or sometimes even of telling the truth at all"; "the ordinary use of rhetoric,

which attempts to make society presentable, is becoming hypocritical and disguising the reality it presents beyond the level of social safety"; "freedom has nothing to do with lack of training; it can only be the product of training"; or, "we are not getting any nearer heaven, and . . . it is time to return to the earth."

1 2 3 4 5   122480   92 91 90 89 88